S0-ADM-766

Private Capital Flows
to Emerging Markets
After the Mexican Crisis

GUILLERMO A. CALVO
MORRIS GOLDSTEIN
EDUARD HOCHREITER

Editors

Private Capital Flows to Emerging Markets After the Mexican Crisis

Institute for International Economics
Washington, DC
Austrian National Bank
Vienna, Austria
September 1996

Guillermo A. Calvo is Distinguished University Professor at the University of Maryland at College Park, and Advisor to the Minister of Economy in Argentina.

Morris Goldstein, is the Dennis Weatherstone Senior Fellow at the Institute for International Economics, and a former Deputy Director of the Research Department at the International Monetary Fund.

Eduard Hochreiter is Senior Adviser and Head of the Economic Studies Division of the Oesterreichische Nationalbank in Vienna, and Lecturer at the University of Economics in Vienna.

INSTITUTE FOR INTERNATIONAL ECONOMICS
11 Dupont Circle, NW
Washington, DC 20036-1207
(202) 328-9000 FAX: (202) 328-5432
http://www.iie.com

C. Fred Bergsten, *Director*
Christine F. Lowry, *Director of Publications*

Typesetting and Printing by Automated Graphic Systems

Copyright © 1996 by the Institute for International Economics. All rights reserved. No part of this book may be reproduced or utilized in any form or by any means, electronic or mechanical, including photocopying, recording, or by information storage or retrieval system, without permission from the Institute.

For reprints/permission to photocopy please contact the APS customer service department at CCC Academic Permissions Service, 27 Congress Street, Salem, MA 01970.

Printed in the United States of America
98 97 96 5 4 3 2 1

Library of Congress Cataloging-in-Publication Data

Private capital flows to emerging markets after the Mexican crisis / Guillermo A. Calvo, Morris Goldstein, Eduard Hochreiter, editors.
    p.   cm.
    Includes bibliographical references.
    1. Capital movements. 2. Capital movements—Government policy.
    I. Calvo, Guillermo. II. Goldstein, Morris, 1944– . III. Hochreiter, Eduard.
    HG3891.P74 1996   96-35399
    332'.042—dc20   CIP

    ISBN 0-88132-232-6

The views expressed in this publication are those of the authors. This publication is part of the overall program of the Institute, as endorsed by its Board of Directors, but does not necessarily reflect the views of individual members of the Board or the Advisory Committee.

Contents

Preface

The Institute has placed high priority on the issue of capital flows to developing countries throughout its history. Some of our earliest publications, mainly by William R. Cline, helped shape initial thinking and policy toward the Third World debt crisis of the 1980s. A subsequent study by John Williamson, supported the adoption of debt relief schemes in the latter part of that decade. All of those efforts stressed the need to provide a foundation for renewed and more broadly diversified private flows to the emerging market economies, as they came to be called in the 1990s, and Cline's review of the debt crisis period (*International Debt Reexamined,* 1995) noted that impressive levels of such flows had resumed in recent years.

The Mexican crisis of late 1994 and early 1995, however, highlighted the potential reversibility of capital inflows and the vulnerability of countries that were relying heavily on them. In September 1995 the Institute and the Austrian National Bank thus convened a group of leading policymakers, academics, and private-market participants to discuss the wide-ranging implications of that crisis. The aim was to increase understanding of the main origins of the crisis and especially to draw lessons about appropriate policies for emerging economies receiving large capital inflows, about the strengths and weaknesses of new players and new instruments in global capital markets, and about the adequacy of existing surveillance and crisis prevention/crisis management arrangements on the part of the international financial institutions (especially the International Monetary Fund).

This book presents the results of those deliberations. The seven papers analyze the anatomy of the Mexican crisis and the outlook ahead (Leiderman and Thorne); the experience of the transition economies of Central and Eastern Europe with their own surge of capital inflows in the 1990s (G. Calvo, Sahay, and Végh); the way governments are now managing their borrowing in international capital markets (Giovannini); how securitized debt instruments and institutional investors affect the dynamics of currency and debt crises (Gilibert and Steinherr); the factors that influence the contagion of financial disturbances across countries (S. Calvo and Reinhart); the combination of macroeconomic and exchange rate policies that seem to be the most successful in dealing with surges of capital inflows (Montiel); and the contribution that early warning systems, international lenders of last resort, and orderly workout procedures can make to the prevention and management of international financial crises (G. Calvo and Goldstein).

Each of the papers is accompanied by the reflections of at least two discussants. These include the accounts of two central bank governors (Governor Roque Fernández[1] of Argentina and Governor Josef Tošovský of the Czech Republic) on the experience of their own countries with large shifts in private capital flows, and appraisals of the causes and implications of the Mexican crisis from the markets (Hale, Lipsky, Ramirez de la O, Wadhwani, and Walter), from academics and think tanks (Cline, Dooley, Portes, and Williamson), and from other officials at national governments and international institutions (Åkerholm, Koromzay, Mishkin, Rojas-Suárez, Truman, and Turner). Broader perspective on these issues was also provided in round table and summing-up discussions by Andrew Crockett (general manager, Bank for International Settlements) and Stanley Fischer (first deputy managing director, IMF). Finally, Ariel Buira (deputy governor, Bank of Mexico) kindly agreed to share the Mexican authorities' own assessment of the crisis—an assessment that on some counts (e.g., the stance of monetary and fiscal policy in 1994, Mexico's competitiveness just prior to the crisis, the risks associated with Mexico's 1994 current account deficit) differed markedly from the assessment of other conference participants.

Much has happened since the conference took place. I therefore want to add a brief postscript on how several themes emphasized at the conference relate to recent or ongoing policy initiatives and developments.

First, there was broad consensus that countries with *weak banking systems* have one hand tied behind their backs in trying to deal with large shifts in international capital flows. Banking-sector fragility incites runs, puts sharp constraints on the willingness of monetary authorities to induce or

---

1. In August 1996, Governor Fernández left his position at the Central Bank of Argentina to become minister of the economy.

even permit an increase in domestic interest rates when capital inflows ebb or reverse themselves, and makes it harder to keep credit flows (linked to large capital inflows) from being channeled into unproductive activities. For this reason, efforts launched at the 1996 G-7 summit in Lyon, France to improve prudential standards in emerging-market banking systems (perhaps including consideration of an international banking standard) appear particularly timely.

Second, the Mexican crisis confronted the official sector with a difficult dilemma: either allow Mexico to default on its *tesobono* obligations and risk a deep recession in Mexico along with a possibly wide-ranging contagion to other emerging-market economies, or intervene with an official rescue package of unprecedented scale and risk, weakening the operation of market discipline in the future. A "third option" for an *orderly workout* was not available at the time. There was a Paris Club for restructuring of official debt and a London Club for restructuring of commercial bank debt—but no formal or informal framework for sovereign bonds. In this sense, most conference participants would probably regard the G-10 deputies report of June 1996, *Resolution of Sovereign Liquidity Crises,* as a step that should make any future Mexico-type crises a little easier to deal with. At least the implicit "rules of the game" should be somewhat clearer the next time.

Third, and along similar lines, most of our conference participants would likely welcome the agreement on two other initiatives. The IMF's Special Data Dissemination Standard should be helpful in combatting another problem highlighted by the Mexican crisis: inadequacies in the coverage, quality, and timeliness of countries' *published economic and financial data.* Such information on the creditworthiness of borrowers is a necessary (though by no means sufficient) condition for stronger market discipline. Opinion, however, is more divided on what the IMF could do beyond that to rein in errant macroeconomic and exchange rate policies at an earlier stage. In this connection, the proposal to have the IMF publish its Article IV consultation reports and to take a more activist role in sharing its views on exchange rate misalignments with the markets elicited strong views on both sides.

The other initiative is the Fund's Emergency Financing Mechanism (EFM), which despite its name deals only with procedural matters. Several European countries were upset that they were not consulted adequately in the run-up to the IMF loan to Mexico. The US Treasury and IMF management responded that the urgency of the situation precluded more *extensive consultation.* The procedural changes incorporated in the EFM are designed to improve such consultation, as well as to speed up the Fund's response to calls for emergency financial assistance.

Fourth, several conference participants drew attention to the role of a healthy cushion of *owned or borrowed reserves* in discouraging speculative attacks. In this regard, the subsequent agreement to enlarge the General Arrangements to Borrow (GAB), and regional arrangements to pool reserve holdings at times of strong exchange market pressure (such as the repurchase agreements recently worked out by several Asian countries), are a move in the right direction.

Fifth, those at the conference who stressed the greater resilience of a capital market dominated by nonbank capital flows and by nonbank institutional investors have received some support from the *resurgence of net private capital flows to developing countries* in the last three quarters of 1995, to a point where the (estimated) total for 1995 as a whole exceeded that in either 1994 or 1993. Many would also regard this resurgence, along with Mexico's return to the international bond market in the second half of 1995, as reflecting positively on both the official rescue package of more than $50 billion and on the strength of Mexico's adjustment efforts in the aftermath of the crisis. Also worthy of note in 1995 was the large expansion in net private flows to the transition economies of Central and Eastern Europe.

At the same time, this resurgence of private capital flows should not obscure another theme frequently voiced at the conference: that the volatility of these markets and their sensitivity to both interest rate developments in the industrial countries and confidence shocks elsewhere should make developing countries wary of leaning on them too heavily, and that these same considerations argue for paying due attention to the *composition of capital inflows*. This means that developing countries should concentrate on improving domestic saving performance, be less concerned by large inflows of foreign direct investment than of portfolio flows, and perhaps most important, avoid a penny-wise, pound-foolish strategy of heavy reliance on short-term, foreign currency-denominated debt. While it is probably still too early to know whether this message is being taken to heart, it is relevant to note that net foreign direct investment in developing countries increased in 1995 whereas net portfolio flows to them declined sharply.

Finally, on the issue of *exchange rate policy*, there appeared to be an increased interest in the wake of the Mexican crisis in regimes that would allow countries to make a more orderly exit from rigid nominal exchange rate anchors to greater exchange rate flexibility. In addition to a simple widening of exchange rate bands within a traditional adjustable peg system, crawling exchange rate bands (à la Chile, Colombia, and Israel) seemed to be attracting increased support—as analyzed by John Williamson in his new study for the Institute entitled *The Crawling Band as an Exchange Rate Regime: Lessons from Chile, Colombia, and Israel*. Part of this may reflect a finding emphasized in one of the conference papers, that host emerging economies that adopted tight monetary and fiscal policies, along with some exchange rate flexibility, were apparently better able to avoid real exchange rate appreciation and consumption booms—characteristics often linked with higher vulnerability to Mexico-type crises—than countries that oriented their strategy more closely to the maintenance of a nominal exchange rate anchor with an unchanged fiscal policy.

But I hope all of this will merely whet readers' appetite for the extensive analysis of these issues that follows. I deeply appreciate the cosponsorship of both the conference and the volume by the Austrian National Bank and especially the major contributions made to both by executive directors Thomas Lachs and Adolf Wala, and by co-editor Eduard Hochreiter (senior adviser and head of the Economic Studies Division). Co-editor Morris Goldstein and I also greatly appreciate the cooperation of co-editor Guillermo Calvo, professor of economics at the University of Maryland and now senior economic adviser to the government of Argentina, in organizing and completing the volume.

The Institute for International Economics is a private, nonprofit institution for the study and discussion of international economic policy. Its purpose is to analyze important issues in that area and to develop and communicate practical new approaches for dealing with them. The Institute is completely nonpartisan.

The Institute is funded largely by philanthropic foundations. Major institutional grants are now being received from the German Marshall Fund of the United States, which created the Institute with a generous commitment of funds in 1981, and from the Ford Foundation, the Andrew Mellon Foundation, and the C. V. Starr Foundation. A number of other foundations and private corporations also contribute to the highly diversified financial resources of the Institute. As noted, the Austrian National Bank provided substantial funding for this project.

The Board of Directors bears overall responsibility for the Institute and gives general guidance and approval to its research program—including identification of topics that are likely to become important to international economic policymakers over the medium run (generally, one to three years), and which thus should be addressed by the Institute. The Director, working closely with the staff and outside Advisory Committee, is responsible for the development of particular projects and makes the final decision to publish an individual study.

The Institute hopes that its studies and other activities will contribute to building a stronger foundation for international economic policy around the world. We invite readers of these publications to let us know how they think we can best accomplish this objective.

C. FRED BERGSTEN
Director
August 1996

INSTITUTE FOR INTERNATIONAL ECONOMICS
11 Dupont Circle, NW, Washington, DC 20036-1207
(202) 328-9000 Fax: (202) 328-5432

C. Fred Bergsten, *Director*

BOARD OF DIRECTORS	ADVISORY COMMITTEE

BOARD OF DIRECTORS

*Peter G. Peterson, *Chairman*
*Anthony M. Solomon, *Chairman,
  Executive Committee*

Leszek Balcerowicz
Raymond Barre
W. Michael Blumenthal
Miguel de la Madrid
George David
*Jessica Einhorn
George M. C. Fisher
Maurice R. Greenberg
*Carla A. Hills
W. M. Keck II
Nigel Lawson
Lee Kuan Yew
*Frank E. Loy
Donald F. McHenry
Ruben F. Mettler
Minoru Murofushi
Kaneo Nakamura
Suliman S. Olayan
Paul H. O'Neill
I. G. Patel
Karl Otto Pöhl
Edzard Reuter
David Rockefeller
Stephan Schmidheiny
Paul A. Volcker
*Dennis Weatherstone
Marina v.N. Whitman
Lynn R. Williams
Andrew Young

Ex officio
*C. Fred Bergsten

Honorary Directors
Alan Greenspan
Reginald H. Jones
Akio Morita
George P. Shultz

ADVISORY COMMITTEE

Robert Baldwin
Barry P. Bosworth
Susan M. Collins
Rimmer de Vries
Wendy Dobson
Juergen B. Donges
Rudiger Dornbusch
Gerhard Fels
Robert J. Flanagan
Isaiah Frank
Jacob A. Frenkel
David D. Hale
Mahbub ul Haq
Dale E. Hathaway
Nurul Islam
Peter B. Kenen
Lawrence R. Klein
Lawrence B. Krause
Anne O. Krueger
Paul R. Krugman
Roger M. Kubarych
Robert Z. Lawrence
Jessica T. Mathews
Rachel McCulloch
Isamu Miyazaki
Michael Mussa
Richard R. Nelson
Sylvia Ostry
Rudolph A. Oswald
Tommaso Padoa-Schioppa
Jacques J. Polak
Dani Rodrik
Jeffrey D. Sachs
Lawrence H. Summers
Alan Wm. Wolff
Robert B. Zoellick

Member of the Executive Committee

The 1994 Mexican Crisis and Its Aftermath: What Are the Main Lessons?

Leonardo Leiderman and Alfredo E. Thorne

In the wake of strong speculative attacks on the peso in late 1994, Mexican authorities widened the exchange rate band on 20 December and then three days later switched to a float. The peso depreciated by about 50 percent against the dollar between 20 and 31 December. The authorities' decision to abandon the band represented an explicit acceptance that the previous exchange rate policy was unsustainable and thus led to a crisis of confidence and to capital outflow. As a result, Mexico had to reduce its current account deficit by about 8 percent of GDP in 1995. Both the magnitude and international consequences of the crisis were unexpected: it reminded the international community that Mexico's successful reformers of the 1990s, who attracted most of the capital inflows, were also exposed to new and diverse risks.

The Mexican crisis came on the heels of a successful stabilization and a period of intense economic reforms. By implementing a heterodox stabilization program, Mexico successfully reduced the annual inflation rate from more than 150 percent in the early 1980s to single digits in

Leonardo Leiderman is professor of economics at the Berglas School of Economics, Tel-Aviv University. Alfredo E. Thorne is vice president for economic research at J. P. Morgan, Mexico. The views and conclusions expressed in the paper are those of the authors and should not be attributed in any way to the affiliated institutions. The authors would like to thank Mohamed El-Erian, Stanley Fischer, Daniel Oks, Phil Suttle, Klaus Schmidt-Hebbel, and the seminar participants' for their insightful comments and suggestions and Lara Christianson and Rossana Polastri for their valuable research assistance.

the 1990s. It also engaged in a major structural reform program, making the economy more competitive and limiting the role of the public sector.[1]

The behavior of the capital account of the balance of payments in recent years is a key, transparent manifestation of the changing patterns in the Mexican economy. Indeed, after the foreign debt crisis of the mid-1980s, net capital inflows began in the late 1980s and reached $3.6 billion in 1989. A sharp increase in net capital inflows was then observed in the early 1990s, and these reached a record high of $29.4 billion in 1993. Accompanying these changes, Mexican equity prices (in dollars) were 10 times higher at the start of 1994 than their level at the start of 1989.

Yet the 1994 crisis took place—despite all these successes and the relatively sound fiscal and monetary fundamentals in preceding years. The crisis renewed memories of Latin America's debt crisis in the mid-1980s, which started with Mexico defaulting on its international debt and ended almost a decade later, when most Latin American countries had recovered.

Several authors have analyzed the economic conditions leading to the 1994 crisis (e.g., Dornbusch and Werner 1994, including the comments by G. Calvo and S. Fischer; Leiderman, Liviatan, and Thorne 1994; Calvo 1995; Hausmann 1995; Steiner 1995; International Monetary Fund, *World Economic Outlook*, 1995; Sachs, Tornell, and Velasco 1995; Burki and Edwards 1995; Lustig 1995). Differences among these papers are more questions of emphasis than basic disagreement about the origins of the crisis.

We believe a "consensus view" would stress the existence of both "flow" and "stock" problems. On the flow side, a sharp rise in the current account deficit to about 8 percent of GDP was to a large extent financed by highly volatile, short-term capital inflows. Thus, the whole external equilibrium became quite vulnerable to external or internal shocks that could change foreign investors' sentiments about Mexico. The economy was vulnerable not only because the sizable, short-term capital inflows were probably unsustainable, but also because of the authorities' implicit commitment to avoid marked movements in nominal exchange rates. Yet, as we will argue, it was precisely this exchange rate commitment that probably increased the weight of short-term portfolio flows in total capital inflows.

On the stock side, the rapid growth of domestic monetary aggregates and the conversion of *cetes* into dollar-denominated *tesobonos*—at a time of considerable erosion in official foreign exchange reserves—raised financial vulnerability of the public sector, as well as the chances of a banking crisis. Here, the increased risk of default mainly reflected the potential foreign exchange illiquidity of the authorities. To these, one may

---

1. For a discussion of the Mexican reforms and their impact on the economy, see Aspe (1993).

add the impact of growing doubts about fiscal and monetary fundamentals, along with a sequence of inadequate policy responses to adverse shocks in 1994. Taken together, these factors made Mexico extremely vulnerable to a self-fulfilling attack.

Although important and sizable, the 1994 crisis had shorter-lived effects on other developing countries than did the debt crisis of the 1980s. There is evidence that net capital inflows to developing countries continue to be strong, following marked declines in portfolio flows in the first two months of 1995, and that the Mexican government and private Mexican companies continue to have access to world capital markets. Similarly, most emerging markets' equity prices rebounded in late 1995. And there are good reasons to believe that following the implementation of an economic adjustment program and a sharp recession, the "worst" might be over for the Mexican economy.

We do not intend to provide a complete description of the events leading to the crisis. Instead, we emphasize key aspects of the crisis and its aftermath. These include the role of fundamentals and the existence of growing doubts about the degree of fiscal discipline in 1994; a crucial delay in the shift of nominal anchors and in the introduction of substantial exchange rate flexibility, along with their effect on the composition of capital inflows; the information content of policy reactions to adverse shocks in 1994 and its possible implications for the likelihood of a self-fulfilling attack on the peso; and the analysis of the crisis's aftermath, with particular emphasis on the economic adjustment and its differences with the pattern of adjustment in the 1980s, and on the causes of the September 1995 confidence shock.

Balance of Payments Crises in Theory

There is a voluminous literature on currency crises and speculative attacks.[2] While some models stress the role of unsustainable fundamentals (such as monetary and fiscal policy) in precipitating a crisis, others focus on the role of self-fulfilling expectations. With the benefit of hindsight, this section discusses theoretical frameworks that offer insights into the Mexican crisis. The discussion also provides some analytical discipline for the interpretation of the empirical evidence presented later.

Crises Due to Unsustainable Policies

In the basic framework introduced by Krugman (1979), balance of payments crises arise because of a discrepancy between the monetary and

---

2. For recent discussions of work in this area, see Eichengreen, Rose, and Wyplosz (1995) and Calvo (1995).

fiscal fundamentals required to support the authorities' commitment to peg the nominal exchange rate and the actual behavior of these fundamentals. In particular, when monetary and fiscal policy are more expansionary than is consistent with the peg, (e.g., as under monetized government budget deficits), international reserves begin to fall, and eventually a crisis erupts.

Krugman (1979) considered a small, open economy in which residents consume a single tradeable good. Domestic supply of the good is exogenous, and the domestic price of the good equals the foreign price times the nominal exchange rate (i.e., purchasing power parity holds). In principle, agents can hold three types of assets: domestic money, domestic bonds, and foreign bonds, which are perfectly substitutable. To simplify matters, the money stock is assumed to be equal to the monetary base (there are no banks)—that is, equal to the sum of domestic credit and the domestic-currency value of foreign reserves held by the central bank. Foreign reserves earn no interest, and agents are endowed with perfect foresight.

In this framework, if domestic credit expansion (which here is financing a government budget deficit) is excessive, international reserves are run down at a rate proportional to the rate of credit expansion. Consequently, any finite stock of international reserves will be depleted in a finite period. Assume that nominal exchange rate policy is summarized by the central bank's announced rule that it will peg the exchange rate until reserves reach a specified lower bound. At that lower bound, the central bank will withdraw from the market and shift to a floating exchange rate regime. Under these conditions, a positive rate of growth of domestic credit that exceeds the growth of domestic demand for money will lead agents to anticipate that reserves will fall gradually to the lower bound and ultimately that there will be a shift of regime. To avoid losses when the pegged exchange rate regime collapses, the economic agents will take anticipatory actions that will force a crisis before that point is reached.

With an eye toward the Mexican case, this model predicts that expansionary monetary and fiscal policies would be observed prior to speculative attacks. Put differently, in the preattack equilibrium, there is a basic incompatibility between the policy fundamentals and the fixed exchange rate regime—an incompatibility that cannot be sustained with a finite stock of international reserves. That scenario should also be associated with a gradual depletion of the central bank's international reserves over time. In the preattack equilibrium, this gradual depletion of reserves could be accompanied by rising nominal interest rates, rising wages and prices, overvaluation of the real exchange rate, and a widening of current account deficits.

The foregoing framework stresses government budget deficits and excessive domestic credit creation as the roots of the balance of payments problem under a nominal exchange rate peg. In reality, however, there have been numerous speculative attacks and currency crises that were not preceded by the developments predicted by the standard approach. This observation has provided a strong motivation for development of alternative crises models.

Policy Switches and Self-Fulfilling Speculative Attacks

An alternative class of models develops the notion that a pegged (or targeted) exchange rate can be attacked even in the absence of a basic incompatibility between the behavior of fundamentals and the exchange rate regime. In these models (as developed by Flood and Garber 1984; Obstfeld 1986, 1994), self-fulfilling attacks can arbitrarily shift the foreign exchange market between multiple equilibria.

What is critical for this result is the assumed *contingent* nature of the authorities' policy rule. Under normal conditions, monetary and fiscal policies follow their paths, and there is no threat to the exchange rate regime. However, if the exchange rate is attacked, the authorities are assumed to shift to more accommodative fiscal and monetary policies compatible with a more depreciated exchange rate. Thus, agents' anticipation that monetary and fiscal policy will loosen following an attack may generate the anticipation of capital gains on foreign assets.

The possibility of validation of an attack makes multiple equilibria viable simultaneously. In the Krugman model, the markets anticipate a crisis—based on the behavior of fundamentals and on the fixed nominal exchange rate—and spark an attack. In contrast, in these later models the attack itself provokes the crisis, and the attack need not be preceded by falling international reserves, by an overvalued exchange rate, and by a deterioration in the current account.

The original formulation of these models assumed an exogenous trigger for the shift in economic agents' expectations (from less to more accommodative policies) that leads to the attack. Recent models have discussed economic conditions that may endogenously affect the public's perception of future changes in the policy regime. For example, if the present anti-inflationary policies of the government are likely to increase the rate of unemployment—and if policymakers and the public perceive such a result as an increasing cost of this policy—then the public may forecast a greater probability of a switch to a more inflationary regime. This revised forecast may in turn spark a speculative attack. In this example, the crisis (or attack) need not be preceded by the precrisis developments laid out in the Krugman model. Instead, domestic recessionary phenomena and/or political factors should characterize the precrisis period.

For this framework to be useful, it is essential to find major events that could have coordinated the actions and expectations of economic agents. In the case of Mexico, a combination of social and political turbulence

Figure 1   Current account balance and real exchange rate index, 1989–95

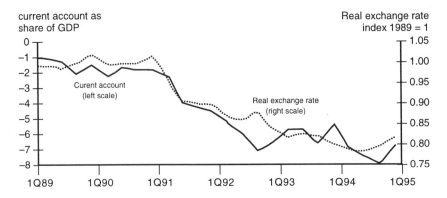

current account as share of GDP

Real exchange rate index 1989 = 1

and adverse shocks in 1994, together with a slowdown in economic growth and a prolonged deterioration in external competitiveness, may have provided such a basis for an expected expansionary shift in macroeconomic policy. As time passed, nominal exchange rate targeting was also increasingly blamed for the marked overvaluation of the peso and for a prolonged recession (e.g., Dornbusch and Werner 1994).[3] It was suggested that these developments would ultimately endanger stabilization and that they needed to be reversed (at least partially) by means of a devaluation.

As adverse political and economic shocks cumulated over the course of 1994, each successive shock probably served as a focal point for downgrading the authorities' credibility and for increasing expectations of a regime shift toward less restrictive policies.

Growing Doubts about Fiscal Fundamentals

Almost all explanations of the Mexican crisis based on the alleged nonsustainability of precrisis policies and economic conditions stress the sizable current account deficit and real exchange rate appreciation as key concerns. These two factors could have undermined Mexico's creditworthiness, prompting a crisis in confidence. Figure 1 plots the behavior of the current account balance and the real exchange rate of the peso. It is noteworthy that the current account deficit (expressed as a percentage of

---

3. On the use of nominal exchange rate targeting at the start of Mexico's disinflation and on the need to shift to an inflation-target anchor, see Leiderman, Liviatan, and Thorne (1994); see also Stanley Fischer's comments to Dornbusch and Werner (1994). These issues will be discussed below.

GDP) reached an average level in 1992–94 that was higher than that reached by the Mexican economy before the debt crisis in 1982.

True, these were worrisome developments. Yet it would have been hard to justify sounding the alarm of a major balance of payments crisis based on these developments alone. While economic analysis suggests that large current account deficits are unsustainable in the long run, as countries cannot borrow indefinitely, this need not be the case over the course of several years in which an economy is undergoing a major transformation.

As is well known, Mexico introduced major economic reforms in the 1980s. These included a marked tightening of the fiscal stance, trade liberalization, entry into the General Agreement on Tariffs and Trade (GATT) and the North American Free Trade Agreement (NAFTA), privatization, deregulation, and, beginning in late 1987, a major disinflation effort. As a result of these changes, Mexico regained access to world capital markets, and foreign investors began to pour funds into its economy. Substantial capital inflows from abroad generated a capital account surplus, which financed both an increased deficit in the current account and central bank accumulation of international reserves. From this perspective, real exchange rate appreciation and deterioration of the current account could represent the economy's equilibrating (endogenous) response to reforms and to renewed foreign capital flows.

Unlike the run-up to the debt crisis of the 1980s, this time Mexico had reduced its public-sector debt substantially, from about 80 percent of GDP in the 1980s to 22 percent in 1993. Moreover, this time most of the current account deficit was financed by private nondebt flows. Therefore, the risk of a government default was less likely, and any creditworthiness assessments depended more on the performance of the private sector than on that of the public sector. However, because growing amounts of peso-denominated Mexican assets were held by foreign investors, a key risk was that of unexpected devaluation. As we show later, currency risk became sizable only in late 1993 and early 1994; currency risk was much lower in 1992–93.

Since the size of public-sector debt in early 1994 was not a leading indicator of a crisis, a reasonable alternative is that investors began to be concerned about the allocation of capital inflows between consumption and investment and about the private economy's ability to generate future income to repay its new debts. It is commonly argued that creditworthiness is an increasing function of the portion of capital inflows allocated to increased investment (as opposed to increased consumption). A striking feature of the Mexican capital inflows episode is the allocation of capital flows between a decline in saving (or increase in consumption) and an increase in investment. In table 1, we compare Mexico with five other developing countries that experienced strong capital inflows in 1989–93.

Table 1 Effects of capital inflows on saving and investment[a]
(percentages)

Items	Argentina	Chile	Indonesia	Malaysia	Mexico	Thailand
Change in the current account balance to GDP ratio[b]	−2.8	0.8	−2.1	−1.7	−3.6	−5.6
Change in domestic saving	−1.0	2.5	1.4	8.6	−2.9	4.2
Private sector	−4.9	1.4	−1.0	3.7	−8.7	1.5
Public sector	3.9	1.1	2.4	4.9	5.8	2.7
Change in gross investment	1.8	1.7	3.5	10.3	0.7	9.4
Memo items						
Average real growth in GDP	8.0	6.3	6.8	9.1	2.9	10.9
Average rate of inflation	12.0	18.9	7.7	3.3	18.8	5.2
Cumulative real exchange rate appreciation	24.0	4.4	1.6	8.7	32.3	6.5

a. Estimates correspond to the following periods: 1991–93 for Argentina, 1990–93 for Chile, 1988 for Indonesia, Malaysia and Thailand, and 1989–93 for Mexico.
b. Equals the difference between the change in domestic saving and in gross investment.

Source: Banco de Mexico, *Indicadores Económicos*; IMF, *International Financial Statistics.*

The comparison is particularly telling. In contrast to countries such as Indonesia and Thailand—where most of the increase in the current account deficit as a share of GDP was explained by a sharp increase in the investment ratio—in Mexico only a small proportion (less than 20 percent) of the inflows were used to finance investment. The bulk of the inflows financed a decline in the national saving ratio. Moreover, the evidence indicates that countries that invested a large proportion of their capital inflows also experienced accelerated economic growth. The only country that bore some resemblance to Mexico was Argentina, but even in this country the case was less extreme.

There were several economic reasons for the consumption boom in Mexico. First, the private sector probably revised upward its expected permanent income in the new economic environment (including NAFTA). Second, the enhanced access to international credit and capital probably meant that previous liquidity constraints were now at least partially reduced. Third, the exchange rate–based stabilization policy implemented after 1987 was not perceived as a fully credible strategy—a feature common to many heterodox stabilizations in other emerging markets. As such, there was probably a reduction in the expected relative price of present versus future consumption—especially of imported goods and services, which provided an incentive for a rise in consumption. The weight of each of these factors in the observed consumption boom remains to be determined in future work.

While the foregoing has become a relatively standard characterization of the allocation of Mexican capital inflows into investment and saving, there are two statistical flaws in this analysis. The first is shown in table 1, which estimates private saving using the concept of nominal public-sector saving—that is, it defines total public-sector saving to include nominal interest payments on the public-sector debt as a current expenditure. During periods of high inflation, nominal interest payments include the compensation for the erosion in the principal resulting from high inflation rates; this concept therefore overestimates current expenditure. Moreover, since private saving and private disposable income are estimated as residuals, they record the inflation component on the domestic public debt as private disposable income, thus overestimating private saving and disposable income during periods of high inflation and underestimating them during periods of low inflation. Strictly speaking, the inflation component should not be regarded as a government expenditure or as private income because it does not represent flows derived from productive activities.

A second important flaw is in the treatment of the development banks' net lending to the private sector. The official estimate—that is, the nominal public-sector deficit—excludes development banks' net lending. However, development banks undertake expenses that would otherwise be absorbed by the public sector. One example is the unrecoverable loans granted to sectors that the government intends to protect (e.g., agriculture and small-enterprise loans). They should be recorded as expenses in the definition of public-sector deficits.

The problem in making this correction lies in estimating correctly these expenses—that is, in estimating development banks' quasi-fiscal deficit. To overcome this difficulty, we have decided to proxy the quasi-fiscal deficit with development banks' net lending (as it is commonly done in the IMF's definition of public-sector deficits). Although this definition overestimates the true size of the quasi-fiscal deficit (because it assumes that none of the loans will be repaid), it nonetheless provides a more accurate estimate of the true fiscal stance than the official estimate.

Correcting the official estimates for these two effects—namely, the treatment of the interest rates and of development banks' net lending—leads to different conclusions about the role of private-sector saving and fiscal policy stance in the capital inflows episode. To illustrate the differences from official estimates, we record three definitions for the public-sector deficit and for private saving for 1989–94 (figures 2 and 3).[4] The three

---

4. To estimate the inflation-corrected fiscal deficit and private-sector saving, we used a methodology similar to that of Arrau and Oks (1992; see also Thorne 1991; World Bank, *World Development Report* 1988). The main differences between our methodology and Arrau

Figure 2 Estimates of fiscal stance, 1983–95

percent of GDP

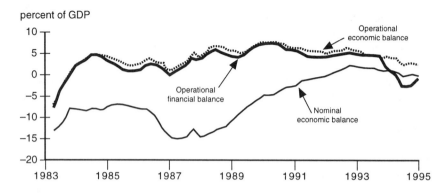

Figure 3 Private saving, 1983–95

percent of GDP

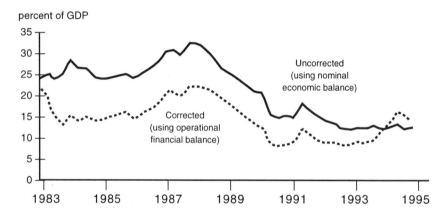

fiscal deficit variables in figure 2 are the *nominal economic balance*, which is the official measure of fiscal stance; the *operational economic balance*, which is the nominal economic balance corrected for the inflation component in both domestic and external debt; and the *operational financial balance*, which is the operational economic balance less the net lending of the development banks.

Although the assumptions used to construct the scores are open to debate, suffice it to say that conclusions on fiscal stance reached with these three estimates are very different. While the nominal economic

and Oks's is the treatment of the inflation tax. While Arrau and Oks treated the inflation tax as an explicit tax and recorded it as government tax revenues, we treated it as an involuntary tax and did not include it as a government revenue. The effect of this difference is that in Arrau and Oks private saving is smaller than in our estimates because of the inflation tax on private disposable income.

balance suggests a fiscal tightening from 1989 to 1993, the inflation-corrected fiscal balances (the operational economic and financial balances) indicate that in 1989 the fiscal sector was in surplus and remained tight until the third quarter of 1993. But after that the operational financial balance points to a strong fiscal expansion, which was the result of the net credit expansion of development banks. By that measure, the fiscal expansion in the last quarter of 1993—about 3 percentage points of GDP—was as large as that over the previous four years. We can therefore conclude that the sharp fiscal adjustment reported in the official estimates using the nominal economic balance overestimates the true fiscal adjustment during 1989–93. The inflation-corrected definition of the public-sector deficit indicates that the fiscal adjustment took place before 1989.

Since then, there was a small fiscal expansion, but the fiscal balance was kept in a strong position. In fact, fiscal policy only changed in the third quarter of 1993, coinciding with the slowdown in economic growth and with the arrival of adverse external and domestic shocks.

The redefinition of fiscal balances has important consequences for calculations of private saving ratios. Figure 3 reports two definitions of the private saving ratio consistent with the definitions of the nominal economic and operational financial balances reported in figure 2.[5] The main result is that the fall in the inflation-corrected, private-sector saving ratio is less dramatic than in the official (or standard) estimates. In fact, when corrected for the inflation component and for the net lending of development banks, private saving fell by 1.2 percentage points of GDP between 1989 and 1993, and by 3.4 percentage points if we make no correction for the net lending of development banks.

The main explanation for this less-marked fall in private saving is that official estimates of private-sector disposable income do not adjust for the effect of interest rates and of development banks' quasi-fiscal deficit. Following the introduction of the anti-inflation program in late 1987, the government paid relatively high *ex post* real interest payments on the domestic debt; this in turn increased private disposable income. Thus, some of the private consumption boom in 1989–93 probably resulted from the marked increase in private disposable income.

This effect is underestimated in the official statistics, which make no correction for the inflation component. As such, private disposable income in the official estimates changed little between the periods of high and low inflation and of high and low real interest rates. Also, the rapid expansion in development banks' net lending to the private sector in 1993–94 had the effect of increasing private-sector disposable income and thus private-sector saving. Because these loans contain either an interest

---

5. To facilitate the comparison in figure 3, we omitted the estimate of private saving using the operational economic balance.

rate subsidy or were not repaid, they were in fact transfers to the private sector.

To sum up, various budget and public-sector indicators suggest that in 1993 and 1994 there was a marked shift toward a relaxation of the fiscal stance in Mexico. In addition to the effects of inflation correction on the budget, there was a sharp cumulative rise of about 3 percent of GDP in net credit creation by public-sector development banks. Furthermore, while the debt-management conversion from *cetes* to *tesobonos* in 1994 resulted in a fall in government interest payments relative to GDP (because of the lower interest rates paid on dollar-denominated *tesobonos*), this shift increased the government's exposure to exchange rate risk. It also increased the public sector's vulnerability to a rollover risk—particularly under conditions of falling foreign exchange reserves. All in all, 1994 witnessed growing doubts about whether earlier tight fiscal discipline would continue. Nevertheless, this development on its own—given the orders of magnitude involved—was probably not a sufficient indicator of a Krugman-type balance of payments crisis.

Shifting Nominal Anchors—Too Little, Too Late

Exchange rate policy played a key role in the developments that culminated in the December 1994 crisis. Exchange rate policy went through three main phases after stabilization. First, after an initial devaluation of almost 40 percent, the Economic Solidarity Pact (or Pacto) signed in December 1987 established a fixed exchange rate for the peso against the dollar. Fixing the exchange rate meant that the nominal exchange rate was treated as a key nominal anchor in the program. Second, the authorities shifted toward increased flexibility by adopting a preannounced crawling peg after January 1989: the peso/dollar rate was allowed to depreciate by 1 peso per day in 1989, 80 cents per day in 1990, and 40 cents per day in 1991. Third, an exchange rate band was adopted on 11 November 1991.

The foregoing gradual shift toward increased flexibility in the nominal exchange rate is a common feature of heterodox stabilizations (Helpman, Leiderman, and Bufman 1994). While exchange rate anchoring can break inflation inertia and produce rapid disinflation at the start of a stabilization program (especially when accompanied by contractionary measures on fiscal fundamentals), this is commonly followed by a loss of competitiveness, as reflected in cumulative real exchange rate appreciation. Experience indicates that, sooner or later, policymakers begin perceiving this erosion in competitiveness as a serious risk to the ultimate success of the whole program. When this happens, and once it has become clear that fiscal and monetary fundamentals have been adjusted and major disinfla-

Figure 4 Mexico's exchange rate band, 2 January 1991–19 December 1994

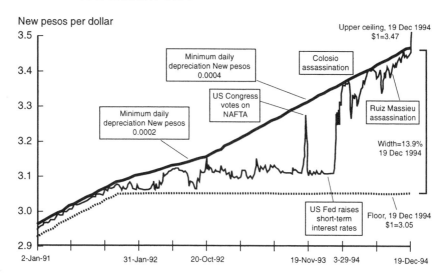

New pesos per dollar

Upper ceiling, 19 Dec 1994
$1=3.47

Minimum daily depreciation New pesos 0.0004

Colosio assassination

US Congress votes on NAFTA

Minimum daily depreciation New pesos 0.0002

Ruiz Massieu assassination

Width=13.9% 19 Dec 1994

US Fed raises short-term interest rates

Floor, 19 Dec 1994 $1=3.05

2-Jan-91 31-Jan-92 20-Oct-92 19-Nov-93 3-29-94 19-Dec-94

tion is being achieved, countries may relax the fixity of the exchange rate by moving toward relatively ample bands, or to a free float.

The problem of shifting nominal anchors refers to the policy dilemma of how and when to move toward increased exchange rate flexibility without necessarily raising expectations of inflation and without jeopardizing the achievements of the disinflation program (Leiderman, Liviatan, and Thorne 1994).[6] An increasing number of countries have resolved this dilemma by adopting official inflation targets when they shifted toward exchange rate flexibility (Leiderman and Svensson 1995). Indeed, the United Kingdom, Finland, and Sweden took this route following their shift to a float in the aftermath of the European currency crisis of September 1992.

In the case of Mexico, it can be argued that despite the shift to a crawling exchange rate band in November 1991, there was little exchange rate variability until the end of 1993 (figure 4). In part this reflected market forces. However, this also reflected the existence of an "inner" band of central bank intervention within the announced band. The presence of this inner intervention band mirrored, to a large extent, authorities' strong desire to keep relying on a nominal exchange rate anchor for disinflation. An additional motivation for the inner band was the apparent attempt

6. In addition, see Stanley Fischer's published comments to the Dornbusch and Werner (1994) paper, focusing on the need to move toward increased flexibility of nominal exchange rates in Mexico.

*reasons for the
inner
band*

in 1993 to minimize foreign investors' uncertainties and to minimize capital flow reversals in a year loaded with political and economic uncertainties (e.g., the presidential elections and the ratification of the NAFTA agreement). This interpretation received some support in late 1993. When the US Congress approved NAFTA, President Carlos Salinas announced the presidential candidate, and the central bank abandoned the inner intervention band. This led to greater exchange rate fluctuations within the wider band as the new sources of uncertainty developed—in particular, the assassination of Luis Donaldo Colosio in March 1994 and the rise in US short-term interest rates starting in February 1994.

It can be argued that, in principle, Mexico had begun to shift its nominal targets before the crisis. On 1 January 1994, the Mexican Parliament enacted the Central Bank Law, giving the central bank full independence and making price stability its key mandate. This clear-cut mandate compels the central bank to concentrate its efforts and resources on the fight against inflation. The mandate also makes the central bank accountable for inflation performance.

To reassure market participants that shifting nominal anchors would not lead to higher inflation, the independent central bank was to consolidate the earlier low-inflation success and to fulfill the official inflation targets. Although the Mexican authorities had announced inflation targets before, these were more a form of price-increase guidelines in the context of the Pacto than the main operational goal of monetary policy. The target inflation rate was 9.7 percent for 1992; inflation ended up higher, at 11.9 percent. For 1993, the authorities announced a target of 7 percent; actual inflation turned out to be 8 percent. And for 1994, the authorities announced a target rate of inflation of 5 percent, and inflation ended at 7 percent—with the major crisis erupting at the end of that year. Before the crisis, the authorities had announced an inflation target of 4 percent for 1995.

While the coexistence of explicit inflation targets and an exchange rate band can result in mutual support between exchange rate and price developments, these objectives can also sometimes conflict, especially if there is an inner, relatively narrow exchange rate band.[7] Much depends on the nature of the underlying shocks.

When such conflicts develop, experience from other countries indicates that it is useful for the authorities to prioritize among their objectives in a clear, transparent manner. Despite the intention to shift toward an inflation target anchor, actual policy in most of 1993 and 1994 was still conducted as if minimizing exchange rate fluctuations within the band, and maintaining the nominal exchange rate anchor, was a main policy

---

7. Some of the arguments in this paragraph are further discussed in Leiderman, Liviatan, and Thorne (1994).

objective. Accordingly, with the 1994 shocks, there was no immediate danger to the inflation target, yet there was substantial pressure on the exchange rate band. Instead of adopting restrictive monetary policy measures to defend the band, the authorities relied on selling foreign exchange to reduce pressure in the foreign exchange market, an action that did not prevent the exchange rate from reaching the upper limit of the band— that is, the maximum depreciation of the peso against the dollar—where it remained for most of the year (figure 4).

As indicated, monetary policy was not extremely tight throughout 1994. While short-term interest rates were raised after the Colosio assassination in March, and the interest rate differential vis-à-vis the United States reached 12 percentage points in April (on three-month Treasury bills), this differential showed a declining trend, mainly reflecting hikes in US interest rates. Thus, despite a marked fall in foreign exchange reserves and substantial exchange rate pressure, monetary aggregates were growing quite rapidly in 1994. There was no active reliance on interest rate hikes to defend international reserves and the exchange rate band. It was only toward the end of the year that interest rates were raised. But this was too little too late, and the 20 December crisis prompted a shift to a float.

Much of the crisis could likely have been avoided with an earlier shift of nominal anchors—say, in the first quarter of 1994—giving monetary policy priority to the inflation target and relying less on targeting nominal exchange rates in a narrow band—together with a tighter monetary policy stance (see also Leiderman, Liviatan, and Thorne 1994).

Not only did the inner-band intervention policy potentially conflict with other nominal targets of monetary policy, it also probably affected the composition of capital inflows by providing incentives to short-term flows. These flows in turn make the economy more vulnerable to adverse shocks. In the short run, exchange-market intervention can substantially reduce the degree of foreign exchange risk associated with foreigners' peso-denominated investments.

In table 2, we report the composition of capital inflows for Mexico and for five other countries that also experienced strong capital inflows. Mexico stands out as the country with the highest proportion of portfolio flows in total capital flows—about two-thirds. This pattern is especially clear in 1993, when, out of the net capital inflows of about $29 billion, only about $5 billion was in the form of foreign direct investment (FDI). In the other countries, FDI accounts for a much larger proportion of capital inflows.

Although a large share of portfolio flows was invested in private Mexican enterprises and contributed to their modernization, most of these investments were highly liquid assets. Investors could sell them at short notice. In fact, some of these assets were quoted in the form of American Depositary Receipts (ADRs) on the New York Stock Exchange, thus mak-

Table 2 Size and composition of capital inflows in selected countries[a]

Items	Argentina	Chile	Indonesia	Malaysia	Mexico	Thailand
Annual average capital inflows						
In billions of dollars	10.2	2.3	3.4	1.8	18.7	8.6
As a percentage of GDP	4.5	7.0	3.6	4.3	5.9	11.2
Components of capital inflows (percent of total inflows)						
Portfolio investment	36.6	21.7	−2.7	−9.1	67.1	5.5
Foreign direct investment	42.0	31.1	27.5	124.1	21.1	20.2
Other	21.4	47.2	75.2	−15.0	11.7	74.3
Memo item						
Increase in net reserves	36.0	76.2	26.0	47.6	20.3	42.5

a. Estimates correspond to the following periods: 1991–93 for Argentina, 1990–93 for Chile, 1988 for Indonesia, Malaysia and Thailand, and 1989–93 for Mexico.

Source: Banco de Mexico, *Indicadores Económicos*; IMF, *International Financial Statistics.*

ing them highly liquid for foreign investors. While investors prized the high liquidity of these assets, it also made the flows more volatile and more prone to reversals. A substantial part of the portfolio flows reflected the actions of mutual funds and large institutional investors in the United States, for which small changes in market perceptions can lead to rapid portfolio shifts.

Moreover, the evidence on the importance of external factors in explaining capital inflows into Latin America suggests that even if conditions in the domestic economy were unaltered, changes in the international economy can cause outflows of capital and trigger crises in confidence (Calvo, Leiderman, and Reinhart 1993; Chuhan, Claessens, and Mamingi 1993). Overall, casual cross-country evidence seems to indicate that there could be a connection between the composition of capital inflows and the extent to which nominal exchange rates are allowed to vary in the short run.

In sum, the strong reliance on the nominal exchange rate anchor and on selling foreign exchange reserves to calm the markets probably increased the economy's vulnerability to capital outflows. As long as investors believed that the authorities were able to defend the exchange rate band and as long as capital inflows continued, the current account deficit could be regarded as sustainable. Yet a finite stock of foreign exchange reserves underpinned this strategy. Thus, after almost a year with the exchange rate at the top of its band, and with a substantial erosion of foreign exchange reserves, confidence was quickly lost, and the current account deficit came to be regarded as unsustainable. To explain when and how this happened, we need next to explain what led to changes in market perceptions.

What the Policy Response to Shocks Reveals

In models of policy switches and self-fulfilling speculative attacks, the authorities' response to shocks can provide important signals to market participants. For a country that depends heavily on capital inflows, as Mexico did, policy responses that are perceived as enhancing the prevailing fundamentals can reassure the market and help sustain capital inflows. *signalling* Symmetrically, policy responses that the market perceives as weakening the fundamentals can undermine confidence and lead to capital-flow reversals. Each time the policy response is perceived as inadequate, the level of the sustainable current account deficit falls as investors become less willing to finance the deficit.

In this context, a crisis can arise following a sequence of inadequate policy responses. Modeling market participants' reaction to policy responses is a difficult task that is beyond the scope of this chapter. Nevertheless, it is useful here to focus on the market reaction to shocks as an indicator of how policymakers' actions affected market confidence.

We treat each shock as an event that can change the behavior of market variables. Three groups of variables were selected for the analyses: policymakers' responses, market responses, and indicators of illiquidity or vulnerability to policy shocks.

To assess the authorities' responses, we picked three policy variables that are under the direct control of the government and/or the central bank (figure 5). These variables are Banco de Mexico's holdings of international reserves, Banco de Mexico's net credit expansion to the economy, and public-sector debt management (proxied here by the proportion of *tesobonos* and *cetes* in total government securities). These variables are reported monthly from August 1993 to December 1994.

To assess market response, we focused on the following five variables: the weekly 90-day *cetes* interest rates; the weekly foreign exchange risk, defined as the difference between the *cetes* and the *tesobonos* interest rates;[8] the weekly country (or default) risk, defined as the difference between the rates on *tesobonos* and those on US Treasury bills; the daily position of the exchange rate relative to the ceiling of the exchange rate band; and the exchange rate expected 30 days earlier relative to the realized exchange

---

8. *Cetes* are a local currency-denominated government security, and *tesobonos* are a dollar-indexed government security. Therefore, differences in the yield on these two instruments should proxy the expected risk of an exchange rate devaluation.

Figure 5 Effects of shocks on reserve holdings, net domestic credit, and government debt management, August 1993–November 1994

International reserves
millions of dollars

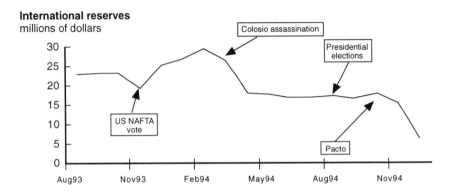

Base money and net domestic credit
billions of dollars

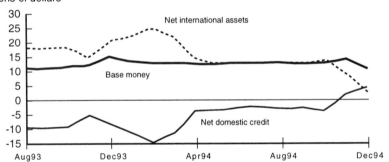

Share of *tesobonos* and *cetes* in total government securities
percent

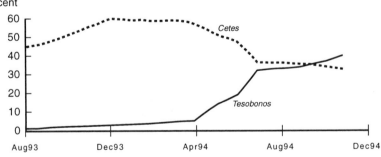

Figure 6 Indicators of vulnerability to speculative attacks, August 1993–August 1995

Ratio of reserves to base money
percent

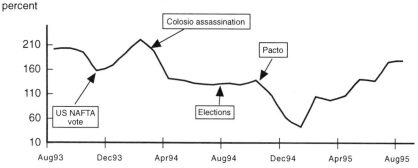

Ratio of reserves to liquid public-sector debt
percent

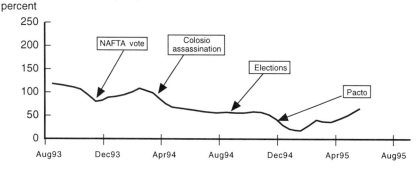

rate. In our time-series analysis, we centered each shock at time zero and provided sufficient lags and leads on each variable to determine how shocks affected their paths. In the case of weekly variables, we found that lags and leads of 12 weeks relative to the timing of the shock did the job, and for the daily variables, 60-day lags and leads seemed appropriate. We have indicated cases in which two or more shocks happened simultaneously.

Our two indicators of potential illiquidity and vulnerability to speculative attacks were the ratio of international reserves to base money and the ratio of international reserves to liquid public-sector debt (sum of *tesobonos* and *cetes*; see figure 6).[9] When either of these two indicators fall markedly below 100 percent, there is the danger of a self-fulfilling

---

9. Stock-type variables such as these have been the focus of much of Calvo's (1995) discussion of the Mexican crisis; see also published comments on the Dornbusch and Werner (1994) paper.

speculative attack based on the fear of illiquidity and default—much as under a banking crisis.

In general, if the policy response enhances the economic fundamentals, we expect the shock to only temporarily alter the behavior of the variable. As confidence improves, the variable then should return to its previous path. Likewise, if the shock is regarded as temporary, one can expect the time series data to return to its previous trend. In contrast, if the shock is viewed as permanent, then the whole time-series profile of the variable might change.

If the response to the shock weakens the economic fundamentals, the variable's behavior might be altered, and its path may reflect a loss of confidence. For instance, suppose there is a sudden, temporary capital outflow and assume that the authorities' response did not weaken policy fundamentals. We would then expect to observe a depreciation of the exchange rate immediately upon the realization that a shock has occurred, followed by an appreciation later on. In the case of a permanent financial shock, such as an increase in international interest rates, we would expect the new equilibrium nominal exchange rate to be higher (that is, more depreciated) than before. This is because the shock would have made Mexico less attractive relative to other investment opportunities and thus induced a portfolio shift. In analyzing these variables, one should also not rule out the possibility of pure speculative bubbles. These would manifest themselves via changes in market perceptions without changes in the fundamentals. In this case, we might observe temporary departures in the variables' time-series behavior even though policy fundamentals remained unchanged.

We applied this methodology to six domestic and external shocks to the Mexican economy between September 1993 and December 1995 that we found most significant (figures 7 through 12). First was the external shock of 11 November 1993—the date when the US Congress voted on NAFTA. One week before the vote, Ross Perot, the former third-party candidate in the US presidential elections, launched his opposition to NAFTA; this sent the Mexican markets into turmoil. Second was the US Federal Reserve external shock of 4 February 1994—the date when the US Federal Reserve pushed up interest rates in an attempt to cool down inflationary pressures. Third was 24 March 1994, the date that Mexican presidential candidate Luis Donaldo Colosio was assassinated. Fourth was the domestic shock of 24 September 1994—when the members of the social pact (or Pacto) reaffirmed their commitment to jointly determined targets and to the exchange rate band. Fifth was the 20 December 1994 crisis, when the government decided to widen the band by 15 percent in a futile attempt to stabilize the market. And sixth was the expectations shock of September 1995, when the market adjusted its inflation and growth expectations. This also coincided with the start of relatively large exchange rate and interest rate fluctuations.

Figure 7   Effects of shock accompanying US Congress' vote on NAFTA, 11 November 1993

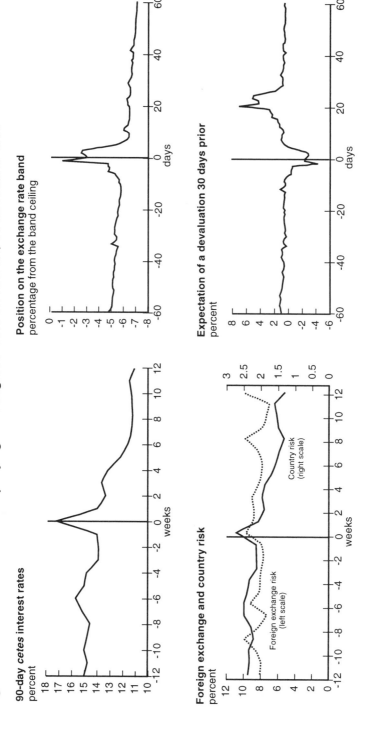

90-day *cetes* interest rates
percent

Position on the exchange rate band
percentage from the band ceiling

Foreign exchange and country risk
percent

Foreign exchange risk
(left scale)

Country risk
(right scale)

Expectation of a devaluation 30 days prior
percent

Although we could have added other shocks, our analysis indicates that the ones selected were the most important and offer sufficient variety to enable us to explain the changing expectations of market participants on the way to the December 1994 crisis.[10] Of particular interest is how the pattern of policy adjustment to shocks was distributed as swings in the exchange rate within the band, changes in international reserves, and shifts in nominal interest rates.

The NAFTA Shock

This shock represented a threat to the stability of the Mexican economy. Evidence in figures 5, 6, and 7 indicates that this was a temporary shock and that the authorities' response to it was adequate. Specifically, the authorities reacted initially by selling some international reserves, then by sharply contracting net domestic credit and by increasing interest rates. This apparently discouraged speculative capital outflows. Overall, the market reacted as if this was a temporary shock. Market-determined variables (figure 7) displayed small deviations from the trend, and these variables approximately returned to their previous levels after the shock. Note that *cetes* interest rates increased sharply and then fell and that the exchange rate variables show a sharp depreciation followed by a strong appreciation.

US Federal Reserve Shock

The evidence on this shock was ambiguous, mainly because the market reaction reflected the joint effect of two concurrent events: the adverse effect of the increase in US interest rates and the positive effect of NAFTA approval. Interestingly enough, market reaction variables (figure 8) show very little impact of the increase in US interest rates. In fact, *cetes* interest rates kept falling until about eight weeks after the shock (that is, until the Colosio assassination). Currency and country risk also showed a downward trend, and there were expectations of exchange rate appreciation. Presumably, the positive response of these variables can be explained by the strength of capital inflows in late 1993 and early 1994. The only variable that showed an atypical response was the position of the exchange rate within the band: it showed a depreciation within the band about 10 days before the Colosio assassination. This, however, could have resulted from pure daily speculation.[11]

---

10. Ironically, the Chiapas uprising on 1 January 1994 and the September 1994 assassination of the secretary general of the PRI party, José Francisco Ruiz Massieu, show effects too insignificant to be included as shocks in our analysis. Also, we have excluded the March 1995 policy shock in which the authorities announced their reinforcement of the 9 January stabilization program; we regard this as part of the December 1994 crisis.

11. In fact, there is some anecdotal evidence that the depreciation within the band resulted from the fact that market participants were expecting an appreciation and shortened their dollar positions, which led to a shortage of dollars in the market. When some of the dollar

The Colosio Shock

This was far and away the most powerful shock. Evidence in figure 5 suggests that the authorities responded as if it were a temporary shock. Moreover, the policy response appears to have endangered the commitment to defend the exchange rate band. To defend the prevailing regime, the authorities sold large amounts of reserves—more than $10 billion. As a result, indicators of illiquidity and financial vulnerability fell to risky but still not extreme levels (figure 6). The ratios of reserves to base money and of reserves to public-sector liquid debt fell to less than 150 and 80 percent, respectively. Simultaneously, the central bank appears to have strongly expanded net domestic credit (figure 5).[12]

This monetary response took place in a context in which public finances were expanding and were further strained by the Colosio shock; fiscal expansion peaked in the second quarter of 1994 (figure 2). In an apparent attempt to contain potential social unrest, the government stimulated economic growth through aggregate demand policies—in particular, development banks' net lending, which reached about 4 percent of GDP by end-1994. In addition, the government offered to convert *cetes* into dollar-denominated *tesobonos*, thus taking over the foreign exchange risk of the short-term public-sector debt.[13] These three responses—the sale of international reserves, the increase in net domestic credit, and the loosening of the fiscal stance—led to an erosion in the economic fundamentals.

Figure 9 suggests that the market reacted strongly and that it probably viewed the Colosio shock as permanent. Note that there is sharp deterioration in all five market-reaction variables. *Cetes* interest rates, foreign exchange risk, and country risk exhibited a quasi-permanent shift in their trends. Similarly, the exchange rate remained pegged to the top of the band, at which point there were still expectations of additional future depreciations. Admittedly, the economy could have taken longer to recover from a shock as powerful as the Colosio assassination; this possibility is not allowed for in figure 9. But even after looking at longer

---

commitments fell due and the market demanded dollars, the exchange rate depreciated. Moreover, and presumably to dissuade speculative attackers, Banco de Mexico kept a tight monetary policy.

12. Although there were various reasons for the sharp expansion in net domestic credit to the economy, there are two that we believe were most important. First is the fact that Banco de Mexico was targeting base money. Therefore, keeping the supply of base money unaltered while losing foreign exchange reserves requires a net credit expansion. Second and perhaps more compelling is the weak condition of the banking system. Admittedly, Banco de Mexico and the government were concerned that a sharp contraction and the resulting high real interest rates could lead to bank insolvency (Gil-Díaz and Carstens 1996).

13. In fact, as Oks (1991) argued convincingly using the 1980s evidence on Mexico, the likelihood of a debt default and exchange rate devaluation increases the higher the proportion of the public debt held in foreign exchange and the shorter its maturity.

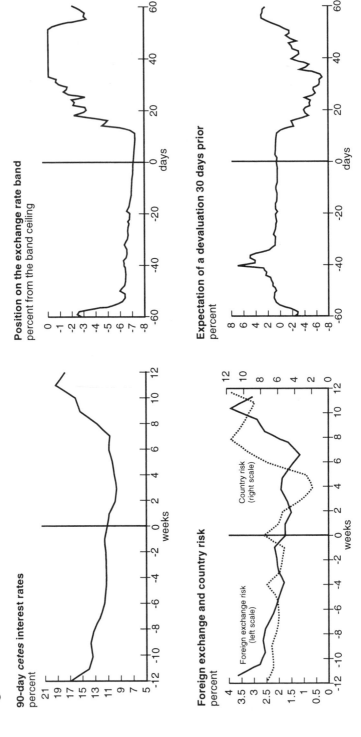

Figure 8   Effects of shock associated with US Federal Reserve's interest rate hike, 4 February 1994

Figure 9 Effects of Colosio assassination, 24 March 1994

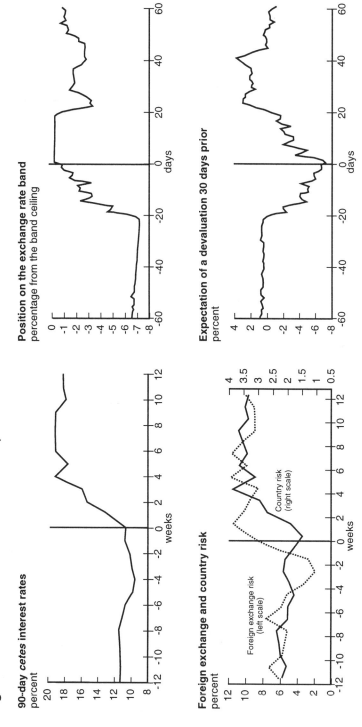

90-day *cetes* interest rates
percent

Position on the exchange rate band
percentage from the band ceiling

Foreign exchange and country risk
percent

Foreign exchange risk
(left scale)

Country risk
(right scale)

Expectation of a devaluation 30 days prior
percent

25

periods, we find no clear return of market-reaction variables to their preshock trends.

The Pacto Shock

This was a favorable domestic shock. After Ernesto Zedillo won the presidential elections with a strong majority on 2 August 1994, the government felt it necessary to renew the social pact (Pacto) originally laid out in 1987 so as to reassure the markets of its commitment both to the exchange rate band and to low inflation. The government therefore expected the market to react positively.

Judging from market reaction variables reported in figure 10, the market had doubts that the Pacto framework was sustainable. *Cetes* interest rates and foreign exchange risk had been headed downward just before the Pacto's signing, but immediately afterward, both climbed before stabilizing. Moreover, there is some anecdotal evidence that the authorities attempted to slow the increase in domestic interest rates by limiting supply in the *cetes* auctions.

Exchange rate variables also suggest that the Pacto brought little reassurance to the market. The exchange rate kept fluctuating very close to the band's ceiling without showing signs of appreciating, and the expected exchange rate was flat. Although the assassination of PRI Secretary General Francisco Ruiz Massieu on 28 September could explain the lack of positive reaction, there is no direct evidence that this negative news was strong enough to reverse the potential positive economic effects of the Pacto's renewal.

Eruption of the Crisis

The interesting feature here is not so much what happened on the date the peso was attacked but rather the events that preceded 20 December 1994. One way to interpret the crisis is that the sequence of adverse shocks during 1994 combined with inadequate policy responses to exacerbate the crisis.

Immediately after the Pacto was renewed, and presumably reflecting a lack of confidence in its ability to compensate for the economy's substantial vulnerability, the market started attacking the peso. As with previous shocks, the central bank responded initially by selling reserves. But this time the interest rate was left unchanged—quite contrary to expectations. In fact, the central bank expanded net domestic credit to the economy (figure 5), which might have both sustained the low interest rates and contributed to the strength of the attack by providing liquidity to the market. Interest rates only increased on the day the crisis erupted—that is, when it was too late (figure 11). The exclusive reliance on reserves as

Figure 10 Pacto shock, 24 September 1994

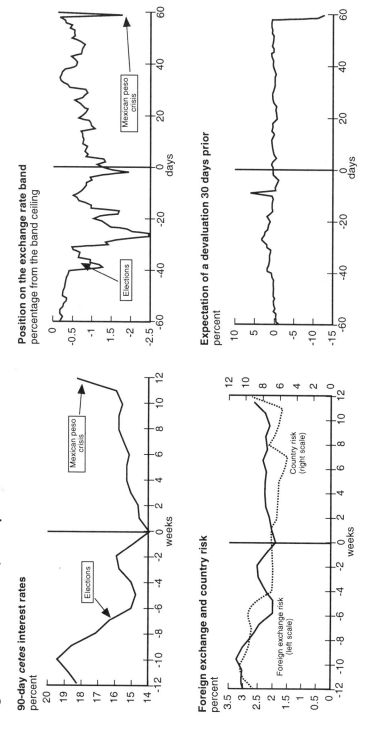

90-day *cetes* interest rates
percent

Position on the exchange rate band
percentage from the band ceiling

Foreign exchange and country risk
percent

Expectation of a devaluation 30 days prior
percent

Figure 11   Mexican peso crisis, 20 December 1994

90-day *cetes* interest rates

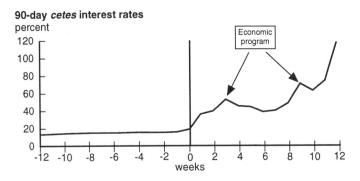

Foreign exchange and country risk

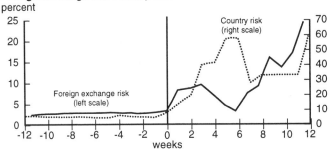

Expectation of a devaluation 30 days prior

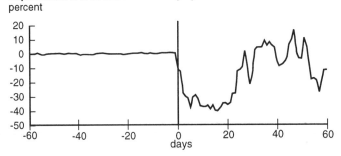

the instrument for defending against the attack pushed potential illiquidity and financial vulnerability to highly dangerous levels (figure 6). As suggested earlier, when these indicators fall below 100 percent, further speculative attacks could result in a major devaluation in which the exchange rate would shoot well beyond the top of the band.

The market reaction to the crisis thus had the hallmarks of a major crisis in confidence. The *cetes* interest rate and foreign exchange risk increased sharply, and the exchange rate exhibited marked instability.

To recapitulate, some of the shocks Mexico experienced in 1994—especially after the Pacto shock—prompted inadequate policy responses, which produced a loss of confidence. Policymakers appeared to believe that the shocks were temporary. Accordingly, they insisted on maintaining their commitment to the nominal exchange rate band. They did this not via an especially tight monetary policy, but rather by selling foreign exchange reserves. Put in other words, the authorities were reluctant to accept that each shock reduced the level of the sustainable current account deficit and thus rejected the conclusion that tighter monetary and fiscal policies were needed. Moreover, despite a low and decreasing level of reserves in early October, the authorities *increased* their reliance on the sale of reserves and on expansionary monetary policy—just when the opposite was needed. The signal embodied in this action further undermined market confidence and probably led to the final attack in November and December 1994—a result consistent with the observed sharp fall in international reserves (figure 5).

Why did the authorities adopt what *ex post* turned out to be inadequate policies? This is a complicated question in political economy. We can, however, put forward a few considerations. In responding to shocks in 1993–94, there were basically two main options—each with its own risks and virtues. A first option was for the authorities to shift the nominal anchor to explicit inflation targets and to allow shocks to be absorbed mainly by exchange rate fluctuations. The main risk here was that wider exchange rate fluctuations could have destabilized inflation expectations. In addition, it might have deterred some capital inflows, as foreign investors realized that exchange rate risk had increased. Thus, both higher inflation and capital outflows could emerge under this option. Alternatively, the authorities could have kept their commitment to the exchange rate band and to the Pacto. Here, the main risks were defense of the nominal exchange rate commitment under adverse shocks requiring relatively tight aggregate demand policy and possibly low economic growth along with it. Moreover, success depended on the level of foreign exchange reserves turning out to be adequate and on the shocks being transitory.

The resolution of the policy dilemma was affected by the upcoming election, by the Chiapas uprising, and by the Colosio assassination. The government was under pressure both to maintain nominal stability, as

Figure 12   Stock market index, 6 January 1995–15 December 1995

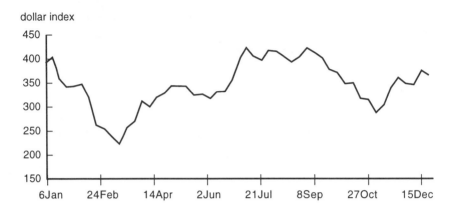

dollar index

reflected in the exchange rate commitment, and to expand the economy. For a while, buoyed by its strong international reputation as a major reformer, this strategy worked. However, once it became clear that defending the nominal exchange rate commitment was becoming increasingly difficult with fast-shrinking international reserves, and that tighter—and not more expansionary—aggregate demand policies were needed, market participants probably realized that existing policy was inconsistent and unsustainable. The crisis therefore erupted.

In terms of the theoretical explanations discussed earlier, it is difficult to favor one model exclusively over the other. On the one hand, there were shocks that fit the weak economic fundamentals highlighted by Krugman; to be sure, there were growing doubts about the extent of fiscal discipline in 1994 and afterward. The Colosio shock also exhibited behavior sympathetic to the Krugman model. On the other hand, there were shocks that fit nicely with explanations based on policy switches and self-fulfilling speculative attacks. NAFTA and the US Federal Reserve shocks, for example, follow that latter pattern.

The Aftermath of the Crisis

We now turn to an analysis of the aftermath of the crisis, starting with the consequences for the economy of devaluation and then assessing progress with adjustment. Based on the evidence now in hand, we conclude that the 1995 crisis was shorter and deeper than the 1982 crisis. Also, we study the postcrisis confidence shock of September 1995 and argue that so long as fundamentals remain weak, the economy will be exposed to future confidence crises. However, trends in international flows and in the stock market index suggest that capital flows are slowly returning to Mexico (figure 12).

A Vicious Circle

The first phase of the crisis was marked by confusion and lost confidence in the authorities. The devaluation and the switch to a floating rate did not immediately restore credibility. On the contrary, these actions, though unavoidable, aggravated the crisis: they failed to stop capital outflows, and they induced nominal instability and inflationary pressures.[14] In addition, the devaluation did not attenuate the illiquidity problems of a government that had to redeem short-term, public-sector debt indexed to the dollar (i.e., the *tesobonos*). Thus, the risk of default was still there.

While the devaluation could help generate the required current account adjustment to deal with the flow problem, it was only upon the invocation of the Exchange Stabilization Fund—funded by the United States and the IMF—that the stock problem began to be resolved.[15] In the meantime, investors, fearing the possibility of default, liquidated their Mexican assets and started a massive outflow of capital that made the crisis self-fulfilling. International prices of Mexico's foreign debt reached very low levels, and the private sector was unable to regain international credit lines.

While the Mexican government announced an emergency program on 9 January, the vicious circle began to break down only in February with the signing of an IMF stand-by agreement for $17.8 billion—the largest stand-by in IMF's history. In March, after the IMF had marshaled the Exchange Stabilization Fund with the assistance of the United States, it became evident that Mexico was on its way toward meeting its short-term debt obligations (i.e., the *tesobonos* that were coming due). Moreover, on 9 March the authorities announced an economic program aimed at producing the needed current account adjustment. It committed them to the following key measures:

- tighter fiscal measures that would generate a small budget surplus in 1995;

- tighter fiscal and monetary policy to control inflationary pressures once the Pacto expired;

- specific inflation targets of 42 percent in 1995, 20 percent in 1996, and single-digit inflation in 1997, and a net domestic credit target (or ceiling) of 10 billion in new pesos;

---

14. Memories of past experience with high inflation returned. In several of these cases, there had been sharp devaluations immediately after a shift in presidential administrations that prompted wage and price setters to make rapid nominal adjustments, which fueled inflationary pressures.

15. The argument that a step devaluation would not resolve the stock problem and that foreign assistance would be needed for that purpose appeared well before the crisis in Calvo's comments on Dornbusch and Werner (1994).

Figure 13   Country risk and *tesobonos* falling due, February 1995–November 1995

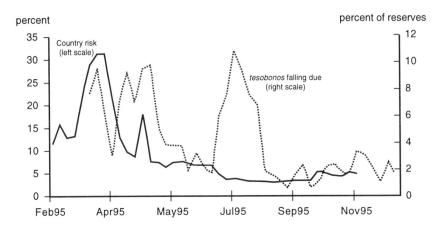

percent   percent of reserves

Country risk (left scale)

tesobonos falling due (right scale)

- a relatively clean float, with no intervention in the foreign exchange market;
- help for banks in overcoming liquidity pressures and avoiding a systemic banking crisis;
- a social safety net aimed at protecting the poor and social sectors that the crisis had affected most deeply.

The 1995 Economic Adjustment

A full assessment of the economic adjustments under the program would be beyond the scope of the paper. Instead, we offer preliminary analysis that focuses on the key achievements of the program, the key characteristics of the current account adjustment, the comparison with the 1980s adjustment, and the reasons for the crisis in confidence on 29 September 1995. Finally, we explain why capital flows are returning—albeit slowly—to Mexico.

Key Achievements

When the 9 March economic program was launched, the authorities and market participants stressed three key short-run risks: the risk of default on short-term government debt that was scheduled to mature in 1995, the risk of escalating inflation, and the risk of a systemic banking crisis (e.g., similar to the one experienced in Chile in 1982).

By the end of December 1995, the government had redeemed almost all the $29 billion in *tesobonos* that were outstanding at the beginning of the year. This seems to have had an important effect on the market's risk perception. This is shown in figure 13, in which we show the close

**Figure 14　Expected inflation and actual inflation, November
1994–December 1995**

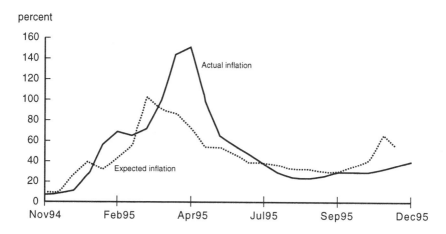

correlation between *tesobonos* falling due (as a percentage of foreign exchange reserves) and a measure of country risk (defined as the difference between the interest rate on *tesobonos* and that on US Treasury bills). The figure shows that country risk was very high in early 1995 when the market had doubts about the government's ability to deal with the stock problem—that is, to meet the amortizations of *tesobonos*. Despite the large amount of *tesobonos* falling due in July and August, the figure shows that the market perception had changed and that country risk had diminished considerably.

Another important feature of the adjustment program has been inflation control. Although the market was likely skeptical about the authorities' ability to meet the 42 percent inflation target rate for the year's end, the recent reduction in the monthly rate of inflation from 8 percent in April 1995 to just over 3 percent in December 1995 was impressive. Despite the progress by the last quarter, consumer prices registered a 52 percent increase in 1995.

The available evidence likewise suggests a moderation in inflation expectations. This is shown in figure 14, where we plot the actual annualized biweekly inflation rate and a market-based measure of the expected inflation rate (where the expected inflation rate is defined as the difference between the nominal interest rate on 91-day government *cetes* and the inflation-adjusted rate on *ajustabonos*—i.e., inflation-indexed bonds). A close correlation between the two series is apparent. Note, too, that the expected inflation rate is typically a leading indicator for inflation. From March 1995 through the year's end, the moderation in the expected inflation series translated into a marked, consistent decline in the actual inflation rate.

Table 3   Real GDP by type of expenditure, 1995

	Percent change over year 1994, nsa	Percentage point contribution to real GDP growth
Real GDP	−6.2	−6.2
Domestic demand	−14.4	−15.1
Private consumption	−6.9	−5.0
Government consumption	−6.4	−0.7
Total investment	−42.7	−9.4
o/w fixed investment	−29.1	−5.5
External demand	8.2	8.9
Exports	36.4	6.3
Imports	−12.1	2.6

Sources: Inegi, national account for the first three quarters of 1995, and J. P. Morgan's projections for the fourth quarter of 1995.

Furthermore, the government apparently also prevented a systemic banking crisis from erupting. Although banking problems persist and banks still hold large proportions of bad loans, the government has avoided a major collapse. The three most important measures have been a subordinated debt scheme, or Procapte, to recapitalize banks; ad hoc schemes to deal with insolvent banks; and the government purchase of banks' bad debts. The first program ensures that banks experiencing a temporary loss of capital will be able to replenish it. But if the banks' liquidity problems persist, the government may take over the bank by converting the subordinated debt into capital. This has been an efficient mechanism for making bonds more susceptible to market discipline. Also, the government has engaged in restructuring, recapitalizing, and reprivatizing banks that fell into insolvency. An example is the Probursa Bank, which was sold to the owners of Banco de Bilbao y Viscaya.

Current Account Adjustment

Turning to the external sector, available evidence indicates that external adjustment is proceeding stronger and faster than expected. By December 1995, accumulated trade surpluses had reached over $7 billion with the current account reaching a small deficit of about $300 million.

More important is the relative contribution to the current account adjustment of the external and the domestic sectors (table 3). Underlying the marked adjustment in the trade balance is a rapid growth in exports— about 30 percent in 1995 over 1994—led by both the sizable real devaluation of the peso and strong US demand. Also significant was the sharp decline in import demand—around 25 percent—reflecting mainly the domestic recession. Table 3 shows that the 6.4 percent fall in GDP in 1995 can be decomposed into a positive contribution of 8.8 percentage points by the external sector and a negative one of 15.2 percentage points by the domestic sector.

Behind this rapid turnaround in the current account are at least two key factors that probably reflect structural changes in the economy. First is the modernization of investment and export industries that took place before the crisis, along with the anticipation of increased competition under NAFTA. Second is the response of the domestic private sector. Unlike earlier business cycles, in which it took domestic expenditure a long time to respond to changes in economic policies, consumption this time responded very quickly, and labor markets showed considerable flexibility. To summarize, markets in Mexico may now respond more rapidly and efficiently to changes in economic policies than they once did.

1982 and 1995 Compared

Comparing the 1982 and 1995 crises makes apparent three key aspects of the economic adjustment and underscores several select characteristics of the 1990s current account crisis (figure 15). One key difference lies in the causes. In the 1980s, wrong economic fundamentals were clearly the main driving force. Overexpansion of the public sector and its greater indebtedness accounted for most of the large current account deficit. In the 1990s, although faulty fundamentals played a role in the origin of the crisis, it was the deterioration of fundamentals accompanying the policy responses to external shocks, along with the induced expansion in private expenditure, that accounted for the large current account deficit.

Delving further, we believe there are several variables that developing countries such as Mexico should examine when a current account crisis is marked by heavy reliance on capital flows and by self-fulfilling speculative attacks.

First, there is the speed of the adjustment. Comparing the two crises in terms of the performance of the noninterest current account in relation to GDP, it is striking that much faster current account adjustments characterized the crisis in 1995. While in both crises the size of the adjustment exceeded 10 percent of GDP, adjustment occurred in only two quarters in 1995 versus more than six quarters in 1982–83. In fact, data indicates that the Mexican economy bottomed out between the second and third quarters of 1995.

The more compressed period for adjustment in the recent crisis owes much to the reliance on short-term capital. Because most of Mexico's external financing in the 1980s consisted of bank financing, policymakers were able to negotiate a gradual reduction in the current account deficit. This option was unavailable in the 1990s; the sudden suspension of access to international capital markets meant that the economy had to sharply reduce its current account deficit by reducing domestic aggregate expenditure. This is apparent in the close coincidence between the sharp fall in GDP and the swing in Mexico's noninterest current account balance; this link was much weaker in the 1982 crisis.

Figure 15   Economic adjustment, 1982 and 1995

Noninterest current account balance
percent of GDP

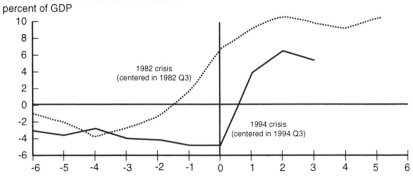

Real GDP
percent change over previous year

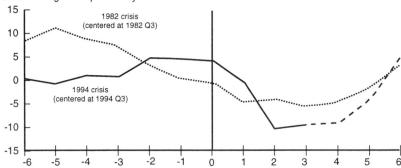

Real interest rates
percent

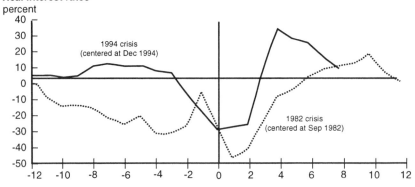

Public-sector primary balance
percent of GDP

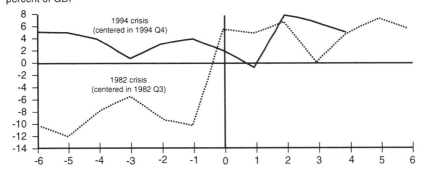

Inegi unemployment rate
percent of labor

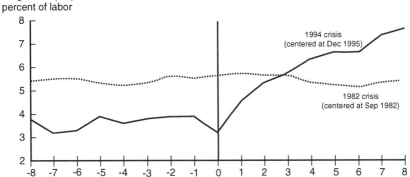

Private-sector claims
percent of GDP

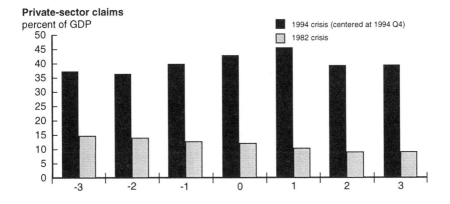

Second, there is the issue of burden sharing between the private and public sectors. Again, the different causes of the two crises carried different implications. In the 1995 crisis, most of the adjustment was accounted for by the private sector, while in 1982 the public sector absorbed most of the burden. We see this in the sharper increase in unemployment in the 1990s crisis. The need to reduce aggregate private expenditure also explains the sharp increase in real interest rates in the 1990s crisis. This, combined with the fact that the private sector was highly indebted, goes a long way toward an understanding of why there was such a rapid response to tight monetary and fiscal policies. In contrast, there was less need to increase interest rates by tightening monetary policy in the 1982 crisis because the public sector undertook most of the adjustment.

Third, we need to introduce the vulnerability of the banking system. Because the financial sector played such a key role in ensuring the adjustment of the private sector, the banks became the Achilles' heel of the 1995 adjustment program. Policies aimed at reducing excess private domestic demand and the current account deficit and at increasing interest rates had the undesirable consequence of also weakening the financial condition of the banking system. The higher the real interest rates, the less likely it was that the borrowers could repay loans and the more likely it became that there would be a systemic banking crisis. While this cannot be an argument for avoiding economic adjustment, it underscores the difficulties of engineering a sharp macroeconomic adjustment when the country's banks are in weak financial condition.

The Postcrisis Confidence Shock

By late September 1995, most of the economic factors that led to the December crisis seemed to have been corrected: the government had repaid most of the *tesobonos* stock, the public sector was in a strong surplus, the current account was in balance, and, most important, the authorities had committed to a flexible exchange rate regime. Yet in early October, the peso experienced a new attack, and the economy came close to repeating the 1994 crisis. Real activity was still weak, the banking system was vulnerable to exchange and interest rate volatility, signs of the economic rebound were unclear, and Mexican policymakers again made some mistakes that rendered expectations self-fulfilling. This episode underscored the vulnerability of the Mexican economy to dramatic changes in expectations.

With the benefit of hindsight, it can be argued that the confidence shock was not a major one. Yet again, inadequate policy responses raised market concerns about the authorities' willingness to tighten monetary policy and to let interest rates increase. Again, the authorities seemed to harbor worries that high interest rates could lead to bank failures and to a deepening of the recession, to the point where social pressures would force the government to abandon the economic program. Again, a speculative bubble emerged that could have evolved into a currency crisis, with policy responses weakening the economic fundamentals.

The shock began in late September, when market participants adjusted their inflation expectations upward and their growth expectations downward. Before the inflation rate for the first half of September was published, economic projections were optimistic about inflation and growth. Thus, *cetes* interest rates and measures of foreign exchange and country risks showed a declining trend before 29 September (figure 16). Likewise, the market was then expecting a strong appreciation of the exchange rate. In retrospect, market participants were overly optimistic about the evolution of economic fundamentals. For example, because future inflation was expected to decline significantly, real interest rates (using three-months forward inflation) approached zero in the second half of September (figure 17). The publication of the inflation rate for the first half of September quickly reversed expectations, accompanied by an increase in interest rates, a weaker peso, and greater exchange rate volatility (figure 12).

Since the Mexican authorities perceived this market adjustment as not being rooted in economic fundamentals, they tried to limit the increase in primary *cetes* interest rates. This can be seen from the difference in primary and secondary *cetes* rates (figure 18). Anecdotal information suggests that market participants were concerned about a repetition of the mistakes made in the months preceding the December 1994 crisis, when the authorities limited interest rate increases and loosened monetary policy. The loss of confidence in policy and the fears of weak economic fundamentals then induced the market to sell the peso. Thus, there was another case of self-fulfilling expectations.

After realizing their mistakes, the authorities tightened monetary policy and interest rates overshot to about 80 percent. In the end, tight monetary policy, combined with intervention in the foreign exchange rate, calmed the markets. Also, the authorities reaffirmed their commitment to the economic program, strengthened the banking system by removing its bad debts, and committed itself to tight fiscal and monetary policies for the remainder of 1995 and for 1996.

Continuation of Capital Inflows to Emerging Markets

In another contrast with Mexico's debt crisis of the early 1980s, this time "tequila effects" were short-lived. Net capital flows to developing countries averaged over $130 billion a year from 1990 to 1994, with flows to Mexico amounting to nearly 20 percent of the total. While there was a sharp fall in capital inflows to developing countries immediately after the eruption of the 1994 crisis—particularly portfolio flows to Latin America—a gradual return of capital to that region is under way, and foreign direct investment appears to be little changed. For the aggregate of all developing countries, most forecasts are that net capital inflows in 1995 will be on the order of $130 billion, only slightly below the $142 billion figure for 1994. Clearly, this will be a more supportive environment for recovery of the Mexican economy than was the case in the aftermath of the 1982 crisis. The recent sovereign debt issues the Mexican government

Figure 16   Expectations adjustment shock, 29 September 1995

90-day *cetes* interest rates

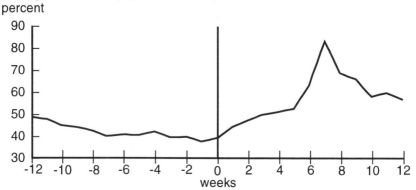

Foreign exchange and country risk

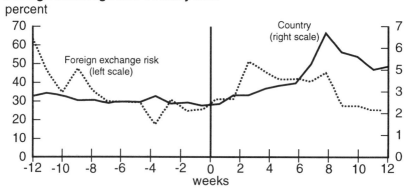

Expectation of a devaluation 30 days prior

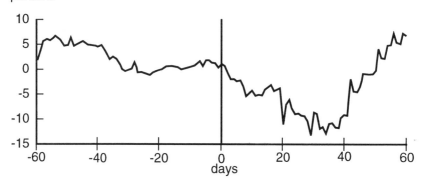

Figure 17 Real interest rates, primary auctions, December 1994–October 1995

28- and 91-day *cetes* percent per annum

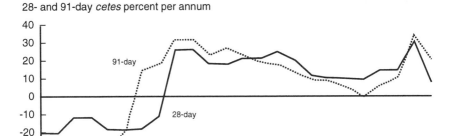

a. Using three months' forward inflation.

Figure 18 Primary and secondary *cetes* markets, 3 October 1995–16 November 1995

91-day *cetes* percent per annum

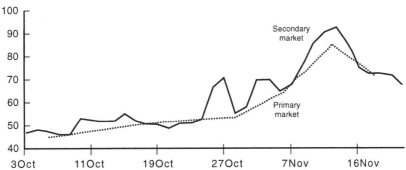

placed in the international market, along with private Mexican companies' continued issuance of debt, support this assessment (Gavin, Hausmann, and Leiderman 1995).

These developments, together with Mexico's progress on economic adjustment, have been reflected in a rebound (i.e., an improvement) in measures of foreign exchange and country risk, as well as in a recovery of equity market prices in Mexico and in other emerging markets. It is noteworthy that Mexico's shift to a floating exchange rate has been accompanied by a recent fall in foreign exchange risk (defined as the difference between the interest rate on *cetes* and *tesobonos*).

Overall, it appears that the Mexican crisis has vividly illustrated to foreign investors the considerable risks of short-term portfolio investment in emerging markets. While this episode is likely to make these investors more cautious and selective, we believe the growth of private capital flows to emerging markets are likely to continue. For individual emerging-market economies, the risks of sudden (and perhaps self-fulfilling) capital flow reversals will be a continuing feature of the operating environment.

We would not want our renewed optimism about the potential for the Mexican economy to obscure the important short-term and medium-term risks that still remain. These risks could make the recovery prolonged and difficult. Perhaps the two most important ones are banking system problems and social pressures (*cum* their political implications). Mexican banks still appear to hold a large share of bad loans, and international experience suggests that this can lead to high interest rate spreads or to an undue allocation of credit toward problematic borrowers. Either outcome could put more pressures on public-sector resources. In addition, stagflation, a sharp increase in unemployment, and a fall in both real wages and the standard of living could together generate social and political pressures that might endanger the implementation of the present economic adjustment strategy. Over the medium term, Mexico's external adjustment will require greater reliance on domestic saving—to finance both domestic investment and the repayment of the new foreign debts obtained in the context of the recent crisis.

References

Arrau, P., and D. Oks. 1992. *Private Saving in Mexico*. Working Paper Series No. 861. Washington: World Bank.

Aspe, P. 1993. *Economic Transformation the Mexican Way*. Cambridge, MA: MIT Press.

Burki, S. J., and S. Edwards. 1995. "Latin America After Mexico: Quickening the Pace." Washington: World Bank. Manuscript.

Calvo, G. A. 1995. "Testimony on the Loan Guarantee Package for Mexico before the Senate Banking, Housing, and Urban Affairs Committee." Washington, 31 January.

Calvo, G. A. 1995. "Varieties of Capital-Market Crises." Unpublished manuscript. University of Maryland.

Calvo, G. A., L. Leiderman, and C. Reinhart. 1993. *Capital Inflows to Latin America: The Role of External Factors*. IMF Staff Papers No. 40. Washington: International Monetary Fund.

Chuan, Punam, Stijn Claessens, and Niandu Mamingi. 1993. *Equity and Bond Flows to Latin America and Asia: The Role of Global and Country Factors*. World Bank Policy Research Working Papers No. 1160. Washington: World Bank.

Dornbusch, R., and A. Werner. 1994. "Mexico: Stabilization, Reform, and No Growth." *Brookings Papers on Economic Activity* 1: 253–97. Washington: Brookings Institution.

Eichengreen, B., A. K. Rose, and C. Wyplosz. 1995. "Exchange Rate Mayhem: The Antecedents and Aftermath of Speculative Attacks." *Economic Policy* (21 October): 251–312.

Flood, R., and P. Garber. 1984. "Collapsing Exchange-Rate Regimes: Some Linear Examples." *Journal of International Economics* 17: 1–13.

Gavin, M., R. Hausmann, and L. Leiderman. 1995. "The Macroeconomics of Capital Flows to Latin America: Experience and Policy Issues." Working Paper. Washington: Inter-American Development Bank.

Gil-Díaz, F. 1995. "A Comparison of Economic Crisis: Chile in 1982, Mexico in 1995." Banco de Mexico. Presented at Forum 95 of the Managed Futures Association, Chicago, July.

Gil-Díaz, Francisco, and Agustín Carstens. 1996. *Some Hypotheses Related to the Mexican 1994–95 Crisis*. Banco de Mexico Research Paper no. 9601. Mexico, D. F.: Banco de Mexico.

Hausmann, R. 1995. "The Mexican Crisis: Lessons for the Region." Office of the Chief Economist, Inter-American Development Bank, Washington (February). Photocopy.

Helpman, E., L. Leiderman, and G. Bufman. 1994. "A New Breed of Exchange Rate Bands: Chile, Israel, and Mexico."*Economic Policy* 19 (October): 259–306.

Krugman, P. R. 1979. "A Model of Balance of Payments Crises." *Journal of Money, Credit, and Banking* 11 (August): 311–25.

Leiderman, L., N. Liviatan, and A. Thorne. 1994. "Shifting Nominal Anchors: The Experience of Mexico." *Economía Mexicana* 4, no. 2: 197–237.

Leiderman, L., and L. E. O. Svensson. 1995. *Inflation Targets*. London: Centre for Economic Policy Research.

Lustig, N. 1995. *The Mexican Peso Crisis: The Foreseeable and the Surprise*. Brookings Discussion Papers in International Economics No. 114. Washington: Brookings Institution.

Obstfeld, M. 1986. "Rational and Self-Fulfilling Balance-of-Payments Crises." *American Economic Review* 76: 72–81.

Obstfeld, M. 1994. *The Logic of Currency Crises*. National Bureau of Economic Research Working Paper No. 4640. Cambridge, MA: NBER.

Oks, D. 1991. *Devaluation Expectations and Interest Rates in Mexico: The Role of Domestic Debt Management*. Latin America and the Caribbean Region Discussion Paper No. IDP-098. Washington: World Bank.

Reisen, H. 1995. "Managing Temporary Capital Inflows: Lessons from Asia and Latin America." OECD Development Center Working Paper. Paris: Organization for Economic Cooperation and Development.

Sachs, J., A. Tornell, and A. Velasco. 1995. "The Collapse of the Mexican Peso: What Have We Learned?" Harvard University Working Paper. Cambridge, MA: Harvard University.

Steiner, R. 1995. "The Mexican Crisis: Why Did It Happen and What Can We Learn?" Washington: World Bank. Manuscript.

Thorne, A. 1988. "Why a Market Solution to Financial Crisis Might be Infeasible." Washington: World Bank.

Thorne, A. 1990. "Turkey: The Internal Transfer Problem." Working Paper. Washington: World Bank.

Williamson, J. 1988. "The Mexican Currency Crisis." Statement before the Foreign Affairs Committee of the Canadian Senate, February.

Comment

William R. Cline

Leiderman and Thorne have provided a fine analytical review of the Mexican crisis. My comments will focus on important nuances and the outlook. At the outset, I would like to recapitulate my own interpretation of the causes of the December 1994 peso crisis.

Causes

First, the peso became overvalued in 1993–94, because the government held on too long to the exchange rate anchor. The potential costs of external disequilibrium began to outweigh the anti-inflationary benefits of the anchor. An implication is that Mexican authorities were too fearful that the social pact would collapse if the peso were to devalue faster. At least after the Colosio assassination, it would seem that the government could have appealed for public support in a national emergency to continue the Pacto despite the significant real devaluation.

Second, the basic problem was that there was a regime shift from excessive capital inflow in 1992–93—linked to NAFTA expectations and low US interest rates—to a backward shift in the supply curve of foreign capital after the Colosio shock. Yet the trade account could not adjust instantaneously, at least not without serious recession.

Third, the Mexican authorities were too willing to accept the convenient (Nigel) Lawson thesis as their analytical paradigm. This provided seeming

William R. Cline, currently on leave as senior fellow at the Institute for International Economics, is managing director at the Institute for International Finance, Washington.

justification for not worrying about an external deficit as large as 8 percent of GDP on the grounds that there was no accompanying fiscal deficit.

Fourth, the situation was aggravated by substantial short-term government debt. Mexico had not indulged in a domestic stretchout to parallel the external Brady Plan with an internal government debt restructuring.[1] Holding much of the domestic debt in short-term *cetes* was penny-wise and pound-foolish. Although a longer-term debt structure would have involved higher interest costs, it would have largely avoided the potential for a run. The shift to dollar-indexed *tesobonos* in the second quarter of 1994 merely added fuel to the fire by making the comparison between the amount of these instruments and the level of external reserve holdings the gauge of credibility.

Fifth, the ultimate collapse was driven by the market perception of a vast imbalance between $29 billion in *tesobonos* held largely by foreigners and only $6 billion in external reserves in December.

Sixth, with the benefit of hindsight, it would have been desirable to devalue substantially when the Colosio shock occurred. Similarly, it would have been desirable to hold on tenaciously to the bulk of foreign reserves that still existed rather than to spend almost all of them to defend the quasi-fixed peso.

Seventh, the $50 billion rescue package built around the US Treasury and IMF commitments was the right international policy response. *Tesobono* default would have been a tragic jettisoning of a credit reputation built up at great cost during the 1980s. There is the related question of whether the specific policy package that came as the price of the support involved monetary overkill. I will return to that issue.

The Leiderman-Thorne Analysis

Turning to the Leiderman-Thorne findings, I particularly liked the empirical documentation that the Colosio assassination was the key regime shifter. These results debunk the argument that the US Federal Reserve's tightening was anywhere near as important. The methodology is attractive: examining the weeks before and after the shock to detect transitory as opposed to persistent shifts in the foreign exchange risk spread and other indicators. Here I would note a puzzle in the timing of the exchange rate move within the band, which occurred 20 days *before* the assassination. I would add that the paper's "ambiguous" result on the Fed shock suggests that the various studies (including earlier work by Leiderman) heavily emphasizing this influence should be taken with a grain of salt.

---

1. This was unlike the response of Argentina, with its Bonex Plan, and Brazil, with the Collor Plan. Of course, these plans had serious problems of their own.

I agree with several of the summary lessons drawn by the two authors: the current account deficit should be kept moderate, there should be greater reliance on direct investment rather than more volatile portfolio flows, and the government should have abandoned the exchange rate anchor early in 1994.

The paper does raise several points on which I am less in agreement. The initial theoretical emphasis on monetary expansion plus the authors' judgment that there was excessive money growth in 1994 seem to diverge from at least some of the facts. The head of the central bank, Miguel Mancera, published a chart in the *Wall Street Journal* in January 1995 showing that M1 had risen by only about 6 percent in 1994, less than the nominal rise of GDP by over 10 percent.

The real problem was not the surge in money growth but that there was a persistent effort to avoid the contractionary shock to the money supply that would have resulted from a decline in foreign exchange reserves in the absence of sterilization. Yet the quasi-fixed exchange rate anchor effectively put Mexico on a quasi gold standard. A first principle of the gold standard is that when there is a loss of reserves, the money supply must contract so that prices can fall. Sterilization meant that the government was trying to elicit the beneficial expectations effects of a quasi gold standard without paying the price of reducing the money supply and accepting recession when there is a balance of payments deficit. In this regard, if it were taken as given that the desired policy was to maintain the exchange rate after the Colosio shock, then the consistent policy response would have included acceptance of a sharp fall in the money supply.

Similarly, the paper's treatment of fiscal policy is not fully persuasive. The old stylized fact was that Mexico shifted the primary balance from a deficit of 8 percent of GDP in 1981 to a surplus of 8 percent in the late 1980s, a swing equivalent to five Gramm-Rudman-Hollings reforms in a period when the United States could not achieve even one. Leiderman and Thorne would establish a new stylized fact that Mexico gave back 6 percent of GDP fiscal correction from 1989 to 1994, or two of the five Gramm-Rudmans. They place this swing at 3 percent from 1989 to 1993 and another 3 percent through the development banks in 1994.

One problem with this view is that development-bank lending is not equivalent to deficit spending unless it is fully expected that borrowers will default. More broadly, however, the analysis seems to ignore the context of fiscal policymaking. The Brady deal improved confidence and made it possible to reduce domestic interest rates sharply (and gave some interest relief on external debt as well). With a much smaller government interest burden, there was less need to run a high primary surplus. Indeed, the government consciously increased social spending as a way of taking out its dividend from lower interest costs. In short, the authors seem to exaggerate the supposed shift toward a loose fiscal policy.

In their discussion of private saving, the authors are ambiguous. First they seem to say that there was indeed such a collapse but then they suggest that the problem was with government saving instead. In this connection, a new stylized fact has emerged to the effect that private saving collapsed by nearly 10 percent of GDP (Edwards 1995). However, saving data are notoriously suspect, primarily because they are derived residually from investment and balance of payments data. Other data do not seem to support the notion of a collapse in Mexican saving. The International Monetary Fund's *International Financial Statistics* reports that private consumption rose from 72.8 percent of GDP in 1989 to 73.5 percent in 1993. This increase is too small to be consistent with the idea of a consumption binge fueled by a drop in private saving.

Finally, let me add a quibble. The authors are too tolerant of a current account deficit of 8 percent of GDP, which they state did not "justify sounding the alarm." Here they give too much implicit endorsement to the Lawson thesis.

Is the Worst Over?

This is the subtitle of the paper. However, the paper is thin on one important piece of the answer and silent on another.

The first is the banking crisis. The paper says little about it, yet it is important to know how serious it is (probably, very) and how sufficient the indexed accounts and other corrective measures are (probably, not fully).

The second is the issue of the strategy of monetary shock adopted in early 1994, partly as the consequence of US Treasury arm-twisting. It was no coincidence that on the day Treasury announced the $20 billion Exchange Stabilization Fund package, Mexico pushed the *cetes* rate to 70 percent. These high rates did not fully persuade foreign investors. Indeed, the credit-rationing model (Stiglitz and Weiss 1981) might have suggested that investor doubts about the desperation of such rates would have limited their response. However, the high rates did impose a contractionary shock on the economy. Real GDP fell by 10 percent in the second quarter of 1995 relative to a year earlier.

The high interest rates also aggravated the banking crisis. As Calvo and Goldstein point out in chapter 7, nonperforming loans were already high in 1994, at about 8 percent of assets. With the high interest rate strategy of 1995, the nonperforming ratio rose to 14 percent. This in turn caused pressure for Rube Goldberg offsets, such as the government's new loan subsidy program.

Returning to the subtitle's query, the good news is that Mexico has carried out a massive external-sector adjustment. Much of this adjustment is initially from recession, but the exchange rate devaluation sets the stage for lagged adjustment through expenditure switching instead of expenditure reduction. It is especially encouraging that in the first half of 1995, exports rose by 32.8 percent above their level in the same period of 1994, whereas imports only fell by 6.6 percent (IMF, *International Financial Statistics*, 1995, 391). This was a much less contractionary adjustment than occurred at the outbreak of the 1980s debt crisis, when exports rose by only 10 percent from 1981 to 1983 whereas imports fell by 65 percent (IMF, *International Financial Statistics*, 1994).

Moreover, through mid-September the requisite virtuous circle seemed to be in the process of realization. The model required a sufficient period of exchange rate stability so that investors would no longer be able to resist the temptation of high peso interest rates, which would mean capital inflows that would permit further exchange rate stability and lower domestic interest rates. Following this script, the exchange rate did stabilize in the range of 6¼ per dollar in April through September, and interest rates did decline from a peak of 80 percent in March to 35 percent by September.[2]

Moreover, the *bête noire* of the Mexico story had been caged: the $29 billion in *tesobonos* had been cut to only $3 billion, as the government paid off the obligations with the help of some $12 billion drawn from the US commitments and another $8 billion or so from the IMF. There had been enough relief on the capital account (including through new international bond flotations of about $2 billion) that reserves were back up to about $13 billion by September.

The not-so-good news is that the jury is still out on Mexico's stabilization. The sharp decline in real wages and the loss of an estimated 1 million jobs in the recession mean there will be political pressure domestically and, perhaps more important, jittery nerves among foreign investors, who are skeptical of claims of stability under these circumstances. Nor is it clear that the banking crisis has been overcome.

Real interest rates were too high even at September's *cetes* rate of 35 percent. If forward-looking inflation was 25 percent, then the (compounded) *cetes* rate at that time meant a real interest rate of 12 percent. By November the rate was even higher.

On balance, though, the odds are considerably better than even that the jury will return a favorable verdict. If Mexican politics hold together, export-led growth should be feasible, especially if the government leans toward a crawling peg rather than returning to an exchange rate anchor (the latter would leave stagnation as the only external adjustment mechanism). As of August, a substantial amount of real devaluation remained

---

2. However, in the fourth quarter there was a slide in the peso that took the rate from about 6½ to the dollar in mid-September to about 7½ in mid-November, and the rate briefly reached 8¼ before the central bank intervened with some $200 million (*Wall Street Journal*, 10 November, 1995; *Financial Times*, 10 November 1995). The peso's fall had not been halted by raising *cetes* back to around 50 percent.

in place, as the number of real pesos per dollar was still about one-fourth higher than in mid-1994.[3]

Finally, with respect to the implications of the Mexican crisis for the international capital markets, allow me to quote what I wrote in January 1995 (Cline 1995, 505):

> ... the likelihood [is] that eventually there [will] be a settling down in anxiety, and that countries with good policies ... [will] be able to borrow from the capital markets.... [Foreign investors are more likely to be] sophisticated and discriminating rather than shift to a monolithic new revulsion from emerging markets.

So far, this prognosis seems to be holding up relatively well.

References

Cline, William R. 1995. *International Debt Reexamined.* Washington: Institute for International Economics.

Edwards, Sebastian. 1995. "Why Are Latin America's Saving Rates So Low: An International Comparative Analysis." Presented at the First Annual Latin American Conference on Development Economics, World Bank, Rio de Janeiro, June.

Stiglitz, Joseph, and Andrew Weiss. 1981. "Credit Rationing in Markets with Imperfect Information." *American Economic Review* 71, no. 3 (June): 343–410.

---

3. From August 1994 to August 1995, the peso/dollar rate rose by 83 percent (from 3.38 to 6.19 per dollar). Domestic inflation was 42 percent in the first eight months of 1995, and there was a cumulative total of 46 percent over the year ending August 1995 (WPI; IMF, *International Financial Statistics*, 1995). The real peso/dollar rate was thus 25.8 percent more attractive to exports and unattractive to imports than in mid-1994. By mid-November, at an exchange rate of 7.5 and with monthly inflation running at 2 percent or less, this real change had widened to about 40 percent.

Comment

Rogelio Ramirez de la O

This is a competent paper containing a good mix of information and interpretative work about developments in Mexico during 1994. It also enriches the previous literature on the Mexican crisis, which on the whole has been too focused on describing events and not enough on adding new insights. The authors combine the description of events with a straightforward measurement of market responses after the government reacted to these events. This allows us to see that some key market indicators did not return to their pre-shock levels after the Colosio assassination. For example, neither the peso's level within the exchange rate band nor the authors' preferred proxy for expected exchange rate devaluation returned. Similarly, after the anti-inflation pact was signed on 24 September, nominal interest rates did not return to their pre-shock level. The same applied to nominal interest rates after the 20 December shock, when the government lifted the upper boundary of the exchange rate band by 15 percent.

Given the shocks and the market responses, the authors go on to analyze the government's policy stance. They confirm what other observers had noted: the Bank of Mexico injected domestic credit at a time and under circumstances that created an increased risk of financial crisis.

These findings provide useful insights into the exchange rate crisis at the end of last year and will contribute to a healthy discussion. For one thing, they invalidate the Bank of Mexico's claim that, after the speculative attacks against the peso subsided, the situation regained its previous stability—a claim apparently meant to justify the bank's conclusion that

Rogelio Ramirez de la O is president of Ecanal, SA, Mexico City.

there was no need to reexamine the exchange rate regime or policy. We know, of course, that one principal indicator never returned to its previous level—namely, the stock of international reserves. But this paper shows that other indicators did not illustrate a return to stability either.

The authors' brief review of exchange rate crisis theory is useful but not indispensable to their main propositions. Their analysis focuses on specific events and policy responses to them, and this throws sufficient light on a fundamental inconsistency between the government's nominal exchange rate target and the short-term fiscal and monetary expansion of 1994.

My comments cover both aspects of the peso devaluation as well as suggestions for additional research.

Importance of Medium-Term Developments

The authors focus on the short term, especially 1994. This is an illuminating approach for examining specific shocks and policy responses, but it does not make much allowance for certain trends. These trends can be useful for helping to understand what caused the government to follow such a risky policy against its publicly stated intentions. In other words, we want to know why the government or the Bank of Mexico failed to take some particular action with regards to monetary or fiscal policy. Was it simply a matter of human error, or did the decision reflect real constraints from taking the right policy action?

If trends constrained monetary and fiscal policy in 1994, then the origin of the crisis must be sought in an earlier period. For example, the authors argue that one reason the Bank of Mexico was reluctant to raise interest rates was the precarious situation of the commercial banks. This issue is very important, as financial deregulation and privatization was an integral part of the stabilization/reform package Mexico had implemented earlier.

It would likewise be helpful to understand if a process of prolonged exchange rate appreciation, *cum* other elements of stabilization, gradually generated the Mexican crisis or rather if the authorities' inappropriate response to external shocks was at fault. The authors seem at times to suggest that different policy management would have produced significantly different outcomes. They do not say so categorically, however. At the same time, the authors do not really tell us how the economy became gradually trapped in a need for a tight policy and how much room for manoeuvre this trap really allowed.

In my opinion, the shocks accelerated the moment the government found itself caught between low economic growth on the one hand and an expansive policy that would prove harmful to the peso exchange rate on the other. But even without shocks, the inherent features of the stabilization plan eventually would have posed a delicate policy dilemma.

Table 1   Mexico: signs of economy's weakening before crisis, 1991–94

	1991	1992	1993	1994
Positive signs				
Public-sector balance (percent of GDP)	− 0.5	0.5	− 2.8	− 4.2
Consumer inflation (percentage change from December to December)	18.8	11.9	8.0	7.0
Foreign capital inflows (billions of dollars)[a]	22.6	25.8	29.3	11.0
Negative signs				
GDP annual growth (percent)	3.6	2.8	0.4	3.5
Ex ante interest rate, cetes, 28-day average (percent)	4.8	6.4	8.4	− 15.4[b]
Ex post interest rate, cetes, 28-day average (percent)	− 1.3	1.1	5.6	6.7
Current account balance (billions of dollars)	− 14.6	− 24.4	− 23.4	− 29.4

a. Includes "errors and omissions."
b. Average rate over expected annual inflation of 38 percent in 1995.

Source: Bank of Mexico, 3 March 1995.

Table 1 highlights this point by summarizing several paradoxes of Mexico's development. Quite independently of the political shocks, table 1 reveals that there was a medium-term trend at work. Well before 1993, the economy exhibited signs of increasing weakness, despite Mexico's huge foreign capital inflows. Let's consider how this weakness affected subsequent policy decisions.

To what degree did Mexico's stabilization plan generate endogenous conditions that would gradually weaken its capacity to maintain relatively high economic growth and a given nominal exchange rate target? Many analysts point to the high level of the real exchange rate, but there were other ingredients of the plan that also contributed to the problem. One of them was the insufficient synchronization between trade liberalization, which happened rapidly, and asset-market liberalization, which was slower; this probably explains why foreign direct investment was not greater. Constraints on asset markets also contributed to an excessive exposure of the private sector to foreign debt rather than foreign equity. Mexican shareholders remained unwilling to share company control with foreign partners, and the government did not counter this unwillingness with its capital market policies.

The same phenomenon in part explains the excessive prices Mexican investors paid for Mexican banks. This in turn influenced their attitudes to risk as well as the quality of management during a consumer lending boom. Table 2 looks at this boom in commercial bank lending—and again

Table 2 Commercial bank lending, 1987–94
(billions of 1994 new pesos, except where noted)

	1987	1990	1993	1994	1995	Real increase 1987–94 (percent)
Real wages adjusted for productivity (1987 = 100)	100.0	103.6	104.8	102.6	84.0	2.6
Outstanding bank credit (1987 new pesos)	420.004	382.843	624.699	872.300	n.a.	107.7
Manufacturing industry	52.954	67.190	90.145	122.100	n.a.	130.6
Housing	10.156	19.988	82.437	108.300	31.4	966.4
Subsidized low-income	10.156	19.988	28.906	37.100	28.3	265.3
Middle-income	0.000	0.000	24.303	37.000	52.2	n.a.
Other	0.000	0.000	29.228	34.200	17.0	n.a.
Consumption	7.979	27.983	44.644	44.500	−0.3	457.7
Credit cards	0.000	0.000	31.583	31.200	−1.2	n.a.
Durable consumer goods	0.000	0.000	13.061	13.300	1.8	n.a.
Housing + consumption	18.135	47.971	127.081	152.800	n.a.	742.6
Credit for trade, retail, wholesale	21.036	49.047	92.822	128.900	n.a.	512.7
Average real peso exchange rate (new pesos per 1987 dollar)	1.000	0.710	0.583	0.594	0.834	−40.6

n.a. = not available

Source: Bank of Mexico, Indicadores Económicos, various years.

highlights why the banking problem became such a key factor in the 1994 crisis.

Given that many of these forces were unfolding over a span of several years, any examination of market-related developments during 1994 needs to revisit the dynamics of the original stabilization policies and the specific trade-offs it created. The authors point to one such trade-off— namely, that between protecting the commercial banks (by not allowing large increases in interest rates) and stemming the decline in private capital inflows (by initiating such increases in interest rates). But there are others. For example, another such trade-off was the need to support a badly hit agricultural sector with resources from Procampo ($3.8 billion in 1994) versus the need to maintain a tight overall macroeconomic policy framework. Yet a further important trade-off was that between maintaining confidence in the exchange rate and allowing fiscal policy to become more expansionary. Indeed, the stance of fiscal policy became clearly expansionary as early as the autumn of 1993, when there was an explicit effort to alleviate some of the effects of declining output. However, the market seemingly did not recognize this shift in fiscal policy until later.

We will never know whether this 1993 relaxation of fiscal policy would have been enough by itself to cast doubts on the sustainability of the exchange rate. Probably not. The fact is, however, that it was the stagnating output in 1993 that forced the change in fiscal policy, and it was the same background that forced the accelerated disbursement of public-sector capital spending in 1994, following the outbreak of the Chiapas rebellion. Incidentally, the authors do not give the Chiapas conflict—and the possible tensions it created within the Cabinet—enough attention as a shock, although I admit that it is difficult to capture its effect in a specific event.

These trade-offs help to explain why the government could not adopt a more restrictive policy later on when it became necessary. But even more interesting, the notion that the many factors that created the trade-offs originated in the stabilization process itself highlights the point that the government missed the opportunity to review its stabilization strategy and to reformulate it. This would have reinforced the overall objective of stability. This review never took place in Mexico; perhaps this explains why the complacency with the slow pace of structural reforms (in labor, energy, and social security) and with the growing external deficit. Likewise, it sheds light on why President-elect Zedillo was less than enthusiastic in November 1994 to reconfirm the terms of the anti-inflation pact signed by the previous administration in September. It may also explain why a strong reaffirmation of exchange rate stability was absent from his inaugural speech.

Theories of Exchange Rate Crisis

The authors survey two strands of theory. One is Krugman's relatively simple model, which provides a solid first approximation of the problem. This model has the merit of relating the precrisis fiscal and monetary expansion to the economic fundamentals that are necessary for sustaining the exchange rate. Use of this model is helpful because it focuses on the important question of whether there was a departure from fundamentals in the Mexican case. As I have argued above, it would be inaccurate to say that there was no deterioration in fundamentals in Mexico.

The second model examined is that of self-fulfilling speculative attacks, in which an incompatibility need not exist between the fundamentals and the exchange rate regime. These models propose the existence of multiple equilibria. In my opinion, they do not fit the Mexican case, where economic fundamentals, at least in 1994, strongly suggested that there was a potential exchange rate problem. The very fact that there was a massive shift out of peso-denominated *cetes* into dollar-indexed *tesobonos* is a good reminder of this. But there were also increasing references in the press and in business and government circles to the rigidity represented by the exchange rate.

Given the relaxation of fiscal policy outlined above, the conditions became ripe for a speculative attack. We should recall that in Mexico there is no memory of any period of lasting exchange rate stability. Changes in administration or in the Treasury team could trigger negative market responses. In that sense, the market reaction that was observed might have taken place even without complete information on the government's expansionary policy. In fact, at the time investors were ready to sell the peso, information was incomplete on how much the government had loosened policy. The greater frequency of public discussions about the depth of domestic recession (including statements by the new PRI campaign candidate promising more growth) may have sufficed to justify a change in perception.

In sum, the authors may be giving too much weight in their paper to the theory of self-fulfilling speculative attacks independent of economic fundamentals. They also probably anticipate too soon the end of the Mexican crisis—again because structural medium-term developments cloud the horizon. Especially important in this regard is the banking crisis, which both imposes limitations on any future economic recovery and carries the potential for further deterioration.

2

Capital Flows in Central and Eastern Europe: Evidence and Policy Options

Guillermo A. Calvo, Ratna Sahay, and Carlos A. Végh

In sharp contrast to the last decade, an abundance of capital has been flowing from industrial to developing countries since the early 1990s. During 1990–92, capital inflows to Latin America amounted to $117 billion (1.2 percent of GDP), roughly the same amount the region received during the entire 1982–89 period. Similarly, capital inflows to Asia during 1989–92 amounted to $144 billion, or 3.2 percent of GDP. In several instances, domestic factors, such as structural reforms and successful stabilization programs, have played a key role in attracting capital flows. At the same time, despite wide variations in policy performance among individual economies, foreign capital has flooded entire regions. This suggests that external factors, such as low international interest rates and recessionary conditions in industrial countries, have been major factors in explaining these capital movements.[1]

Guillermo A. Calvo is a professor of economics at the University of Maryland. Ratna Sahay is a senior economist at the International Monetary Fund (IMF), Washington. Carlos A. Végh, currently on leave as a senior economist at the IMF, is a visiting associate professor at the University of California at Los Angeles. The authors would like to thank Gerard Bélanger, Peter Dittus, Giorgio Gomel, Val Koromzay, Donald Mathieson, Carmen Reinhart, Peter Wickham, and conference participants for very useful comments. We are grateful to the IMF desk economists for providing data and helping us in their interpretation, and to Ravina Malkani for her invaluable research assistance.

1. For a detailed analysis, see Calvo, Leiderman, and Reinhart (1993, 1994a, 1994b) and Schadler et al. (1993).

Table 1 Central and Eastern Europe: balance of payments, 1987–93
(billions of dollars)

Year	Balance of goods, services, and private transfers[a]	Balance on capital account[a]	Balance on capital account plus net errors and omissions[a]	Overall balance[b]	Official transfers
1987	0.9	−4.4	−3.5	2.6	0.0
1988	3.4	−9.5	−6.4	2.9	0.0
1989	0.0	−4.1	−1.4	1.4	0.1
1990	−3.3	−4.5	−4.7	8.0	0.3
1991	−2.9	−8.0	−8.0	10.9	0.3
1992	−2.7	2.4	1.6	1.1	0.4
1993	−9.2	13.2	12.2	−3.0	0.2

Note: The countries included are Bulgaria, the former Czechoslovakia (until 1991), the Czech Republic (1992–93), Hungary, Poland, Romania, and the Slovak Republic (1992–93).

a. Balance on goods, services, and private transfers is equal to the current account balance less official transfers. Official transfers are included in the capital account.
b. A minus sign indicates an increase in reserves.

Source: IMF, *World Economic Outlook* data base.

In contrast to Latin America and Asia, the transition economies of Central and Eastern Europe as a group exported capital in 1990–91. This was most likely triggered by the collapse of the communist regimes during these two years, which aggravated the internal and external macroeconomic imbalances of the 1980s. The advent of market-oriented reforms in these economies, however, began to reverse this trend, especially in such countries as the former Czechoslovakia and Hungary. This reversal in capital flows began in 1992–93 when the capital account (including errors and omissions) swung from a deficit of $8 billion in 1991 to a surplus of more than $12 billion by 1993 (table 1).[2] Preliminary evidence indicates that the capital account improved further by US$1 billion in 1994. Furthermore, the Mexican crisis in late December 1994 appeared to have had little effect on these economies in 1995.

This paper examines capital flows in Central and Eastern Europe, exploring emerging trends and analyzing policy options for these countries in light of the experiences of Latin America and Asia. The paper first documents the external-sector developments of individual countries and examines in detail the magnitude, nature, and effects of capital flows in Central and Eastern Europe. It then assesses and analyzes the main issues raised by the current episode of capital flows into this region, such as their inflationary consequences and their impact on financial vulnerability. Finally, it takes up sterilization issues.

---

2. This swing in the flow of capital toward Eastern Europe in 1992–93 coincides with the ebbing of investment opportunities in Latin America and Asia.

External Sector Developments in Eastern and Central Europe

Before turning to a detailed discussion of capital flows in Eastern and Central Europe, we will present a broad picture of developments in the external sector of the following transition economies: Bulgaria, the Czech Republic, the Slovak Republic, Hungary, Poland, and Romania.

The Pre-Reform Period

The timing of the demise of the economic and political systems in Central and Eastern Europe in 1990–91 was not a coincidence. With the exception of the former Czechoslovakia, the buildup of internal and/or external macroeconomic imbalances during the 1980s was common to all transition economies. Even Hungary, which began to reform its economy in the late 1960s and experienced relatively low inflation, had accumulated a substantial stock of external debt by the end of the 1980s. Having pursued extremely lax financial policies and borrowed heavily abroad in the 1980s, Bulgaria, Poland, and Romania experienced severe debt-servicing difficulties. All three countries were forced to reschedule their external debt payments.

Following a debt rescheduling in 1986, Nicolae Ceausescu's economic policies in Romania were dominated by the desire to reduce external dependence at all costs. Consequently, and with little regard to the adverse effects on the domestic economy, the saving-investment balance in Romania was manipulated to ensure current account surpluses to repay (and sometimes even prepay) external debt. The domestic counterpart of the large current account surpluses in the late 1980s were savings generated by steep taxation of state enterprises and a sharp contraction of social spending.[3] By March 1989, nearly all debt had been repaid. The primary cost to the Romanian economy of this extreme inward-looking policy was a sharp decline in both the quality of investment and economic growth, as well as a rapid deterioration in living standards.

During 1985–89, convertible-currency debt in Bulgaria nearly tripled as the economy became increasingly dependent on imported inputs. At the same time, the economy performed poorly, and the competitiveness of Bulgarian exports declined sharply. By 1989, Bulgaria was forced to cut imports and draw down reserves to such dangerously low levels that, in March 1990, a moratorium on external debt was declared.[4] Poland,

---

3. In fact, a decree in 1989 forbade Romanian entities from contracting new external debt (Demekas and Khan 1991).

4. Bulgaria was a particularly hapless case because it had a net creditor position vis-à-vis the Council for Mutual Economic Assistance (CMEA) countries.

Table 2 Central and Eastern Europe: key macroeconomic developments, 1987–93 (percent of GDP)

Indicator	Bulgaria	Czech Republic[a]	Hungary	Poland	Romania	Slovak Republic[a]
Current account balance						
1987–91	− 4.4	1.2	− 0.9	− 1.2	3.5	1.2
1992–93	− 7.2	0.8	− 5.4	− 1.5	− 7.1	− 1.1
Gross capital formation (current prices)						
1987–91	31.5	27.9	25.3	27.5	29.2	27.9
1992–93	17.8	20.5	21.1	15.8	29.6	24.7
Total consumption (current prices)						
1987–91	70.8	65.6	73.6	70.1	69.1	65.6
1992–93	88.8	73.1	83.5	85.0	76.8	81.7
Private final consumption (current prices)						
1987–91	54.2	44.3	62.6	56.0	n.a.	44.3
1992–93	73.1	54.1	70.7	62.2	n.a.	55.6
Government final consumption (current prices)						
1987–91	16.6	21.3	11.0	14.2	n.a.	21.3
1992–93	15.8	15.5	12.8	22.8	n.a.	26.2

n.a. = not available

a. Data for 1987–91 are for the former Czechoslovakia.

Source: IMF, World Economic Outlook data base.

beset by high inflation, was also weighed down by significant debt during this period and went into arrears in 1990. Both countries had very large capital outflows in the late 1980s concurrently with current account deficits (tables 2 and 3).

While Hungary's macroeconomic policies in the late 1980s can be best characterized as shifting between expansion and restraint, the government remained current in the payment obligations on its large external debt (table 3). Perhaps more than the uncertainty surrounding Hungary's national elections and its erratic economic policies, the emergence of debt-servicing arrears in two heavily indebted neighboring CMEA countries in 1990 raised concerns in the international community regarding Hungary's debt-servicing capacity. Consequently, Hungary's trend of rising capital inflows in the late 1980s—a trend enjoyed only by Hungary in the region—was reversed in 1990.

The former Czechoslovakia's experience in the late 1980s is distinct from other transition economies because—unlike Bulgaria, Hungary, and

Table 3 Central and Eastern Europe: external sector indicators, 1987–93

	Bulgaria	Czech Republic[a]	Hungary	Poland	Romania	Slovak Republic[a]
Capital account balance (percent of GDP)						
1987–91	−4.0	−0.5	2.1	−5.2	−2.0	−0.5
1992–93	−8.5	4.5	9.3	1.1	6.8	1.3
Capital account, net direct investment (percent of GDP)						
1987–91	0.2	0.5	1.3	0.0	0.0	0.5
1992–93	0.5	2.7	5.6	0.5	0.3	−0.6
Cumulative net official borrowing (billions of dollars)						
1988–91	1.0	0.7	2.5	3.9	−2.7	0.7
1992–93	1.4	0.2	0.1	−1.1	2.8	n.a.
Cumulative net commercial borrowing (billions of dollars)						
1988–91	4.1	0.0	−0.4	2.0	−2.3	0.0
1992–93	1.6	2.0	1.8	1.4	0.3	n.a.
Total ratio of external debt to GDP						
1987–91	57.4	18.4	70.8	65.6	9.7	18.4
1992–93	121.7	24.1	64.2	56.4	16.9	19.7
Ratio of official to nonofficial debt						
1987–91	0.4	0.1	0.1	1.8	0.5	0.1
1992–93	0.4	0.2	0.2	1.6	2.2	n.a.
Debt-service ratio						
1987–91	33.8	9.9	31.9	13.3	12.9	9.9
1992–93	19.8	n.a.	44.4	10.3	7.6	n.a.

n.a. = not available

a. Data for 1987–91 are for the former Czechoslovakia.

Source: IMF, World Economic Outlook, data base.

Poland—it had very little external debt (table 4), and, unlike Romania, it had pursued balanced macroeconomic policies. In response to more stringent lending practices by international commercial banks in the early 1980s, the former Czechoslovakia successfully pursued export-oriented economic policies during the 1980s. By the end of the 1980s, its external

Table 4   Central and Eastern Europe: economic indicators, 1989–93

Indicator	1989	1990	1991	1992	1993
Real GDP growth					
Bulgaria	−0.5	−9.1	−11.7	−5.6	−4.2
Czechoslovakia	5.0	−0.4	−15.9	−8.5	..
Czech Republic	4.5	−1.2	−14.2	−7.1	−0.3
Hungary	0.7	−3.5	−11.9	−4.4	−2.3
Poland	0.2	−11.6	−7.6	2.6	3.8
Romania	−5.8	−5.6	−12.9	−10.1	1.3
Slovak Republic	n.a.	n.a.	−14.5	−7.0	−4.1
Inflation rates (period average)					
Bulgaria	6.4	23.9	333.5	82.0	72.8
Czechoslovakia	1.4	10.8	59.0	11.0	..
Czech Republic	n.a.	n.a.	56.5	11.1	20.8
Hungary	17.0	28.9	35.0	23.0	22.5
Poland	251.1	585.8	70.3	43.0	35.3
Romania	0.9	4.7	161.1	210.3	256.0
Slovak Republic	n.a.	n.a.	61.2	10.0	23.2
Fiscal balance (percent of GDP)					
Bulgaria[a]	−1.4	−12.7	−15.1	−14.8	−18.5
Czechoslovakia	−3.1	−0.4	−2.0	−3.6	..
Czech Republic[b]	n.a.	n.a.	n.a.	0.4	0.5
Hungary[c]	−1.3	0.5	−2.5	−8.0	−6.9
Poland[d]	−7.4	3.1	−6.5	−6.6	−2.9
Romania[a,b]	8.8	0.9	0.6	−4.6	−0.1
Slovak Republic	n.a.	n.a.	n.a.	−13.1	−7.5
External debt (billions of dollars)[e]					
Bulgaria	9.2	10.2	11.6	12.5	12.8
Czechoslovakia	7.9	8.2	9.9	n.a.	..
Czech Republic	n.a.	n.a.	n.a.	7.6	10.5
Hungary	20.0	21.3	22.7	21.4	24.6
Poland	40.2	48.9	48.3	48.7	48.7
Romania	0.8	1.1	2.1	3.4	4.4
Slovak Republic	n.a.	n.a.	n.a.	2.3	3.4
GDP (billions of dollars)					
Bulgaria	21.9	7.6	7.9	8.3	10.3
Czechoslovakia	n.a.	n.a.	n.a.	n.a.	..
Czech Republic	34.9	31.6	24.3	27.3	30.8
Hungary	NA	32.9	30.9	35.5	36.1
Poland	66.8	62.3	78.1	83.8	85.6
Romania	22.1	22.7	27.6	19.4	26.0
Slovak Republic	n.a.	n.a.	10.0	10.7	11.1

.. = not applicable; n.a. = not available.
a. General government.
b. Cash basis.
c. Consolidated state budget.
d. General government balance on a commitment basis, except external interest, which is on a cash basis.
e. Includes nonconvertible currency-denominated debt.

Sources: National authorities; IMF staff estimates.

debt was minimal and it had accumulated substantially more reserves (measured in months of imports) than any other country.[5]

The Post-Reform Experience

While, as described above, the transition economies went through diverse experiences during the 1980s, the period 1990–91 proved, in many ways, to be a common turning point for all these countries. The following factors were decisive: the breakup of the CMEA, the opening of these economies to the rest of the world, the adverse terms-of-trade shock (stemming mainly from market-determined prices of oil and other raw material in the new regime), and, most important, the uncertainties generated by the huge upheaval of the economic and political systems. As a result, the current account for the region as a whole swung sharply into deficit, and speculative capital outflows led to a depletion of reserves (table 1).

All transition economies launched ambitious stabilization programs together with structural reforms in 1990–91.[6] Faced with unprecedented declines in output and rising inflation (table 4), these countries urgently turned to the international community for financial support. With the notable exception of Bulgaria, the capital account turned positive in net terms for all countries in 1992–93. Official assistance was given across the board, while some countries also benefited from private flows (table 3).

Given initially favorable conditions and its remarkable progress in adapting to them, the former Czechoslovakia was best positioned to benefit from a relatively favorable external environment (tables 5 and 6). At the end of 1990, it unified and pegged its exchange rate to a basket of currencies and aggressively built up reserves. This was made possible in 1991 and the first half of 1992 by a strong current account surplus, inflows of official assistance, and foreign direct investment triggered by direct sales of public assets and mass privatization in 1991–92.[7] Developments in the second half of 1992 were mainly influenced by the uncertainties regarding the breakup of the country. As a result, there was a temporary reversal in the current account and a decline in capital inflows leading to a drawing down of reserves.

The formal split of the former Czechoslovakia in January 1993 left the Czech Republic in a relatively favorable position. During 1993 and the first quarter of 1994, its trade deficit was reversed, and inflows of foreign

---

5. See Prust et al. (1990) for a more detailed discussion.

6. For a detailed discussion of the stabilization programs, see Bruno (1993, chapter 7), Sahay and Végh (1996a), and Fischer, Sahay, and Végh (1996a).

7. A surge in imports resulting from trade liberalization did not materialize due to large declines in output. The country also showed great versatility in reorienting exports to the industrial countries.

Table 5 Central and Eastern Europe: stabilization programs and external debt

Country	Stabilization program	External debt
Bulgaria	First comprehensive program started in March 1991; still continuing.	Moratorium on debt since March 1990; most debt is commercial. Agreement with London Club reached in mid-1994.
Czech Republic	Following price jump in 1991, inflation brought down quickly; no major stabilization issue.	Low external debt (about 30 percent of GDP in 1993) and debt service (9 percent of goods and nonfactor services).
Hungary	Gradual reform since 1968, accelerated since 1988.	External debt about 50 percent of GDP (1993); most debt is commercial, current on servicing.
Poland	Comprehensive program in early 1990; lax policies in 1992; economy began to stabilize in 1993.	Large external debt; significant arrears exist that are being resolved.
Romania	Comprehensive program began in April 1991; still continuing with limited succession on inflation.	Mostly medium- and long-term official debt (debt-service ratio of about 10 percent in 1993).
Slovak Republic	Since breakup, an IMF program, the System Transformation Facility, approved in mid-1993; successful stabilization of former state continuing after temporary uncertainty following breakup in early 1993.	External debt about 31 percent of GDP at end-1993, and debt service about 9 percent of exports of goods and services.

capital resumed. The accumulation of external reserves was spectacular during this period (figure 1). The dissolution caused greater disruption for the Slovak Republic as the fiscal deficit widened considerably (table 4), mainly due to a loss of transfers from the Czech Republic, and capital fled the new country. By early 1993, reserves had reached very low levels. Tight financial policies, a one-step devaluation of 10 percent, and some temporary external controls in 1993 partly revived capital inflows and bolstered external reserves.

Capital flows into Hungary, which had stopped in 1990, reemerged in 1991 and gained momentum in 1993. The current account during this period began to decline and turned sharply negative in 1993 (from a small surplus in 1991–92 to a deficit of over $4 billion). Nevertheless, the net result was a substantial increase in reserves (figure 1) brought about, in part, by foreign direct investment but mainly by a sharp increase in bond issues in international markets by the National Bank of Hungary.

While both Poland and Bulgaria faced severe debt-servicing difficulties and large macroeconomic imbalances at the start of the 1990s, Poland

Table 6 Central and Eastern Europe: exchange rate and capital account regimes

Country	Exchange rate regime	Capital account transactions
Bulgaria	Managed float; exchange rate determined in domestic interbank market.	Relatively free for incoming capital.
Czech Republic	Pegged to basket of currencies (the composition changed in May 1993 with higher weight to the deutsche mark).	Most incoming capital flows not subject to licensing; foreign equity participation, Czech bond issue abroad, and foreign suppliers credit are free; enterprise borrowing subject to licensing; most capital outflows are subject to CNB approval and some (e.g. enterprise lending) not allowed; liberal policy on foreign direct investment and repatriation.
Hungary	Fixed to a basket; adjusted periodically on basis of inflation rate differentials.	Attractive for inflows; limits on outflows; interbank foreign exchange established.
Poland	Fixed to a basket; crawling peg policy followed since October 1991.	Parliament sets annual upper limit on public sector external indebtedness; foreign investment liberalized in mid-1991; limits on outflows exist.
Romania	Flexible since November 1991, determined in daily auctions by National Bank of Romania.	All inward and outward transfers of foreign exchange must be authorized by the central bank; foreign investments laws are liberal.
Slovak Republic	Fixed to a basket of five currencies; weights adjusted from time to time.	Registered enterprises can freely obtain suppliers' credit. Foreign direct investment abroad subject to approval from National Bank, usually given if it facilitates exports. No limit on equity participation by nonresidents; foreign investors can freely repatriate earnings.

recovered much faster on both fronts. In contrast to Bulgaria, Poland succeeded in reviving output and curbing inflation by end-1993 (table 4). Even though both countries received significant debt relief from the Paris Club and made progress with the London Club, Poland faces a more favorable external environment because most of its past debt is official while Bulgaria's is predominantly commercial. External accounts for both countries reflect increasing current account deficits in 1992–93 countered by a swing in the capital account in Poland since 1992 and in Bulgaria since 1993. In Bulgaria, capital flows are dominated by exceptional financing by international financial institutions.

Figure 1 Central and Eastern Europe: total reserves minus gold, 1990–94 (millions of dollars)

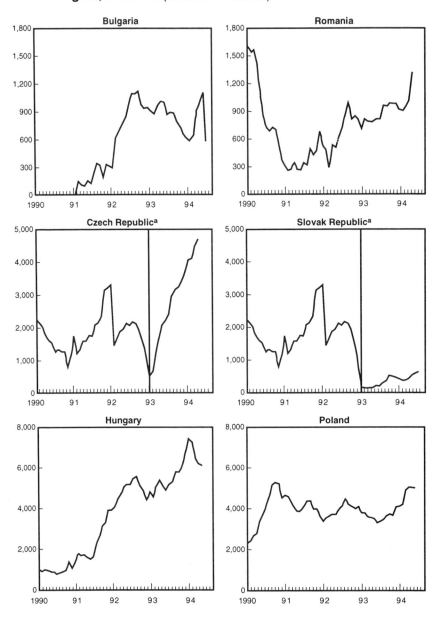

a. Czechoslovakia through end of 1992 (breakup indicated by a vertical line).

Sources: IMF, *International Financial Statistics* data base; national authorities.

Since the start of its reform program in 1991, Romania has been plagued by high inflation and poor economic performance (table 4). Since Ceausescu's downfall, internal imbalances have been reflected in current account deficits (table 2). While capital has begun to flow in since 1991, it is predominantly medium- and long-term financing from official creditors.

Evidence on Capital Flows in Central and Eastern Europe

During the 1970s and the 1980s, the Eastern European economies' access to international capital markets was comparable to that of other developing countries. Hence, the ripples of the 1982 international debt crisis were also felt in Eastern Europe, as capital inflows declined temporarily in response to Western banks' tightened lending practices toward the rest of the world. The former Yugoslavia, which had accumulated a substantial stock of hard-currency debt by the late 1970s, was hit the hardest by the worldwide credit squeeze and soaring interest rates in international capital markets in the early 1980s.

Despite tighter access to Western capital, the region (with the exception of Czechoslovakia) continued to borrow abroad and eventually became heavily indebted. Romania (by the mid-1980s) and Bulgaria and Poland (by 1990) were forced to reschedule their external debt. In light of the difficult external and macroeconomic situation, the late 1980s were a period of increasing capital outflows and reserve losses, which climaxed with a loss of reserves of $10.9 billion in 1991. For the period 1987–91, capital outflows for the region as a whole totaled $24 billion, financed mostly by a loss of international reserves of $25.8 billion (table 1). The region's deteriorating macroeconomic condition and the rapidly collapsing economic structure led to a substantial reduction in private consumption and investment.

During 1990–91, as the Eastern European economies embarked on macroeconomic stabilization programs and far-reaching structural reforms, they also turned to the international community for financial support. In a remarkable turnaround, the capital account (including errors and omissions) improved by $9.6 billion in 1992 (from a deficit of $8 billion to a surplus of $1.6 billion) and by a further $10.6 billion in 1993 (table 1). Given the alarming rate at which the stock of international reserves was being depleted, it is not surprising that the initial improvement in the capital account in 1992 was fully utilized to cut dramatically into reserve losses, with the overall balance of payments improving by $9.8 billion, and the current account balance remaining essentially unchanged. In contrast, during the following year only $4.1 billion (roughly 40 percent) of the additional $10.6 billion that flowed into the region was accumulated as international reserves. The rest ($6.5 billion) was used to finance a

Table 7 Central and Eastern Europe: composition of capital account,[a] 1987–93 (billions of dollars)

Year	Total	Foreign direct investment	External borrowing	Asset transactions	Errors and omissions
1987	−3.5	0.0	−3.1	−1.4	0.9
1988	−6.3	0.0	−9.5	0.1	3.1
1989	−1.5	0.5	−2.5	−2.2	2.6
1990	−5.0	0.5	−5.0	−0.2	−0.2
1991	−8.3	2.3	−11.3	0.7	0.0
1992	1.2	3.0	−1.0	0.1	−0.9
1993	11.9	3.5	8.2	0.5	−0.2

a. The countries included are Bulgaria, the former Czechoslovakia (until 1991), the Czech Republic (1992–93), Hungary, Poland, Romania, and the Slovak Republic (1992–93). The capital account figures reported in this table differ from those in table 1 because the latter include official transfers.

Source: IMF, World Economic Outlook data base.

more than threefold increase in the current account deficit, which reached $9.2 billion in 1993. The increase in the current account deficit mostly reflected increases in private consumption.[8] Preliminary data for 1994 show that the capital account improved further by $1 billion, which was used to finance higher current account deficits as well as to accumulate more reserves.

The orders of magnitude involved are worth noting. Table 4 indicates that the GDP for the region as a whole in 1993 was about $200 billion. Hence, capital inflows during 1993, which amounted to $12.2 billion, represented 6.1 percent of GDP for the region as a whole. This figure is not only impressive in absolute terms but is also considerably larger than that observed in most countries in Latin America and Asia (Calvo, Leiderman, and Reinhart 1994a).

Composition of Capital Flows

The significant changes in the capital account during 1987–93 primarily mirror developments in external borrowing (table 7). In particular, external borrowing hit a low of minus $11.3 billion in 1991—the year in which capital outflows peaked. This reflects the culmination of a period during which debt servicing was in full swing for virtually all countries, and when fresh loans were either drying up (as in the cases of Bulgaria, Poland, and, to some degree, Hungary), or countries were following a deliberate policy of not increasing external liabilities (Romania and the former Czechoslovakia). During 1992–93, all countries received external

---

8. This pattern of using the initial wave of capital inflows to finance mainly a buildup of reserves and later on to finance widening current account deficits was also observed in Latin America. In Asia, however, capital inflows were predominantly used to build reserves.

assistance from official creditors, and some (Hungary and the Czech Republic) raised funds in international capital markets. In 1993, net external borrowing accounted for almost 70 percent of the capital inflows. This pattern is similar to that observed in 1990–91 in Latin America, where net external borrowing accounted for more than 70 percent of net capital inflows. The corresponding figure for Asia was about 50 percent.

The second notable feature in the composition of the capital account is that, starting from negligible amounts during the late 1980s, foreign direct investment has rapidly gained momentum during the 1990s (table 7). This could be expected given the sudden opening up of these economies and the massive privatization of state enterprises in some countries. As a share of GDP, foreign direct investment was also significant in the region during 1992–93, particularly in the Czech Republic and Hungary (table 3). On average, foreign direct investment was about 1.5 percent of GDP during 1992–93, compared with about 1.1 percent in Latin America in 1990–92 and 3.0 percent in Asia in 1989–92. Unlike Asia and Latin America, portfolio investment in the region was negligible during 1987–93. Within the region, it was a significant proportion of total capital inflows in the Czech Republic, accounting for nearly 25 percent of capital inflows in 1993. More recently, however, portfolio investment seems to have risen sharply. Regional data for 1994 indicate that portfolio investment increased almost $1 billion.

Consumption and Investment

As table 1 indicates, $6.3 billion of the $20.2 billion increase in capital inflows in 1992–93 were used to finance a rise in the current account deficit, which reached $9.2 billion (roughly 4.5 percent of the region's GDP) in 1993. The larger current account deficits in 1992–93 reflected mainly increases in consumption rather than investment (tables 2 and 8). In fact, total consumption as a share of GDP rose significantly from 1987–91 to 1992–93 across all countries, ranging from an increase of 18 percentage points for Bulgaria to between 7 and 8 percentage points for the Czech Republic and Romania. Most of this increase has been reflected in private consumption rather than government consumption (tables 2 and 8). On the other hand, during the same period, gross capital formation declined in practically all countries, particularly in Bulgaria and Poland. Whereas in Asia investment as a share of GDP rose about three percentage points during 1989–92, the trend in Latin America was similar to that in the transition economies, with investment falling and consumption rising during 1990–92.

Real Exchange Rate Appreciation

If domestic consumption—rather than investment—increases in response to capital inflows, there is likely to be upward pressure on the real

Table 8   Central and Eastern Europe: consumption, 1991–93
(millions of dollars)

	Bulgaria	Czech Republic	Hungary	Poland	Romania	Slovak Republic
Total consumption						
1991	6.5	22.2	24.8	61.4	21.6	22.2
1992	8.0	19.4	27.5	67.9	14.9	8.8
1993	9.4	22.4	27.8	78.2	15.0	9.0
Private final consumption						
1991	5.4	13.5	20.7	45.5	n.a.	13.5
1992	6.6	15.0	23.1	53.6	n.a.	5.7
1993	7.7	17.6	23.5	62.2	n.a.	6.4
Government final consumption						
1991	1.1	8.8	4.1	15.9	n.a.	8.8
1992	1.5	4.5	4.4	14.3	n.a.	3.1
1993	1.7	4.8	4.3	16.0	n.a.	2.6

n.a. = not available

Source: IMF, World Economic Outlook data base.

exchange rate. The reason is that domestic consumption tends to fall relatively more on nontraded goods, while domestic capital formation is likely to be more import-intensive (Calvo, Leiderman, and Reinhart 1994b). Figure 2 illustrates the fact that, to varying degrees, the real exchange rate indeed appreciated in virtually all the transition economies during 1992–93. In the majority of Latin American countries also, the real exchange rate appreciated during 1990–92. This trend was less common in Asia during the same period.

Among the transition economies, the appreciation of the real exchange rate was most noticeable in Bulgaria, the Czech Republic, Hungary, and Poland. In the latter two cases, it began even before 1992. The regional trend toward real exchange rate appreciation is strongly supported by the cross-country correlation of real effective exchange rates presented in table 9. This table reveals a sharp switch from very low (or even negative) coefficients during 1990–91 to very high coefficients during 1992–93 for practically all the countries, suggesting a stronger degree of co-movement in real effective exchange rates.

Reserve Accumulation

While almost all countries intervened in the foreign exchange markets to build reserves in 1992–93, intervention was most noticeable in the Czech Republic and Hungary. The Hungarian authorities deliberately accumulated reserves to take advantage of their increased access to markets abroad at low interest rates, partly in anticipation of the need to meet

Figure 2 Central and Eastern Europe: real effective exchange rates,ᵃ 1990–94 (Jan 1991 = 100)

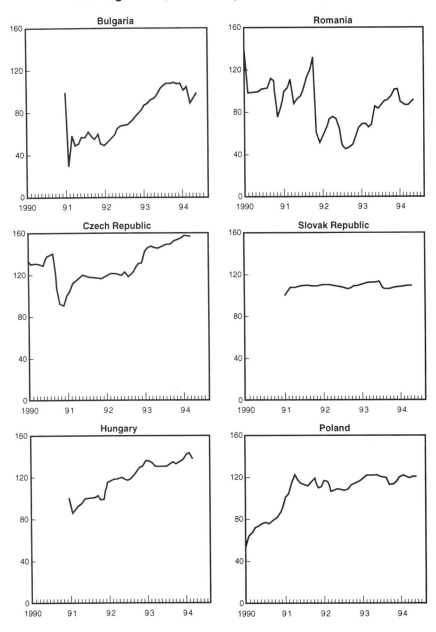

a. An increase in the index indicates an appreciation.

Source: National authorities.

Table 9 Cross-country correlations: real effective exchange rates, 1990–94[a]

	Bulgaria	Czech Republic	Hungary	Poland	Romania	Slovak Republic
1/90 to 12/91						
(Number of observations: 24)						
Bulgaria	1.000					
Czech Republic	−0.360	1.000				
Hungary	0.550	0.394	1.000			
Poland	−0.383	−0.462	0.089	1.000		
Romania	0.073	0.326	0.061	−0.218	1.000	
Slovak Republic	−0.499	0.950	0.241	0.656	−0.091	1.000
1/91 to 3/94						
(Number of observations: 27)						
Bulgaria	1.000					
Czech Republic	0.921	1.000				
Hungary	0.862	0.935	1.000			
Poland	0.624	0.733	0.730	1.000		
Romania	0.728	0.786	0.652	0.417	1.000	
Slovak Republic	−0.078	0.092	0.119	0.467	−0.048	1.000

a. The sample period for cross-country correlations for Bulgaria, Hungary, and the Slovak Republic is 1/91 to 12/91 (data for 1990 are not available for these three countries).

Source: IMF, *International Financial Statistics* data base; national authorities.

large debt repayments in 1995–96. This strategy, of course, increased their debt burden in 1992–93.

To the extent that movements in the capital account are reflected in the reserve account, changes in reserves are a reasonable proxy for the inflows, although, as noted, the proportion of inflows going into reserve accumulation has changed. Figure 1 illustrates that reserves, in general, rose for most countries since 1992. The cross-country correlations (table 10) were also fairly high since 1992. No obvious pattern emerges before that.[9]

A Case Study: The Czech Republic

The period of capital inflows probably raised the most concerns in the Czech Republic. The steep increase in reserves in the Czech Republic (figure 1) resulted from the current account being marginally in surplus when the economy was being flooded by foreign capital. A closer examination of the composition of capital inflows during 1993 reveals that nearly half of the inflows reflected borrowing by Czech enterprises, while the

9. One exception to the high values of cross-correlations was Bulgaria, where the authorities intermittently intervened in the foreign exchange market to prevent rapid depreciation of the currency.

Table 10 Cross-country correlations: total reserves minus gold, 1990–94

	Bulgaria[a]	Czech Republic[b]	Hungary	Poland	Romania	Slovak Republic[b]
1/90 to 12/91						
(Number of observations: 24)						
Bulgaria	1.000					
Czechoslovakia	0.674	1.000				
Hungary	0.781	0.725	1.000			
Poland	−0.468	−0.474	0.082	1.000		
Romania	0.743	0.182	−0.403	−0.750	1.000	
1/92 to 4/94						
(Number of observations: 28)						
Bulgaria	1.000					
Czech Republic	−0.646	1.000				
Hungary	0.004	0.838	1.000			
Poland	0.152	0.658	0.502	1.000		
Romania	0.447	0.851	0.672	0.405	1.000	
Slovak Republic	−0.495	0.870	0.647	0.523	0.911	1.000

a. The sample period for cross-country correlations between Bulgaria and the other countries is 1/91 to 12/91 (data for Bulgaria for 1990 are not available).
b. The sample period for cross-country correlations for the Czech Republic and the Slovak Republic is 1/93 to 4/94 (the two countries were created in 1993:1).

Sources: IMF, *International Financial Statistics* data base; national authorities.

rest resulted mainly from foreign direct and portfolio investment.[10] Nearly 70 percent of enterprise borrowing was undertaken by the private sector, of which about half was lent by neighboring European countries, such as Germany and Austria.

The monetary authorities' policy response was to sterilize some of the inflows through the sale of Czech National Bank bills. In addition, reserve requirements were raised from 9 to 12 percent in August 1994. Because of the ample external reserve position in 1994, the Bank also repaid the remaining outstanding debt due to the IMF in advance.

Some have argued that the rise in external borrowing in 1992–93 by domestic enterprises reflected a substitution of domestic credit for foreign credit. This supposedly occurred because of a mismatch between deposit and loan maturities, in that the latter were relatively long-term. Consequently, local banks were generally reluctant to extend medium- and long-term credit, which was partly reflected in a wide gap between lending and deposit rates. Thus, some of these inflows are arguably linked to the inefficiencies in the domestic financial system.

---

10. Portfolio investment, in large part, reflects the resale to foreigners of stocks received by domestic residents during mass privatization of state enterprises in 1991–92.

If banks were reluctant to extend credit, it should have been reflected in a decline in the loan-to-deposit ratio (given unchanged reserve requirements) and/or an increase in excess reserves. An examination of the data on these series shows that the loan-to-deposit ratio remained virtually unchanged during 1993.[11] Also, the reserve requirement ratio was not raised during this year. Second, excess reserves did not increase in absolute terms or relative to total reserves during 1993.

The unwillingness of banks to extend credit could have been reflected in their unwillingness to accept deposits. One preliminary way of investigating this would be to check whether the spread between lending and deposit rates increased and to assess whether the growth in deposits could be considered too low. The data reveal that while the spread was large (about 6 to 7 percentage points), it declined marginally from end-1992 to end-1993; also, the deposits grew 22 percent during the same period, virtually matching the growth rate in the previous year.[12] Therefore, on the basis of these data, we cannot establish that banks were not accepting deposits.

Thus, enterprises may have borrowed abroad not because domestic banks were reluctant to lend but because of a genuine shortage of credit in the economy, despite the fact that interest rate spreads (particularly with respect to deutsche mark interest rates) had generally declined (table 11). The Czech government's improved credibility (due to sustained stabilization and structural reforms) and the pickup of economic activity could be expected to lead to an increase in the real demand for money. Under these circumstances, the appropriate monetary policy response would appear to be to increase the money supply either by allowing capital inflows and not sterilizing them or by increasing base money at a more rapid pace.[13]

Capital Inflows into Eastern and Central Europe: An Assessment

Given the relatively low initial levels of absorption present in these economies—reflecting the planned economies' highly inefficient use of available physical and human resources—it is logical to see the recent increase in consumption as reflecting a move toward that equilibrium level of

---

11. The loan-to-deposit ratio declined slightly from 1.12 at end-1992 to 1.06 at end-1993.

12. Although the growth in deposits was similar in nominal terms, in real terms growth was lower in 1993 since period-end annual inflation increased from 12 percent in 1992 to 18 percent in 1993. Also, economic growth picked up somewhat in 1993.

13. This argument is further strengthened by the fact that the money multiplier declined during 1993, recording a significant fall of over 35 percent in March 1994 as compared to a year earlier.

Table 11 Czech Republic: T-bill spreads, 1993 Q1–1994 Q1 (percent a year)

	Foreign interest rates		Devaluation-adjusted domestic interest rates[a]				Interest rate spreads			
			Dollars		Deutsche mark		Dollars		Deutsche mark	
	US T-bill	German T-bill	T-bill	CNB bill	T-bill	CNB bill	T-bill	CNB bill	T-bill	CNB bill
1993 Q1	3.0	7.1	n.a.	5.3	n.a.	10.1	n.a.	2.3	n.a.	3.0
Q2	3.0	6.6	17.8	17.7	13.1	12.9	14.9	14.7	6.5	6.4
Q3	3.0	6.0	3.8	6.9	10.6	13.9	0.7	3.9	4.6	8.0
Q4	3.1	5.4	8.0	10.2	4.6	6.7	4.9	7.1	-0.8	1.3
1994 Q1	3.3	5.1	10.6	12.5	5.5	7.3	7.3	9.2	0.4	2.2

n.a. = not available

a. CNB bills are issued by the Czech National Bank, while T-bills are issued by the government.

Sources: Czech authorities; IMF, *International Financial Statistics* data base.

consumption that would be consistent with a productive use of all available resources. Because the structural reform process that leads to a full utilization of resources is a gradual one, the private sector is likely to borrow from abroad to satisfy its consumption needs until full productive potential is realized. Therefore, current capital inflows would be financing a permanently higher level of consumption, rather than a temporary binge triggered by lack of credibility (as in Calvo and Végh 1993).

Insofar as capital inflows are not financing unsustainably high levels of consumption, the oft-mentioned negative effects of capital inflows should be of much less concern. In particular, real exchange rate appreciation, rather than reflecting an unsustainably high level of consumption, would reflect the fact that the increase in desired absorption faces an infinitely elastic supply of traded goods and a relatively inelastic supply of nontraded goods. Hence, whatever future adjustment may be needed in the current account should come about through an increase in income (though higher production of goods), which would reflect an increasingly efficient use of resources, rather than a fall in absorption. Capital inflows would bridge the gap until the higher production actually materializes. Furthermore, any attempts to reduce these capital inflows would be welfare-reducing.

Two other factors may also account for the observed real exchange rate appreciation. As argued in the previous section, there has been a large surge of foreign direct investment into these economies. Such a "bunching" of foreign direct investment, which will probably persist, is likely to require inputs of nontraded goods—labor and materials—whose availability necessarily involves a time lag. The demand for these nontraded inputs will bid up the relative price of nontraded goods (i.e., will contribute to a real exchange rate appreciation). Again, this change in relative prices should reverse itself once the first and probably the largest wave of foreign direct investment has taken place.

Unlike the two factors mentioned above, which in principle should call for a temporary real exchange rate appreciation, the upgrade and expansion of the capital stock to its new steady-state level should lead to a permanent appreciation of the real exchange rate, as the higher capital stock raises the marginal productivity of labor and thus increases the demand for labor. In sum, the current real exchange appreciation is likely to reflect both permanent and temporary components. A real exchange appreciation, per se, should not cause concern because it reflects—under all three scenarios—a change in relative prices required by the current adjustment process. Attempting to interfere with these relative price changes would only slow the adjustment process and thus reduce welfare.[14] These arguments contrast with those applicable to Latin America

---

14. To the extent that these inflows cause volatility in real effective exchange rates, however, they can adversely affect exports (Grobar 1993).

in the early 1990s, where a case could be made for slowing the inflows since these may have been financing unsustainably high levels of absorption. Therefore, the policy choice in the transition economies would consist of letting the real exchange rate appreciation occur either through an appreciation of the nominal exchange rate or through higher inflation.

A somewhat surprising piece of evidence is that higher investment ratios have not yet materialized. Two explanations come to mind. First, roughly similar investment ratios may be hiding important differences regarding the efficiency of investment. If that were the case, investment in "efficiency units" would have increased even if investment ratios did not. Second, to the extent that structural reforms have proceeded more slowly than anticipated, investment activity can only be expected to pick up with a lag.[15]

An interesting aspect of the evidence presented in the previous sections is that, contrary to what has been observed in other cases of capital inflows, the cross-correlations for the real exchange rates are higher than that for international reserves (tables 9 and 10). Several factors may lie behind this pattern. First, one could argue that even in the absence of capital inflows, the real exchange rate would have tended to appreciate throughout the region as price liberalization brought prices of nontraded goods closer to equilibrium levels and consumption began to increase from the very depressed levels corresponding to the collapse of the communist systems. Second, the relatively low cross-correlations for international reserves are likely to reflect dissimilar policy responses to capital inflows. In the Czech Republic and Hungary, the extent of intervention in foreign exchange markets exceeded that of the rest.[16]

Problems and Policies: A First Look

As already illustrated, capital inflows led to an increase in consumption and an appreciation of the real exchange rate in the transition economies. We have argued that, unlike in Latin America, these developments could have reflected an adjustment toward a new equilibrium and may not necessarily have warranted an intervention by policymakers at that time. In fact, capital flows may have helped build reserves and allowed larger current account deficits, with the latter improving living standards in

---

15. It is worth noting that gross capital formation as a share of GDP has, indeed, begun to rise in some countries—Bulgaria, the Czech Republic, and Hungary—according to preliminary data for 1994. Further analysis of the investment and growth prospects in the transition economies can be found in Fischer, Sahay, and Végh (1996b).

16. Furthermore, in some countries there appears to have been a deliberate policy to keep the nominal exchange rate undervalued during the initial stages of reform to ensure external competitiveness.

these economies either directly—through a greater variety (and better quality) of imports of final goods—or indirectly—through imports of high-quality capital and intermediate goods. Apart from bringing financial resources, foreign direct investment is generally also accompanied by highly skilled human capital. If this all sounds like good news, why should countries be concerned?

Despite these positive aspects of capital inflows, some causes of concern for the authorities remain:[17]

- If capital inflows are used to finance a temporary consumption boom, then eventually expenditure will have to fall in order to service the associated debt accumulation.[18]

- Even if outside funds are used for capital accumulation, the resulting surge of domestic activity to install the new capital may call for an overshooting of the real wage. Thus, eventually the real wage will have to fall, creating adjustment problems, unless the labor market exhibits very high flexibility.

- Capital inflows induce growth in monetary aggregates that far exceeds the inflation target and/or a large appreciation of the nominal exchange rate. The former is likely to be associated with higher-than-planned inflation, while the latter gives rise to an immediate loss of international competitiveness through the resulting appreciation of the real exchange rate. Moreover, excessive growth of monetary aggregates is also likely to result in an eventual real exchange rate appreciation.

The best reaction to the first two concerns listed above is likely to be a deepening of reforms in order for market forces to operate free of distortions, a process that takes time. A second-best solution would be to attempt to slow the flow of funds to the private sector and/or to provide incentives for the latter to decrease current expenditure. Examples of second-best policies are direct controls on, or taxation of, new international loans (usually adjusting for loan maturity); higher taxes (to lower private expenditure); and higher interest rates on government debt (to attract international funds away from the private sector).[19]

Direct controls are hard to implement because the private sector has many ways in which to camouflage financial transactions. Higher taxes

17. For a more comprehensive discussion, see Calvo, Leiderman, and Reinhart (1993, 1994a and b).

18. A related concern is that the consumption boom will contribute to an appreciation of the real exchange rate and undermine export competitiveness. This expenditure cycle might not necessarily occur if funds were used for productive capital accumulation because output would grow and contribute to financing the debt.

19. This is closely related to the sterilized intervention policy discussed later.

are not likely to be effective unless the tax hike is substantial—a highly unpopular move—or perceived to be long-lasting, which may be hard to justify when the policy is aimed at offsetting short-term developments.[20] Finally, higher interest rates on debt may be effective but could discourage the most important type of expenditure—namely, investment. Investment projects are guided by their internal rate of return. In contrast, consumption projects may not, and in general will not, be self-financing. Consumption loans are often guided by whether the consumer can afford to pay the credit installment. Consumer credit is normally extended until the individual's credit-service obligations reach a given critical level. Thus, below that critical level, interest rate hikes are likely to have a relatively small impact on consumption. Another negative aspect of the interest rate option is that, to the extent that interest rates rise above international levels, such a policy will generate a larger fiscal deficit, which is likely to worsen as the interest rate differential attracts foreign capital flows.

The most widely and quickly perceived problem caused by a surge of capital inflows, however, is monetary. This may be partly explained by the fact that monetary phenomena surface very quickly. A capital inflow puts pressure on the foreign exchange market, which forces the central bank to decide right away whether to let the exchange rate appreciate or intervene to buy foreign exchange. Thus, in the very short run—when there is no time for changing regulations, and little is known about the nature of the capital inflows episode—the central bank has two options: sterilized or nonsterilized intervention. Sterilized intervention consists of buying foreign exchange by issuing government (interest-bearing) debt, while nonsterilized intervention takes place through the issuance of domestic money (i.e., non-interest-bearing government debt).

In practice, at the beginning of an episode of capital inflows episodes, policymakers have tended to prevent the exchange rate from appreciating through sterilized intervention (Frankel 1993). Later, as the cost of sterilized intervention mounts, sterilization is abandoned in favor of nonsterilized intervention, or some form of taxation.[21]

A Simple Analysis

In this section we will develop a simple analytical tool that should prove useful in understanding some of the more subtle implications of capital

---

20. If there was no fear of capital flow reversal, then the associated developments would be mostly sustainable over time.

21. Sterilized intervention is costly because domestic interest rates (adjusted for the rate of devaluation) tend to exceed international ones. Some examples of taxation are a higher cash/deposit reserve requirement or a tax on foreign assets (Reinhart 1991).

Figure 3   Monetary effects of capital inflows

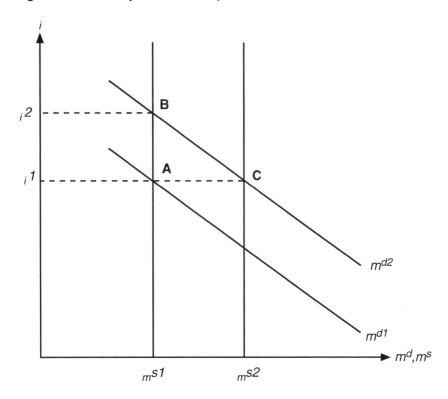

inflows. In figure 3 we draw a standard demand for real monetary balances, m^{d1}, which is inversely related to the nominal interest rate, i. The real money supply is given by m^{s1}. The initial equilibrium is represented by point A. Suppose that, starting from this initial equilibrium, structural reforms or the opening of new markets make profitable a certain number of new investment projects. As a result, investment rises and, with it, construction activity and employment. Thus, the demand for domestic money is likely to rise reflecting the higher activity level (captured by the shift to m^{d2} in figure 3). For a constant real money supply, m^{s1}, the new equilibrium is at point B. We thus see that a rise in the demand for money results in a higher interest rate (i.e., the increase from i^1 to i^2).

To carry the analysis one step further, let us assume a simple economy in which the price level and the exchange rate are the same ($P = E$). Let M and E denote the supply of money and the exchange rate (i.e., the price of foreign exchange in terms of domestic currency), respectively. Thus, by definition, the supply of real monetary balances, m^s, is equal to M/E. The higher real money demand provokes an incipient capital inflow and/or a nominal appreciation of the exchange rate (i.e., a fall in the price level).

As noted above, the central banker's first instinct is not to let the supply of money expand. Thus, real supply of money would be constant, as in the above experiment, and domestic interest rates will rise. In order to keep both M and E constant, however, the central bank must buy all the foreign exchange that is offered at that exchange rate and then quickly sell the same amount of public debt in order to mop up the new money. In other words, the central bank has to engage in sterilized intervention.

Two implications should be highlighted. First, if the domestic interest rate exceeds the international one, then, assuming a fixed exchange rate, the central bank would have undertaken a loss-making operation. Second, by raising interest rates, the new projects "crowd out" outstanding projects, especially those that depend on domestic financing.

Alternatively, the central bank could have acquired the new supply of foreign exchange by issuing domestic money (nonsterilized intervention), i.e., by letting M increase so as to keep the initial interest rate constant (point C in figure 3). Because domestic money yields no return, and reserves can be invested in US Treasury bills, for example, the central bank can now make a profit. Moreover, outstanding projects are not crowded out. Thus, under the present circumstances, nonsterilized intervention clearly dominates sterilized intervention.

Finally, the central bank could provoke the same shift in money supply (with the equilibrium changing from point A to point C) by lowering the exchange rate, E, by means of a nominal appreciation. The implications are very similar to the nonsterilized intervention case, with one important difference: to the extent that the appreciation was not fully anticipated by the public, lenders (in domestic currency) will gain and borrowers will lose in real terms (in terms of goods and services).

In practice, not all promising projects are started at the same time. Thus, as new projects filter in, the demand for money rises and, with it, the domestic interest rate, if the central bank maintains its sterilization policy. Thus, all the negative aspects of sterilized intervention mentioned above are exacerbated over time. Furthermore, even if there are no new investment projects, the central bank may still experience serious difficulties. That would be the case, for example, if sterilization policy raises interest rates to levels that look attractive to "portfolio investors," i.e., investors interested in short-term liquid assets. Under these circumstances, the economy would be flooded with foreign funds in search of domestic deposits. The amount that must be sterilized will skyrocket and, as a result, central bank losses are likely to become unsustainable.[22]

---

22. The policy choices just discussed would remain essentially unchanged even when capital inflows are not responding to an increase in real money demand (see Rodriguez 1993). In the face of such an "exogenous" capital inflow, policy makers would still need to choose between letting the exchange rate fall (with a fall in interest rates)—which would be captured by a rightward shift in the real money supply in figure 3—or engaging in sterilization, thereby preventing the real money supply from increasing and interest rates from falling.

Figure 4　Colombia: deposit interest rate, 1980–94

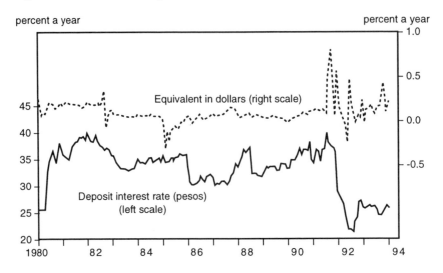

The recent experience in Colombia is very revealing. Capital started to flow in around 1990. The central bank first followed a strict sterilization policy and then abandoned it toward the end of 1991. Figure 4 shows interest rates relatively flat from 1990 to end-1991 and then falling sharply by about 10 points in 1992. Interestingly, the same chart shows that its dollar equivalent does not fall.[23] It becomes considerably more volatile and, if anything, rises slightly. Figure 5 shows that upon abandoning sterilization, the money supply (M1) rises sharply, while inflation remains about the same or falls. This change of policy is also reflected in figure 6; during sterilization the ratio of M2 to reserves falls sharply (like in Central and Eastern Europe, see figure 7); after sterilization stops, this ratio flattens out.[24]

Fear of Inflation and Financial Vulnerability

The above discussion gives strong support to nonsterilized intervention and currency appreciation as policy responses to a surge in capital inflows. In this section, however, we focus the discussion on a case in which the nominal exchange rate is kept constant throughout.

23. The dollar equivalent, i^*, is defined as follows: $1 + i^*_t = (1 + i)/(1 + \epsilon_{t+1})$. Where $\epsilon_{t+1} = E_{t+1}/E_t - 1$.

24. See Bento (1994) for an interesting analysis of interventionist measures used to contain the surge of capital inflows in Portugal in 1990–92.

Figure 5   Colombia: M1 growth and inflation, 1987–94
(month over month; percent)

percent, 12-month change

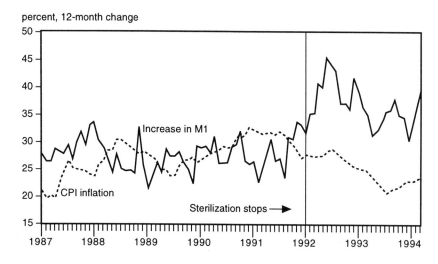

**Figure 6   Colombia: ratio of M2 to international reserves,
1987–93**

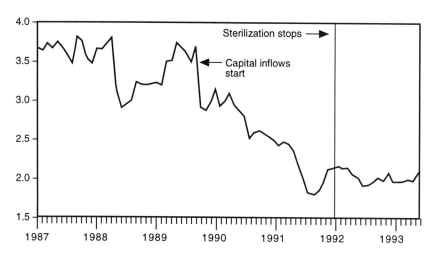

A major objection to nonsterilized intervention stems from the fear
that the resulting expansion in money supply will fuel inflation. This
consideration had no role to play in the previous section because we
identified the price level, P, with the exchange rate, E. However, this
assumption is highly unrealistic. In practice, domestic prices are not so
closely linked to international ones. This is particularly true for "services,"

Figure 7   Central and Eastern Europe: ratios of M2 to reserves, 1990–94

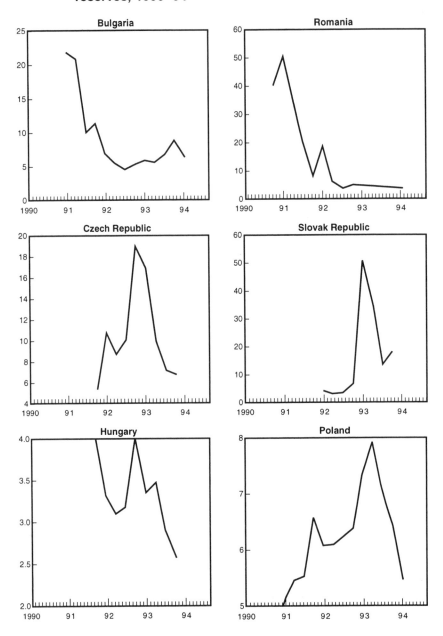

Sources: IMF, International Financial Statistics; national authorities.

which do not face strong competition from abroad. Goods that have no international markets are usually referred to as "home goods." We will denote their price, in terms of domestic currency, by P^h. Thus, the price level could be expressed as a weighted average of the prices of home and international goods; for example, one could define $P = \theta E + (1 - \theta)P^h$, where θ is a number between 0 and 1.[25] In the present setup, the real exchange rate, e, is defined by the equation $e = E/P$.

The popular view referred to above often relies on extending the closed-economy monetarist statement—that prices are caused by money—to an open economy. Thus, it is conjectured that nonsterilized intervention, by allowing M to grow, will foster a rise in P^h and, consequently, in P. Therefore, if capital inflows persist for a while, inflation (i.e., the rate of growth of P) would increase. We will now argue that such a view is valid only under certain, but sometimes relevant, circumstances.

First, we will show a case where the view is not valid. Suppose the relevant price level for the concept of real monetary balances is P. Furthermore, assume, as in the previous section, that a surge in economic activity gives rise to an increase in the demand for money, which leads to a capital inflow. If money supply stays put by means of, say, sterilized intervention, then two things may happen: (a) given the price level, the nominal interest rate i will rise (as in figure 3), and (b) given the nominal interest rate, the price of home goods, P^h, will tend to fall. Thus, capital inflows could be accompanied by a deflation, not inflation as the popular view would have it.

The explanation for the apparent contradiction between an episode of capital inflows and deflation is straightforward. If capital inflows have been brought about by an increase in the demand for money, no inflationary forces need to be set in motion. A good illustration of a case in point is the Portuguese experience in 1990–92 (Bento 1994). In brief, Portugal became a member of the European Community (now the European Union, or EU) in 1986. Since then, it began to adopt macroeconomic policies that facilitated a sequence of EU convergence programs. Perceiving a reduction in the country risk and an increase in the expected profitability of the economy, capital (mostly foreign direct investment) began to flow in, reaching 5 to 6 percent of GDP during 1989–92. Inevitably, these inflows caused a significant appreciation of the real exchange rate to which the authorities responded by imposing capital controls (since mid-1990). One of the consequences of these measures was a sharp disinflation of about 7 percentage points in 1992.[26]

As we said above, however, there is an important instance in which the popular view holds true. Suppose the capital inflows occur during a

---

25. In the previous section we have implicitly set $\theta = 1$.

26. The disinflation reported here excludes the 2 percentage points of the increase in the consumer price index (CPI) caused by a VAT adjustment.

stabilization program that is not fully credible. As argued in Calvo and Végh (1993), if a stabilization program is not fully credible and individuals expect inflation to resume in the near future, prices of home goods will tend to rise (before the expected abandonment of the program). Thus, the demand for nominal monetary balances will rise in tandem with those prices. Suppose that there is no international capital mobility (at the margin); then keeping the money supply constant may, according to previous arguments, put downward pressure on prices, preventing lack of credibility from generating larger-than-planned inflation.[27] Under capital mobility, the same result could be obtained by means of sterilized intervention. Consequently, if keeping inflation within the program's limits is an important policy objective, then partial sterilization of capital inflows may be called for.

A more fundamental criticism has to do with the greater financial vulnerability that might occur through nonsterilized intervention. As a general rule, nonsterilized funds will find their way through the banking system usually causing an increase in bank deposits. If banks are not subject to 100 percent reserve requirements, an increase in bank deposits will lead to an expansion in bank credit. Bank credit, in turn, is likely to be of longer maturity than bank deposits. Thus, a sudden and significant deposit withdrawal may generate a banking crisis. Clearly, the probability of a crisis will be a function of the stability of funds channeled through the banking sector and, of course, of the extent of the maturities mismatch of deposits and loans. In the very short run, when the nature of the capital inflows episode is still not well understood, it may thus be advisable to resort to sterilized intervention. Later on, however, measures should be taken to lessen the extent of the maturities mismatch. As an intermediate step before fundamental measures are undertaken, it may be desirable to increase banks' reserve requirements, at least at the margin. This has the advantage of carrying lower fiscal costs than standard sterilization but is still prone to generating the above-mentioned "crowding out" effect on outstanding projects.

At the heart of financial vulnerability is the deposit/loans maturity mismatch. To some extent this problem may be associated with certain bank regulations. A prominent example is bank deposit insurance. Deposit insurance is a very common feature of banking systems around the world. It serves the obvious purpose of covering depositors, especially small ones from bank failures. However, one key function served by deposit insurance is to enhance the liquidity of bank deposits (by lowering the costs of assessing the financial health of the institution on which a check is drawn, for example) and, thereby, to enhance the role of banks in domestic payments mechanisms. On the other hand, deposit insurance

---

27. For a formal proof of this proposition, see Calvo and Végh (1993).

is likely to induce banks to extend longer-term credit than they would otherwise, because they are assured of an automatic credit line from the central bank in case of a sudden deposit withdrawal. One proposal aimed at eliminating this moral-hazard problem that has received a great deal of attention (although we are not aware that it has been implemented anywhere in its pure form) consists in subjecting sight deposits to 100 percent reserve requirements and treating time deposits as mutual funds. This proposal, known as the Chicago Plan, was spearheaded by Henry C. Simons in 1936. According to this scheme, time deposits are a claim on the assets acquired by the bank against those deposits. The value of the claim will represent the market value of those assets and is bound to fluctuate. If the bank fails, for example, the value of time deposits could possibly collapse. Therefore, there would be de facto full deposit insurance on M1 and no insurance on the rest of banking liabilities.

Space limitations do not allow a full discussion of these issues.[28] We would like to note, however, that the Chicago Plan may run into difficulties if the public expects that the central bank may not allow the value of time deposits to collapse. In these circumstances, the public would expect some kind of implicit deposit insurance. Thus, if, contrary to expectations, the central bank allows the value of time deposits to plummet, serious financial strain might ensue—possibly forcing the hand of the central bank to bail out banks *ex post* and invalidating the Chicago Plan.

Sterilization: Relevant Monetary Aggregates

Sterilization may fail to be effective if it targets the wrong monetary aggregate. If vulnerability is a key issue, for instance, then sterilization should aim at controlling the expansion of bank liabilities as a whole ("broad money"), taking into account the quality of banks' assets. In particular, if Treasury bills in local currency are deemed completely safe and liquid, then perhaps a suitable variable to target would be broad money *minus* banks' holdings of Treasury bills.

On the other hand, if sterilization is driven by fear of inflation, then targeting broad money (without subtracting anything from it) could be more appropriate. Sometimes, however, the latter may not be enough. A relevant example is a "dollarized" economy, in which dollar deposits constitute an important fraction of broad money. Controlling the banking "dollar" component may not be enough because that would leave out foreign currency (on which there is no reliable and/or timely information), and foreign checking accounts.[29]

---

28. In particular, we do not analyze the Mexican crisis, which exposed the fragility of the domestic financial sector to volatile capital flows (see, e.g., IMF 1995).

29. Dollarization is already becoming a major policy challenge in economies in transition (Sahay and Végh 1996b).

In practice, central banks use sterilization to target narrow monetary aggregates, such as M1. This would clearly be inappropriate in a highly "dollarized" economy. In general, however, targeting M1 will be inappropriate in economies where time deposits are also perceived as being highly liquid.[30] The problem that arises, though, is that the larger the monetary aggregate, the harder it is for sterilization to alter its total amount. Take the limit case in which government bonds are very liquid. In such a case, standard sterilization will simply change the composition of "money" in favor of bonds and against cash and sight deposits, but it will fail to change its total amount. Thus, no perceptible effect on prices is likely to take place.

Even if a relatively narrow monetary aggregate such as M2 is targeted, sterilization may not be effective. It is not unusual in developing countries for banks to be the main holders of government debt (see Calvo and Végh 1995). Consider the following example: the legal cash/deposit reserve requirement is 10 percent, and there is an inflow of capital of 100 million (or local currency) taking the form of time deposits. If the government does not issue public debt, this amount will be "multiplied" and is likely to result in an increase in M2 larger than 100 million. Instead, if the government issues 90 million in public debt, it will be able to soak up the additional loanable funds, and the "bank multiplier" will be 1. Effective as it is, however, this would not be enough to sterilize the initial 100 million increase in liquidity, M2. To do so would require luring the funds away from banks. Otherwise, a new sterilization round could simply attract more foreign funds into the banking system—resulting in an increase in M2 accompanied, most likely, by an increase in domestic interest rates.

Conclusion

Central and Eastern Europe have experienced a dramatic turnaround in the capital account beginning in 1992, after an extended period of capital outflows. International capital has flowed unevenly into the region, although the degree of co-movement in some key macroeconomic indicators has increased in comparison to the 1987–91 period, indicating that the phenomenon is regional and not just country-specific. This phenomenon has strong parallels in Asia and Latin America. It began later but, like in the other regions, one can observe, for example, a tendency for real exchange rates to appreciate, and for international reserves to increase sharply. Our analysis suggests that until end-1993 there were no particular

---

30. We suspect that the liquidity of time deposits is particularly high in high-inflation countries.

reasons to be concerned about the inflows of capital to Central and Eastern Europe—at least given its recent characteristics and extent.[31]

A more detailed analysis does show some worrisome developments, along with very good ones. One positive development, for example, in contrast to Latin America, is a significant increase in foreign direct investment. The latter, however, has not been reflected in higher investment ratios. Actually, those ratios have fallen, while consumption, as a share of GDP, has increased throughout. We believe that, on the whole, the increase in consumption ratios is a normal development because, prior to reform, those ratios were lower than those in comparable market economies. Thus, the pattern of consumption could perhaps represent a redressing of a previous imbalance rather than an unsustainable "consumption boom," unlike in some Latin American countries. Still, the fall in investment is somewhat worrisome if "efficiency units" of current investment are not rising.

As in other capital inflows episodes, one also finds an expansion in monetary aggregates, showing that sterilized intervention has played a relatively minor role. This seems to have been a reasonable monetary strategy because capital inflows are usually characterized by a sharp increase in the demand for money. The paper also discusses the possible dangers of nonsterilized intervention. A major point of concern in this regard is that the resulting expansion of domestic credit to the private sector, accompanied by the likely maturity mismatch between loans and deposits, may increase the degree of financial vulnerability.

Preliminary evidence from 1994 and early 1995 reveals that capital has continued to flow into the region, albeit unevenly, despite the Mexican crisis. Investors appear to be continuing to respond to domestic market conditions rather than to external developments. Moreover, the nature of the flows seems to be changing: with the creation of capital markets, portfolio and foreign direct investment are growing more rapidly than external borrowing. Systemic risks and financial vulnerability in these markets remain key concerns, however, particularly in light of the fragile banking systems of transition economies.

References

Bento, Victor. 1994. "The Management of Exchange Rate Pressures: The Portuguese Experience with Capital Controls." Banco de Portugal. Photocopy.

Bruno, Michael. 1993. *Crisis, Stabilization and Economic Reform.* Oxford: Oxford University Press.

---

31. However, more recent data show that there may be some cause for concern regarding Hungary's external situation, as short-term foreign currency denominated bonds are increasingly being issued by the government to finance the fiscal deficit.

Calvo, Guillermo A., Leonardo Leiderman, and Carmen M. Reinhart. 1993. *Capital Inflows to Latin America: The Role of External Factors.* IMF Staff Papers No. 40. Washington: International Monetary Fund.

Calvo, Guillermo A., Leonardo Leiderman, and Carmen M. Reinhart. 1994a. "The Capital Inflows Problem: Concepts and Issues." *Contemporary Economic Policy* 12: 54–66.

Calvo, Guillermo A, Leonardo Leiderman, and Carmen M. Reinhart. 1994b. "Inflows of Capital to Developing Countries in the 1990s: Causes and Effects." IMF. Photocopy.

Calvo, Guillermo A., and Carlos A. Végh. 1993. "Exchange Rate-Based Stabilization under Imperfect Credibility." In Helmut Frisch and Andreas Worgotter, *Open-Economy Macroeconomics.* London: MacMillan Press.

Calvo, Guillermo A., and Carlos A. Végh. 1995. "Fighting Inflation with High Interest Rates: The Small Open Economy Case under Flexible Prices." *Journal of Money, Credit, and Banking* 27 (February): 49–66.

Demekas, Dimitri G., and Mohsin Khan. 1991. *The Romanian Economic Reform Program.* IMF Occasional Paper No. 89. Washington: International Monetary Fund.

Fischer, Stanley, Ratna Sahay, and Carlos A. Végh. 1996a. "Stabilization and Growth in Transition Economies: The Early Experience." *Journal of Economic Perspectives* (Spring): 45–66.

Fischer, Stanley, Ratna Sahay, and Carlos A. Végh. 1996b. "Economies in Transition: The Beginnings of Growth." *American Economic Review* 86: 229–33.

Frankel, Jeffrey A. 1993. "Sterilization of Money Inflows: Difficult (Calvo) or Easy (Reisen)?" IMF. Photocopy.

Grobar, Lisa M. 1993. "The Effect of Real Exchange Rate Uncertainty on LDC Manufactured Exports." *Journal of Development Economics* 41: 367–76.

International Monetary Fund (IMF). 1995. *International Capital Markets: Developments, Prospects, and Policy Issues.* Washington: IMF.

Prust, Jim et al. 1990. *The Czech and Slovak Federal Republic: An Economy in Transition.* Occasional Paper No. 72. Washington: International Monetary Fund.

Reinhart, Vincent. 1991. "The 'Tobin' Tax, Asset Accumulation, and the Real Exchange Rate." *Journal of International Money and Finance* 10: 420–31.

Rodriguez, Carlos A. 1993. "Money and Credit under Currency Substitution." *IMF Staff Papers* 40, no. 2: 414–26.

Sahay, Ratna, and Carlos A. Végh. 1996a. "Inflation and Stabilization in Transition Economies: An Analytical Interpretation of the Evidence." *Journal of Policy Reform* 1: 75–108.

Sahay, Ratna, and Carlos A. Végh. 1996b. "Dollarization in Transition Economies: Evidence and Policy Implications." In Paul Mizen and Eric Pentecost, *The Macroeconomics of International Currencies: Theory, Policy, and Evidence.* London: Edward Elgar. Forthcoming.

Schadler, Susan, Maria Carkovic, Adam Bennett, and Robert Kahn. 1993. *Recent Experiences with Surges in Capital Inflows,* Occasional Paper No. 108. Washington: International Monetary Fund.

Comment

Norbert Walter

Coming from an institution that deals frequently with Central and Eastern Europe and having worked as a consultant for countries and companies representing various industries in this area, I know that one can often lose sight of the macroeconomic picture. These papers are extremely helpful in reminding us of this potential problem. I would like to comment on some practical issues, however, and add some personal observations concerning German unification.

First, I felt the paper placed too much emphasis on statistics. I have learned the hard way that statistics of countries in structural transition can be unreliable, as can the application of concepts of Western macroeconomic analysis on the basis of such statistics. Some of the concepts are ill-advised anyway. Countries that were formerly divided, even those considered advanced in the use of statistics, such as Germany, have encountered a number of registration problems once united.

Second, the paper does not address the issue of the initial conditions of the transformation process. The condition we find in our textbooks apply only if we start from an equilibrium. But if we start from massive undervaluation, such a process probably tells a totally different story, which must be examined very carefully indeed. I would suggest that quite a few of the countries started from considerable disequilibrium rather than from anything that could be called equilibrium. Even a measured real appreciation may not mean very much for international competitiveness if it reflects the decontrolling of local prices, such as rents. Addi-

Norbert Walter is chief economist, Deutsche Bank Group, Frankfurt.

tionally, productivity gains in the traded goods sector are considerably higher in transition countries than in industrialized countries in the West because of a natural catching-up process in technology.

Third, many politicians and economic policymakers in those countries had to "square the circle"—that is, develop policies that probably were not optimal in the first place. In order to gain credibility, however, they had to pursue certain measures that were, so to speak, existential for any policy action thereafter. Even if a Cambridge-trained economist is deeply convinced about a concept, voters in a transition economy may still not believe in it, nor may international investors. We bankers, as the intermediators learned very directly, know that most of our customers have not read the books of the great postwar economists. Thus the concept of achieving autonomy in monetary policy by using flexible exchange rates may not be as attractive as that of gaining an anchor for discipline by fixing the exchange rate.

Many complex issues need to be addressed. For example, overconsumption may appear to be a one-way road to ruin, but it should also be discussed in a totally different context. If one becomes addicted to a certain consumption level, one will probably want to earn a higher income than before because one is so attracted by the new consumption pattern. Therefore, the work effort that goes into the labor market may be much higher after people have experienced a different lifestyle that includes travel, modern cars, or attractive clothing. If we do not consider such dynamic aspects, there is a risk that certain developments will be interpreted incorrectly.

East Germany offers a telling example of investment statistics. Germany "invested" in firms through the Treuhandanstadt. While this was considered an investment, it was very inefficient, to say the least, because it went into production that should have been closed down in the first place. It is very important, therefore, that we should look not only at investment, but also at the efficiency of investment. I am convinced that countries in Central and Eastern Europe, as well as many other emerging countries, badly need management skills to go along with capital flows. We must thus examine closely the structure of capital flows. Loans and portfolio investments may not bring with them the management skills that foreign direct investment would provide. Therefore, the willingness of countries in Central and Eastern Europe to allow foreign management to participate in the modernization of their economies is very important and more relevant than macro views based on current account statistics or on whether intervention is sterilized or not.

Let me give you an example. Hungary's high current account deficit in 1994 was considered a problem. Hungarian authorities understood this, and corrective measures were taken in order to control it by 1995. Therefore, increased capital inflows into economies in transition—for example, Hungary, the Czech Republic, and Poland—would have yielded a higher return on investment than could have in Western sunset industries, such as those in East or West Germany.

Finally, let me touch upon one of my pet subjects: the money supply in emerging-market economies. When I ask international monetary experts about the money supply of the United States, the United Kingdom, and Germany, for example, I am amazed that many of these experts basically have no idea of the numbers except for German M3. My conclusion is that, with the exception of Germany, they regard monetary aggregates as so unstable that they do not think it is worthwhile to have even a rough idea of what is going on. Yet, for the same experts, monetary aggregates in the transition economies are a big issue. How should one interpret monetary aggregates in countries whose economies are partly dollarized, and how should we attach significant importance to money supply targeting for demand management?

A number of papers for this conference also discuss policy options for countries facing simultaneous current account deficits and pressure for a real appreciation. I believe there are quite a few options for these countries. The example of the Czech Republic is clear: speed up the liberalization of financial markets, open them up for your own citizens, and repay foreign debt (early). These are consistent measures.

I think that a monetary policy geared toward the exchange rate—be it a crawling peg, a basket, or a fixed rate for some time and corrected thereafter in a meaningful way—is a superior strategy for economies in transition.

Comment

Val Koromzay

I found this a useful, thought-provoking paper that nonetheless left me somewhat uneasy. In particular, there is a certain looseness in the connections between the data and some of the conclusions, and I have trouble with the view that nonsterilized intervention should be considered the right response to capital inflows. The paper does note that there are situations where such a response might not be appropriate, and I would argue that such situations are likely to predominate. The problem perhaps is that the paper focuses on one country—the Czech Republic—as if it could be taken as a typical example for the region. The paper would benefit if another sample country, such as Hungary, were also included in the analysis. Hungary did pursue a strategy of nonsterilized intervention in 1992–93, with the result of accelerating domestic demand and a rapid shift from a current account surplus to an unsustainably large deficit. At least with hindsight, most observers would agree that this was the wrong policy. The appropriate policy response to capital inflows is a complicated matter, not well-served by generalizations. It also depends very much on particular country circumstances, including such variables as the degree of external indebtedness, the fiscal position, and inflation.

I would like to comment briefly on six issues raised in the paper and put them in a somewhat broader context.

First, the data. The paper does us a service by pulling together data on these economies' external transactions that are not easy to assemble. It is

Val Koromzay is deputy director, Department of Economics, OECD, Paris. The views expressed in this comment are those of the author and should not be interpreted as necessarily reflecting those of the OECD or its member governments.

a pity that is has not been updated to include 1994, and even the first half of 1995. At the same time, I would stress that the data are messy and possibly subject to misinterpretation. In the case of Poland, for example (and *a fortiori* for Bulgaria), getting a clear picture of the balance of payments involves sorting out how "exceptional financing" is treated in the accounts. Some explanation of how the authors have dealt with this would be useful. As another example, there is probably a large bias in the Polish data due to crossborder shopping by Germans with the result that exports are underrecorded and capital inflows correspondingly overstated.

Second, I question the usefulness of treating the six countries covered as an area, rather than individual cases. One would imagine that as these countries move firmly onto a "convergence path" towards Western European standards of living and economic development, similarities will deepen. Over the period covered by the analysis, however, the differences among the countries seem to be more significant than the similarities. The paper notes the very big differences in "initial conditions" for the transformation, and it seems clear that these differences have persisted and even intensified. For example, Bulgaria and Romania still do not have real access to international financial markets; foreign direct investment into the region has been highly skewed; and macroeconomic stabilization is in very different phases in the different countries. The evidence presented to suggest a regional dimension to developments in the area— namely the cross-correlation in real exchange rate and reserve movements—is not all that powerful in view of the huge differences in the levels of these variables. But even if there is some kind of underlying "area dimension" to capital inflows, any assessment of the policy implications needs to be done on a country-by-country basis.

Third, the link between consumption demand and real appreciation is not convincing. The paper argues that observed real appreciations are explained by the fact that domestic demand has centered on consumption rather than investment. I could follow this logic if the author were trying to explain an equilibrium adjustment in a smoothly functioning economy. I am less persuaded that this is really the driving force in the present case. I would argue that real appreciation is fully explained by the fact that the authorities have generally sought to use the exchange rate to bring inflation under control in the wake of the initial liberalization shocks— themselves associated with undervaluation. Anyone who tried to shop in Poland in January 1990—when, in dollar terms, those Polish goods available seemed almost free—would have predicted rapid real appreciation.

Fourth, on a related point, I question the judgment that the rise in consumption following liberalization is entirely equilibriating and even if it is, whether the author's reasoning is right. Surely there was a substantial degree of repressed consumption demand in these economies prior to liberalization linked both to rationing and unavailability of many consumer goods. At least a temporary consumption binge was predictable (and generally predicted by the authorities, which is one reason they opted for coupling liberalization with sharp devaluation). I am not sure that the average consumer in the transition economies is even now convinced that transition will raise their "permanent incomes" so much that they can afford to borrow against the future. My sense is that anxiety rather than confidence is the dominant characteristic of most households.

Fifth, and here I am moving to the policy section of the paper, I would emphasize the importance of trying to assess the reasons for capital inflow when thinking about the policy response. The paper does this by contrasting a scenario where the inflow is driven by an increased demand for money with one where it is the result of "partially credible stabilization efforts." I have some problem with the former scenario and its analytical development. It seems to me that an "increased demand for money" in the transition economies is actually associated with higher desired saving, not higher planned consumption. This is because bank deposits constitute the dominant form of financial saving. Obviously, in a situation where households desire to save more and domestic demand thereby weakens, the current account would tend to improve. If capital is also flowing in, the net foreign assets of the banking system would be rising, and there would be a good case for allowing the resultant increased liquidity to feed through into easier monetary conditions. I question, however, a causal link between the desired saving and the capital inflow. I think this scenario is not very convincing on this point; perhaps it could be rethought.

Finally, I will comment on why Czech firms are borrowing abroad. It may be, as the paper suggests, that this is indeed just a reflection of too tight monetary policy rather than the structural weaknesses of the Czech banking system. In Hungary, where I know the situation better, structural problems are very relevant, however, and I suspect that similar problems arise in the Czech Republic. Those enterprises that can borrow abroad find it advantageous because they get better service and longer terms. These are obviously prime borrowers. Domestic banks would love to attract these customers and (in Hungary) there are reports of very favorable terms being offered in some cases. Thus, it is nonprice rather than price differences in the product that are decisive. If this is right, there are strong implications for financial fragility. If the best borrowers go abroad, there is a danger that domestic banks will be saddled with a lesser grade portfolio. This points to the urgency of improving the competitiveness of domestic banks.

I would like to conclude my remarks with a more general observation about the role of capital inflows in the transition economies. When transition started, many observers (including myself) envisaged that these economies would move onto a convergence path characterized by high rates of capital accumulation because the initial capital stock was not appropriate to a market economy and would largely have to be scrapped. Physical capital was in fact scarce relative to the rather high stock of human capital. At the same time, inherited standards of social protection and collective consumption suggested that national savings rates might not be very high. Large-scale capital inflows thus appeared necessary, and the task was to define the policies that could attract and sustain them. Such policies, encompassing a variety of structural reforms, effective macroeconomic discipline, and a competitive real exchange rate, have proved difficult to put in place, though continuous progress is being made. Insofar as the transition economies are moving onto such a convergence path, the logic would be that capital inflows would be the counterpart of current account deficits, in which case the question of whether to sterilize would be moot.

It is clear, however, that these economies are not yet there. The paper has noted the failure of investment to take off. In addition, macroeconomic stabilization is not yet achieved. Thus, the paradigm of "partially credible stabilization" is relevant for all countries of the region, with the partial exception of the Czech Republic, and even there inflation still needs to be brought down. There are no easy rules for how to manage policies to achieve stabilization. Capital flows in both directions can and do complicate matters a great deal, with the risk of large real exchange rate swings as the policy balance shifts between fighting inflation and maintaining competitiveness. Ultimate success depends on steadfastness of purpose, coolness of judgment, and, I suspect, good luck.

3

Borrowing in International Capital Markets: Lessons from Experience

Alberto Giovannini

The organizers of this conference assigned to me a different title—"Borrowing and Overborrowing in International Capital Markets: Rules of Thumb and Lessons from Experience"—which I have taken the liberty of editing. I eliminated the word "overborrowing" because I am not sure how to define it. Moreover, the problems I will discuss here are unaffected by whether a country is deemed to borrow too much or not. I also eliminated the expression "rules of thumb." While in daily practice borrowing certainly requires such rules, they are not per se of great interest. I will instead concentrate on some conceptual issues raised by government activities in private markets. These issues affect daily activities as well as government strategies.

This chapter discusses some aspects of government borrowing in private capital markets. The distinction between domestic and international borrowing activities could be of some use in this discussion, but I largely omit it. Because the process of liberalization of international capital flows, accompanied or followed by deregulation of domestic financial markets, has multiplied the possibilities of arbitrating domestic and international securities (that is, securities issued within and outside domestic financial markets), the distinction between domestic and international markets is now becoming less important than in the past.

Alberto Giovannini is senior adviser of Long-Term Capital Management in London, research associate of the National Bureau of Economic Research in Cambridge, Massachusetts, and research fellow of the Centre of Economic Policy Research in London.

The 1980s have witnessed a sea change in the attitudes of governments toward financial markets. Much of the postwar governmental wisdom in this area was the product of the IMF-World Bank-GATT structure, which saw free international trade in goods as an essential element of the postwar liberal organization of world markets but left out—without much explanation—free international trade in financial assets. This institutional structure was the product of the interwar experience, during which governments' ill-conceived and ill-fated initiatives in the foreign exchange markets were seriously disrupted by international speculation. Powerful intellectual support for restricting international capital movements came from the work of John Maynard Keynes, who stressed the limits on domestic monetary policy arising from international capital mobility.

Thus, during much of the postwar period, the leading countries in the world were—at most—cautious about deregulating international capital flows and domestic financial markets.

This attitude has been reversed over the decade of the 1980s, fundamentally changing the character of government activities in financial markets, both as regards monetary policy and debt management. To understand the nature of this change, consider the hypothetical case of a government that has full control of financial markets. Under this regime, government financial transactions, be they money market operations by the central bank or issuance of securities by the treasury, are essentially allocation decisions and can be carried out through administrative acts. Under the polar opposite regime of free financial markets, government authorities are just another actor in the marketplace, with perhaps some informational advantages. In practice, of course, even today's relatively free and deregulated financial markets are still characterized by substantial, and often well-justified, forms of government control. However, there is no doubt that the recent process of deregulation has forced governments to change the way they approach financial markets. The objective of this paper is to discuss in particular government borrowing activities.

The paper is organized as follows. First I discuss the evolution of government borrowing activities in recent years and the causes and role of deregulation. I then list the key questions that need to be tackled when managing government borrowing. In the next section, I isolate the problems raised by asymmetric information between markets and authorities. After discussing potential roles of international institutions, I conclude by summarizing the main points of the paper—and trying to identify the lessons that the title promises to deliver.

I want to make clear that this paper is inspired by my experience in addressing the problems of the management of government debt in Italy. The paper deals with issues that are common in many industrial countries but does not mention the peculiarities of the problems and experience of developing countries. I trust, however, that several of the "lessons" that I suggest here might apply also to developing countries.

Background: The Evolution of Government Debt Management

In a recent paper, Mussa and Masson (1995) have highlighted some common characteristics in the evolution of government debt among industrial countries. For many industrial countries, the origins of the current high levels of government indebtedness are to be found in expansions of government spending in the 1970s. Interestingly enough, during the 1970s the large increases in government primary deficits were not accompanied by corresponding increases in the ratio of government debt to income.

The explanation of this apparent puzzle lies in the behavior of the nominal cost of debt relative to the nominal rate of growth of the economy: while large primary deficits exerted powerful upward pressures on the ratio of debt to GDP, inflation much exceeded the cost of government debt, thus largely offsetting the effects of primary deficits.

What was behind this "stickiness" or nonadjustment of nominal interest rates? It was a combination of two phenomena: unexpected inflation and financial repression. In several industrial countries (among them France and Italy), domestic financial markets were, until the late 1980s, far less developed than in the United States. Because of capital controls, interest rates could be kept artificially below the levels warranted by expectations of inflation and currency depreciation. It is well known that government revenue from financial repression is higher in countries with higher domestic inflation (Giovannini and de Melo 1993).

The growth of government debt (relative to income) accelerated as a result of the disinflation of the early 1980s. This sharply increased the average cost of government debt (again, relative to the nominal growth of GDP) and was in some cases accompanied by further fiscal expansion. In the second half of the 1980s, countries such as Italy found themselves with a much reduced rate of inflation relative to the previous decade, but also with persistently high real interest rates and a very large stock of government debt. The question at this point was whether the apparently high real interest rates were caused by lingering expectational problems of the disinflation process alone or also represented some sort of vengeance of financial repression. In other words, did capital controls and inefficient domestic markets add significantly to the cost of government debt in countries that have lower inflation?

In Italy the belief that capital controls entailed efficiency costs to government debt was shared by several policymakers. On the one hand, the elimination of capital controls, in compliance with the Single European Act, was viewed mostly as a coronation of the disinflation effort and as a "commitment" technology aimed at strengthening the anti-inflationary resolve of the authorities. On the other hand, the reforms in debt management of the late 1980s reflected the view that more efficiency in debt markets would save Italian taxpayers money. Italy's experience in the reform of the government bond market is by no means unique. Indeed, Italy followed the example of France, which acted early on to improve the efficiency of the French franc government bond market.

My main point here is that after the mid-1980s, few industrial countries considered the imposition or strengthening of capital controls an effective tool of economic policy. And free financial markets, together with very large stocks of government debt, compelled many sovereign borrowers to adopt methods of debt management that were borrowed from private market practice.

The new methods of debt management combined reforms of debt markets with modification of market practices. I list below the four broad areas of important reforms:

- reforms of primary markets: more regularity and predictability in auctions of government debt securities;

- reforms of secondary markets: new rules on participating institutions aimed at encouraging transparency and competition;

- encouragement for the development of derivatives markets;

- reform of the tax treatment of government securities, to facilitate access by foreign professional investors and to promote arbitrage.

The general aim of these reforms has been to increase both the efficiency and transparency of debt markets. A comprehensive description and discussion of these reforms in government debt management would require a separate paper. Here, I want to concentrate on more general conceptual problems underlying such reforms, and more broadly, underlying the activity of debt management by governments.

The Conceptual Problems of Government Debt Management

As suggested earlier, the sheer impact of the cost of debt on the budget is the most powerful motivation for governments to adopt private market practices in managing national debt. The liberalization of both international capital flows and domestic financial markets makes private market techniques more applicable for minimizing cost.

Yet sovereigns are special market participants, for a number of reasons. First of all, their objective is not the maximization of shareholders' value, although it might be likened to it. Second, sovereigns are not competitive market participants: their size is very large relative to the market (however defined) and their prerogatives in certain markets are exclusive. These two facts together imply a third feature that differentiates government borrowers: what they do in the marketplace has important implications for monetary policy. In what follows, I consider a number of general questions underlying the management of debt by sovereigns.

What Is the Appropriate Level of Risk for Sovereigns?

Debt management could be formalized as a programming problem: the maximization of some objective function subject to a set of constraints. However, there are some difficult issues that need to be tackled when setting up such a problem.

Suppose that the government's main objective is to minimize, in an expected sense, the cost of national debt given a pattern of financing requirements. But cost minimization is not enough, since it is conceivable that different levels of expected cost of debt are plausibly associated with different levels of risk. How much risk should governments be allowed to take?

Risk aversion on the part of private agents or corporations originates from tastes and institutional constraints, including the nondiversifiability of human capital risk and the presence of liquidity constraints and bankruptcy costs. However, such motivations as tastes and institutional constraints seem to suggest that governments might be able to sustain much more risk than the private sector.

One justification for the absence of significant risk on the part of governments could be obtained from the tax-smoothing model. Suppose for simplicity that government spending is exogenous and that the cost of raising taxes is a convex function of the amount of taxes raised. The tax-smoothing model implies that, in general, increases in volatility of the cost of debt would partially increase the volatility of taxes and therefore would imply costs. In general, however, it is unlikely that the "welfare" effects of the volatility of the cost of debt would be significant.

Imperfect and asymmetric information could, however, be reasons for caution. Low risk aversion would result in higher volatility of the stock of government debt (if it was to be marked-to-market) and therefore higher volatility of the government's borrowing requirement. The question is, how would high volatility in the borrowing requirement be interpreted? In a world of imperfect information about the dynamics of government spending and about the (implicit) rule followed by the government, the borrowing requirement becomes a more important signal of future policies. For these reasons, governments might find it appropriate to limit the volatility of the borrowing requirement; this in turn implies limiting the volatility of the cost of debt. In addition, the political significance of the borrowing requirement represents another reason for limiting the risks of government debt management.

What Is the Appropriate Measure of the Cost of Debt?

Given some appropriate level of risk for debt management program, sovereigns next need to face the question of the proper measurement of the cost of debt. The standard measure of return used in finance is based on marking to market all securities in a portfolio. Governments, however, are quite unfamiliar with that method, and most public accounting is not consistent with the principles underlying mark-to-market measurement. In addition, marking to market is fully consistent only under the assumption that a given portfolio can, at all times, be liquidated at the given market prices. Finally, other things being equal, mark-to-market measurements of the cost of debt are much more volatile than the cash-based measures normally used in public accounting. This raises the problem discussed above of the cost of debt signaling government policy.

What Is the Appropriate Measure of Performance?

The appropriately measured cost of government debt should be compared with some benchmark to evaluate the performance of debt management. Fund managers in private markets often use the return on aggregate indices as the benchmarks that they try to beat. What benchmarks should governments adopt? Clearly, governments cannot take their domestic markets as exogenous with respect to their own debt management activity; thus indices of the domestic market do not appear appropriate. But indices of world markets are also difficult to apply. The conversion of foreign returns into domestic returns requires use of the forward foreign exchange rate, which—given foreign interest rate—is itself determined by the spot exchange rate and the domestic interest rate.

Once the problem of measuring performance is solved, governments need to determine the nature and degree of publicity of government transactions as well as how to implement public oversight of debt management. As regards publicity, it is easy to supply numerous examples to argue that the absence of publicity about government operations could maximize their effectiveness in the marketplace. However, the need for checks and balances often makes it difficult to maintain confidentiality.

A related problem is that of monitoring debt management. Since debt management involves risk taking, it requires the delegation of substantial responsibilities to individuals. How much should such individuals be monitored, and by whom? In monetary economics, the complexity of the debate on the independence of central banks underscores the issues associated with public delegation of substantial economic powers to individuals whose actions can profoundly affect national welfare. Existing oversight bodies in many industrial countries are often not equipped to assess the transactions undertaken by management bodies in the government. These institutions might require substantial changes to allow proper and efficient monitoring of the debt management function.

Can Debt Management Respect the Principle of Central Bank Independence?

The principle of central bank independence implies that relations with national treasuries should be at arm's length. However, debt management has important implications for the fluctuation of liquidity. The sheer volume of debt issuance can affect money market rates significantly. In addition, many securities issued by governments are short-term bills, which influence money market rates directly. Finally, the issuance of debt denominated in foreign currency can generate sharp fluctuations in the relative demand for foreign exchange, with potentially large impacts on the value of the currency.

These examples suggest that arm's-length relations between national treasuries and central banks might be costly. In principle, central banks could mechanically offset the effects of government financial transactions on their targets, without direct communication with the government. In practice, however, lack of communication can be a source of serious disruptions. Conversely, once debt management is run jointly with the central bank, the problem of preserving the central bank's independence comes to the fore. That same concern would arise more strongly were the central bank to be given full responsibilities in the debt management function.

Markets, Authorities, and Information

The issue of asymmetric information between markets and governments takes on two related dimensions. The first is the problem of maximizing the value of information that governments own, through their own financial transactions. The second is the issue of publicizing information about government policies and their intentions over the medium to long term.

On the value of information that governments own, the appropriate starting point is the celebrated analysis by Milton Friedman (1953). The active use of information in the market, as Friedman correctly puts it, amounts to speculation. Of course, such speculation by governments serves a desirable social function whose value would be measured by the profits it enables governments to reap.

It is difficult, however, to determine which information in the hands of governments is really valuable, and what is the optimal way to exploit such information. The risk is that rather than efficiently transmit information to markets through their transactions, governments become involved in market manipulation, with adverse effects in the form of excess volatility.

The fact that there is little uniformity in the debt management methods that different countries actually adopt suggests that it is no straightforward matter to decide which inside information is valuable and what is the best way for governments to exploit it in their market transactions. In some countries, notably the United States, the management of government debt is rather passive. Emphasis is given to the predictability and regularity of government actions. In some other countries, the way the government deals with the market suggests that the objective is to systematically surprise market participants and to obtain the benefits that such surprises might bring about.

Recently, governments have adopted a more transparent style in their relations with private markets. Traditional shyness has given way to systematic relations with the investor community. In some cases the need for timely communication is felt keenly: for example, authorities in Argentina now provide daily information about the country's foreign exchange reserves on the Internet. This process is certainly desirable, because it forces government authorities to communicate their intentions clearly and consistently. At the same time, contact with a typically impartial audience such as the financial community permits government officials to discuss their work without the constraints imposed by the political debate. Yet even the release of information to the investor community is an activity that requires careful planning and management, because of the impact of economic and financial news in the marketplace.

The Role of International Institutions

In recent years the process of liberalization of international financial markets has generated some fascinating events. Governments of rich countries have been compelled to reverse dramatically their policies in response to pronouncements of independent, private rating agencies. These occurrences have highlighted the potential severity of information asymmetries affecting the world financial markets: in the absence of information asymmetries, the signals provided by the reports of rating agencies would have no impact.

What is more unsettling, the impact of these agencies' declarations is clearly disproportionate to the know-how about macroeconomics or public finances that their personnel possess. One is also hard pressed to justify that impact by pointing to the considerable independence that rating agencies enjoy.

These observations lead me to conclude that international institutions, and the IMF in particular, could play a very constructive role in the elimination of inefficient information asymmetries in world financial markets. The IMF's resources and know-how greatly exceed those of private credit-rating agencies. The multilateral nature of the IMF contributes to its reputation for fairness and independence. As Morris Goldstein (1995) has also recently advocated, one way the IMF could contribute to the elimination of information asymmetries would be by publishing the findings of its Article IV consultations; indeed, some member countries already release such reports on their own accord. The publication of investment information is not necessarily in contrast with the lending activities of the Fund, since the motive of such lending is not profit maximization.

Summary and Concluding Remarks

Recent years have witnessed a sea change in the approach of governments to market transactions. This chapter has illustrated the origins of this change and has explored some of its consequences.

What are the lessons I take away from that experience? The main lesson is that the adoption of market practices by governments is not a trivial, straightforward affair. It requires tackling a host of conceptual and practical problems. Among the conceptual problems, the identification of the objectives of government activity as well as the creation of appropriate performance measures and monitoring mechanisms take priority.

Another problem, both conceptual and practical, regards the degree of activism in the marketplace. This problem can be solved only by clarifying to the maximum extent possible what is the value of the information that governments possess, and what is the best way of extracting that value. In general, I have tried to argue here that governments could gain significantly by adopting a more systematic approach in the management of the information they possess. Finally, I have suggested that international financial institutions have a natural and valuable role to fulfill by supporting the orderly development and growth of international capital markets.

References

Friedman, Milton. 1953. *Essays in Positive Economics*. Chicago: University of Chicago Press.

Giovannini, Alberto, and Martha de Melo. 1993. "Government Revenue from Financial Repression." *American Economic Review* 83, no. 4: 953–63.

Goldstein, Morris. 1995. *The Exchange Rate System and the IMF: A Modest Agenda*. POLICY ANALYSES IN INTERNATIONAL ECONOMICS 39. Washington: Institute for International Economics.

Mussa, Michael, and Paul Masson. 1995. "Long-Term Tendencies in Budget Deficits and Debt." In *Budget Deficits and Debt: Issues and Options*, Federal Reserve Bank of Kansas City.

Comment

John Lipsky

Alberto Giovannini's paper—a *tour d'horizon* of the issues confronting government borrowers—is both thorough and sobering. He enumerates the myriad questions that must be taken into account in designing an "optimal" plan for the issuance and management of public debt. The complexity of these questions underscores Giovannini's principal point: namely, that it is very difficult either in theoretical or in operational terms to define an objective function for government debt management. The temptation, therefore, is for public borrowers to adopt private-sector standards for debt management—that is, cost minimization—even though the applicability of this principle to the public sector obviously is incomplete. Giovannini also offers some observations on the prospective role of the IMF as a conduit for improved economic data.

I am in agreement with most of Giovannini's points. However, I would draw some stronger conclusions from his discussion of public debt management with regard to broader public finance issues. Specifically, Giovannini's arguments lend support to the goal of maintaining a cyclically neutral budget, as well as to aggressive privatization of publicly owned enterprises. Moreover, with regard to Giovannini's observations about the role of the IMF, I suspect that there are more potential problems with the IMF acting as a data clearinghouse than have been recognized. At the same time, elevating capital account convertibility to the same status that current account payments already enjoy under the Fund's Articles of Agreement would powerfully improve the efficiency of international capital markets and reduce their volatility.

John Lipsky is chief economist and managing director at Salomon Brothers Inc., New York.

As enumerated by Giovannini, the problems that must be confronted in designing an "optimal" borrowing strategy are daunting. They include:

- tax smoothing;

- information asymmetry;

- measuring the cost of debt;

- establishing appropriate benchmarks for debt managers;

- publicizing activities;

- establishing oversight of debt managers;

- resolving potential conflicts with central bank independence;

- exploiting proprietary information.

Of course, private-sector borrowers also have to deal with many of these issues, with the important difference that public-sector entities ultimately have recourse to the power of the state; they can send in the police, as it were. Nonetheless, Giovannini emphasizes that there is no clear-cut answer to these questions. Their complexity is an implicit endorsement of implementing a cyclically neutral budget as a matter of principle. In this case, public borrowing would net to zero over the business cycle, making moot the widespread concerns about rising public-debt/GDP ratios in the industrial countries and their apparent link to high real long-term interest rates and sluggish growth. Even proposals such as public-sector capital budgeting do not really seem up to the task, as investors tend to view such tools in the hands of politicians as "smoke and mirrors" rather than means to conceptual clarity. Moreover, the difficulty in specifying an objective function for public debt management constitutes an argument in favor of more aggressive privatization programs: such action expands the conceptually clearer role of market discipline.

The problem of "overborrowing"—whatever that is—is not confined to the public sector alone, of course. After all, Chile's debt crisis of the early 1980s afflicted mainly private-sector borrowing, while the recent Mexican crisis was driven by public-sector debt. In both these cases, as well as in others, financial markets ultimately applied their severe sanctions. These incidents suggest that market discipline is effective, but messy. This applies to the industrial countries as well, as British Prime Minister John Major and former Chancellor Norman Lamont can testify eloquently. There are numerous worthy proposals to make the process of market discipline work more smoothly, but the basic point here is that such discipline exists.

It is hoped, therefore, that the role of sovereign borrowing will diminish over time, reflecting expected progress on privatization and the growing support for reduced budget imbalances. This is especially likely if fiscal reform efforts include a scaling back of the generous but probably unsustainable transfer programs—financing health care and retirement income—that are common in the industrial countries. At the same time, the role of securitized financial markets—and of cross-border private-sector capital flows—should continue to grow rapidly. This prospect reflects the likely combination of what might be termed "supply side" factors, including (1) sustained low industrial-country inflation—at least compared to the past 20 years, (2) the inevitable industrial-country shift to a defined-contribution format for providing retirement income, (3) the impact of international trade liberalization on improving resource allocation and economic efficiency, and (4) the relatively rapid economic growth in the nonindustrialized countries. "Demand side" factors that will support the rapid growth of securitized markets include prospective increases in national and private saving rates in the industrial countries.

Lest I seem to be stating the obvious, let me clarify the broad point here: portfolio capital flows are and should be relatively stable compared to other financing forms. This claim runs contrary to what appears to be the informed conventional wisdom on the matter, in that portfolio flows—especially short-term flows—typically are viewed to be both highly volatile and the typical cause of external payments crises.

In contrast to the widely held perception, the latest Mexican payments crisis was not caused by, and does not reflect, some inherent instability in private-sector portfolio flows. Instead, just as in the 1982 international debt crisis of the developing countries, a key contributing factor was an important systemic ambiguity rather than an inherent weakness. In 1982, the external payments crisis afflicting major debtor countries was exacerbated by the lack of a clear assignment of responsibility for the solvency and liquidity of the debtor countries' overseas branch banks. This ambiguous responsibility for the large-scale (by contemporaneous standards, at least) interbank liabilities of offshore branches of debtor-country commercial banks represented a sufficiently worrisome systemic Achilles' heel as to justify unprecedented official participation in providing emergency financial support. The goal of the IMF-led bailout was at heart an effort to avoid an international banking crisis of an unknown scale.

With the latest Mexican peso crisis, the systemic ambiguity comprised the lack of clear responsibility for the solvency and liquidity implications of a potential default on securitized sovereign debt—in this case, the *tesobono*. The implications of a default involved banks, as well as other financial institutions. This key ambiguity made it impossible for officials to receive a clear answer to their question, "What happens if we do nothing?" Indeed, these officials were willing to commit an unprecedented amount of funds to avoid finding out the answer.

This brings me to Giovannini's final point, namely that the IMF could fulfill a useful role in avoiding such problems by providing better economic data on debtor countries. There can be little doubt that better information would be useful and that this function would be even more helpful if the data were supplied in a standardized, Fund-approved format. More complete data releases are occurring already, without the Fund's involvement, as borrowers are finding that fuller disclosure lowers their borrowing costs. No doubt, Fund involvement would induce even more openness. Unexamined in the discussion of the Fund's potential role as an expanded data source, so far, is the Fund's potential liability for the figures' reliability. At present, the Fund publishes its *International Financial Statistics* monthly, but the data they contain are provided by the member countries. The Fund makes no claims for the figures' accuracy. Fund sanctioning of official data releases would imply some degree of responsibility.

There is another course of action open to the Fund that should be even more powerful in improving the efficiency and stability of international capital markets: elevating capital account convertibility to the same status already afforded current account payments under the Fund's Articles of Agreement. Such a move would provide an effective basis for assigning lender-of-last-resort responsibility for securitized borrowing. Under such a provision, it would be more straightforward to determine who bears the ultimate responsibility for liquidity and solvency of financial institutions in a world of securitized finance. In most cases, the responsibility would devolve to the home-country institutions of the borrower. For example, potential buyers of Mexican bank debt would understand that the responsibility for the debt's soundness was that of the Mexican authorities. Thus, standard market discipline should become more effective in setting market-clearing prices for official—and unofficial—issues of securitized debt.

Comment

John Williamson

In response to a question put to him at the conference, Ariel Buira asked, "Was the [Mexican] current account deficit too large? How can you judge that?"

These are important questions, to which I have on several occasions offered an answer. It is tautological that the steady-state current account deficit cannot safely exceed the rate of growth of nominal income multiplied by the maximum safe debt/income ratio.[1] It is convenient to measure the growth of nominal income using the international currency in terms of which debt is measured—that is, the dollar—which implies that the trend rate of inflation can be taken as 3 percent. If one accepts the rule of thumb according to which the debt/income ratio cannot safely exceed 40 percent, then the formula states that the steady-state current account deficit should not exceed 2.4 percent of GDP for a country with a trend growth rate of 3 percent, should not exceed 3.2 percent of GDP for a country with a trend growth of 5 percent, and should not exceed 5.6 percent of GDP for a country with a trend growth rate of 10 percent. While there can be scope for a prudent country to exceed these limits for short periods if its initial debt/income ratio is low or if its deficit is clearly temporary, I have used these results to argue that a country like Mexico

John Williamson, senior fellow at the Institute for International Economics, is currently on leave as regional chief economist for South Asia at the World Bank, Washington.

1. Let D = foreign debt and Y = nominal income. $\hat{Y}/Y = \hat{D}/D$ in steady state, so $\hat{D}/Y = (\hat{D}/D)(D/Y) = (\hat{Y}/Y)(D/Y)$.

should not allow its structural deficit to exceed about 3 percent of GDP, or an East Asian country to go above about 5 percent of GDP.

As you will have gathered from Ariel Buira's speech (chapter 11) I have not convinced everyone who matters of the validity of this approach. Indeed, I have to say that I myself do not find it wholly intellectually satisfying. At the very least, it needs critical scrutiny: we should ask such questions as whether the 40 percent rule of thumb is convincing, whether more open economies or economies with higher investment rates can accept less constraining limits,[2] whether the form of the capital inflow matters (e.g., whether a large inflow of foreign direct investment, or FDI, permits a higher prudent level of deficit), and so on.

I therefore suggested to the organizers of this conference that it would be worthwhile for them to commission a paper with a title like "Rules of Thumb to Evaluate When Countries Are Overborrowing" (or, what amounts to the same thing, "Rules of Thumb to Evaluate When Lenders Are Overlending"). I urged them to seek a fresh mind to address this topic, which the discussion at this conference already has suggested is indeed an important one. I thought they had accepted my suggestion, and I saw no harm in their decision to broaden the title somewhat by adding "borrowing" to "overborrowing" and "lessons of experience" to "rules of thumb."

They certainly found a fresh mind to address the topic. Unfortunately, Alberto Giovannini's mind is so fresh that he decided to change his assigned title, in the process emasculating any discussion of the topic that I had conceived we needed a paper to address. I have to say that I was not at all convinced by the defense he offered for his change of title. Yes, of course "overborrowing" is difficult to define, but it surely happens, as Mexico illustrated all too vividly (not to mention two countries much closer to Austria—namely Italy and Hungary). Most interesting concepts are in fact difficult to define, but that is no excuse for dismissing them. And surely rules of thumb are of great interest when they are the only guidance we can offer (they are intellectually unsatisfying, but that is another matter).

While I regret what is not in the paper, I do not in fact disagree with much that is in it. However, I am less convinced than Giovannini as to the benefits of governments emulating the markets rather than aiming to complement them. For example, I worry that the short-termism of marking to market and of judging performance on that basis contributes to speculative bubbles, which I think governments ought to try to prick rather than acquiesce in. I would have liked a definition of market "manipulation,"

---

2. Could that factor explain, for example, why Singapore got away with running a deficit of 10 percent of GDP for a decade, while Mexico came to grief with a deficit of only 8 percent? The former amounted to perhaps 25 percent of investment, while the latter was some 40 percent.

and I am curious to know whether the thesis that market manipulation leads to excess volatility is advanced as an empirical generalization or an ideological certainty, and to see what the supporting evidence is. I was interested to note the conclusion that central bank independence is costly, coupled with a blank refusal to treat this as a serious reason for questioning what has become a new sacred cow. But my main regret is that the change in the focus of the paper leaves me bereft of any improvement in my formula.

4

Private Capital Flows to Emerging Markets after the Mexican Crisis

Pier-Luigi Gilibert and Alfred Steinherr

An important and well-known event of the late 1980s and early 1990s has been the recomposition of capital flows directed to developing countries that accompanied a robust increase in overall flows. Commercial bank lending, which supported the bulk of the debt rescheduling in the early 1980s following Mexico's bank debt moratorium in August 1982, and to a lesser extent official flows (i.e., financial aid, concessionary and conditional loans) have given way to a substantial increase in other private inflows—that is to both short-term and long-term portfolio placements and direct investments.

According to the International Monetary Fund (IMF), while the total external debt of developing countries increased by almost 40 percent to $1.6 billion between 1987 and 1994, the external debt owned to nonbank private sources, which was some 14 percent of the total at the end of 1987, had reached almost 27 percent by the end of 1994 (table 1). This is now expected to grow to about 31 percent by the end of 1996. Conversely, external bank debt fell from 41 percent of the total in 1987 to 28 percent over the same period, contracting in absolute terms in the process. This trend is even more pronounced if one focuses on certain groups of developing countries. Developing countries in the Western Hemisphere, for instance (i.e., mostly Latin American countries), saw the relative impor-

Pier-Luigi Gilibert is head of division in the Financial Research Department of the European Investment Bank, Luxembourg. Alfred Steinherr is director general and chief economist at the European Investment Bank, Luxembourg.

Table 1   Developing-country debt by type of creditor, 1987–96
(billions of dollars)

Creditor	1987	1990	1994	1996[a]
Official	520.2	608.1	737.5	797.8
Commercial banks	482.2	421.7	450.0	440.9
Other private	163.6	268.9	435.6	558.0
Total	1,165.9	1,298.7	1,623.1	1,796.7

a. Forecasts.

Source: IMF, World Economic Outlook, May 1995, table A 39, 180.

tance of external private nonbank debt increase almost threefold, from about 13 percent to 38 percent of overall foreign debt, while that of commercial bank debt was halved from 62 percent to 31 percent.

Extensive macro- and microeconomic reforms in developing countries' financial markets, expectations of high returns, as well as recessionary forces taking hold in many industrialized economies, promoted these quantitative and qualitative shifts in international capital flows. By and large, the effects of these changes on the recipient countries have been welcomed, even though they may at times have complicated macroeconomic management (Schadler et al. 1993).

One notable change has been the appreciation in the real exchange rates of the recipient countries. This, in combination with an increase in the money supply, a fixed exchange rate, and an absence of an appropriate policy of fiscal consolidation aimed at increasing domestic saving, has induced large, and ultimately unsustainable, current account deficits. It is well known that Mexico's current account shortfall steadily increased in the 1990s to reach 8 percent of GDP in 1994. These trends, in turn, eroded investors' confidence and provoked sudden large-scale disposals of foreign funds invested in liquid forms (i.e., local bonds and stocks). The Mexican crisis of December 1994 is a case in point.

The issue of "sustainability" of a given capital inflow is thus important, especially for middle- and upper-income developing countries that have emerged as acceptable investment targets in the eyes of the international financial community because they have achieved a degree of political stability, financial sophistication, and market openness. Continuing to pursue such goals may, however, clash with the necessity of maintaining macroeconomic control and avoiding the disruptions provoked by cycles of feast and famine in the availability of finance for growth. This subject has been extensively explored in recent literature.

The other side of the coin is represented by what is "sustainable"— that is, what is realistic and feasible to expect in the medium term—in the eyes of investors wishing to enter these emerging markets. For instance, a collective decision to go in or to withdraw from an emerging market following reappraisals of desirable portfolio allocations may be both self-defeating and disruptive. The question of the speed with which ideal portfolio allocation decisions in emerging markets are reached is also of prime importance, as are the mechanisms whereby unsustainable "excesses" are remedied (and at what costs). Emerging market authorities may also wish "to throw sand in the wheels," both to avoid such "excesses" and as a means to manage any adjustment process once the excesses are finally recognized.

In short, the issue of sustainability is ultimately linked to the notion of equilibrium in portfolio choices. Prolonged periods of overinvestment in any particular market will eventually prove unsustainable and give rise to the possibility of speculative bubbles. Once awareness of this possibility finally descends on lenders or investors (possibly following seemingly unrelated events—e.g., the two Chiapas uprisings in Mexico in January and December 1994, as well as the assassinations of presidential candidate Luis Donaldo Colosio in March and of prominent politician Francisco Ruiz Massieu in September), the bubble bursts and the subsequent crisis, which often extends well beyond its origin, is the adjustment mechanism whereby equilibrium is restored.

This paper first reviews the evidence of private nonbank (particularly equity) capital flows to emerging markets thus far in the 1990s, with a view to discussing the "sustainability" and appropriateness of the ensuing portfolio distribution from the viewpoint of investors. In particular, it examines recent enthusiasm for buying into Latin American securities markets by a new breed of players (e.g., investment funds and, through them, individual investors, rather than banks). We also wonder if, by following banks' overlending to this area in the late 1970s and early 1980s, we again witnessed in the 1990s the same type of overconfident investment behavior, leading up to the well-known cycle of overexposure, sudden generalized withdrawals, and ruinous financial market declines. The closing section then presents a few considerations on the possible differences in the nature of the adjustment process when nonbank investors are called on to bear the brunt of the losses, and when marketable securities rather than loans are the vehicles through which such losses materialize.

Recent Experience of Private Flows to Emerging Markets

Between 1990 and 1993, developing countries received nearly $160 billion worth of (gross) foreign direct investment (i.e., flows that do not give rise to an external obligation), and about $140 billion in net portfolio investments (table 2). Although Asia and Latin America absorbed 40 to 45 percent each of this total flow of some $300 billion, Latin America was by far the largest recipient of nonbank portfolio flows, while Asia accounted for the bulk of direct investments. If these financial flows are

Table 2 Private nonbank capital flows to developing countries, 1990–93 (billions of dollars; gross figures)

	FDI	PI	Total	Percent of exports
Developing countries	156.4	138.6	295.0	8.2
Western Hemisphere	45.0	65.6	110.6	21.1
Asia	79.3	47.7	127.0	6.1
Others	32.1	25.3	57.4	5.9

FDI = foreign direct investment.
PI = portfolio investment (equity, bonds, and investment funds).

Sources: For private capital flows: de la Dehesa (1994, tables 1 and 3). For export data: World Bank, 1994a, tables 10 and 11, 80.

Table 3 International equity issues by selected emerging countries, 1992–95 (billions of dollars)

	1992	1993	1994	1995[a]
Main emerging economies	8.0	12.0	17.0	5.3
Argentina	1.0	3.0	1.4	n.a.
Chile	0.1	0.8	1.7	n.a.
Mexico	3.0	1.4	n.a.	n.a.
India	n.a.	1.5	1.9	0.2
Philippines	n.a.	0.1	1.0	1.3
Taiwan	n.a.	0.2	0.3	0.1

n.a. = not available

a. First half.

Sources: Institute of International Finance, *Country Reports*, various issues; *International Equity Review*, July 1995, no. 1.

related to some indicator of both economic dynamism and ability to repay (e.g., total exports) Latin America, for which the $110 billion of inflows accounted for about 21 percent of total cumulated exports in this period, appears to be the area receiving the most generous treatment by foreign investors. Unfortunately, as later experience proved, this absorption of an immoderate quantity of notoriously fickle capital laid Latin America open to the danger of sudden and massive withdrawals.[1]

To cash in on this surge of investors' enthusiasm, and benefit from widening funding possibilities, companies from emerging markets, often in the framework of privatizations but also to finance growth or acquisitions, stepped up their equity offerings on the international market (table 3). This, in turn, enhanced opportunities available to western investors

---

1. The nature of private capital traditionally flowing into Mexico, characterized by a predominance of opportunistic short-term investments and a scarcity of direct investments, was recognized, with great lucidity and a stiff dose of fatalistic pessimism, by a noneconomist almost 30 years ago: "The truth is that the resources of our nation as a whole are insufficient to 'finance' our development or even to create what the experts call an 'economic infrastructure,' the only solid basis for real progress. We lack capital, and the rhythm of internal capitalization and reinvestment is still too slow. Thus our essential problem, according to

to achieve better international portfolio diversification, and provided new means of acquiring emerging market securities beyond those available through direct purchases in local bourses.

Foreign investment is as subject to fads and fashions as any other field, and the "discovery" of emerging markets has not been an egalitarian process. Some countries, for example, appear to have attracted a disproportionate amount of attention, such as Mexico and Argentina, and seem to have benefited enormously from this increased interest in emerging economies. Together, they received almost $13 billion in foreign equity funds between 1990 and 1993, while China, Korea, India, Thailand, and the Philippines together totaled less than half that figure (de la Dehesa 1994, table 2, 5). One cannot but draw a parallel with the experience of bank loans to these same countries in the early 1980s, when excessive lending by commercial banks to Latin America was followed, after 1982, by a lengthy and laborious process of debt rescheduling to reduce the debt overhang.

After the Mexican "crisis" of December 1994, when various investment funds, rather than commercial banks, bore the brunt of the price adjustment, it seems opportune to ask whether the same drama was again played out, albeit with a different cast of actors.

Criteria for International Portfolio Diversification and Emerging Markets

Although the world economy is already largely integrated, world financial markets are not. This is best illustrated by the fact that national saving and investment are highly correlated (Feldstein 1995). As a consequence, current account imbalances—especially for emerging economies—are restrained in size and limited in time. A current account deficit of 5 to 10 percent of GDP is still generally considered to be "unsustainable" and typically leads after a few years to expectations of policy corrections, such as more restrictive monetary policy and exchange rate devaluations.

In a perfectly integrated world financial market, national saving and investment would be completely dissociated, and assets in national portfolios would roughly reflect the share of each economy in the world economy. This is a long-term view, and a far cry from the current situation

---

the experts, is to obtain the resources vital to our growth. But where, and how? One of the remedies most frequently offered by the 'advanced' nations—especially the United States— is that of private foreign investments. In the first place, everyone is aware that the earnings from these investments leave the country, in the form of dividends or other benefits. . . . There is also the fact that private capital is not interested in the sort of investments we need: those offering long terms and accepting small profits. On the contrary, it searches for opportunities that promise better and more rapid earnings. The capitalist cannot and will not involve himself in a general plan for economic development" (Paz 1967, 170–71).

Table 4 Real rates of growth and GDP shares

	Average annual growth of real GDP (percent)		Share of world GDP (percent)		
	1983–93	1994–2003[a]	1990	1993[b]	2003[a]
G-7 industrial countries	2.8	2.7	47.7	47.8	45.5
East Asia	7.9	7.6	16.9	20.8	31.6
South Asia	5.2	5.3	0.3	0.3	0.4
Latin America and Caribbean	2.2	3.4	8.0	8.5	8.7
World	3.3[c]	3.2	72.9	77.4	86.2

a. Forecasts.
b. Estimates.
c. 1981–90.
Source: For actual and forecasted GDP growth rates: World Bank (1994a) for GDP shares in 1990, IMF, *World Economic Outlook*, May 1994.

in which emerging markets still play only a very marginal role in portfolios of the industrial countries. From such a long-term perspective one should expect a massive investment in emerging markets for two reasons. First, there should be a "portfolio adjustment" as foreign investors move from the current situation to the unconstrained optimal degree of diversification. This process will necessarily take many years, as it will require both a more complete opening of the financial markets of emerging economies as well as the building of institutions to improve the efficiency of their markets and to create the necessary hedging instruments. This process alone would require years of substantial flows into emerging markets.

The second reason for a large investment in emerging markets is that emerging economies are and will be growing more rapidly than the industrialized countries, so the world share of the emerging economies will be increasing over time. Several emerging economies do indeed present excellent opportunities for efficient portfolio diversification because they combine ample natural resources, skilled work forces, open trade policies, and the ability to benefit from technology transfers from nearby industrialized countries. This is reflected in above-average growth potential and, as a consequence, in rising importance in the world's projected income distribution (table 4). Not all emerging markets share these advantages equally, however, so that selectivity will still characterize such capital flows.

On the basis of current forecasts, the portfolio weight of East Asia (comprising countries such as China, South Korea, Malaysia, and Thailand) would in principle have to increase by as much as 50 percent in the next 10 years or so to match its growing importance in the world economy, while that of Latin America should hardly have to change. Another indicator is provided by export growth performance. Between 1981 and 1992, Latin American merchandise exports to high-income countries (HICs) grew at an average annual rate of 3.3 percent, while HIC merchandise trade expanded by 6.3 percent. This implied a 1992 market share of only 2.6 percent. In contrast, merchandise exports from both East and South Asia grew at an average annual rate of 10.7 percent, and achieved a combined market share of 7 percent (World Bank 1994a, 80). The story for commodities exports is similar.

Thus, even accounting for the possibility that portfolio allocations at the beginning of the current decade showed an imbalance, it is hard to characterize as anything but a disequilibrium an allocation that divides private capital inflows to Latin America and Asia equally and that sees portfolio flows go predominantly to Latin America.

To gain a sense of the magnitudes involved, consider the following long-term scenario. According to table 4, in 1993 the emerging economies accounted for about 30 percent of world production. Yet the share of emerging economies in the equity held by US, European, and Japanese portfolios represented only a few percentage points. Thus, a portfolio reallocation to bring the emerging market share close to its weight in the value portfolio would amount to over 20 percent of world equity. By 2003 the share of production is expected to increase to 40 percent. Thus, the superior growth performance of emerging markets would add 10 percent to their share of world equity.

Capital flows will not go in only one direction, however. As the emerging economies themselves mature they will become net investors abroad, diversifying their portfolios according to the optimal worldwide structure. Thus, portfolio reallocation effect and the net effect is likely to be small. The major reason for sustained net inflows into emerging markets is therefore likely to be the same as growth performance.

It is not difficult to see why Latin American financial markets became so popular with industrial country investors and what the consequences of this infatuation were in terms of rising market valuations. Confining ourselves to stock markets, figure 1 shows that, in 1990–94, the International Finance Corporation (IFC) composite emerging market index for Latin America, even when expressed in US dollars, outperformed all the other "natural" benchmarks in the United States (here, the S&P 500), Japan, and Europe. This was true to an even greater extent in Mexico.

To put these Latin American returns into perspective, we have deducted from them the riskless rate of return, taken here to be the three-month US Treasury bill rate (some 4.7 percent during the period). These "excess" returns on the various regional stock indexes are shown in table 5 together with their respective volatilities. Sharpe ratios (i.e., the ratios between the mean and the standard deviations of excess returns) appear in the last columns of table 5. The main conclusion is that the IFC composite index for Latin America shows the best excess returns, even taking into account its relatively high volatility. That is, Latin American stock markets produced the best return per unit of risk. Asian emerging markets fared less

Figure 1 Regional stock market indexes, 1990–94[a]
(monthly observations)

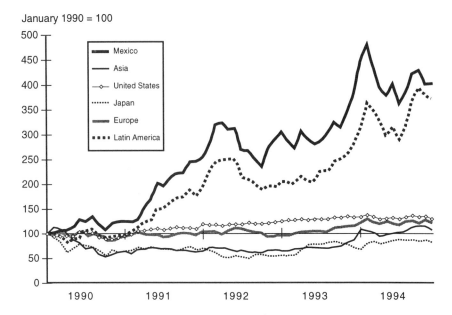

January 1990 = 100

a. The IFC Latin America Index includes Argentina, Brazil, Chile, Colombia, Mexico, Peru and Venezuela. The IFC Asia Index includes China, South Korea, Philippines, Taiwan, India, Indonesia, Malaysia, Pakistan, Sri Lanka and Thailand.

Sources: Asia, Mexico, and Latin America: International Finance Corporation; Japan and Europe: Morgan Stanley; United States: S&P500.

Table 5 Excess returns, volatilities and the Sharpe ratios for the main regional stock markets, 1990–94[a] (annual percentages)

	Average	Standard deviation	Sharpe ratios
Latin America	21.9	26.9	0.81
Asia	−3.8	25.7	−0.15
United States	0.2	11.4	0.01
Japan	−9.4	30.7	−0.31
Europe	−1.1	15.6	−0.07

a. The IFC Latin America Index includes Argentina, Brazil, Chile, Colombia, Mexico, Peru and Venezuela. The IFC Asia Index includes China, South Korea, Philippines, Taiwan, India, Indonesia, Malaysia, Pakistan, Sri Lanka and Thailand.

Sources: Asia, Mexico, and Latin America: International Finance Corporation; Japan and Europe: Morgan Stanley; United States: S&P500.

well, but still performed better than the Japanese index. Overall, however, the stock markets of the developed world seem to have produced rather poor results compared with the safe alternative of investing in US government securities.

The question then arises whether such results for Latin America are "rational" or instead represented the product of a speculative "bubble" that the Mexican debacle of December 1994 has punctured for good. On closer inspection, there are grounds for thinking that the realized returns on Latin American equities in the early 1990s are, by any standard, anomalous. Consider that, in the late 1980s, stock market indexes for Latin American countries averaged five to six times earnings, versus far higher levels (in the 20s) for Asian emerging markets. Assuming a risk premium of 5 percent for a US-based investor, and a risk-free rate of 8 percent (the three-month T-bill rate in 1989), it follows that the expected growth rate of earnings implied by such stock market valuations was about 3 to 5 percent per year, for a payout ratio of 40 to 50 percent. On the whole, this is not inconsistent with Latin America's average growth performance (over 1983–93) of about 3 percent (table 4). By early 1993, however, Latin American price/earnings (P/E) ratios had been driven up to about 20 or more, implying expected earnings growth rates in excess of 10 percent.[2] This is a rhythm that, though still reasonable for Asian countries, was clearly unsuitable for most Latin American countries, at least based on past norms, the area's economic potential, and economic projections at that time.

Equity valuations in Latin America only started to decline, however, in the second half of 1994. This downward trend accelerated powerfully toward the end of the year and into the first quarter of 1995, when some of these markets lost up to 40 percent in dollar terms (IMF 1995, 40). This fall in equity prices moderated later on because the US government was relatively swift in putting together a rescue package and several Latin American authorities introduced stabilization plans. But by end-June 1995, the IFC Latin America stock index was still down by just over 20 percent compared with end-1994, while Asia's was up by nearly 4 percent.

To corroborate further the view that Latin American stock prices were pushed by the inflow of foreign capital to unrealistic levels, and that

---

2. The simplest version of the "dividend growth model" states that the price of a stock (P) is equal to its current dividend (D) divided by the difference between the required rate of return (r) and the expected earnings growth (g) or:

$g = r - D/P$

In turn, dividends are linked to earnings (E) via the payout ratio ($d = D/E$). Thus:

$g = r - d (E/P)$.

Setting r = 13 percent, d = 50 percent and P/E = 5(20), gives g = 3 percent (10.5 percent). According to Glen et al. (1995), Colombia, Chile, Malaysia, Pakistan, Thailand, and Turkey had payout ratios of about 50 percent, while Argentina, India, Indonesia, Mexico, and Venezuela averaged between 20 and 30 percent.

Table 6 Correlations among returns on main regional stock market indices, 1990–94[a] (computed from monthly returns)

	Latin America	Asia	United States	Japan	Europe
Latin America	1.00				
Asia	0.30	1.00			
United States	0.38	0.22	1.00		
Japan	0.28	0.17	0.26	1.00	
Europe	0.27	0.34	0.62	0.44	1.00

a. The IFC Latin America Index includes Argentina, Brazil, Chile, Colombia, Mexico, Peru and Venezuela. The IFC Asia Index includes China, South Korea, Philippines, Taiwan, India, Indonesia, Malaysia, Pakistan, Sri Lanka and Thailand.

Sources: Asia, Mexico, and Latin America: International Finance Corporation; Japan and Europe: Morgan Stanley; United States: S&P500.

this had little to do with informed portfolio choices, consider that the correlation (covariance) between US dollar returns on Latin American stocks and those on the S&P 500 was about 0.4 (1.1 percent) over 1990–94 (table 6). Over this period, the variance of the returns on US equities was 1.3 percent, for a US-based investor, Latin American stocks therefore had a "beta" of around 0.9. Given the levels of the risk-free rate and risk premium mentioned above (i.e., 4.7 percent and 5 percent, respectively), it follows from a naive extension of the Capital Asset Pricing Model (CAPM) to regional stock market indexes that the US dollar required rate of return on Latin American equities was about 9 percent, or about one-third of the realized return. An analogous calculation performed for Asia would have yielded, with a comparable "beta" of 0.5, a required return on stock investments in that region of about 7 percent, against an average realized return of about 1 percent. In other words, while Latin America "overperformed" with respect to expectations, Asia did the reverse. A correction might be seen as justified.[3]

Extending the reasoning from stand-alone rates of return and their variability to portfolio considerations, Asian stock markets in general seemed to have provided better opportunities to diversify into emerging market equities. Based on the correlation matrix presented in table 6, for a Europe-based investor (last row), the returns on both Asian and Latin American markets displayed lower correlations with a broadly based European stock market index than did those for Japan or the United States. For a Japanese investor, Asia's stock markets seem to have offered the best opportunities for lowering portfolio risks, while both Latin

3. A more appropriate use of portfolio theory would be to select a country index in Latin America and compare it to the US S&P 500. Suppose we pick the Mexican index. The correlation between the two over the five-year period 1990–95 is equal to 0.39, and Mexico's "beta" is thus 0.93. The required rate of return on Mexico's stocks is thus 9.4 percent (= 4.7 percent + 5 percent × 0.93) against a realized rate of return of about 28 percent.

Table 7 Comparison of emerging stock markets

Emerging market	Number of listed companies	Market capitalization (billions of dollars)	As percent of GDP
Latin America			
Argentina (1993)	180	43.9	17
Brazil (1992)	565	45.3	12
Chile (1993)	263	44.6	102
Mexico (1992)	195	139.1	42
Asia			
India (1992)	6,540	65.1	21
Korea (1993)	693	139.4	42
Philippines (1993)	180	40.3	74
Thailand (1992)	305	58.3	56
Developed Countries (1994)			
United States of America	7,030	4,942	74
Japan	1,782	3,592	76
United Kingdom	2,002	1,150	111

Sources: IFC, *Emerging Stock Markets Fact Book*, 1993; IMF; OECD.

America and Europe's markets seem to have offered less valuable diversification opportunities—even relative to the US market.

Finally, on diversification grounds, US investors would have been better off acquiring exposure to Asia's emerging markets, followed by Japan. Latin America does not appear to have offered significant diversification advantages for US-based stock investors. The reason could probably be found in the synchronization of the two regions' economic cycles, a fact that recent trade liberalization measures (such as the North American Free Trade Agreement) might have increased.

All the above conclusions, however, should be hedged by several considerations. Indeed, creating an internationally diversified portfolio that includes emerging market securities, is fraught with difficulties and subject to several constraints posed by the still limited breadth and efficiency of these markets (see table 7). First, domestic bourses may not be freely accessible, as different types of restrictions may prevent acquisition of local stocks. Some regulatory authorities restrict aggregate shareholdings of domestic stocks by foreigners, or else limit foreign placements in individual companies. Some impose minimum holding periods; others restrict the repatriation of dividends. Furthermore, suitable hedging mechanisms may not be in place to reduce price or currency risks, an important consideration in view of the high volatility often displayed by these markets.

Finally, stocks of local companies may not be sufficiently liquid to allow what would be, by stock market standards of industrial countries, normal size orders to go through without provoking adverse price movements. For instance, with respect to the Argentine stock market, it has been noted that, "in 1992, the top ten stocks accounted for 66 percent of trading volume. Less than 100 firms have one trade per month, and over a third of the listed companies are not traded even monthly.... The publicly held shares of the three major privatized companies—Telefonica, Telecom, and Argentine energy company YPF—alone represented 58.5 percent of the total market capitalization on 29 October 1993.... The small market capitalization of most stocks is suggestive of non-viable size, lack of public accountability and strong family control.... Most Argentine stocks are very illiquid mainly due to the small floating stock of shares (actual floating stock is around 5 to 10 percent of all shares). This gives rise to the possibility of material price manipulation by insiders/dealers with large holdings. Despite significant price and volume increases, continuous trading in corporate shares is restricted to only 15 shares" (World Bank 1994b, 40–41, 48).

Other problems are of more recent origin, but may persist for a long time. For instance, it is reported (Wood 1995) that, following extensive privatizations through the use of vouchers, as many as 1,700 Czech companies are now quoted on the Prague stock exchanges. Not only is the market illiquid, however (less than $1 million in shares are traded daily), opaque (only average prices are disclosed) and therefore prey to insider trading, but it is also fragmented with three exchanges in operation. Moreover, it is unclear who owns and controls these quoted enterprises— the 15 largest investment funds hold more than 40 percent of all equities, but are in large part owned by the commercial banks, who in turn are still partly state owned.

By shifting the location of trade to more efficient foreign markets and by submitting companies to a vetting process by Western stock exchange specialists and authorities, American/Global Depository Receipts (ADRs or GDRs) have proved to be moderately successful solutions to some of these problems. They have also increased the funding capacity of local companies. The market for ADR in emerging market stocks has thus significantly expanded, though it still remains a small one if set against normal institutional investors' requirements.

All things considered, therefore, the relatively high rates of return available in certain (segmented) emerging markets may well prove illusory and their potential as a source of diversification unrealized (see Claessens and Rhee 1994).

Nature of the Adjustment Process

At least two major, and related, features distinguish the Latin American external debt (or, better, financial) crisis of 1994–95 from that of 1982 and will affect the ensuing adjustment process. One concerns the types of the investors involved; the other, the nature of the financial claims used.

Table 8 External debt and debt-service rations, 1982 and 1994

Region	Total external debt (billions of dollars)		Debt owed to nonbank creditors (billions of dollars)		Debt-service ratios (percent of total exports)	
	1982	1994	1982	1994	1982	1994
Latin America	331.2	523.9	66.2	197.4	53.1	16.2
Asia	186.8	550.4	30.6	102.5	12.2	3.5
Africa	122.4	245.3	24.0	27.1	21.0	11.3
Middle East	113.9	303.4[a]	30.1	108.6[a]	6.3	4.6[a]

a. Includes "Europe."

Sources: IMF, *World Economic Outlook,* May 1990 (tables A46 and A49) and May 1995 (tables A39 and A42).

These two differences render the solutions found in 1982 of little use in the present context, except perhaps for the prompt and confidence-building interventions of both the US government and the IMF. Quantitative differences exist as well.

By year-end 1982, or just after Mexico's default on its external bank debt rocked world financial markets, Latin America's foreign debt stood at some $330 billion, of which $225 billion (or 68 percent) was owed to commercial banks. This total debt required annual repayments representing 53 percent of total regional exports. As already mentioned, by end-1994, out of a total Latin American external debt of $524 billion (which would imply a debt-service ratio of only 16 percent), almost 40 percent was held by the nonbank private sector (see table 8). In the 1982 crisis the global banking system was involved; however, this time US nonbank institutional investors suffered the most.

Drawing quantitative parallels between the two episodes is thus not easy, and only rather crude comparisons can be offered. By end-1982, the $225 billion debt that Latin America owed creditor banks was equivalent to some 4 percent of the total assets of the banks of the Group of Seven (G-7) countries plus Switzerland. By contrast, the $197 billion worth of Latin American nonbank private external debt was equivalent to about 2 percent of the total collective assets of US nonbank financial institutions, pension funds, and insurance companies. Thus, the 1995 Latin American financial crisis is perhaps about half the size of the 1982 crisis—a factor that has surely played a part in what so far has been a relatively smooth absorption of the recent emerging market turmoil.

A further difference stems from the process of securitization of the external debt of many less-developed countries, particularly in Latin America. Foreign bank lending has been displaced by the issuance of tradable debt instruments sold to foreign investors. One consequence of this process is that the quality and reliability of foreign debt statistics become more doubtful. Indeed, when nearly half the reported total external debt of a country is in the hands of private foreign investors, external debt indicators (such as debt-service ratios, the level of foreign liabilities in relation to GDP, international reserves) can become misleading, both because the portion of domestic debt (e.g., Treasury bills) held by foreign investors is often unknown or not revealed, and because the distinction between short- and long-term debt is blurred.

Take for instance the behavior of industrial country investors facing the collapse of emerging market debt prices. Like depositors facing an impending crisis in their local bank, they pay little regard to the systemic implications of their behavior, nor are they likely to be sensitive to appeals from authorities not to dump the securities at any price. This "herd behavior" is exacerbated by the absence of contractual maturities (e.g., equities) or by the existence of a market (e.g., domestic government securities). The entire amount of debt or quasi-debt securities held by foreign investors should therefore probably be counted as being potentially short-term. The fall in market prices necessary for these instruments to be willingly held by a new set of investors severely diminishes these countries' ability to rollover old debt, or to issue new debt. If so, the improvements in the external financial position of developing countries between the early 1980s and the mid-1990s may be largely illusory.

The fact that a new class of investors is involved in the crisis, however, also has positive implications. For instance, despite the fact that the bond-holders are numerous and uncoordinated, we now are discovering that a country's external debt crisis can successfully be managed when a large number of nonbank investors are the main protagonists.[4] True, both the US and emerging-market governments were swift to recognize the potential costs and to seek ways to reduce the damage and build confidence, but price reductions of over 50 percent in a few months are probably as close to a stress test as market reality can produce. That any major distress was avoided is as much a tribute to the authorities' prompt actions as it is to the resilience of self-correcting market mechanisms.

Moreover, the stability of industrial countries' banking systems is no longer imperiled, as it was in the mid-1980s, by the financial difficulties of certain sovereign borrowers. Rather, the recession induced by austerity measures taken in some developing countries to redress the current account are seriously undermining the soundness of the local banking system. First, investment funds are, unlike banks, unleveraged operators. That is, except for "hedge funds," they do not finance their "bets" with borrowed money. Portfolio losses due to falling emerging stock and bond markets are absorbed by their own funds and do not threaten other creditors in any significant sense (although the bank borrowings of some "hedge funds" might indeed be cause for concern). These losses are ultimately spread

---

4. It has often been argued that an advantage of a universal banking system over a market-based one is that the predominance of a few large, influential bank creditors increases the chances of an orderly (if long) resolution of debt crises.

among a large number of private investors. As a consequence, the possibility of "contagion" or of a "domino effect" is sharply reduced. One must always guard against the possibility, though, that, if small investors really panic and redeem their shares in investment funds believed, perhaps incorrectly, to hold depreciating assets, this might give rise to a wholesale liquidation of stocks and bonds. In the event, both US bonds and stock prices kept rising, and the 1994 emerging-market crises had surprisingly few effects on domestic financial markets in industrial countries.

Indeed, the chances of a generalized financial "meltdown" seem to have been significantly reduced, both because only a small section of retail investors bought into emerging debt and equity markets, and because any ensuing loss would generally be absorbed by the financial system as a whole (rather than by any one section of it). Although a few local companies with dollar-denominated debt securities have indeed experienced debt-service difficulties, the relatively low levels of bank debt have meant that no demand for extensive corporate or sovereign bank debt rescheduling has been or is likely to be made. The possibility of widespread redemptions of investment fund shares by panicked small investors is reduced further by the nature of certain underlying contractual obligations (as, e.g., emerging market securities owned by closed-end funds, pension schemes, or insurance companies). These allow for losses either to be reversed or "diluted" over a longer-term holding period. Nonetheless, this episode underlines the need for transparency in investment activity and for stronger capital adequacy regulations for investment banks and institutional investors.

Finally, the "herd instinct" displayed by nonbank investors and the nature of the claims involved, have contributed to a rather rapid adjustment process—with little of the drawn-out, behind-the-scenes, high-level haggling among bank creditors, sovereign borrowers, and multilateral institutions that was so pervasive in the debt crisis of the mid-1980s. This time the dimensions of the crisis were immediately apparent, losses were more swiftly recognized, and remedies more promptly taken. In other words, all the shock seems to have come upfront and all the bad news (and perhaps more than that) immediately discounted, so that emerging market authorities were jolted into action.

Strangely enough, a main casualty seems to have been the dollar. Although dollar appreciation was ascribed to the proximity of Latin America to the United States. It is more probable that the US currency just happened to undergo a crisis of its own, which the prospect of lower US net exports to Latin America might have temporarily exacerbated. The dollar's decline thus had little to do with the financial crisis touching emerging markets.

Conclusions

This paper has advanced two arguments. First, we believe that the 1990s inflow of private capital into Latin America's emerging economies, and into Mexico in particular, primarily reflects an infatuation lacking solid financial justification. For instance, Latin American equity valuations were then implying rates of return that neither historical evidence nor then current projections justified. Moreover, in terms of portfolio diversification, Latin American equities presented few advantages over other markets in emerging nations, such as those in Asia, or in industrialized countries. Therefore, Mexico's financial crisis should be seen as the bursting of a speculative bubble. To prevent similar episodes and to protect Western investors against their own actions, a certain degree of "re-regulation" via administrative controls on the part of the host country authorities (e.g., mandatory minimum holding periods for foreign equity purchases) might be justified. In this way, not only would speculative excesses be prevented, but capital inflows would be rerouted toward the more stable and long-term form of direct investments (as has been the case in Asia). At the same time, better oversight over institutional investors' leveraged operations and improved disclosure of their exposure to potentially risky investments could allay small investors' preoccupation with (often unfounded) fears of systemic tremors.

Our second main point is that the emerging market crisis of 1995 has little in common with the one that erupted in August 1982. This time, a large share of emerging countries' debt was held by the nonbank financial sector of the industrial countries (particularly the United States), rather than by their banks. Furthermore, this debt was mostly held in the form of tradeable instruments, typically market-to-market, rather than as bank loans, valued at their historic cost and thus open to ambiguous (i.e., optimistic) valuations. A different investor base and the use of new instruments also appears to have altered significantly the nature of the adjustment process, making it faster, more brutal, and possibly less manageable than was the case when the creditors were mostly banks. At the same time, however, the threat of contagion and systemic instability has been reduced, the extent of the damage is easier to assess, and the dynamics of the adjustment process—while amenable to conscious management and dangerously prone to short-term "overshooting"—are prone to greater self-correction (as long as the scale is not overwhelming).

Ultimately, and spurred on by the fundamental forces of portfolio diversification and the quest for higher returns, private capital flows to emerging markets will resume, and the absorption problems and risks of instability witnessed in the recent episode will reappear. Improved macroeconomic management in recipient countries, particularly policies designed to promote domestic savings and fiscal consolidation, will be the most appropriate way to rebuild and maintain investor confidence in the longer run.

On a shorter term basis, however, financial innovation can play a significant role, as demonstrated by the successful $500 million Mexican debt issue convertible into bank shares in July 1995. Completing the available menu of risk sharing and hedging instruments (e.g., local currency and stock index futures) and improving the local financial infrastructure with the aim of increasing liquidity and lowering transaction costs will widen investor choice, prevent capital flight, and soften the impact of adverse events or expectations.

As noted by Merton (1990), capital controls in emerging markets can be easily circumvented. For example, institutional investors in industrial countries could swap the return on notional amounts of their well-diversified industrial country equity portfolios against the yield on an equal value portfolio of emerging market stock indexes held by local residents (while the two principal amounts and streams of returns were denominated in a common currency, for instance, in dollars). Such swaps would effectively transfer the risk/return profile of emerging market stocks to foreign investors and vice versa, thus providing the desired diversification to both sets of investors at minimal transaction costs, and without generating initial capital inflows or the risk of sudden future withdrawals of funds.

References

Claessens, S., and M. Rhee. 1994. "The Effect of Barriers to Equity Investment in Developing Countries." In J. A. Frankel, *The Internationalization of Equity Markets*. Cambridge, MA: National Bureau of Economic Research; University of Chicago Press.

de la Dehesa, G. 1994. "The Recent Surge in Private Capital Flows to Developing Countries: Is It Sustainable?" Per Jacobsson Lecture. Madrid: Asociación Española de Banca Privada.

Feldstein, M. 1995. "Too Little, Not Too Much." *The Economist*, 335 (24 June): 72–73.

Glen, J. D., Yannis Karmokolias, Robert R. Miller, and Sanjay Shah. 1995. *Dividend Policy and Behavior in Emerging Markets: To Pay or Not to Pay*. International Finance Corporation Discussion Paper No. 26. Washington: International Finance Corporation.

Merton, R. C. 1990. "The Financial System and Economic Performance." *Journal of Financial Services Research* 20, no. 5: 263–300.

Paz, O. 1967. *The Labyrinth of Solitude: Life and Thought in Mexico*. London: Penguin Press.

Schadler, S., M. Carcovic, A. Bennett, and R. Kahn. 1993. *Recent Experiences with Surges in Capital Inflows*. Occasional Paper No. 108. Washington: International Monetary Fund.

Wood, B. 1995. "The Perils of Prague." *Institutional Investor*, international ed., 20, no. 5 (May): 99–104.

World Bank. 1994a. *Global Economic Prospects*. Washington: World Bank.

World Bank. 1994b. *Argentina Capital Markets Study*. World Bank Report No. 12963-AR. Washington: World Bank.

Comment

David D. Hale

The history of the Mexican peso crisis of 1995 is likely to serve as a case study for seminars on international financial crisis management well into the early decades of the 21st century. Mexico's experience vividly illustrated all the fragilities of the post–Cold War boom in securitized capital flows to developing-country financial markets. It also raised new questions about the role of international financial institutions, such as the International Monetary Fund, in an era when the private sector was supposed to have replaced the public sector as the primary source of capital for developing countries. The provisional verdict on the crisis is that portfolio capital flows can be highly volatile if policymakers mismanage critical issues of confidence, such as an exchange rate adjustment, but that international organizations can help contain the damage if they move quickly.

In 1994, numerous gatherings celebrated the 50th anniversary of the Bretton Woods conference and examined the future of the international institutions created there. Most commentators agreed that the growth of private-sector capital flows to emerging markets would force the IMF to focus its efforts on the world's most backward regions. In early 1995, however, the US Treasury and the IMF were so alarmed by the financial crisis engulfing Mexico that they organized the largest international aid program since the Marshall Plan to help the government avoid default on its dollar-linked securities. Mexico's recent history suggests that both private investors and governments still have a great deal to learn about

David D. Hale is first vice president and chief economist at Zurich Investments, Inc., Chicago.

the stability of capital flows, financial markets, and exchange rate policy in the new global economic order made possible by the end of the Cold War.

Major Weaknesses of the Global Financial System

The first vulnerability in the post–Cold War global financial system that the Mexican crisis exposed was the low saving rate of the Western Hemisphere. Except for Chile, every nation in the Western Hemisphere is an external debtor and has a saving rate well below the levels prevailing in East Asia as well as many European countries. Mexico was able to boost its rate of investment in the face of a low domestic saving rate by importing large amounts of capital vis-à-vis its stock and bond markets. American investors were large buyers of Mexican financial assets during the early 1990s because the low level of interest rates prevailing in the United States and a growing awareness of the benefits of global portfolio diversification encouraged an unprecedented demand for foreign securities. In 1993, for example, US capital outflows to purchase foreign securities reached a level equal to 1.7 percent of GDP or a level in excess of Marshall Plan transfers to Europe during the late 1940s.

The United States was able to export capital on a large scale despite its low private saving and large full-employment budget deficit because foreign investors were enthusiastic buyers of US securities during the bull market of 1992–93. Moreover, the Japanese government was willing to spend $60 billion supporting the US dollar when private capital inflows slowed. This transnational chain made Mexico's capital account highly vulnerable to changes in American interest rates and foreign investor perceptions of the dollar, not just market concerns about Mexico's burgeoning current account deficit. Mexicans began to sell the peso aggressively in December because they feared that in an environment of rising US interest rates, there would not be sufficient surplus liquidity in the savings-deficient US economy to finance a Mexican current account deficit equal to 8 to 9 percent of GDP at an exchange rate that was higher in real terms than the peso on the eve of the 1982 debt crisis.

The second fragility exposed by the peso crisis was the greatly increased sensitivity of securitized capital flows to adverse news events compared with that of commercial bank lending and foreign direct investment— the primary sources of private capital for developing countries before the 1990s. Managers of mutual funds have very different attitudes toward currency devaluations than commercial banks or multinational companies. Commercial banks with dollar loans do not object to currency depreciation in developing countries with large trade deficits because they can improve the credit rating of the country by boosting exports at the expense of domestic consumption. Multinational corporations also can benefit from a currency devaluation if they are using the country as an export base. The portfolio managers of mutual funds and pension funds operate under very different constraints. Although they understand that currency devaluations are sometimes a necessary component of an economic restructuring program, they do not like unpredictable exchange rate policies when they are large holders of debt and when the equity market is dominated by companies oriented toward domestic consumption.

The Mexican devaluation was traumatic because of the heavy concentration of US investment in peso-denominated securities without any available currency hedges, the refusal of practically all Mexican policymakers to admit to American fund managers that devaluation might even be a policy option, and the lack of any export sectors in the Mexican stock market significant enough to compensate for the large losses that occurred in the banking and domestic consumption sectors as the peso declined. As a result of the confidence engendered by the North American Free Trade Agreement (NAFTA) and the outstanding communications of key economic ministers, Mexico under then-President Carlos Salinas achieved a degree of intimacy with the American financial community unprecedented for a non-English-speaking developing country. During the early 1990s, it was able to finance nearly two-thirds of its expanding current account deficit through sales of securities to US investors, whereas in most developing countries, portfolio investment still accounted for only 20 to 30 percent of capital inflows.

Mexico's ability to import capital via security markets was greatly enhanced by the tremendous expansion then occurring in the US mutual fund industry. As a result of the low interest rates prevailing in the United States during the early 1990s, US mutual fund assets expanded from the equivalent of barely 10 percent of bank deposits in the early 1980s to nearly 90 percent by 1994. Bond and equity funds accounted for practically all of the growth in mutual fund assets, and the volume of money invested in international funds expanded from a few billion dollars to nearly $100 billion. Wall Street further encouraged diversification into emerging-market debt and equity by investing heavily in new research, trading, and investment banking departments targeted on Latin America and East Asia. Despite the obvious deterioration in Mexico's economic position in 1994, some of these firms also tried to downplay the issue of peso currency risk because of concern that it would jeopardize the transactions flow required to support their expensive overhead at a time when Wall Street's domestic business was in recession.

As the growth of securitized capital flows to developing countries is a recent phenomena, there has been no other developing-country financial crisis comparable to Mexico's in the modern era. Many occurred in the half century before World War I, however, when securities markets were also major channels for capital transfers between rich and poor countries.

In fact, most of the great upheavals in both the US and Latin American stock markets during that period resulted either from financial shocks in Europe that reduced demand for all foreign securities, or political events here that undermined foreign investor confidence in Western Hemisphere currencies.

The best analogy to the recent Mexican crisis is the dollar crisis of 1893. Grover Cleveland had just become president, and investors began to sell the dollar out of concern about his commitment to maintaining its link to the gold standard. As money left New York, US interest rates rose sharply, and Cleveland had to negotiate an emergency gold loan from an Anglo-American banking syndicate in order to maintain the dollar's gold parity. Once the markets regained confidence in his commitment to a stable dollar, however, interest rates fell and the crisis eased. The major differences between the two eras were that private bankers rescued Grover Cleveland from a devaluation because there were no official lenders of last resort and the US economy was in recession before the crisis. Mexico, however, experienced a severe slump because the central bank attempted to avoid moderate monetary tightening in 1994.

The third weakness that the Mexico crisis exposed was the inadequacy of the monetary regimes of many developing countries to sustain investor confidence in their commitment to low inflation during periods of economic and political transition. Mexico pursued an accommodative monetary policy during 1994 because its policymakers were concerned about the health of the country's banks. The entrepreneurial stockbrokers who had taken over Mexico's banks during the privatization boom of the early 1990s had encouraged aggressive lending policies and permitted the stock of nonperforming loans to expand to nearly 8 percent of assets even before the onset of the recent economic crisis. As with the Bank of England, the Reserve Bank of Australia, and the Federal Reserve during the early 1990s, the Mexican central bank felt compelled to take monetary policy risks on the side of ease in order to prevent a further deterioration in bank credit quality. When the rundown of foreign exchange reserves threatened to shrink the monetary base, the central bank responded by creating more domestic credit.

Foreign investors did not initially understand what was happening because of the long lags in obtaining Mexican monetary data, but it is now widely accepted that Mexican monetary policy in 1994 was overly expansionary. The Mexican central bank could rationalize accommodative actions when the US Treasury intervened to support the peso during the second quarter of 1994, but it persisted with this policy after the election despite the weakness of the country's foreign exchange position. Economists will long debate whether the Zedillo administration could have avoided the peso crisis by hiking interest rates aggressively when foreign exchange reserves resumed their decline in December 1994. Whatever the motives for postponing higher interest rates, however, the Zedillo team and the American academic enthusiasts for devaluation, such as Professor Rudiger Dornbusch, clearly failed to appreciate the differences between importing capital from US banks during the 1970s and US mutual funds during the early 1990s. Whereas US banks could afford to take a long-term view of devaluation because their loans are usually dollar-denominated, mutual fund managers have to mark their assets to markets every day and can suffer redemptions when investor confidence changes abruptly.

The tensions facing Mexico's policymakers in December 1994 were not unique for a middle-income, capital-importing developing nation, but the scale of the subsequent crisis will cause emerging-market investors to focus far more attention on the quality of national monetary institutions and banking supervision in the future. Does the central bank of a developing country enjoy modest or significant autonomy from political interference? What is the health of the domestic banking system, and how great is its capacity to withstand interest rate hikes? How effectively has the central bank supervised the expansion of the banking system and its propensity for risk taking? Is exchange rate stability a primary objective of monetary policy, or is the exchange rate secondary to other policy objectives? How timely and transparent are official reports about monetary conditions and the conduct of monetary policy?

Enhancing Monetary Credibility

In the last great age of securitized capital flows, most developing countries tried to enhance their credit rating and access to foreign investment by linking their exchange rate to the gold standard. They experienced periodic crises when global recession and falling commodity prices significantly curtailed their export income, but on the whole, the gold standard facilitated a tremendous expansion of global private investment through securities markets. The magnitude of the recent Mexican crisis suggests that developing countries will have to reexamine their assumptions about monetary policy if they want to encourage the recent boomlet in capital flows via security markets to continue. They will not be able to recreate a global monetary system comparable to the pre-1914 gold standard, but they can pursue a number of unilateral policies to enhance their monetary credibility with both foreign investors and their own citizens.

Some countries can establish investor confidence simply by establishing independent central banks, while others should consider converting their central banks into currency boards similar to those that now exist in Hong Kong or Argentina. Under a currency board, all monetary growth has to be underpinned by an expansion of foreign exchange reserve assets to make the currency fully convertible. Currency boards were very common in the British colonies before World War II and were then discarded when they became independent. Interest in them is reviving because they offer countries with weak central banking traditions or histories of high inflation an opportunity to establish credible monetary policies more quickly than would be possible with ordinary central banks. Hong Kong established its currency board during a financial crisis in 1983, and it has withstood a decade of great volatility in both Chinese politics and US interest rates. Argentina turned its central bank into a de facto currency board during 1991 in order to establish monetary credibility coincident with the introduction of a far-reaching economic liberalization program. Estonia established a currency board in 1992 to accelerate its transition into a low-inflation economy as it left the ruble currency zone, and Lithuania has been following suit. In fact, Estonia has achieved great monetary credibility that it currently enjoys real interest rates of −10 percent, compared with real interest rates of 70 to 80 percent in the ruble currency zone.

In early 1995, there was extensive discussion about Mexico introducing a currency board using the IMF and US Treasury. Supporters contended that it would help restore credibility to Mexican monetary policy more quickly than a conventional IMF austerity program and would thus reduce the upward pressure on Mexican short-term interest rates (then 70 to 80 percent) resulting from the peso's collapse. They also argued that it was appropriate to reinforce Mexico's increasing commercial and financial links with the United States by encouraging further convergence in monetary policy. The US Treasury opposed the idea, however, because of concern that the introduction of a new exchange rate target so soon after the crisis would simply encourage investors to drain Mexico's new reserves by selling any peso securities they had left. They also did not want to constrain the central bank's ability to play lender of last resort to troubled commercial banks. American officials instead favored a conventional economic austerity program encompassing high real interest rates, public spending cuts, tax hikes, and further privatization of government assets in order to reduce Mexico's need for external capital.

Instead of introducing a currency board, Mexico attempted to reestablish anti-inflation credibility with a monetary policy that establishes a firm target for the growth of net domestic credit, not the exchange rate, while shifting responsibility for bank bailouts to the government's deposit insurance agency. Some analysts have described the new Mexican monetary regime as a "mini currency board" because it puts heavy emphasis on restraining the growth of the monetary base irrespective of the policy's impact on the level of interest rates. Mexico's announcement of the new monetary regime in March 1995, immediately had a beneficial impact on investor attitudes and encouraged speculative buying of the peso. During the second quarter of 1995, the peso appreciated further while prices of both Mexican equities and bonds rallied sharply.

What remains to be seen is whether Mexico can sustain a severely restrictive monetary policy in the face of the recession now engulfing the economy. Mexico needs 1 million new jobs per year to employ those leaving school and since the first half of 1995, the economy has lost more than 1 million jobs. The official unemployment rate for urban areas rose to 6.3 percent in April 1995 from 3.2 percent at the end of 1994 and continued to rise through the summer of 1995. Real wages fell more than 10 percent, and real personal consumer expenditures declined at a 16 percent annual rate during the first quarter of 1995.

The financial counterpart to the sharp fall in real private spending was a large decline in the monetary base. By mid-1995, the real monetary base had contracted 34 percent from its level at year-end 1994. Monetary growth has slowed sharply in response to the high levels of nominal interest rates that prevailed during early 1995, when money market yields touched 80 percent. Credit growth also has suffered from the structural weakness of the banking system, which in 1995 had official nonperforming loans in excess of 10 percent, compared with 7 percent in late 1994. As a result of high real interest rates, lending to households and business fell 10 percent and 15 percent, respectively, during the first five months of 1995.

As workers accepted large declines in real wages in a vain effort to protect employment, the inflation rate peaked in April 1995, and the central bank began to ease monetary policy. Money market yields fell to 40 percent, and equity prices rallied significantly. The rally in financial asset prices helped stabilize the peso by encouraging renewed capital inflows as the trade account moved into a large surplus.

The second and third quarters of 1995 marked the low point of Mexican economic crisis because of the lagged effects of the financial shocks that occurred during the first quarter. The economy soon stabilized in GDP terms, however, because of the huge improvement in the trade account. The first-quarter contraction in private spending was so intense that it reduced the consumption share of GDP to 60 percent from 67 percent in 1994, while the trade account improved by an amount equivalent to 8.0 percent of GDP. The collapse in Mexican private spending was so severe and exports so robust that the country generated a small current account surplus in 1995 whereas a $33 billion deficit (7.0 percent of GDP) had been forecast before the peso's devaluation. Such an adjustment would be the equivalent of a $600 billion shift in the composition of US GDP or a sum four times as large as the average output loss in an American recession. A revival of Mexican private spending will depend upon how quickly the Mexican central bank can reduce interest rates without precipitating a peso crisis.

In April 1995 it did not appear that Mexico could reduce interest rates significantly until late 1995, but several factors permitted the central bank to ease much sooner than expected. First, the international aid package and the sharp decline in imports allowed Mexico to rebuild foreign exchange rates to the $10 billion to $11 billion level from less than $5 billion immediately after the peso crisis of December 1994. Second, Mexico greatly reduced its stock of short-term dollar-linked debt and during recent weeks has been able to roll over a large volume of maturing *tesobono* securities without investors requesting their conversion into dollars. Third, Mexico has been able to resume selling securities in the international financial markets, whereas after the 1982 default it did not regain access to the markets for more than seven years. Finally, the slowdown in the US economy has encouraged the Federal Reserve to reduce US interest rates by 75 basis points and bond yields to drop more than 150 basis points from the peak levels of late 1994. The US easing encouraged a large rally in the financial markets of many developing countries as well as in the prices of dollar-denominated securities, such as Brady bonds. Mexico shared in this rally through large price gains for both its domestic securities and dollar-denominated bonds.

Mexico could not have avoided default during early 1990 without financial assistance from the US Treasury and the IMF. As a result of the recent improvement in private investor confidence, however, it has been able to reduce short-term interest rates without jeopardizing the value of the peso. Mexico still intends to take down the remaining $10 billion available to it from the US credit facility, but it is possible to construct scenarios in which it will not need to borrow the full amount if the current rally in Mexican financial asset prices can be sustained long enough to trigger a revival of private capital inflows. In the first half of 1995, Mexico borrowed $1.25 billion through short-term swaps that have been repaid and an additional $8 billion that is scheduled for repayment after 1997. Mexico also has $13.8 billion of loans from the US Agency for International Development, $2.5 billion of credit from the US Department of Agriculture, and $2.7 billion from the US Export-Import Bank, but most of these loans were made prior to the recent peso crisis.

As a result of the severity of the current recession, Mexico's inflation rate could drop back to the 15 to 20 percent range if the peso stabilizes in a trading range of 6.0 to 7.0. The Mexican central bank will want to keep the peso strong during the near term to help Mexican companies service their foreign currency loans and improve investor confidence in the country. What remains to be seen, however, is whether they will want to adopt a long-term policy of targeting the real exchange rate though occasional devaluations to offset the inflation differential with the United States.

In recent months, there has been widespread discussion about Mexico establishing a target for the peso's real exchange rate on the model of Chile's exchange rate regime. The goal of the Chilean system has been to promote trade competitiveness by continually adjusting the nominal exchange rate to offset inflation differentials. This system kept Chilean inflation in the 20 to 30 percent range for several years after it was intro-duced in 1984, but it provided a sufficiently firm anchor for monetary policy that the economy enjoyed steady output growth. As with Chile, such a system in Mexico would probably cause inflation to stabilize at a higher level than the single-digit level that prevailed before the peso crisis. It would, however, lock Mexico into an economic policy that emphasized export growth rather than domestic consumption. Under the previous fixed rate regime, by contrast, many analysts felt the peso had become commercially overvalued by at least 20 to 30 percent.

The most difficult part of the Chilean model for Mexico to imitate would be the imposition of capital controls. Chile has imposed numerous restrictions on portfolio capital inflows and the timing of outflows to prevent them from undermining its monetary policy objectives, especially the real exchange rate target. Neither the United States nor the Mexican government favor exchange controls, while Mexico's OECD membership could preclude such controls. If Chile emerges as a model for Mexican policy, however, it is an option that will be revisited periodically. Indeed, some Mexican officials suggest the country should leave the OECD because its joining the membership during 1994 was premature and imposes restrictions on Mexican policy that may be unsuitable as a result of the crisis.

The US and global financial environment should be more helpful to Mexico's attempt at economic stabilization than it was during much of 1994 and early 1995. US consumer spending slowed sharply in mid-1995, so the Federal Reserve eased policy for the first time since 1992. The stabilization of US interest rates encouraged large rallies in US stock and bond prices and thus increased the willingness of some foreign investors to reenter the Mexican market. The decision of the US government to hold short-term interest rates steady as the dollar fell in early 1995 forced Japan and Germany to reduce their own interest rates. It has worked so far, however, because the US trade deficit approached $200 billion in 1995. Such a policy was risky because the recent slowdown in retail spending has lessened investor anxiety about the risk of overheating in the American economy. As in the late 1980s, the ability of the United States to force more reflationary monetary policies upon Europe and Japan through a lower dollar could create a global bull market in financial asset prices with positive spillover effects on Mexico as a result of the high yields still available on its bonds and money market instruments.

International Implications of the Mexican Crisis

As a result of Mexico's leadership role in the economic liberalization movement that swept the developing world during recent years, the peso crisis will have greater demonstration effects for other developing countries than any global economic shock since 1989.

The peso crisis has already provoked some countries to reconsider the speed at which they will liberalize their financial systems. South Korea, for example, will probably slow its application to join the OECD because membership requires countries to eliminate capital controls. In countries with long traditions of statist economic policies, such as India, political factions opposed to economic liberalization will seize upon Mexico's crisis as an excuse to slow removal of barriers to greater foreign trade and capital mobility.

The Mexican crisis is also reviving debate about the role of the IMF as a lender of last resort for developing countries. If Mexico had not been able to obtain international financial assistance in February 1995, it would likely have defaulted on its dollar-linked government securities. The United States played a decisive leadership role in providing Mexico with such assistance because the Clinton administration perceived that it was in America's self-interest to prevent the country from sliding into an economic depression. The United States agreed to provide Mexico with $20 billion of direct assistance from its Exchange Stabilization Fund, and it lobbied for a significant expansion of the IMF loan over the protests of Germany and other European countries. The IMF loan to Mexico was 3.5 times larger than any previous IMF credit, while the total package was the largest international aid program since the Marshall Plan. It is doubtful, however, that the United States would have acted so vigorously for any other nation in the Western Hemisphere except Canada. If other developing countries encounter liquidity problems as severe as Mexico's they will be totally dependent upon the IMF to resolve them (as was Argentina in March 1995).

The IMF was originally established to provide short-term liquidity to industrial countries experiencing liquidity problems, and since the 1970s it has emerged as a major short-term lender to developing countries as well. During the 50th anniversary celebration of the IMF and the World Bank in 1994, it was often argued that the IMF should focus on only the poorest regions, such as Africa, because Latin America and Asia were increasingly gaining access to large flows of private capital. As a result of the Mexican crisis, however, IMF officials contend that their organization still has an important role to play in providing liquidity and economic advice to middle-income developing countries, not just the basket cases of the developing world.

What remains unclear is whether the industrial nations will be prepared to expand the IMF's capital to give it a large lending role. At last year's IMF meeting, Germany was strongly opposed to proposals from Michel Camdessus for expanding the IMF's Special Drawing Rights (SDR) quotas by $50 billion. Camdessus wanted to adjust the IMF's SDR quotas for the new members from the former Soviet bloc. The United States and Britain proposed a compromise alternative of $17 billion, but the developing nations voted it down. Now that the Mexican crisis has demonstrated how vulnerable even successful developing countries can be to sudden shifts in private capital flows, these countries will probably review their demands for an expansion of the IMF's lending resources. The Republican takeover of the US Congress probably made it even more difficult for the IMF to obtain new funds from the G-7 countries in 1995 than it was in 1994. In fact, the US Treasury has discussed the possibility of obtaining more IMF capital from the newly affluent nations of East Asia.

Many American investors have mixed feelings about the IMF because the organization is alleged to have helped set the stage for the recent Mexican financial crisis by encouraging the government to devalue rather than defend the currency. In fact, the World Bank lobbied more aggressively for the Mexican devaluation than the IMF, but senior IMF officials were sympathetic to the arguments for a devaluation because they perceived the Mexican current account deficit to be unsustainably large and American investors to be foolishly complacent about the risks of investing in peso financial assets.

The Mexican crisis also provoked more discussion about the need to establish some form of bankruptcy process for countries comparable to that which exists for companies. Mexico, for example, faced far more of a liquidity than a solvency problem during the first quarter because of the maturity structure of its debt. If Mexico had been a company, it would have rescheduled the debt. If Mexico had borrowed primarily from banks rather than mutual funds, it might have been able to restructure the timing of loan repayments. Because the debt consisted of securitized instruments owned by mutual funds, pension funds, and retail investors, however, there was no simple way to reschedule, and Mexico had to seek external assistance. If there had been an established framework for rescheduling securitized debt, Mexico could have used that process to avoid relying upon a lender of last resort, such as the IMF.

The Mexican crisis may also have encouraged more experimentation with private insurance guarantees for internationally tradable government securities comparable to the insurance that was already available for US municipal bonds. In an age of rapidly expanding securitized global capital flows, the private sector should be able to develop systems for pricing insurance guarantees on credit risk and thus play a more effective role in detecting economic policy errors before they evolve into major crises. In the case of Mexico, foreign investors turned more cautious after the Colosio assassination by reducing purchases of peso-denominated *cetes*, but the government filled the gap in its funding needs by offering investors dollar-linked *tesobono* securities. Mexico's growing dependence upon the sale of such securities after June 1994 was a sign that investors had serious doubts about the peso, but the government's ability to sell the *tesobono* instruments permitted it to defer any decisions about making a currency realignment until it was too late to control the magnitude of the devaluation. It is possible that an insurance guarantee company would have made the same mistakes as the government, but it also might have been more forceful in obtaining enough data about Mexico's monetary policy dilemmas to encourage discussion about a currency realignment before reserves were exhausted.

As a result of the large losses that investors in Latin American securities suffered, several observers—including Gilibert and Steinherr—have suggested that the early 1990s boom in developing-country debt and equity markets was merely a bubble resulting from low US interest rates and aggressive marketing by Wall Street investment bankers. Some even compare it to the 1920s boomlet in US purchases of Latin American and Central European bonds from New York commercial banks, which attempted to get rid of bad loans by converting them into securities for sale through their retail distribution networks. There was such widespread public outrage at the scale of the defaults on these securitized Latin American loans that Congress enacted the Glass-Steagall law separating commercial and investment banking.

As tempting as it may be to compare the recent Mexican debacle and earlier Latin American financial manias, there are some important differences. First, Mexico became attractive to foreign investors because of an economic reform program that is still largely in place. The Mexican government pursued a high-risk exchange rate policy that resulted in a financial crisis, but its trade and investment policies have produced a Mexican economy that is more open than at any time since the 1910 revolution. Second, the Mexican reform program is part of a larger global process of economic liberalization resulting from the end of the Cold War and the acceptance of market-oriented economic ideas by hitherto mercantilist countries. The global scope of this revolution will prevent Mexico from reverting to the statist economic model that prevailed before the late 1980s. Third, the Latin American bond defaults of the 1930s or the late 19th century resulted from global economic shocks, such as depression and deflation, not just economic mismanagement in Latin America itself.

The global economic environment will be much more supportive of recovery in Mexico and other developing countries during the next few years than it was during the depression of the 1930s or the deflation of the 1890s. In fact, the growth rates of many developing countries will continue to exceed those of the old industrial nations for many years to come and thus offer ample opportunities for their stock markets to produce superior returns. Although the stock market capitalization of the developing countries has already grown to nearly $2 trillion from only

$400 billion in the late 1980s, it still accounts for barely 15 percent of world stock market capitalization, despite the fact that these countries account for over 40 percent of world output, 70 percent of its land area, and over 80 percent of its population.

The Role of Pension Funds

The emerging-market theme is still such a compelling one for investors that many US pension funds expanded their exposure to the sector during 1995 in the belief that the Mexican crisis created bargain-hunting opportunities in both Latin America and Asia. Latin American mutual funds also suffered far smaller redemptions than the managers initially feared because many investors decided that the Mexican crisis was a buying opportunity, not a reason to abandon the whole region.

The role of private pension funds in emerging markets could be especially important in the future because they account for a large and growing share of saving in many industrial countries. At present, most US corporate pension funds have 7 to 8 percent of their assets ($2 trillion) in foreign markets and 15 to 20 percent of those assets in emerging markets. By 2000, both public and private US pension funds could easily have 10 to 15 percent of their assets in foreign markets and 20 percent of those assets in emerging markets, providing potential capital of $150 billion to $200 billion to developing countries. As the market capitalization of the developing countries is likely to expand more rapidly than the market capitalization of the old industrial countries, this share could expand further during the next century. The public sector, by contrast, is much less equipped to play a major role in providing development finance than it was after World War II because the governments of the G-7 countries now have much higher ratios of public debt and unfunded pension liabilities to GDP than ever before. In the United States and Britain, for example, the ratio of public debt to GDP after 1945 was 125 percent and 200 percent, respectively. Today, both countries have ratios of public debt to GDP in the 50 to 60 percent range and unfunded public pension liabilities two or three times as large as their national incomes. In Canada, Germany, Italy, and other European countries, the ratios are even worse.

Many aspects of the Mexican financial crisis are reminiscent of the shocks that so-called peripheral countries experienced during fluctuations in British capital flows during the late 19th century. The periphery depended upon capital flows from the metropolitan power to purchase critical imports, so interruption of those capital flows forced the country into recession. But while the Mexican crisis had many similarities with the financial crisis of the late 19th century, it also had several features that are unique to the modern era.

The primary reason the Mexican crisis was so severe was the extraordinary appetite that developed in the American fund management industry for Mexican financial assets as a consequence of NAFTA and the low level of interest rates prevailing in the United States during the banking crisis of the early 1990s. After enactment of NAFTA, a growing number of US portfolio managers began to perceive Mexico as an extension of the American economy. As a result, they pushed up equity multiples and downplayed the issue of currency risk despite a large current account deficit that would have provoked far greater caution if Mexico had been located in Asia, Africa, or even the southern cone of Latin America. When the US Treasury intervened to support the peso with swap agreements during the market turmoil that followed the Colosio assassination in March 1994, it also reinforced the impression of many US investors that Mexico was a de facto 13th Federal Reserve district, not just another Latin American emerging market. While there was a good case for the United States to help Mexico stabilize its financial system during a period of extreme political tension, the intervention further contributed to the investor complacency that made the peso's ultimate devaluation so hard to accept. The decision of the Clinton administration to intervene heavily on behalf of Mexico during early 1995 provides further confirmation of America's strategic interest in a stable Mexico, but it also vividly illustrates the moral hazard created by the relationship. If Mexico had taken advantage of the 1994 political crisis to widen the peso's currency target band by 10 to 20 percent, it is quite possible that the peso would still be at 4.5 to 5.0 vis-à-vis the dollar, and the economy would have enjoyed moderate export-led growth, not a severe recession.

Broader Lessons for Public Policy

But while the factors that contributed to the severity of the current Mexican crisis were a unique by-product of the country's special relationship with the US fund management community, the Mexican experience does offer a few broader lessons for public policy in all developing nations.

First, if developing nations want to boost their rate of the investment significantly, it is essential that they also increase their domestic saving rate. There is nothing wrong with importing capital, but heavy dependence upon foreign saving creates potential vulnerabilities when global interest rates are rising or the capital-importing nation itself is going through a political transition.

Second, if countries do increase their dependence upon foreign capital, they should attempt to diversify their sources in terms of both mix and origin. Mexico financed about 75 percent of its current account deficit after 1990 through flows of portfolio capital, whereas most other developing nations obtain only about 20 to 30 percent of their external funds from such a source. Mexico also depended far more heavily upon US mutual funds and pension funds than any other developing country. It needs to reduce its future vulnerability to US interest rates and mood swings in New York and Boston by attracting a larger share of its investments from Europe, Japan, Korea, and other Asian countries.

Third, if countries are to depend heavily upon portfolio capital to finance a large external deficit, they will have to pursue far more transparent and credible monetary policies than have prevailed in Mexico during the modern era. Regardless of whether the solution to this problem is the introduction of a currency board or the establishment of a truly autonomous central bank will depend upon the circumstances of each country, it is certain that the Mexican crisis will greatly intensify investor focus on the quality of national monetary institutions in the future.

Some members of Congress sought to determine whom to blame for the economic tragedy. But this was difficult because the peso collapse was the by-product of several factors converging at the same time, not particular policies or personalities. There were huge errors of judgment in both Mexico City and on Wall Street about the country's capacity to finance a large and growing current account deficit through sales of securities to US investors at a time of rising American interest rates. Some US government officials perceived the risks in Mexico's strategy, but it would have been difficult for them to propose either a devaluation or monetary tightening in the midst of Mexico's first democratic presidential election during this century.

Instead of searching for bureaucratic scapegoats, the US Congress should focus its energy on encouraging Mexico to complete the economic reform process that originally encouraged it to break with a long tradition of mercantilism and seek membership in the GATT, the OECD, and NAFTA. The Mexican peso crisis has provided useful lessons about the conduct of monetary policy in an age of securitized private capital flows and surplus global liquidity resulting from easy monetary policies in the old industrial countries. It should not be allowed to discredit the great progress that Mexico has achieved in removing barriers to trade and investment, privatizing state enterprises, and beginning the transition to a pluralist law-abiding democracy. The peso crisis of 1995 will go down in the history books as a tragic error of policy implementation, not as cause to reverse the country's strategic direction.

Comment

Michael Dooley

The recent Mexican debt crisis invites comparisons with the 1982 crisis, and this paper offers two interesting themes around which to organize such a comparison. The first theme is the economics behind the private capital inflows that set the stage for the crisis. The second theme discusses the consequences for debtors, creditors, and their governments of the changes in market valuations of these positions.

The author regards private market participants as incapable of rational calculation or, at least, incapable of acting on such calculation. The evidence offered is that price earnings ratios in emerging markets reached levels before the 1994 crash that implied expected growth in earnings that were inconsistent with historical trends in both Asia and Latin America. Moreover, historical relationships did not suggest that Latin markets offered significant diversification opportunities, especially Latin American markets for US investors.

This is reminiscent of the difficulty economists had after 1982 in explaining so-called overlending by commercial banks. Explanations based on disaster myopia, incomplete information, or herd behavior—what was called earlier and most colorfully "popular delusions and the madness of crowds"—were popular after 1982, not to mention 1882 and 1782. I do not think this very basic issue has been or will be resolved. Some participants in all markets are poorly informed and not very bright. The question is, do such participants dominate markets? My own view of pre-

Michael Dooley is professor of economics at the University of California, Santa Cruz. He is also a research associate at the National Bureau of Economic Research (NBER) and an editor of the International Journal of Finance and Economics.

1982 bank lending is that it was a rational decision based on an expected bailout by industrial country governments. I would argue that recent capital inflows were also motivated more by implicit government guarantees than by the naive behavior of private investors. In fact, capital flows can be analyzed as transactions between governments and the private sector that incidentally involve transactions captured in balance of payments statistics.

I agree with the author that portfolio theory is not very helpful in evaluating these capital flows. The view that capital inflows to emerging markets reflected efforts by investors in industrial countries to reduce the home bias in their portfolios is not well supported by data. Indeed, capital inflows to Mexico and other emerging markets after 1989 were about the same size as the capital flight from these countries before 1989. Were these recent inflows "correcting" a home bias for industrial country investors or reestablishing the home bias of Mexican nationals? There is no way to force a confession from balance of payments data concerning the motives or even the residence of investors. The distinction between resident and nonresident investors is much less interesting compared with the distinction between private speculators and governments. Perhaps the distinction across residence is important if some nationals receive inside information about the intentions of a government, but in general we would probably make fewer mistakes by considering all private investors as responding to the same incentives.

The government guarantee behind recent capital inflows was the commitment to a fixed exchange rate and the less apparent commitment to the solvency of the domestic banking system. In Latin America, about half of private capital inflows were matched by an official capital outflow in the form of increases in international reserves. The political commitment to fixed exchange rates as an anchor against inflation meant that the government was committed to using the reserves to guarantee the dollar value of private claims. The secondary reserve was the commitment of the US government to political and economic stability in Mexico. This means that bank deposits are implicitly insured and, more important, that firms with large bank credits cannot be permitted to fail. In the event, both sources of guarantees were fully utilized to soften the losses of investors. Some investors did get caught in domestic currency assets and equities, but only the very slow to exit the game suffered.

The second important issue raised by the author is the likely effects of the recent crisis both for the lenders and the borrowing countries. I agree with the author's view that the form of investment is important in evaluating the continuing effects of the crisis. I have argued elsewhere that the extended bargaining between the banks and the governments of the industrial countries blocked a resolution of the 1982 crisis and that this had serious adverse consequences for the debtor countries. While the losses were unresolved, new investment was discouraged. In the recent crisis this at first seems to be much less a problem. The banks are absent this time, and losses to portfolio investors in the industrial countries are not a threat to the financial system in the industrial countries. Thus foreign investors' losses are more easily identified and resolved. Like the author I have argued that this means that the lasting effects of the crisis are likely to be much less severe this time.

But I am now much less optimistic that we will quickly put the recent crisis behind us. The problem is that in several of these countries the removal of government guarantees for exchange rate stability and price level stability have generated lasting increases in domestic real interest rates. In turn, this imposes large economic losses on domestic firms and threatens the solvency of domestic commercial banks. Unresolved but widely anticipated losses on the books of commercial banks in an "insured" banking system generate the same sort of uncertainty about the ultimate allocation of losses that turned a financial crisis in 1982 into a decade-long economic crisis in debtor countries. In fact, the problem may be even more persistent in this case because the governments of developing countries are much less able to recapitalize their banking systems given their own budget constraints. The problem seems to be that market economies do not adapt well to circumstances where new contracts are contaminated by an unknown allocation of a generally recognized but unallocated economic loss. We know that there are substantial losses on bank assets in many Latin American countries. We also know that governments seldom directly allocate such losses to holders of bank deposits. What we don't know is how such losses will be resolved. The usual suspects include taxes, nationalization of banks, capital controls, and a host of unpleasant alternatives. Argentina, for example, appears to have survived the initial loss of confidence associated with the Mexican crisis.

The domestic recession and high interest rates continue to threaten the banking system, however. It seems to follow that the lasting problem this time is not the resolution of a bargaining game between the foreign banks and their governments but between the debtor governments and their commercial banks. The industrial country governments have always had the ability to resolve their banking problems although they chose not to do so for nearly a decade. The unsettling aspect of the recent crisis is that the governments of the debtor countries are in a much weaker fiscal position. It follows that a resolution of their domestic banking crises may be as slow in coming as it was after 1982.

5

Capital Flows to Latin America: Is There Evidence of Contagion Effects?

Sara Calvo and Carmen M. Reinhart

The issue of "spillover" or "contagion" effects has acquired renewed importance in light of the Mexican crisis of December 1994 and the effect of this event on other emerging market economies, particularly in Latin America. In the wake of the crisis, several countries in Asia and Latin America experienced speculative attacks on their currencies, sharp declines in their equity markets, and a deterioration in the terms on which they could borrow from international capital markets.

In Latin America, Argentina and Brazil came under the most severe pressures. Between December 1994 and March 1995, Argentina's banking system lost 18 percent of its deposits and about one-half of its foreign exchange reserves (Banco Central de la República Argentina 1995). At the height of the crisis, Brazil was compelled to implement measures to stimulate capital inflows by reducing or eliminating existing taxes on foreign purchases of stocks and bonds. By April, financial markets had become calmer, and much of the capital that had fled from these two countries began to return. In some instances, equity prices (figure 1) and foreign exchange reserves recovered to precrisis levels; in others not.

The Asian experience followed a different course. Initially, the countries that had attracted sizable capital inflows in recent years—India, Indonesia, Korea, Malaysia, the Philippines, and Thailand (Calvo, Leiderman, and

Sara Calvo is senior economist at the World Bank, Washington. Carmen M. Reinhart is associate professor, University of Maryland at College Park, and a visiting fellow at the Institute for International Economics, Washington.

Figure 1   Latin America: stock prices in emerging markets and the Mexican crisis, 21 November 1994–30 April 1995 (dollars)

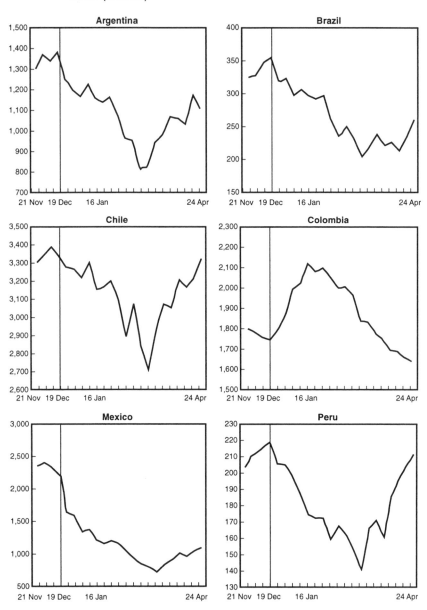

Source: International Finance Corporation.

Reinhart 1994, 1996)—were relatively unaffected by events in Latin America. By mid-January 1995, however, exchange rates in most of those countries (as well as in Hong Kong) came under increased speculative pressures, and equity markets posted large losses (figure 2). In many cases, central banks responded to these events by driving interest rates higher in an effort to defend the currency. As in Latin America, not all countries experienced the same degree of pressure. Although the speculative attack lasted but a couple of days in most instances, the pressures on the Philippines persisted well into March.

Yet, despite its recent relevance, relatively little empirical analysis exists on how small open economies are affected by economic developments in their neighbors and what role financial markets play in the transmission of disturbances. Herding behavior by undiscriminating investors is often blamed for producing common outcomes in countries with heterogeneous fundamentals.[1] Indeed, it is difficult to trace common threads in key economic indicators in many of these economies. Large current account deficits, which are often blamed for Mexico's currency crisis (figure 3), were present in Malaysia and Thailand, and they were also present in Colombia, one of the few Latin American countries relatively unaffected by events in Mexico. Brazil, which experienced considerable turbulence, had a modest current account deficit by almost any criterion at the time of the crisis. The presence of a fixed exchange rate regime has also been suggested as a reason why Argentina and Brazil came under extended pressure. However, Hong Kong and Thailand have pegged their currencies to the dollar since 1984, and the speculative pressures in those countries were confined to a couple of days. The Philippines, on the other hand, has a managed float and yet was the hardest hit of the Asian countries. A sharp and persistent real exchange rate appreciation (possibly leading to an overvaluation of the currency) is another factor commonly blamed for precipitating the Mexican crisis. However, Chile and Colombia (two of the Latin American countries that weathered the crisis relatively well) had also experienced sharp real exchange rate appreciations in recent years (Calvo, Leiderman, and Reinhart 1996). Indeed, the only common thread—among the three countries most affected by the Mexican crisis, Argentina, Brazil, and the Philippines—appears to have been a rich history of failed stabilization plans.

However, not all channels through which contagion can take place among small open economies require the presence of "animal spirits." First, spillovers may arise when two economies have highly integrated capital markets. In this case, shocks to the larger country are quickly

---

1. Eichengreen, Rose, and Wyplosz (1994) argue that such herding behavior played a prominent role in the recent Exchange Rate Mechanism (ERM) crisis, where the attacks on currencies could be justified by poor macroeconomic fundamentals in some instances but not in others.

Figure 2 Asia: stock prices in emerging markets and the Mexican crisis, 21 November 1994–30 April 1995
(dollars)

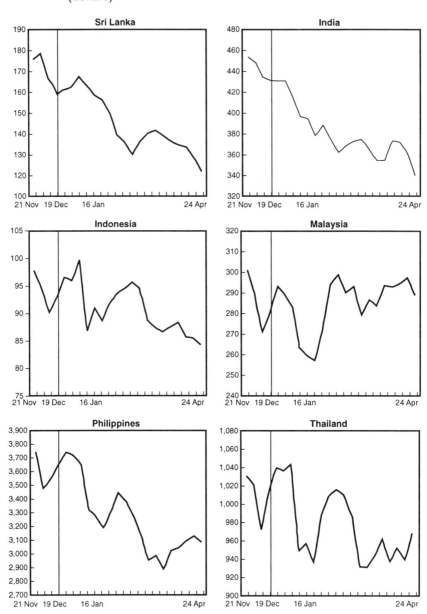

Source: International Finance Corporation.

Figure 3 Current account deficits as a percentage of GDP, from first year of capital inflows to 1994[a]

annual average percent

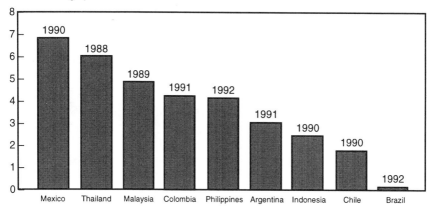

a. The date for each country denotes the year in which the surge in capital inflows began.
Source: International Monetary Fund, *World Economic Outlook.*

transmitted to the smaller one through trade in assets. The most documented example of this type of spillover in Latin America may have been the integration of the financial markets of Argentina and Uruguay (Hoffmaister and Végh 1994; Talvi 1994).[2] Likewise, Mexico during the 1990s appears to have had a growing influence on financial developments in nearby countries in Central America, particularly as the trend toward greater financial market integration and more liberal trade arrangements accelerated (Calvo and Reinhart 1995). An example is the recent arrangement between BANCOMEX and Costa Rican banks, whereby the former offers lines of credit to the latter in order to finance trade between Mexico and Costa Rica (Calvo and Reinhart 1995).

Second, trade patterns and arrangements play a role in the transmission of shocks (Ades and Chua 1993). Prior to December 1994, Mexico had entered into trade agreements with Colombia and Venezuela. In addition, a bilateral free trade agreement between Costa Rica and Mexico went into force on 1 January 1995; however, plans to extend it to the rest of Central America by January 1996 are now uncertain. The large real depreciation of the Mexican peso in early 1995 translated into fewer Mexican imports

---

2. Such "spillover" effects may also characterize the interaction between industrial and developing countries. For instance, recent evidence suggests that volatility spillovers from the US stock market to stock markets in Mexico and Thailand are significant and may have increased in recent years (Folkerts-Landau et al. 1994).

from other parts of Latin America and elsewhere. Further, in markets where Mexico competes with its smaller neighbors, the latter are at a relative disadvantage, increasing the pressure to regain competitiveness.

Third, institutional practices may also be a source of spillover effects. For instance, in response to a large adverse shock (such as the Mexican devaluation) an open-end emerging market mutual fund that is expecting an increasing amount of redemptions will sell off its equity holdings in several emerging markets in an effort to raise cash. However, given the illiquidity that characterizes most emerging markets, the sell-off by a few large investors will drive stock prices lower. Hence, the initial adverse shock to a single country gets transmitted to a wider set of countries. Indeed, among the 12 emerging stock markets shown in figures 1 and 2, only Colombia's (where foreign participation in the stock market had been negligible) recorded a sustained increase in prices following the Mexican crisis.

Yet a fourth mechanism for spillovers takes the form of foreign investors first selecting the larger countries as a place to invest because their equity markets and financial markets are more developed, followed by investment in the regions' smaller countries as investor confidence increases.

Fifth, some recent studies on economic growth have stressed the role of technological factors (Chua 1993; Easterly and Levine 1994) and political instability (Chua 1993) in regional contagion. Thus, the five channels of transmission discussed so far suggest that a large shock in one country can change the fundamentals for other countries in that region.

Finally, there are "bandwagon" effects, in which investor sentiment does not discriminate among different macroeconomic fundamentals across countries. In this case, even if the fundamentals of nearby countries are not affected by a shock to their neighbor, self-fulfilling crises can emerge because investors lump them all together. Hence, the issue of "spillovers" is important for small open economies because it potentially makes them vulnerable not just to external fundamentals in the form of changes in the terms of trade, international interest rates, and the business cycles of large trading partners, but also to other economic and political developments in larger neighbors.

This paper examines whether there was rigorous evidence of contagion in emerging markets in Asia and Latin America during the periods before and after the December 1994 Mexican crisis. We also examine whether there is evidence of "large neighbor effects" in capital flows to and from Latin America during the past 25 years. In the next section, we review the relatively scarce literature on contagion effects among developing countries, and we then examine the behavior of weekly stock returns and returns on Brady bonds for a selected group of emerging markets in the period leading to and following the Mexican crisis, with the aim of determining whether the degree of co-movement across markets varied over time. The aim of the empirical analysis in the penultimate section is to test the hypothesis that there are longer-lived "contagion" or "spillover" effects in international capital flows, over and beyond spillovers, at times of financial crises. The final section outlines the key results of our analysis.

Herding Behavior

This section briefly reviews two strands in the literature on contagion effects in developing countries. The first is herding behavior on the part of economic agents, while the second focuses on "fundamental" channels (e.g., trade, technology).

The literature on banking and financial crises in industrial countries is full of illustrations of contagion effects (see, e.g., Karafiath, Mynatt, and Smith 1991; Park 1991; Smith 1991; Gay, Timme, and Yung 1991; Kaufman 1992; Calomiris and Mason 1994). In the wake of a bank failure (particularly a large or prominent bank), anxious depositors possessing imperfect information about the soundness of other banks rush to withdraw their deposits from the banking system at large. The stampede by depositors generates a liquidity crisis that spreads to other healthy banks. Thus, herding behavior by depositors alters the "fundamentals" for a broader set of financial institutions and the crisis becomes self-fulfilling.

A similar story can be told about investors in international currency and equity markets. Eichengreen, Rose, and Wyplosz (1994) argue that the countries that came under speculative attack during the ERM crisis had largely heterogeneous macroeconomic fundamentals, and only in some cases could the attack be justified by the fundamentals.

Further evidence of contagion in well-developed financial markets comes from the evidence on "excess co-movement" in stock and commodity prices (Pindyck and Rotemberg 1990 and 1993). After taking into account common fundamentals, these authors found residual co-movement across stocks in very different industries with very different fundamentals. Similar results were found in their analysis of primary commodity prices.

With regard to emerging markets, however, relatively little is known about these issues. Doukas (1989) found evidence that sovereign interest rate spreads for Argentina, Brazil, and Mexico had a "contagious" element. "News" about the creditworthiness of a sovereign borrower affected the spreads charged to others. The presence of common factors and "excess sensitivity" to shared international fundamentals has also been detected in other variables which are related to cross-border capital flows, such as the discounts in emerging country funds (Hardouvelis, La Porta, and Wizman 1994). These authors also link the observed co-movement to US fundamentals and "investor sentiment."

More recently, analyzing the behavior of closed-end mutual funds in the wake of the Mexican crisis, Kramer and Smith (1995) note that closed-end funds dedicated to Mexico and other Latin American countries showed a substantial degree of co-movement following the Mexico crisis and developed large premia.[3]

Channels of Contagion

The literature on "large neighbor" effects is still quite limited, but recent papers suggest that contagion effects may play an important role in explaining observed regional differences in growth. Ades and Chua (1993) found that political instability had strong negative effects on neighboring countries' per capita growth rates. They show that such instability disrupts trade flows, reduces investment, and increases military outlays at the expense of other productive activities. Chua (1993) and Easterly and Levine (1994) also stress the role played by technology and human capital in giving rise to regional contagion effects. Such effects, it appears, help explain why Africa has had such a poor growth record (Easterly and Levine 1994).

Other papers have focused on specific countries (Argentina and Uruguay) and on the role played by capital market integration in transmitting disturbances across borders (Hoffmaister and Végh 1994; Talvi 1994). These studies have also found that large neighbor effects are significant.

The Mexican Crisis and Emerging Markets

To examine the issue of contagion effects arising from either herding behavior or the practices of open-end funds, we begin by focusing on some of the most popular emerging markets in Asia and Latin America during the early 1990s. The countries in Asia include India, Indonesia, Korea, Malaysia, the Philippines, and Thailand. The Latin American markets examined were Argentina, Brazil, Chile, Colombia, Mexico, Peru, and Venezuela. Both groups show large differences in foreign investor participation and market liquidity. Foreign participation in Latin America was highest in Argentina, Brazil, and Mexico and smallest in Colombia and Venezuela. Asia's range of variation was also large, with Malaysia and Thailand (the more liquid markets) recording higher shares of foreign participation.

---

3. Although they argue against the use of premia as a measure of investor sentiment, the fact remains that the discount premia showed a high degree of co-movement despite large disparities in fundamentals.

Table 1 presents cross-country correlations on weekly stock market returns in dollars. Two features are worth noting. First, correlations among returns in the Latin American markets increased during the period of market turbulence following Mexico's 1994 devaluation with the only exception being Colombia, where the market continued to strengthen after the crisis began. Second, correlations among the Latin American countries and several of the Asian countries, which had been mostly positive in the earlier period, turned negative. Given the marked discrepancies in macroeconomic fundamentals across countries within the regions (Calvo, Leiderman, and Reinhart 1993, 1994, and 1996), these two observations suggest that contagion in emerging markets may be *regional* rather than global. Although Asian markets were also subject to speculative attacks, these came all at once in mid-January 1995 and were short-lived.

To further explore the issue of co-movement, we employed principal component analysis. We focus on two groups of time series—seven (one per country) for the Latin American countries and six for Asian ones. From these, we constructed a smaller set of series, the principal components, which explain as much of the variance of the original series as possible. The higher the degree of co-movement in the original series, the fewer the number of principal components needed to explain a large portion of the variance of the original series. In the case where the original series were identical (perfectly collinear), the first principal component would explain 100 percent of the variation of the original series. Alternatively, if all the series are orthogonal to one another, it would take as many principal components as there are series to explain all of the variance in the original series. No advantage would be gained by looking at common factors, since none exist. The procedure begins by standardizing the variables so that each series has a zero mean and a unit standard deviation. This standardization ensures that all series receive uniform treatment and that the construction of the principal component indices is not influenced disproportionately by the series exhibiting the largest variation.

The results are summarized in table 2, which first presents the results for both regions and then breaks out the Asian and Latin American markets separately. All groupings tell the same story, although the difference between the pre- and postcrisis periods emerges more clearly from the regional subgroupings. As noted in Calvo, Leiderman, and Reinhart (1993), the first principal component is closely linked to common external fundamentals, such as international interest rates. Not surprisingly, the explanatory power of the first principal component increases markedly during the February 1994 to mid-December 1994 period, given that the US Federal Reserve switched in February 1994 to a policy of actively raising interest rates and tightening monetary conditions. The proportion explained by that component remains stable during pre- and postcrisis

Table 1 Cross-country correlations among emerging-market stock returns, January 1993–April 1995
(weekly returns in dollars)

	Argentina	Brazil	Chile	Colombia	Mexico	Venezuela	Peru	Korea	India	Indonesia	Malaysia	Philippines	Thailand
Heavy capital inflow period (January 1993–January 1994)													
Argentina	1.00												
Brazil	0.14	1.00											
Chile	0.24	0.13	1.00										
Colombia	0.24	-0.02	0.12	1.00									
Mexico	0.31	-0.06	0.22	0.31	1.00								
Venezuela	0.13	-0.04	-0.00	0.26	0.05	1.00							
Peru	0.38	0.08	0.24	0.02	0.15	0.08	1.00						
Korea	0.29	0.12	-0.01	-0.04	0.20	0.04	-0.02	1.00					
India	-0.01	0.14	0.23	0.03	-0.13	-0.02	0.01	0.20	1.00				
Indonesia	0.18	0.08	0.14	0.02	0.14	0.11	0.10	0.10	-0.03	1.00			
Malaysia	0.16	-0.32	-0.13	0.06	0.16	0.32	0.04	0.17	-0.05	0.06	1.00		
Philippines	0.18	-0.03	0.07	0.21	0.40	0.23	-0.01	-0.01	-0.23	0.22	0.39	1.00	
Thailand	0.25	-0.07	0.02	-0.03	-0.03	-0.05	0.12	0.21	0.07	0.03	0.42	0.21	1.00
Moderate capital inflow period (February 1994–mid-December 1994)													
Argentina	1.00												
Brazil	0.32	1.00											
Chile	0.54	0.23	1.00										
Colombia	0.24	0.06	-0.18	1.00									
Mexico	0.49	0.50	0.40	-0.01	1.00								
Venezuela	0.40	0.23	0.27	0.15	0.12	1.00							
Peru	0.37	0.19	0.36	0.28	0.43	0.28	1.00						
Korea	0.26	-0.20	0.36	-0.02	0.19	0.06	0.37	1.00					
India	-0.25	-0.14	-0.01	0.08	-0.16	0.04	-0.38	0.20	1.00				
Indonesia	0.27	0.19	0.32	-0.06	0.37	-0.03	0.12	0.34	0.17	1.00			
Malaysia	0.01	0.08	0.29	-0.02	0.13	0.06	-0.02	0.37	0.43	0.51	1.00		
Philippines	-0.05	-0.02	0.12	0.06	0.04	0.07	-0.04	0.04	0.19	0.24	0.15	1.00	
Thailand	0.44	0.08	0.37	0.09	0.39	0.10	0.09	0.23	0.28	0.45	0.46	0.10	1.00

The Mexican crisis and its aftermath
(mid-December 1994–April 1995)

	Argentina	Brazil	Chile	Colombia	Mexico	Venezuela	Peru	Korea	India	Indonesia	Malaysia	Philippines	Thailand
Argentina	1.00												
Brazil	0.57	1.00											
Chile	0.71	0.81	1.00										
Colombia	−0.12	0.11	0.05	1.00									
Mexico	0.68	0.40	0.34	−0.45	1.00								
Venezuela	0.05	0.27	0.16	−0.13	0.20	1.00							
Peru	0.59	0.55	0.57	−0.14	0.27	0.13	1.00						
Korea	0.23	0.25	0.17	−0.40	0.17	−0.09	0.05	1.00					
India	−0.09	0.12	0.08	−0.16	0.18	0.08	0.12	0.37	1.00				
Indonesia	−0.29	−0.14	−0.15	0.34	−0.31	−0.16	0.02	−0.24	0.28	1.00			
Malaysia	−0.11	−0.24	−0.14	−0.06	−0.08	−0.10	0.11	0.03	0.13	0.63	1.00		
Philippines	0.09	−0.14	0.04	0.10	−0.01	−0.00	0.21	−0.10	0.26	0.69	0.88	1.00	
Thailand	−0.06	−0.04	−0.07	0.23	−0.12	−0.13	0.11	−0.11	0.14	0.84	0.80	0.83	1.00

Source: International Finance Corporation.

161

Table 2 Factor analysis of weekly stock market returns, January 1993–April 1995 (cumulative R^2)

Principal component	January 1993– January 1994	February 1994– mid-December 1994	mid-December 1994– April 1995
Selected Asian and Latin American markets[a]			
1	0.19	0.28	0.29
2	0.33	0.45	0.53
3	0.44	0.55	0.66
Asian markets			
1	0.28	0.42	0.45
2	0.46	0.45	0.65
3	0.54	0.62	0.78
Latin American markets			
1	0.30	0.41	0.57
2	0.52	0.50	0.80
3	0.69	0.56	0.91

a. The Latin American emerging markets include Argentina, Brazil, Chile, Colombia, Mexico, Peru, and Venezuela. The Asian markets include India, Indonesia, Korea, Malaysia, Philippines, and Thailand.

periods. The explanatory power of the second principal component, which we identify with the "Mexico" effect, increases during the postcrisis period. The increase in explanatory power is most marked for Latin America, and the least when the two regions are aggregated. Thus, while it would appear that contagion effects were not altogether absent in Asia, these took on a different modality from that observed in Latin America. Thus, two common factors—the first and second principal components[4]— accounted for 80 percent of the variance of highly volatile weekly stock market returns in the Latin American countries.

Table 3, which presents the correlations among total returns on Brady bonds, paints a similar picture, with correlations rising markedly in the wake of the Mexican crisis. As with equity returns, the correlations are highest among the Latin American countries and lowest for the Philippines, the only Asian country in our sample where Brady bonds exist. Indeed, these correlation patterns appear to be consistent with Doukas's (1989) findings that sovereign interest rate spreads for Argentina, Brazil, and Mexico had a contagious element and that "news" about the creditworthiness of a sovereign borrower affected the spreads charged to others.[5]

---

4. Associated, respectively, with US interest rates and the Mexican "Tequila effect."

5. Doukas used spreads on publicly guaranteed Euro-syndicated loans.

Table 3 Correlations among total returns on Brady bonds, January 1993–April 1995

	Argentina	Brazil	Mexico	Nigeria	Philippines	Venezuela
Heavy capital inflow period (January 1993–January 1994)						
Argentina	1.00					
Brazil	0.23	1.00				
Mexico	0.56	0.22	1.00			
Nigeria	0.41	0.11	0.58	1.00		
Philippines	0.29	0.22	0.32	0.33	1.00	
Venezuela	0.53	0.19	0.55	0.38	0.28	1.00
Moderate capital inflow period (February 1994–mid-December 1994)						
Argentina	1.00					
Brazil	0.57	1.00				
Mexico	0.80	0.47	1.00			
Nigeria	0.48	0.45	0.46	1.00		
Philippines	0.23	0.22	0.23	0.21	1.00	
Venezuela	0.56	0.43	0.55	0.41	0.23	1.00
Mexican crisis and its aftermath (mid-December 1994–April 1995)						
Argentina	1.00					
Brazil	0.80	1.00				
Mexico	0.89	0.73	1.00			
Nigeria	0.68	0.55	0.70	1.00		
Philippines	0.34	0.38	0.43	0.38	1.00	
Venezuela	0.83	0.80	0.78	0.80	0.42	1.00

Source: Salomon Brothers.

Foreign Shocks

We now turn our focus to Latin America to investigate whether there is evidence of more durable forms of regional spillover effects over and beyond those that may arise in moments of crises. It is noteworthy that the surge in capital inflows during 1990–94 in Latin America was not limited to a few large countries. Although the orders of magnitude of change in the capital account balance as a percentage of GDP were, on average, somewhat less for the smaller countries, these nonetheless amounted to a hefty 5 percent of GDP. In the next section, we first revisit the topic of the sensitivity of cross-border capital movements to international interest rates along the lines of Calvo and Reinhart (1995). Second, we test for "spillover" effects in the capital account from the large countries to the smaller ones.

External Variables

The larger country group includes Argentina, Brazil, Chile, Colombia, Mexico, and Peru, while the small country group refers to Costa Rica,

Ecuador, El Salvador, and Uruguay. Since several of these countries have no quarterly balance of payments statistics, we use annual data for the balance on the capital account over the period 1970–93. This is a much longer period than is examined in other studies, such as Calvo, Leiderman, and Reinhart (1993), Chuhan, Claessens, and Mamingi (1993), and Fernandez-Arias (1994). The main advantage of the longer sample is that it captures several important turning points, including the debt crisis.

As noted, the sensitivity of capital flows to external factors such as international interest rates, the business cycle in industrial countries, and rates of return on a variety of foreign assets has been examined in a number of recent papers (see Frankel and Okongwu 1996 for a summary of this literature). The dependent variables potentially affected by foreign variables include international reserves and real exchange rates, bond and equity flows, and total portfolio flows. The main conclusion to be derived is that external variables play a significant role, at least for the larger countries. The measure of capital flows used in this study, the balance on the capital account (including errors and omissions), is more comprehensive than the one used in previous studies. The capital account balance is expressed as a percent of GDP. The real international interest rate used refers to a US three-month Treasury bill rate adjusted by the rate of inflation as measured by the consumer price index—an *ex post* measure of real returns.

International Interest Rates

Given that the available capital account data are annual, thus limiting the number of observations per country to 24 (for a 24-year period), there are considerable efficiency gains from pooling the time-series data of the 11 countries in question. We thus focus on a panel of countries where the dependent variable is the balance on the capital account as a percentage of GDP, while in this simplest of settings the independent variable is a real short-term US interest rate.

To further examine the role of common shocks, and as an intermediate step in analyzing whether there are spillover effects from the larger countries to the smaller ones, we use (as before) factor analysis. This is the same approach as in Calvo, Leiderman, and Reinhart (1993) and is similar to the approach taken in Hardouvelis, La Porta, and Wizman (1994), who examine the extent of co-movement in emerging-country funds discounts.

For the capital account balance/GDP ratio, we constructed principal component indices for the entire 1970–93 period. Concerning the covariation of the balance in the capital account as a percentage of GDP, the share of the total variance explained by the first principal component is about 40 percent for both sets of countries (table 4). The main reason that the proportion of the total variation accounted for by the first common

Table 4   Composition of the "large" and "small" country indices

Country	Capital account balance, 1970–93[a]
Larger countries	
Argentina	0.34
Brazil	0.74
Chile	0.71
Colombia	0.19
Mexico	0.74
Peru	0.74
R^2	0.38
Small countries	
Costa Rica	0.31
Dominican Republic	0.68
Ecuador	0.74
El Salvador	0.06
Uruguay	0.77
R^2	0.42

a. Balance on the capital account includes errors and omissions and is expressed as a share of GDP. The weights attached to each country are the factor loadings associated with the first principal component. The R^2 gives the proportion of the variance of the original series explained by the constructed index (i.e., the first principal component).

Sources: IMF, Information Notice System, *International Financial Statistics, World Economic Outlook*, and the authors.

factor is lower than for other external variables, such as reserves or the real exchange rate, is the long length of the sample period (Calvo, Leiderman, and Reinhart 1993). The most visible example of idiosyncratic behavior during 1970–93 was El Salvador, where 10 years of civil war affected the performance of the capital account. Not surprisingly, its weight in the index is far lower than any of the other countries. Two less obvious examples where country-specific factors play a key role are Colombia and Costa Rica, where capital account developments were heavily influenced by sizable terms-of-trade shocks, such as the boom in coffee prices in the latter part of the 1970s.

To test for spillover effects, we next examine the dynamic interaction of capital account developments between the small and large countries. Here, we test the hypothesis that there are contagion or spillover effects from the large countries to the smaller ones. As noted earlier, mechanisms for spillovers may be in the form of foreign investors first selecting the larger countries as a place to invest in and, as confidence increases, diversifying the portfolio among a broader range of countries or due to highly integrated goods and capital markets (Hoffmaister and Végh 1994; Talvi 1994). We start with the basic relationship that links the balance in the capital account (as a percentage of GDP) for country i to the real rate of interest in the United States and introduce a "large-country index" of the capital account (described in table 4 and denoted by *LCI*), lagged one

Table 5   Latin America: foreign factors and contagion effects
(regression coefficients, number of observations = 264)

Estimation period	US real *ex post* short-term interest rate	Large-country index[a]	Small-country index[a]
1970–93			
Small countries	−0.66 (0.13)	0.90 (0.49)	
Large countries	−0.66 (0.13)		0.60 (0.44)
1979–93			
Small countries	−0.70 (0.15)	2.07 (0.57)	
Large countries	−0.70 (0.15)		0.51 (0.52)

a. The countries that make up the large-country panel are Argentina, Brazil, Chile, Colombia, Mexico, and Peru. The countries in the small-country panel are Costa Rica, Dominican Republic, Ecuador, El Salvador, and Uruguay. Standard errors are in parentheses.

period, as an explanatory variable for the small countries' capital account balances. Hence, in equation (1) below, the dummy variable, d, assumes the value of zero for the large countries and one for the small countries.

$$\frac{KA}{Y}_{it} = \alpha_i + \beta_1 r^*_t + \beta_2 [dLCI_{t-1}] + u_t \qquad (1)$$

The estimation strategy was not complicated by problems of nonstationarity in the variables of interest, since the standard (Dickey-Fuller and Augmented Dickey-Fuller) unit root tests reject the null hypothesis of a unit root.[6] The fixed-effects estimator was used. Hence, in equation (1), the intercept for country i, α_i, varies across countries, while slope coefficients, the βs, are constrained to be the same across countries or, in the case of β_2, for a subset of countries.

At the top of table 5 we report these estimates for 1970–93.[7] The results indicate that a 1 percent decrease in real interest rates in the United States would increase the capital account balance/GDP ratio by 0.77 percent. These results are consistent with the findings of earlier studies. Falling US

---

6. These test results are not reported here but are available upon request.

7. Calvo and Reinhart (1995) test the hypothesis that interest rate elasticities may differ for smaller and larger countries (since the composition of flows also differs for those two groups of countries) and find no significant difference.

interest rates are associated with rising capital inflows to Latin America. A rise in US interest rates (such as the one that occurred after February 1994) would, of course, tend to have the opposite effect.

Hence, it appears that US real interest rates play a significant role in determining the pattern of capital flows, irrespective of whether these are proxied by changes in international reserves and real exchange rates (Calvo, Leiderman, Reinhart 1993), bond and equality flows (Chuhan, Claessens, and Mamingi 1993), aggregate portfolio flows (Fernandez-Arias 1994), or directly measured as the balance on the capital account (this paper). These effects also appear to hold over a wide variation of samples.

To examine whether the trend toward more integrated capital markets has made capital flows more sensitive to changes in international interest rates, we reestimated equation (1) over a more recent subsample (1979–93). There was very little change in the interest rate coefficient, suggesting that if capital controls were in place (even in the earlier years), these were not binding (i.e., were being successfully circumvented).[8] It could also be that the distinction between short-term "hot" money and long-term flows (which was relatively more important in the 1970s) is more tenuous than widely believed, which is the Claessens, Dooley, and Warner (1993) hypothesis. That may also explain why there are no statistically significant differences in the interest sensitivity of the smaller and larger countries even though capital flows to the former are almost exclusively short term.

Table 5 highlights that the lagged large-country index of the capital account enters significantly and with a positive sign, suggesting positive spillover effects. Rising capital inflows to the larger countries would, other things being equal, tend to eventually stimulate increased capital inflows to the smaller countries in the region. This would suggest, for instance, that a successful stabilization program in one or more of the larger countries (which increases inflows to that country) may have positive externalities for some of its neighboring countries. Further, the results for the more recent sample (table 5) suggest that contagion effects may have increased, since the coefficient in the large-country index more than doubles.

To gauge whether there is potential spuriousness in these results, we also investigated whether capital account developments in the smaller economies systematically affected the capital accounts of the larger countries. Hence, the dummy variable, d^*, assumes a value of one for the large countries and a value of zero for the small ones. The small-country index is denoted in equation (2) by SCI.

$$\frac{KA}{Y}_{it} = \alpha_i + \beta_1 r^*_t + \beta_2 \left[d^* SCI_{t-1} \right] + u_t \tag{2}$$

Table 5 (third column) reports the results. Although the lagged aggre-

---

8. See Dooley (1988) and Mathieson and Rojas-Suárez (1993) on the issue of the "effectiveness" of capital controls.

**Table 6   Latin America: effect of changes in Mexico's capital
account balance as a percentage of GDP,
1970–93 and 1979–93** (regression coefficients,
number of observations = 264)

Estimation period	US real short-term interest rate	Mexico
1970–93	−0.14	0.98
	(0.03)	(0.02)
1979–93	−0.74	0.17
	(0.17)	(0.08)

a. Standard errors are in parentheses.

gate index enters with a positive sign, the coefficient is not statistically significant in either of the samples, suggesting a one-way causality from the larger countries to the smaller ones.

Given the prominent historical role played by Mexico in the region and the fact that it alone has accounted for over half of the recent capital inflows into Latin America, it is important to gauge whether developments in Mexico had systematic repercussions in the other countries in the region. To isolate spillover effects from Mexico, equation (1) was reestimated where the large-country index of the capital account was simply replaced by the balance on the capital account (as a percentage of GDP) in Mexico (lagged one year). The estimation results for the entire sample (table 6) show that capital account developments in Mexico had a significant and systematic impact on capital flows to the other countries in the region; the coefficient on the Mexican variable is nearly unity. During the more recent period (1979–93), however, the coefficient on capital flows to and from Mexico declines markedly to about 0.2 (although it remains significant). This implies that a change of 1 percent in the capital inflow/outflow-GDP ratio from Mexico is associated with a 0.2 percent change in the capital inflow/outflow-GDP ratios in the other Latin American countries. In this specification, capital flows appear to have become more interest-sensitive in the recent period.

Although the coefficients on the international interest rate and large-country index coefficient are relatively stable over different samples, irrespective of whether a dummy variable for the debt crisis years is included in the regression or not, the coefficient on the Mexican capital account shows considerable instability across samples (table 6), and its significance hinges on whether a debt crisis dummy is included or not.

Synthesis and Final Remarks

Several results emerge from the preceding analysis. First, there is evidence that the degree of co-movement in weekly equity and Brady bond returns in emerging Latin American markets increased in the wake of the Mexican crisis. Given the heterogeneity in macroeconomic fundamentals across countries, such co-movement could be interpreted as an indication of herd behavior on the part of investors. Alternatively, it could be ascribed to institutional practices in financial markets: an open-end emerging market mutual fund expecting an increasing amount of redemptions will sell off its holdings of equity in several emerging markets in an effort to raise cash. Given the illiquidity that characterizes most emerging markets, the sell-off by a few large investors will drive stock prices in other markets. Second, while the degree of co-movement following the crisis increased in both Asia and Latin America, regional patterns differed, suggesting contagion may be more regional than global.

Third, as in several earlier studies, our results suggest that international capital movements (in our case the balance on the capital account) are all significantly affected by swings in interest rates in the United States. Increases in US interest rates, other things being equal, are associated with capital outflows from Latin America. Small and large countries appear to be equally vulnerable in this respect. Fourth, in addition to external factors, the capital account balance of small countries appears to be affected by developments and trends in the larger countries in the region. These are more persistent forms of contagion than those typically associated with a crisis. Specifically, capital inflows/outflows into the larger countries in the region, other things being equal, tended to encourage increased inflows/outflows in the small countries. The opposite is not true. Capital account developments in the smaller countries appear to have had no systematic impact on the larger countries in the region. Our final conclusion is that whether capital account developments in Mexico alone have significant consequences for other countries in the region depends importantly on the sample period chosen. Hence, this suggests that what may be relevant for the smaller countries in Latin America are developments in a core set of countries in the region rather than developments in a single country.

Sound macroeconomic management is advisable, irrespective of whether the capital account is in deficit or surplus (or whether the country is large or small). However, the main policy implication that emerges from this analysis is that policymakers should be extra cautious in protecting the domestic financial system against the vagaries of international capital flows, as there are grounds to expect that, they respond to a contagious element that may be unrelated to domestic macroeconomic fundamentals.

References

Ades, Alberto, and Hak B. Chua. 1993. *Regional Instability and Economic Growth: Thy Neighbor's Curse.* Discussion Paper No. 704. New Haven, CT: Yale University Economic Growth Center.

Banco Central de la República Argentina. 1995. *Boletin Monetario y Financiero.* June/July.

Calomiris, Charles W., and Joseph R. Mason. 1994. *Contagion and Bank Failures during the Great Depression: The June 1932 Chicago Banking Panic.* NBER Working Paper No. 4934. Cambridge, MA: National Bureau of Economic Research.

Calvo, Guillermo, Leonardo Leiderman, and Carmen M. Reinhart. 1993. "Capital Inflows to Latin America: The Role of External Factors." *IMF Staff Papers* 40. Washington: International Monetary Fund.

Calvo, Guillermo, Leonardo Leiderman, and Carmen M. Reinhart. 1994. "The Capital Inflows Problem: Concepts and Issues." *Contemporary Economic Policy* 12 (July): 54–66.

Calvo, Guillermo, Leonardo Leiderman, and Carmen M. Reinhart. 1996. "Inflows of Capital to Developing Countries in the 1990s." *Journal of Economic Perspectives* 10: 123–39.

Calvo, Sara, and Carmen M. Reinhart. 1995. "Capital Flows to Latin America: Evidence from the Smaller Countries." World Bank. Photocopy.

Chua, Hak B. 1993. "Regional Spillovers and Economic Growth." Center Discussion Paper No. 700. New Haven, CT: Yale University Economic Growth Center.

Chuhan, Punam, Stijn Claessens, and Nlandu Mamingi. 1993 "Equity and Bond Flows to Latin America and Asia: The Role of External and Domestic Factors." World Bank. Photocopy (May).

Claessens, Stijn, Michael Dooley, and Andrew Warner. 1993. "Capital Inflows: Hot or Cool?" In Stijn Claessens and Sudarshan Gooptu, *Portfolio Investment in Developing Countries.* Washington: World Bank.

Dooley, Michael P. 1988. "Capital Flight: A Response to Differences in Financial Risks." *IMF Staff Papers* 35. Washington: International Monetary Fund.

Doukas, John. 1989. "Contagion Effect on Sovereign Interest Rate Spread." *Economic Letters* 29: 237–41.

Easterly, William, and Ross Levine. 1994. "Africa's Growth Tragedy." World Bank. Photocopy (November).

Eichengreen, Barry, Andrew K. Rose, Charles Wyplosz. 1994. *Speculative Attacks on Pegged Exchange Rates: An Empirical Exploration with Special Reference to the European Monetary System.* NBER Working Paper No. 4898. Cambridge, MA: National Bureau of Economic Research.

Fernandez-Arias, Eduardo. 1993. "The New Wave of Private Capital Inflows: Push or Pull?" World Bank. Photocopy (November).

Folkerts-Landau, David, Gary Schinasi, Marcel Cassard, Victor Ng, Carmen M. Reinhart, and Michael Spencer. 1995. "The Effect of Capital Inflows on the Domestic Financial Sectors in APEC Developing Countries." In Mohsin S. Khan and Carmen M. Reinhart, *Capital Flows in the APEC Region.* IMF Occasional Paper No. 122. Washington: International Monetary Fund.

Frankel, Jeffrey A., and Chudozie Okongwu. 1996. "Liberalized Portfolio Capital Inflows in Emerging Markets: Sterilization, Expectations, and the Incompleteness of Interest Rate Convergence." *International Journal of Finance and Economics* 1: 1–24.

Gay, Gerald D., Stephen G. Timme, Kenneth Yung. 1991. "Bank Failure and Contagion Effects: Evidence from Hong Kong." Journal of Financial Research 14: 153–65.

Hardouvelis, Gikas, Rafael La Porta, and Thierry Wizman. 1994. "What Moves the Discount on Country Equity Funds?" In Jeffrey A. Frankel, *The Internationalization of Equity Markets.* Chicago: University of Chicago Press for the NBER.

Hoffmaister, Alexander, and Carlos A. Végh. 1994. "Disinflation and the Recession-Now-Versus-Recession-Later Hypothesis: Evidence from Uruguay." International Monetary Fund. Washington (July).

International Monetary Fund (IMF). 1995. *International Capital Markets: Developments, Prospects, and Policy Issues.* Washington: International Monetary Fund.

Karafiath, Imre, Ross Mynatt, and Kenneth L. Smith. 1991. "The Brazilian Default Announcement and the Contagion Effect Hypothesis." *Journal of Banking and Finance* 15: 699–716.

Kaufman, George G. 1992. *Bank Contagion: Theory and Evidence.* Federal Reserve Bank of Chicago Working Papers Series WP-92-13. Chicago: Federal Reserve Bank.

Kramer, Charles, and R. Todd Smith. 1995. *Recent Turmoil in Emerging Markets and the Behavior of Country Fund Discounts: Renewing the Puzzle of Pricing of Closed-End Mutual Funds.* IMF Working Paper WP/95/68. Washington: International Monetary Fund.

Mathieson, Donald, and Liliana Rojas-Suárez. 1993. *Liberalization of The Capital Account: Experiences and Issues.* IMF Occasional Paper 103. Washington: International Monetary Fund.

Park, Sangkyun. 1991. "Bank Failure Contagion in Historical Perspective." *Journal of Monetary Economics* 28: 271–86.

Pindyck, Robert S., and Julio J. Rotemberg. 1990. "The Excess Co-Movement of Commodity Prices." *The Quarterly Journal of Economics* 100: 1173–89.

Pindyck, Robert S., and Julio J. Rotemberg. 1993. "The Co-movement of Stock Prices." *The Quarterly Journal of Economics* 108: 1073–104.

Smith, Bruce D. 1991. "Bank Panics, Suspensions, and Geography: Some Notes on the 'Contagion of Fear' in Banking." *Economic Inquiry* 23: 230–48.

Talvi, Ernesto. "Fiscal Policy and the Public Sector in Exchange Rate Based Stabilizations: Evidence from Uruguay's 1978 and 1991 Programs." The University of Chicago and the Central Bank of Uruguay. Photocopy (August).

Comment

Roque B. Fernández

Capital Flows and the Liquidity Shock

The liquidity shock that hit Argentina in the wake of the 1994 Mexican devaluation tested the country's new regulatory framework severely. From December 1994 to March 1995, approximately $7.4 billion left the Argentine banking system (some 16 percent of total deposits), central bank reserves fell from $17.6 billion to $12.8 billion over the same period (a drop of 27 percent), and M3 fell by some $8.4 billion (a 15 percent reduction).[1] Furthermore, Argentina's Convertibility Law, which has been crucial to price stability and economic growth, required the central bank to back 80 percent of the monetary base with foreign currency assets and limited the ability of the central bank to act as a lender of last resort.[2]

Given this environment, management of the shock was a delicate balancing act. On the one hand, sufficient liquidity was required in the system as a whole to prevent serious banking failures and maintain confidence in

Roque B. Fernández was governor at the Banco Central de la República Argentina until August 1996, when he became the economics minister.

1. M3 in Argentina is a broad measure of money demand that includes bank deposits in both pesos and dollars.

2. The 1991 Convertibility Law calls for 100 percent backing of the monetary base by liquid reserves. However, during the period covered, 20 percent of the reserves could be held in the form of Argentine bonds denominated in dollars.

the system. On the other hand, too much intervention would upset price signals, reducing the efficiency of private markets in resolving nonsystemic problems. It also would have increased the likelihood of substantial liabilities accruing to the central bank, thus jeopardizing convertibility. This balancing act—often referred to as "constructive ambiguity"—had to be carried out within the narrow limits of the Convertibility Law.

The liquidity shock had four distinct periods, which are discussed below.

Phase One: The First Portfolio Reallocation (December 1994–February 1995)

As an immediate consequence of the Mexican crisis, there was a marked change in the perception of both domestic and foreign investors regarding the risks in emerging markets generally. This sparked a switch from local currency assets to foreign currency assets, and in particular to dollar-denominated instruments. In Argentina, where bank accounts and transactions may be in either pesos or dollars, substitutability is extremely high. In January 1995 there was a marked dollarization of deposits within the banking system, indicating a higher perceived currency risk, and in February there was a general withdrawal from the system, largely of peso deposits (3.6 billion). Meanwhile, dollar deposits fell a mere $109 million.

The increased perception of peso risk also could be seen in interest rates. The 30-day annualized prime rate for peso loans rose from 11.5 to 18.5 percent. In contrast, the equivalent dollar rate rose by only 3 percentage points (from 9 percent to 12 percent), increasing the spread between the peso and the dollar by some 4 percentage points (from 2.5 percent to 6.5 percent).

The central bank adopted two strategies to compensate for the reduction in peso liquidity. First, it injected additional liquidity into the system by reducing reserve requirements, thereby moving some $2.4 billion of reserves into the system.[3] Second, the bank entered into a set of repurchase agreements which provided an additional $369 million. Third, the central bank lent roughly an additional $256 million to banks with liquidity difficulties using collateralized loans. Together, these measures compensated for some 93 percent of the reduction in liquidity due to the decline in deposits over the period.

The second strategy was to redistribute liquidity within the system. This was implemented through a mechanism by which the central bank purchased high-quality loans from banks that had liquidity problems with funds provided by an increase of 2 percent in reserve requirements

---

3. Reserve requirements were reduced in stages (28 December and 22 January) from 43 percent to 30 percent for sight deposits and from 3 percent to 1 percent for time deposits.

from all banks. In this fashion, roughly $700 million was redistributed within the system.[4]

These measures were highly successful in managing the aggregate liquidity problem. Indeed, credit actually rose over the period by some $304 million.[5]

Phase Two: Increase of Withdrawals from the Financial System (March 1995)

In the first half of March 1995, perceptions changed again. For a variety of reasons, there was a perception of a general policy risk in addition to the currency risk. This change in perception stemmed from a small number of well-publicized problems in the banking system and in the corporate sector, mixed with general public uncertainty as the presidential elections drew closer.

The total loss of deposits in March was $4.2 billion, and the fall in M3 accelerated. Interest rates in both pesos and dollars rose substantially. The annualized peso and dollar prime rates reached 45 percent and 30 percent, respectively, although they came down to 28 percent and 20 percent, respectively, by the end of the month.

Given this deepening of the crisis, the central bank again acted to relieve liquidity problems in the financial system. The central bank allowed private banks to count up to 50 percent of their holdings of cash in vault as part of the reserve requirement and, for those banks that purchased loans from institutions with liquidity problems, a system was introduced whereby some of the remaining cash in vault could also be used as official reserves. This policy injected up to a further $1 billion into the financial system. The central bank also stepped up the use of repos and collateralized loans, which together added a further $1.5 billion of liquidity.

These measures, however, compensated for only some 55 percent of the fall in deposits in March and banks were forced to cut credit. The fall amounted to roughly $1.4 billion because the banks found alternative sources to finance the loss of deposits (in particular from external credit lines). The fall in credit in this period was certainly significant, but it should be noted that the fall only represented roughly 3.5 percent of the total stock of credit at the time.

---

4. Previous to this system operated by the Banco Central, there was a completely private system which redistributed a smaller amount of liquidity.

5. The charter of the central bank was amended in February 1995 in order to allow the extended use of repos and collateralized loans but maintaining the limits imposed by the Convertibility Law. The new charter also gave the central bank greater flexibility in managing the assets of institutions that were suspended or closed.

Phase Three: Stabilization of the Withdrawals (end of March 1995–14 May 1995)

During this period M3 fell only by some $32 million; although total deposits fell (by $948 million), peso deposits actually rose. These changes can be explained by a further change in the perceptions of economic agents, and in particular by a reduction in perceived policy risk due to the agreements reached with the International Monetary Fund (IMF) and the flow of funds expected to Argentina from multilateral and other institutions as a result of that agreement. In addition to the IMF agreement, agreement was also reached with the World Bank and the Inter-American Development Bank to fund (together with the receipts of a government bond issue) two trust funds with total resources of roughly $4.5 billion. These trust funds were principally designed to aid in restructuring the private and public banking sectors. Nevertheless, perceptions of risk remained, in large part the consequence of the unresolved political situation. This explains the delay in the recovery of the monetary aggregates, as many waited before replenishing both their bank accounts and other investments within the country until the election result was known.

During this phase, as M3 remained more or less constant, the central bank did not need to further liberalize reserve requirements, and the use of other instruments to increase liquidity was fairly low. In total, a further net increase of $454 million from repos and collateralized loans occurred.

As an additional measure to increase confidence in the banking system, particularly for small depositors, the Argentinean Congress passed a law in April 1995 that created an obligatory, limited deposit insurance scheme to be funded completely by the private banking sector.

Phase Four: The Recovery (15 May 1995 to end of July 1995)

The fourth phase began after the presidential elections took place. With the IMF agreement already in place and with the knowledge that the existing administration would remain in office for another four years, there was a natural reduction in perceptions of policy risk. From mid-May until the end of July, investors increased their holdings of Argentine assets substantially. Total deposits increased by $3.4 billion, with holdings of peso and dollar deposits increasing $1.7 billion each. Total reserves of the central bank increased by $1.3 billion between the election and the end of July, and prime interest rates came down to roughly 14 percent for pesos and 12 percent for dollars.

Financial Structure and Shock Absorption

The policy stance of the Argentine central bank was largely to allow the private market to be the main disciplining device. Nevertheless, the bank stood ready to help institutions with genuine liquidity problems through the availability of repos and collateralized loans. In this fashion, the authorities were able to minimize the number of institutions that were forced to apply for suspension or closure while limiting the potential liabilities of the central bank. In part, this strategy was successful because different types of depositors behaved differently and depositors discriminated between different banks during the crisis. This implied that only a relatively small number of institutions with particular characteristics had severe problems. The different behavior of depositors, the different experience of banks, and the policy response during the crisis are briefly reviewed below.

An interesting feature of the Argentine banking industry is the rather high concentration of deposits by size of depositors. As of December 1994, for example, total certificates of deposit larger than $100,000 accounted for only 2.4 percent of the total number of certificates but represented some 52 percent of total deposits.

An analysis of data over the period of the crisis indicates that large depositors left the Argentine banking system first. Between the end of November and the end of December, for example, accounts larger than $1 million in pesos fell by some 21 percent, whereas accounts of between $100,000 and $1 million fell by about 10 percent; smaller accounts in pesos tended to fall even less. From January to March, the fall in peso deposits was more widespread across different size bands, although smaller deposits remained more stable. Between November and March the largest falls occurred in accounts between $0.75 million and $1 million (some 44 percent), while deposits of less then $5,000 fell by only about 6 percent.

Further, comparing time deposits with sight deposits, it was found that the latter were much more stable over the period. From 21 December to the end of July, sight deposits fell by only 9.2 percent whereas time deposits fell by more than 16 percent. Comparing the period from 21 December to end of July, sight deposits actually rose by some 4.1 percent, whereas time deposits remained down by 12 percent. This difference in behavior is even more marked when the data is analyzed by season. Typically, sight deposits in Argentina fall by more than time deposits during the summer.

Finally, a more systematic time-series analysis of deposit data over the period of convertibility confirms these findings. Taking account of the time series properties of the data (seasonality, serial correlations, etc.), it was found that the volatility of time deposits exceeded that of sight deposits.

Turning to the question of which banks were most affected, we have to consider the evolution of deposits by standard groupings: by ownership (foreign, domestic, private stock bank, mutual cooperative-bank, and public); by type (retail or wholesale); and by size. At the start of the crisis, deposits in public banks and foreign banks actually rose, while those in the other groups fell. Worst hit were the wholesale banks, followed by the small mutual banks. The wholesale banks were also the worst hit in March, losing on average more than 50 percent of their deposits. The large stock banks and the foreign banks fared best over this month. Although they lost deposits, the reductions were lower on average by only 7.8 percent and 0.1 percent, respectively, related to their levels in December. The remaining groups were more severely affected in March. Small stock banks and small mutual banks each lost roughly 32 percent of deposits, while the large mutual and public banks lost 19 percent and 12.5 percent, respectively, from the December figures.

Which characteristics explain which banks lost the most deposits? This question can be addressed through a regression analysis using cross-section data on the loss of deposits across banks and a set of explanatory variables. The results of such an analysis (not reported here) indicate that depositors did indeed discriminate, and that two variables stand out as important explanatory factors. The first is the liquidity of the bank as measured by its actual cash reserves (both in the vault of the central bank and at the bank itself). The second is the interest rate paid on deposits before the crisis began. The latter is interpreted here as a measure of the riskiness of banks' operations. The results indicate that banks that had lower liquidity and that paid higher rates on deposits lost more deposits than the average. Naturally, a regression analysis can only give a partial explanation. However, the preliminary conclusion is that depositors did discriminate quite forcefully during the crisis, punishing in particular the banks that did not maintain high reserve liquidity.[6]

The hard-hit wholesale banks typically had rather large holdings of Argentine government securities, a high concentration of deposits (by size of depositor), substantial income from commissions from trading activities, and a small deposit base relative to assets. Hence, they depended heavily on funding from the interbank market. These characteristics imply that these banks suffered the most from the fall in Argentine asset prices, the low volumes of trading in Argentine markets, high interest rates in the interbank market, and the flight of large depositors. The mutual banks had a relatively larger deposit base than the wholesale banks, but they tended to have weaker balance sheets, paid higher interest rates, and had lower liquidity relative to other banks in the system.

Bank data reveal that the mutual banks were the largest receivers of collateralized loans as a percentage of total deposits. In April 1995 the stock of collateralized loans to this group amounted to roughly 26 percent of their deposits.

6. The banks that were most severely affected also tended to be small. One explanation for this is that depositors simply ran to large banks as they were perceived to be, "too big to fail." The regression analysis however tends to support the importance of liquidity and

Restructuring the Financial Sector

The restructuring of the Argentine banking sector had already begun before the Mexican crisis. Indeed, the central bank through the enforcement of international standards of prudential regulation, and in particular through the implementation of Basel-style capital requirements, was already forcing many banks to consider restructuring as a means to provide further capital. To many observers, however, the restructuring process appeared to be moving at a relatively slow pace. This is perhaps largely attributable to the ownership structure of Argentine banks—in particular, the high number of owner-managed banks.

The liquidity shock following the Mexican devaluation sharply accelerated the restructuring process. Some 53 institutions merged between December 1994 and July 1995. Although these mergers tended to be concentrated in relatively small institutions, the merged institutions held some 15 percent of the total deposits and 13 percent of the total assets of the system. In addition, ten institutions were closed and three had their operations suspended.

The Money and Banking Multiplier

Restructuring alone is not enough to assure a sound financial system. The destabilizing effects of capital flows to emerging economies have frequently been mentioned as a serious threat to stability. Chile and Mexico restricted capital inflows and sterilization policies with different degrees of success. Argentina did not explicitly restrict capital inflows, but, as described above, had to implement several strategic decisions.

Independently of the policy stance taken by different countries, the problem of capital inflows reflects the conventional wisdom of the money and banking multiplier. A system with a fractional reserve requirement would never have enough liquid reserves to withstand massive capital outflows. A fixed exchange rate or convertibility by limiting the lender of last resort capability of the central bank would convert a balance of payments problem to a banking problem.

Powerful and simple, the money and banking multiplier is perhaps the most widely used instrument for monetary targeting and financial programming. In an open economy, simple multiplier effects must be carefully inspected to understand the role of capital flows. In what follows, we will work out a backward determination of the money multiplier—going from monetary aggregates to the monetary base—to deal with the exogeneity of foreign investors' views of finances in emerging economies.

---

interest rate variables rather than size (although there are naturally correlations between the two).

From the definitions of money *(M)* and monetary base *(B)* in terms of currency *(C)*, deposits *(D)*, and reserve requirements *(R)*, we obtain a linear system with five unknowns in two equations:

$$M + C + D \tag{1}$$

$$B = C + R \tag{2}$$

The closed economy "multiplier" results from solving the system under the assumption that B is exogenous, and adding the equations $C = c \cdot D$, and $R = r \cdot D$, where c is a constant and r is a binding legal reserve requirement. The solution is represented by $M = m \cdot B$, where $m = [(l+c)/(c+r)]$.

A Tequila effect for an open emerging economy (with fixed exchange rates) experiencing capital outflows implies that M is determined by foreign investor confidence and that the multiplier determines the endogenous value of the monetary base B.

To illustrate the financial vulnerability from a Tequila effect, subtract the equation (2) from equation (1) to obtain

$$M - B = D - R = L$$

where L represents the loanable capacity generated by deposits. As m 1, a change in foreign investors' mood, that leads to capital outflows and to lower M implies a credit contraction. That is, the comparative statics of the system give $dL/dM = (m - 1)/m > 0$. As loans cannot be immediately recalled, increased capital outflows, by reducing M, produce a banking crisis.

This simple framework can be used to illustrate some policy recommendations. For example, "high reserve requirements" help to reduce financial vulnerability because as $r \to 1$, $m \to 1$ and $dL/dM \to 0$.

Simple and powerful as it is, the multiplier can be very misleading if used to argue that capital outflows—in general—will produce a banking crisis. As emphasized in Fernández and Guidotti (1995), reserve requirements and capital requirements jointly determine the structure of the financial system. Under some conditions explicitly considered in standard prudential banking regulation, capital flows could be largely irrelevant to the stability of the banking system.

Capital requirements mandate a minimum amount of capital (K) as a proportion k of risky assets A (this is a Basel constraint of the form, $K > = k \cdot A$). The balance sheet of the consolidated commercial banking system is

$$A + R = D + K$$

Taking K as a predetermined variable (on the basis that commercial banks are not free to change it at will without the previous consent of the central bank), assuming zero legal reserve requirements (that is, banks are free to determine the "technical" level for R), and assuming that the Basel constraint holds as strict equality, then

$$D - R = L = K\,[(l - k)/k].$$

This means that the loanable capacity out of deposits is independent of M (that is $dL/dM = 0$), implying that capital outflows *cannot* produce a banking crisis if the Basel Constraint (not legal reserve requirements) dominates the expansion and contraction dynamics of banks. As excess supply of international short-run capital can not be immediately converted into "deposits," the capital of commercial banks will first have to increase. This takes time, insulating the domestic system from externally generated short-term financial volatility.

The conclusion of this section should not be taken to imply that capital flows must be ignored. Rather, the problems associated with volatile capital flows can hardly be considered different from the old problems of maturity transformation and bank runs in economies with flexible exchange rates. Adequate regulation, effective supervision, and a central bank with a limited role of liquidity assistance to financial institutions are powerful instruments to manage the volatility of capital flows. Of course, other policies are also feasible, and recent experience may be useful in evaluating the welfare implications of alternative strategies.

References

Fernández, Roque, and Pablo Guidotti. 1995. *Regulating the Banking Industry in Transition Economies: Exploring Interactions between Capital and Reserve Requirements.* Banco Central de la República Argentina.

Powell, Andrew. 1995. Memorandum on the Argentina Financial Crisis. Banco Central de la República Argentina. Unpublished.

Comment

Frederic S. Mishkin

The paper by Calvo and Reinhart provides evidence on contagion effects involving capital flows in the larger and smaller countries of Latin America. To understand their research, it is important to distinguish between two categories of contagion effects. The first is the effect of capital flows in larger countries, such as Mexico, on other countries during normal times. This type of contagion bears directly on the capital inflow problem that has spawned a large literature. The second type occurs during a crisis episode when capital flows shift dramatically, as is the case of Mexico in 1994.

These two types of contagion effects are likely to have entirely different dynamics. During a crisis period, the dynamics of contagion are inherently short run; during normal periods they will be more influenced by longer-run factors. As an example of how contagion effects operate very differently during crisis and noncrisis episodes, consider the co-movement of stock prices across countries. In the stock market crash of 1987, the contagion effects between stock markets in different countries were rapid and huge. Although there are spillovers between stock prices in national markets during normal times (so that there is some positive co-movement), the correlation of stock price movements has been much lower and less immediate than during the 1987 crisis period.

In order to discuss contagion during financial crises, we must first have an understanding of what a financial crisis is. Modern theories indicate

Frederic S. Mishkin is executive vice president and director of research of the Federal Reserve Bank of New York and A. Barton Hepburn Professor of Economics of the Graduate School of Business, Columbia University.

that a financial crisis is a disruption of information flows that prevents financial markets from doing their job, which is channelling funds to the most productive investment opportunities.[1]

How does contagion occur during a financial crisis? A shock occurs in one market which puts market participants in an entirely new environment where they cannot figure out how the financial system will operate. When this happens in one market, it may make it unclear what will happen in other markets. As a result, market participants have greater difficulties in screening out good from bad borrowers or in monitoring and enforcing financial contracts to prevent excessive risk taking. Given the increased informational problems, market participants may begin to pull back in other markets in addition to the one in which the original shock occurred. As this discussion suggests, the contagion during a crisis is very different from the spillovers that occur between markets in normal periods. The information disruption that occurs during a crisis means that the contagion will necessarily occur very quickly and involve short-run dynamics.

The Calvo-Reinhart paper does not focus on contagion during a financial crisis but rather is more concerned with the other category of contagion, that occurring during normal times. The empirical analysis in the paper makes use of regression and factor analysis procedures that focus only on longer run dynamics. As a result, their findings that capital flows move together in small and large Latin American countries cannot tell us much about contagion during a crisis period, when the dynamics are inherently short-run.

Although the methodology of the Calvo-Reinhart paper is not suited to analyzing contagion during crisis periods, there is one result in the paper that does have relevance to what happens during a capital flow crisis. The paper finds that changes in US monetary policy by way of changes in short-term interest rates have important effects on capital flows in emerging markets. Specifically, it finds that when the Federal Reserve tightens monetary policy by increasing short-term real interest rates, this results in a decrease in capital inflows into Latin American countries. This paper adds to the earlier literature on this subject because it uses a longer sample (24 years) with a new set of countries and finds a very strong US interest rate effect on Latin American capital flows.

Before I go on to discuss the importance of this result to our understanding of crisis episodes, I would like to make one technical comment. As it currently stands, there is a problem with the regression procedure used to generate the finding of strong US interest rate effects on capital flows. What is relevant to capital flows is the *expected* real return on US Treasury bills—that is, the *ex ante* real interest rate—and not the actual realized

---

1. For a further discussion of this definition of financial crisis, see Mishkin (1994).

return, the *ex post* rate. However, capital flows are regressed in the Calvo-Reinhart paper on the *ex post* real interest rate, not on the *ex ante* real interest rate as is appropriate.

The problem with the regression can be easily fixed by using standard instrumental variable techniques, which in effect replace the *ex post* rate with the *ex ante* rate by instrumenting out the *ex post* rate using information on past inflation and nominal interest rates. Until the appropriate technique is used, we have to remain somewhat cautious about the result on US interest rate effects on capital flows. However, my own guess about the relationship between *ex post* and *ex ante* real interest rates in the United States is that the paper's finding on the effects of US interest rates will hold up.

The conclusion that US monetary policy has important effects on Latin American capital flows is important because it suggests that a tightening of US monetary policy can decrease capital flows into an emerging market economy, which then makes a capital flow crisis more likely. Does this mean that the Federal Reserve should not tighten policy when domestic conditions warrant it in order to avoid capital flow crises like the one in Mexico? The answer is no. Just as business cycle swings are a fact of life in developed capitalist economies, swings in US interest rates which affect capital flows to a developing country are a fact of life for emerging market economies. They must accept this risk as an inherent part of the environment and adopt policies that prevent financial crises from developing despite fluctuations in capital flows that may arise from foreign interest rate fluctuations.

An excellent example that can help illustrate the above point comes from the history of what was once an emerging market country, the United States. During the nineteenth and early twentieth centuries, the United States was among the most prone to financial crises of the countries tied to the international financial system. One of the important precipitating forces behind these crises was increases in interest rates originating in London capital markets. Was British monetary or fiscal policy the source of the problems in the US financial system? The answer is no. The primary source was a poorly structured banking system which was highly fragmented and which had no central bank to act as a lender of last resort. Indeed, because of the peculiarities of its financial system, the United States experienced a major financial crisis every 20 years or so. This did not occur in other countries despite British interest rate shocks.

What this lesson from history tells us is that emerging market countries must set up an institutional structure for their financial system that protects them from such crises. Such a structure has three primary elements: (1) a regulatory structure that prevents excessive risk-taking on the part of financial institutions, (2) sufficient transparency in monetary and fiscal policy institutions, and (3) appropriate incentives for policymakers to make them accountable to the public they serve, while ensuring that they focus on long-term rather than short-term considerations driven by the political process. Only with attention to these elements will emerging market countries be able to derive the benefits of capital inflows while avoiding potentially disastrous consequences from a capital flows crisis.

References

Mishkin, Frederic S. 1994. "Preventing Financial Crises: An International Perspective." *Manchester School* 62: 1–40.

Comment

Philip P. Turner

This is an interesting and useful paper both because of the statistical evidence it presents about the determinants of capital flows and because of its interesting and important reflections about the sensitivity of small economies to external influences, notably financial forces. Let me consider these two dimensions in turn.

The main statistical findings are two. First, the findings of Calvo and others that capital inflows into Latin America have been inversely related to real short-term interest rates in the United States carries over to five smaller Latin American economies. Moreover, the degree of sensitivity is the same in the small as in the larger economies. According to table 5, the coefficient of 0.66 is the same for both samples. Seeing results as good as these, I suspected that the regressions might have been dominated by the extreme observations associated with the 1982 debt crisis, when abnormally high US interest rates caused a dearth of foreign capital for most of Latin America. But my experiments with interactive dummy variables completely failed to confirm this. I therefore concluded that this is a rather robust, long-standing relationship.

The magnitude of this interest rate effect is quite large. The implication is that a one percentage point rise in real interest rates in the United States will reduce capital inflows into Latin America by the equivalent of 0.66 percent of their GDP.

How does this compare with the effect of higher real interest rates in the United States itself? The answer depends a great deal on the model

Philip P. Turner is submanager at the Bank for International Settlements (BIS), Basel.

of the economy and on the assumptions made. Nevertheless, the results of some simulations recently carried out by Gerlach and Smets (1995) provide an interesting point of comparison. They found that a one percentage point increase in real short-term interest rates in the United States maintained over eight quarters had, as its peak effect, a 1.2 percent reduction in US GDP. Now the Calvo-Reinhart figure—the 0.66 percent of GNP—is just the size of the drop in capital inflows. It does not include any multiplier effects, for example, the effects of more restrictive policies made necessary by lower inflows, etc. When these effects are taken into account, it may mean that the effect of higher US real interest rates may be as large in Latin America as it is in the United States.

The second statistical finding is that swings in aggregate capital flows in the large countries provided an additional explanation for capital inflows into small countries in the following year. But the reverse was not true. This is the evidence for contagion from big to small, but not the other way. The statistical support for this piece of evidence is rather less robust than for the finding about the relation between inflows and US interest rates. As can be seen from table 4 of the paper, the coefficient of the large-country index is rather unstable with respect to the period of estimation. It goes from 0.90 in the period 1970–93 to 2.07 in the period 1979–93. It is, of course, possible that contagion effects may have increased over time as the authors suggest, but one would need to explain why. In particular, why would contagion effects from other Latin American economies have increased while the effects of US interest rates have not altered? It is obviously not because of generalized capital account liberalization.

I am not sure how easy it is to model contagion in financial markets. As Frederic Mishkin pointed out, contagion effects can be quite different in crisis situations than they are in normal times. Another important difficulty is that even the direction of influence may not be very stable over time. The experience of the Mexican crisis was that initial contagion effects were adverse for all the emerging markets in Asia and in Latin America, and in the more balanced Latin American economies as well. But over time, this initial reaction gave way to greater discrimination among different countries. This is not picked up by the studies of simultaneous co-movement analyzed by the authors. The markets began to look more closely at such things as current account deficits, the composition of capital flows, the investment-intensity of domestic demand and so on. Indeed, a cottage industry has grown up among the banks and the security houses ranking the main emerging market economies according to their "soundness." There are signs (e.g., from equity market indices, exchange rates, and interest rates) that the Mexican crisis and the drying up of flows to Mexico actually *increased* the flow of capital to some countries. Hence, initial contagion effects were at first sympathetic (all suffered a

Table 1 International influences: "small" versus "large" countries, 1990–94 (percentages)

	Six "large" countries	Four "small" countries
Net capital inflows as percent of GNP (A)	3.3	2.0
Trade[a] as percent of GNP (B)	13.4	30.7
Net capital inflows as percent of trade (A/B)	24.6	6.5
Deposits with BIS reporting banks as percent of GNP	7.0	24.7

a. Average of exports and imports of goods and services.

Sources: IMF/World Bank statistics; BIS.

decline in inflows), but then became antipathetic/contrary. Because the sign of the short-term effect can differ from that of the medium-term, modeling contagion is tricky. Nevertheless, the attempt in this paper is intriguing and suggestive.

I found the reflective dimension of the paper as intriguing as the statistical. One important observation that recurs in this paper is that small size may itself be an impediment to the development of domestic financial markets that can attract significant foreign interest. The markets may be simply too small, too illiquid, for foreign investors to bother about. The paper points out that, measured in relation to GNP, net inflows in the 1990s in the small countries have been proportionally smaller than into the larger countries—2.0 percent compared with 3.3 percent of GNP.

I think this might be a more significant difference than appears at first sight. It is important to bear in mind that the smaller countries are far more dependent on international trade. Trade averages about 30 percent of GNP for the small countries compared with less than 15 percent for the large countries. Hence, less foreign capital inflow, but more foreign trade. For instance, net inflows in 1990–94 for the small countries in Calvo and Reinhart's sample were the equivalent of only 6 percent of average trade flows. For the large countries, the figure is 25 percent (see calculations in my table 1). I think this is a significant difference. It may mean that foreign exchange flows related to trade dominate flows related to capital movements. If so, the real exchange rate may tend to be more stable because dependence on trade ties down the rate.

Or it may mean that some countries are too small to have their own currencies. The description of extensive dollarization in this paper is interesting, and it prompted me to take a look at BIS international banking data. The Bank for International Settlements (BIS) collects extensive data on banking positions vis-à-vis each and every country, but such data do not include deposits held in other Latin American countries. I discovered that residents in the small countries do indeed have a greater propensity to hold foreign bank accounts than do residents in the larger countries. In the small countries discussed in this paper, for example, residents' deposits with BIS reporting banks amount to about 25 percent of GNP. For the larger countries, the figure is only 7 percent.

The suggestion in the paper that dollarization can reduce a small country's vulnerability to financial crises is also an interesting one and would be worth discussing further. It could be that widespread dollar-denomination in the real economy can reduce the risks of dollar-denominated bank borrowing. After all, this was an important aspect of the difficulties of the Mexican financial system after the crisis. But it still leaves unresolved the question of how to adjust to a large terms-of-trade change if, for example, the dollar price of commodity exports falls. Commodity exporting countries are vulnerable to this and have to find ways of adjusting to it. Also, it may be dangerous to dollarize at an exchange rate that is misaligned. It may be particularly hard to judge this when a country is in the throes of a major structural adjustment.

References

Gerlach, Stefan, and Frank Smets. 1995. *The Monetary Transmission Mechanism: Evidence from the G-7 Countries.* Working Paper No. 26. Basel: Bank for International Settlements.

6

Policy Responses to Surges in Capital Inflows: Issues and Lessons

Peter J. Montiel

The resurgence of capital inflows to developing countries during the early 1990s had attracted a substantial amount of interest from economists even before the outbreak of the Mexican crisis in December 1994. Although the relaxation of external borrowing constraints was a desirable development for many countries, the new influx of capital nevertheless had posed stabilization problems in the forms of potential acceleration of inflation and loss of competitiveness. In principle, a variety of macroeconomic policy instruments are available to address such problems, but the benefits and costs associated with particular instruments (or combinations of instruments) under specific circumstances have not always been clear, and informed observers have differed in their policy prescriptions. It has gradually become evident that these issues have not gone away in the aftermath of the Mexican crisis. Countries that received substantial capital inflows in recent years are likely to continue to do so, albeit at varying rates depending on domestic and international circumstances, and the inflow phenomenon is likely to be extended geographically as market-oriented economic reform continues to spread among developing countries.

This paper examines the range of policies that have been applied by recipient countries in response to capital inflows and attempts to determine whether useful lessons about the benefits and costs of alternative

Peter J. Montiel is professor of economics, Williams College, Willliamstown, Massachusetts, and has held senior research posts at the World Bank and the International Monetary Fund (IMF).

policy responses can be gleaned from this experience. The objective is to identify the menu of policies available to address the problems posed by the receipt of capital inflows, describe the analytical issues that arise from the application of particular policies, and evaluate what can be learned about these issues on the basis of cross-country experience. There are two ways to approach this task. The first is to focus on individual policies and examine what can be learned about each such policy on the basis of country experience. The second is to identify a set of countries that have managed the arrival of capital inflows successfully and attempt to explain this outcome on the basis of their policy strategies. Both approaches are adopted in this paper.[1]

The next section of this paper presents an analytical framework for organizing the policy discussion and describes the policy menu available to the recipient countries within that framework. The issues that arise in evaluating the desirability of each of the individual policies in the menu are also taken up in this section. The following section describes the choices made from the general policy menu by a sample of 14 countries that have received substantial capital inflows in recent years. The lessons emerging from that experience are summarized in the fourth section, while the fifth section adopts the alternative approach, examining the links between successful macroeconomic performance and the general policy mix. The concluding section derives some implications from the analysis of policy strategies.

The Policy Menu

By definition, a policy response represents a departure from a preexisting policy stance. In most of the developing countries that have received substantial capital inflows, it would be fair to describe the monetary component as one in which the authorities defended a predetermined nominal exchange rate while pursuing a target for some monetary aggregate—typically either the net domestic assets of the central bank or the money stock, somehow defined.[2] In this policy context, the motivation for the formulation of a new policy response to capital inflows is the fear that such flows could simultaneously prove inflationary and harmful to

---

1. The paper focuses on stabilization issues, and the policies considered are short-run macroeconomic stabilization policies. The issues of how to design macroeconomic institutions to cope with a world of open capital markets and volatile capital movements, as well as the formulation of microeconomic policies, especially concerning the financial system, are beyond the scope of the paper.

2. The assertion that the authorities pursued both exchange rate and money stock targets obviously assumes that capital mobility was (or was perceived to be) less than perfect. For evidence on the relevance of this assumption for a large group of developing countries, see Montiel (1994).

domestic competitiveness. If domestic interest-bearing assets are perfect substitutes, the macroeconomic mechanism through which such outcomes would result from capital inflows would be an expansion of the monetary base resulting from central bank intervention to sustain the exchange rate.[3] Base expansion would fuel growth in broader monetary aggregates, expanding aggregate demand and putting pressure on domestic prices. In turn, given the nominal exchange rate target, rising prices would translate into an appreciation of the real exchange rate.

Since policy intervention can potentially be directed at various links in this chain, it is useful to classify policy responses according to where along the chain of transmission the intervention occurs. Accordingly, policy interventions are classified as follows:

- Policies designed to restrict the net inflow of capital, either by restricting gross inflows or promoting gross outflows. Such policies would include a variety of capital controls, a widening of exchange rate bands to increase uncertainty, and the elimination of a variety of restrictions on capital outflows.

- Policies that seek to restrict the net foreign exchange inflow (reserve accumulation) by encouraging a current account offset to a capital account surplus. Trade liberalization and nominal exchange rate appreciation would both have this effect. The latter could avoid any foreign exchange accumulation whatsoever.

- Policies that accept the reserve accumulation associated with a balance of payments surplus but attempt to ameliorate its effects on the monetary base. These include various forms of sterilized intervention as well as attempts to limit recourse to the central bank's discount window.

- Policies that accept an increase in the base but attempt to restrain its effects on broader monetary aggregates. Increases in reserve requirements and quantitative credit restrictions are examples of such policies.

- Policies that accept a monetary expansion but attempt to offset expansionary effects on aggregate demand that could result in inflation or real exchange rate appreciation. These essentials consist of tight fiscal policies, which could be implemented in a variety of ways.

The choice of policies from this menu of options will depend, of course, on the benefits and costs of individual policies as perceived by the authorities. The next section examines their benefits and costs from an analytical perspective. In each case, the issues concern both feasibility and optimality.

---

3. If domestic financial assets are imperfect substitutes, the transmission mechanism can be more complex. I consider this case in the subsequent discussion of sterilized intervention.

Restrictions on Gross Inflows

The feasibility of direct intervention in capital inflows has long been questioned on grounds that controls can be easily evaded. The feasibility of controls is likely to vary with the type of control imposed, both across countries and over time.[4]

Indirect evidence on the efficacy of controls is provided by tests of financial integration when controls are known to be in place. If financial integration is high despite the presence of controls, the presumption is that the controls are ineffective. More directly, variations in the intensity of controls, either across countries or over time, can be evaluated as determinants of variations in the measured degree of financial integration. If variations in intensity are not associated with variations in integration, then the presence of controls may not have mattered.

Prior to the recent increase in inflows, the evidence on this issue was mixed. Haque and Montiel (1990), for example, found a high degree of capital mobility in several developing countries during a period when those countries maintained severe restrictions on capital movements, providing indirect evidence that the controls were ineffective. On the other hand, episodic evidence from individual countries—for example, during the time of the Southern Cone policy experiments—suggests that restrictions on foreign borrowing may indeed have been effective, since substantial capital inflows have occasionally followed their removal. Direct regression-based tests of changes in financial integration in response to changes in capital controls dominate such episodic evidence because they satisfy *ceteris paribus* requirements. Using such tests, Calvo and Reinhart (chapter 5) found that, in contrast to the episodic experience, the influence of foreign interest rates on capital movements to 10 Latin American countries was the same across periods with different capital-control regimes.

If capital controls can be made effective, a case for imposing them can be made on either first- or second-best policy grounds. Both cases would have to rely on a preexisting distortion that results in a level of foreign borrowing that is excessive from a welfare point of view. The traditional first-best case arises when the act of foreign borrowing itself creates externalities. If the costs of default on an international loan contract are shared by domestic agents other than the borrowing agent, then individual acts of foreign borrowing will have negative external effects in the domestic economy. Individual agents will tend to overborrow. In that case, a tax

---

4. The incentive to evade depends on differences between foreign and domestic rates of return, and thus on financial policies abroad and at home. The feasibility of evasion, in turn, depends on the structure of trade (which affects the scope for under- and overinvoicing), on the structure of the domestic financial system (which affects the possibility of evasion by altering the channels of financial intermediation), and on the efficacy of policing mechanisms. Such factors explain why the efficacy of controls is likely to differ across countries and over time.

on foreign borrowing will cause each agent to internalize the costs imposed on others, thus making it a first-best policy intervention.

A second-best case emerges when the negative welfare consequences of a preexisting distortion that cannot be removed are magnified by external borrowing. This situation can arise in the context of either static or dynamic distortions in the domestic economy. Static distortions may exist either in the domestic real economy or in the financial system. Their effect may be to cause borrowed resources to be allocated in socially unproductive ways. Although the first-best solution would be to remove the distortion, a second-best option may be to limit foreign borrowing. Dynamic distortions arise when intertemporal relative prices are distorted in such as way as to encourage excessive borrowing—that is, when the real cost of external funds is perceived by private agents to be lower than the "true" value perceived by policymakers. This is the effect of "incredible" stabilization measures and trade reforms, in which the distortion arises from expectations of policy reversal. Although the first-best solution involves the establishment of credibility, in practice this may be impossible to achieve, leaving direct intervention in external borrowing as a second-best option. A second type of dynamic distortion arises if "bubble" or "bandwagon" effects are important in international lending. From the perspective of agents in the borrowing economy, this phenomenom takes the form of a temporarily low cost of external funds. A case for capital controls, however, arises only if the temporary nature of the phenomenon is understood by policymakers but not by private agents. Beyond this, a second-best case for direct intervention can be made on macroeconomic grounds if the costs of distortions introduced by capital controls are less than the costs of applying other stabilization policies.

Encouragement of Gross Outflows

In this case as well, the relevant issues are efficacy and optimality, but the issues arise in a somewhat different way. First, in parallel with the case of inflow restrictions, restrictions on outflows may not be effective. Evidence on this was also mixed prior to the recent inflow episode. Mathieson and Rojas-Suárez (1993), for example, addressed the question directly by testing whether capital flight responded to economic fundamentals in the same manner in countries with and without strong restrictions on capital outflows. They found that while fundamentals continued to influence capital outflows even in the presence of controls, responses to fiscal imbalances were slower, and those to default risk were weaker, in countries with strong capital controls.

Even if outflow restrictions are effective, however, their removal may not have the desired effect of reducing net inflows because the very act of removing such restrictions may attract additional inflows. Two arguments have been adduced to suggest how this could happen. Laban and Larrain (1993) have pointed out that the presence of effective controls on outflows renders inflows irreversible. If future policies affecting the return on loans to domestic agents are uncertain, the option to keep funds abroad while the uncertainty is resolved becomes valuable, and foreign creditors may thus refrain from lending. Removing the outflow restrictions eliminates the irreversibility and thus increases the relative return on domestic lending by eliminating the value of the option to wait. Alternatively, Bartolini and Drazen (1995) have argued that because controls on outflows are often maintained for fiscal reasons (e.g., to facilitate the collection of financial repression taxes), their removal is interpreted by foreign investors as a signal that future capital taxation is less likely, thereby inducing capital inflows. From the standpoint of optimality, a substantial literature on the sequencing of economic liberalization during the 1980s concluded that liberalizing capital outflows should be one of the last steps in economic liberalization, essentially on fiscal grounds.[5]

Trade Liberalization

From a macroeconomic perspective, trade liberalization lowers the domestic currency price of importables directly, and may lower the price on nontradeables indirectly (through a substitution effect). To the extent that liberalization induces a larger trade deficit than would otherwise occur, it absorbs some of the foreign exchange generated by the capital inflow, easing monetary pressures as well. The most controversial issue that arises with respect to trade liberalization as a means to restrict the net inflow of foreign exchange concerns efficacy. Because the trade balance (including services) is the difference between domestic saving and investment, the effect of trade liberalization on the trade balance depends on how saving and investment are affected. Both theory and evidence suggest that the effects of trade liberalization on the trade balance are ambiguous, depending on a host of structural characteristics in the domestic economy as well as on the nature of the liberalization program. The former include the importance of nontraded goods, sectoral factor intensities, the nature of accompanying fiscal policies, and the extent of labor market rigidities. The latter include the incidence of tariffs (whether they fall on intermediate

---

5. The argument was that as long as domestic fiscal stability is not achieved, reliance on revenues from financial repression will be necessary. Financial openness, by providing domestic asset holders an alternative to the domestic financial system, reduces the revenues that can be collected from financial repression and thus requires a higher rate of inflation to finance a given fiscal deficit. The distortions introduced by a higher rate of inflation may be more costly than those associated with controls on capital outflows (McKinnon and Mathieson 1981).

or final goods) and their projected future paths.[6] Empirically, the experience of liberalizing countries—as summarized, for example, in Thomas et al. (1990)—suggests that larger trade deficits have not necessarily followed the liberalization of commercial policy.

Exchange Rate Flexibility

The alternative (to liberalization) of inducing a current account offset to capital inflows through nominal exchange rate flexibility raises issues that concern optimality rather than efficacy. The potentially inflationary implications of capital inflows can be avoided by refraining from intervention in the foreign exchange market. Permitting a (temporary) appreciation of the nominal exchange rate in response to a favorable external interest rate shock (by restricting the scale of foreign exchange intervention) will dampen and possibly reverse the expansionary effect of the foreign shock on domestic aggregate demand by appreciating the real exchange rate. A capital inflow arising from a reduction in external interest rates becomes a *deflationary* shock under fully flexible exchange rates. This outcome will be desirable if domestic macroeconomic conditions are such that policymakers seek to avoid stimulating aggregate demand. Thus, to the extent that capital inflows are permitted to materialize, the desirability of foreign exchange intervention depends in part on the requirements for macroeconomic stability.

The trade-off, however, concerns the implications for domestic resource allocation. If the authorities allow the nominal exchange rate to appreciate in response to capital inflows, the profitability of the traded goods sector will obviously be affected adversely. Aside from possible political economy considerations, policymakers may have two reasons to be concerned with this outcome. First, if the capital inflow is believed to be temporary, an appreciation of the official exchange rate may tend to aggravate the effects of any previously existing domestic distortions biasing domestic resource allocation away from the traded goods sector (and cause the "shadow" value of foreign exchange to exceed its official value).[7] Second, with temporary capital inflows, the associated real exchange rate appreciation will also be temporary, and any costly resource reallocations induced by changes in relative sectoral profitability between the traded and nontraded goods sectors will have to be reversed later, entailing a deadweight loss to society.

---

6. The arguments are reviewed by Ostry (1991).

7. If the inflow is "permanent," the associated real appreciation may be matched by an appreciation of the equilibrium real exchange rate, and thus the wedge between the "shadow" exchange rate and its official value would increase only in association with a temporary overshooting of the equilibrium rate by the actual one.

However, the costs of resource reallocation actually weaken the argument for pegging the nominal exchange rate in the face of a temporary capital inflow. The reason is that such costs represent fixed costs from the perspective of private agents. Thus, the associated resource reallocations would not be undertaken unless the incentives for doing so were perceived to be large or long-lasting.[8] It follows that resource reallocation costs provide an argument for fixing the nominal exchange rate (and thus avoiding the real appreciation from materializing on impact) only if the authorities are better informed about the duration of the shock than the private sector and cannot convey this information to the private sector. If private agents are (or can be made) aware of the temporary nature of the shock, then they will find it in their best interest to avoid the costs of resource reallocation.

The preceding discussion treats the exchange rate as an instrument of short-run stabilization policy. However, the exchange rate also plays another role in small open economies—that of nominal anchor. Indeed, this role is often prominent in stabilization programs, and institutional arrangements have often been devised to enhance the credibility of the anchor. Where the exchange rate plays such a role, the issues are whether institutional arrangements are sufficiently flexible to allow the rate to move and, if so, whether perceptions of the authorities' anti-inflationary commitment would indeed be jeopardized by an appreciation of the nominal rate (albeit one which may need to be reversed if the inflow is temporary). The concern would be that even an appreciation may convey a signal that the exchange rate is not immutable.

Sterilization

The monetary authorities can seek to avoid aggregate demand stimulus with a fixed exchange rate through sterilization. The use of this policy raises a number of feasibility issues. First, sterilization is feasible only if capital mobility is imperfect. And even if capital mobility is less than perfect, sterilization will magnify the cumulative capital inflow. The higher the degree of capital mobility, the larger will be the accumulation of reserves associated with sterilized intervention. Second, sterilization has quasi-fiscal costs because the central bank exchanges high-yielding domestic assets for low-yielding reserves. The magnitude of these costs will be greater the higher the degree of capital mobility and the larger the gap between domestic and foreign rates of return. Thus, the fiscal feasibility of this policy is also at issue.[9] Third, even if sterilization succeeds

---

8. This is the perspective adopted in the "trade hysteresis" literature (see, e.g., Baldwin and Krugman 1989).

9. This argument can be overstated, however. To the extent that higher domestic interest rates are required to offset expected depreciation and to compensate creditors for exchange-

in limiting domestic monetary expansion, it may not insulate the economy from the effects of capital inflows. This would be true under two sets of circumstances. If domestic interest-bearing assets are perfect substitutes among themselves, insulation will fail if the shock that triggers the inflows affects domestic money demand. In this case, with shifting money demand but fixed supply, domestic interest rates will change. If domestic interest-bearing assets are imperfect substitutes, then a capital inflow may be associated with a shift in the composition of demand for domestic interest-bearing assets as well as with an increase in the total demand for such assets. In this case, unless the composition of domestic assets emitted in sterilization operations matches that demanded by creditors, the structure of domestic asset returns will be altered.

The empirical evidence cited above suggesting imperfect capital mobility over recent decades implies that sterilized intervention has been a viable policy option for most developing countries. By and large, studies that have examined the effectiveness of sterilization have supported this conclusion.[10] However, recent capital account liberalization in many developing countries may have changed this situation, increasing the effective degree of financial integration for liberalizing countries. Thus, whether sterilization remains viable after liberalization is an open empirical question.[11]

Policies to Influence the Money Multiplier

If sterilization is incomplete, a foreign exchange inflow will expand the monetary base. Monetary expansion can still be avoided, however, by a commensurate reduction in the money multiplier achieved through an increase in reserve requirements or other restrictions on credit expansion. Feasibility issues arise here. First, if reserve requirements are changed selectively for different components of banks' liability portfolios, their effects may be evaded as bank creditors shift to assets not affected by changes in reserve requirements. Second, even if changes in reserve requirements are applied broadly across bank liabilities, domestic credit expansion could materialize through nonbank institutions (disintermediation). The scope for doing so—and thus for avoiding an increase in domestic aggregate demand—depends on the sophistication of the domestic financial system.

With regard to optimality, measures directed at the money multiplier avoid quasi-fiscal costs but do so through implicit taxation of the banking

rate risk, for example, the government would recoup some of these outlays in the form of a capital gain on its foreign exchange reserves in the event of a devaluation.

10. See the references in Montiel (1994).

11. Frankel (1995) discusses this issue at greater length, and provides some empirical estimates of changes in financial integration.

system. The economic implications of this tax will depend on how the tax burden is shared among bank shareholders, depositors, and borrowers. Nonetheless, the likely effect of this policy will be to shrink the domestic financial system, an outcome that runs counter to the trend toward financial liberalization in most reforming economies and which may have adverse implications for economic growth (King and Levine 1993).

Fiscal Contraction

If domestic monetary expansion is not avoided, or if an expansionary financial stimulus is transmitted outside the banking system, the stabilization of aggregate demand will require a fiscal contraction. Feasibility and optimality issues arise in this context as well. Concerning feasibility, fiscal policy may simply prove too inflexible to be available as a tool to respond to fluctuations in capital movements. The budgetary process in most countries may not respond quickly enough, and the lag in response may aggravate the problems created by volatile capital movements. Second, even if fiscal policy can be changed, the desired effects on domestic demand (and thus on the real exchange rate) will be forthcoming only if expenditure cuts fall on nontraded goods.

From the perspective of optimality, issues arise in the case of fiscal adjustment that are similar to the issues of nominal exchange rate changes. That is, should fiscal policy be designed to anchor long-run expectations of inflation and taxation, or should it have countercyclical objectives? In principle, these goals are not mutually exclusive, since short-run deviations from the medium-term fiscal stance can be designed to achieve stabilization objectives. The problem, however, is that if government credibility is lacking, adherence to the medium-term stance in the face of shocks may be the surest way to achieve it. In a nutshell, the issue is whether the achievement of fiscal credibility is compatible with the adoption of feedback rules for fiscal policy.[12] Finally, if the stabilization objective is adopted, changes in marginal tax rates in response to temporary capital inflows should be avoided so as not to distort intertemporal choices.

Cross-Country Variation in Policy Response

This section examines the frequency with which policies of each of these types was adopted in recent years by countries that experienced surges of capital inflows and the modalities of their implementation. The discussion that follows is based on a sample of 14 developing countries for

---

12. If such a rule were to be applied symmetrically, it would imply that capital outflows should elicit an *expansionary* fiscal response.

which information on policy responses is readily available. They include Indonesia, Korea, Malaysia, the Philippines, and Thailand in East Asia, as well as Argentina, Bolivia, Brazil, Chile, Colombia, Costa Rica, and Mexico in Latin America. Capital flows to other regions are more recent and less information is available, but Egypt and Sri Lanka are included as well. As a group, these countries accounted for over 70 percent of portfolio and direct investment flows to developing countries between 1989 and 1993. A chronological description of policy formulation and macroeconomic outcomes for each country is provided in Montiel (1995), from which the following cross-country information is taken. A summary of the policy measures undertaken in individual countries is provided in table 1.[13]

Measures to Impede Gross Inflows

Controls, taxes, or other impediments to inflows were adopted in several countries and have taken many forms. The most straightforward of these consist of quantitative restrictions on foreign borrowing. Such restrictions were adopted in Sri Lanka during 1993 in response to inflows. Similarly, Indonesia restricted borrowing abroad by public sector entities in 1991. In Mexico, quantitative controls took the form of limits on banks' foreign currency liabilities.[14] Malaysia imposed a wide range of quantitative restrictions on inflows for several months in 1994. These included restrictions on sales of securities abroad by domestic nonfinancial enterprises as well as limits on bank foreign exchange liabilities.

Rather than relying on quantitative restrictions, some countries have imposed explicit or implicit taxes on external borrowing, thereby increasing the cost of such transactions.[15] The most common form of such taxation has been requiring banks with foreign exchange liabilities to maintain a nonremunerated account at the central bank equal to a specified ratio of such liabilities. Such requirements have been adopted in Chile (1991 and subsequently), Colombia (1993), and Mexico (1991).[16] In each of these countries, reserve requirements were supplemented with other measures

---

13. The dates in the first column of the table refer to the year in which the surge in capital inflows began. Dates that appear in the remaining columns indicate when significant new measures of the types indicated by the column headings were implemented (not the period over which such measures were actually in effect). The last column describes important policy measures that do not fit readily under the column headings.

14. Although this measure may have represented a prudential component in bank supervision, it serves the function of restricting capital inflows through the banking system.

15. In other cases, measures of this type have been applied in addition to quantitative controls.

16. In the Mexican case, reserve requirements applied only to the foreign currency liabilities.

Table 1 Policy responses to surges in capital inflows

Country	Restrictions of inflows	Liberalization of outflows	Trade liberalization	Nominal appreciation	Sterilized intervention	Higher reserve requirements	Tighter fiscal	Other
East Asia								
Indonesia, 1990	1991	—	—	—	1990–92	—	1990–94	Restrictions on swap operation, 1991
Korea, 1989	1994(?)	1990–94	1992–94	Sporadic	1990–92, 1994	1990	—	—
Malaysia, 1988–89	1994	1988–94	1988–94	1993	1989–93	1991–94	1988–92	Credit controls
Philippines, 1988	—	1992	1991–94	1992 (small)	1990–93	1990	1990–92	Forward cover arrangements discouraged, 1994
Thailand, 1988	—	1990–94	1990	—	1988–93	—	1988–93	Accelerated debt repayment, 1988–90. Withholding tax imposed on interest paid on foreign loans, 1990.
Latin America								
Argentina, 1991	—	—	—	—	—	—	1991–93	
Bolivia, 1990	—	—	—	—	1992	—	—	
Brazil, 1991	1993	—	—	—	1991–92	—	—	3 percent financial transaction tax imposed on the proceeds of foreign bond sales.

Country							
Chile, 1990	1991–93	1990–94	1991	Slight, 1991–92 Large, 1994	1990, 1992–93	1992	—	Widening of exchange-rate band, 1992.
Colombia, 1991	1991–94	1991–94	1991	Slight, 1991 Large, 1994	1991–93	1991	—	Exchange rate band adopted, 1994
Costa Rica, 1991	—	1992	1992	1992	Limited, 1991	—	1991–93	Dirty float from March 1992 to October 1993.
Mexico, 1989	1991–92	1991	—	—	1991–93	—	—	Exchange rate band adopted in 1991.
Other								
Egypt, 1991	—	—	—	—	1991–94	—	1991–93	
Sri Lanka, 1990	1993	1993	1993–94	1993	1991–93	1991–93	—	

to increase the cost of carrying foreign exchange liabilities. Chile applied a stamp tax to foreign loans, while Colombia imposed a "commission" on the sale of foreign exchange to the central bank. Other ways of taxing foreign borrowing were through the extension of withholding taxes to interest paid on foreign loans in Thailand (1990), as well as through the imposition of interest rate ceilings on deposits held by foreign institutions as part of Malaysia's comprehensive program of capital controls in 1994. Explicit "Tobin taxes"—that is, foreign exchange transactions taxes applicable to certain classes of financial transactions—were introduced by Brazil in November 1993 and were expanded late in 1994.

Finally, some countries sought to discourage inflows by increasing the risks associated with foreign borrowing. Chile, Colombia, and Mexico all adopted exchange rate bands and widened them during the inflow episode. Chile, in particular, permitted extensive variation of the exchange rate within its band, while the other countries intervened more systematically within the band to stabilize the exchange rate. Indonesia (1991) restricted the use of swap facilities by commercial banks and increased their cost, thus increasing the risks to such banks of maintaining a foreign currency exposure.

Quantitative controls and taxes on gross inflows were generally not adopted early in the inflow episode but rather after a preferred alternative response—typically, sterilized intervention—had been weakened or abandoned. Capital controls have not always become permanent. Malaysia, for example, dismantled the panoply of controls imposed in early 1994 later in the year, while Brazil reduced the scope of its financial transaction taxes in March 1995.

Encouragement for Gross Outflows

Many countries relaxed controls on capital outflows. Korea has promoted foreign investment by domestic residents, while Korea, Malaysia, and Thailand have all accelerated the repayment of external debt. Thailand, Chile, and Colombia removed a number of restrictions on capital outflows. This involved such measures as explicitly permitting residents to invest abroad, removing restrictions on repatriation of capital and interest by foreign direct investors, eliminating ceilings on tourist expenditures by residents, discarding export surrender requirements, and extending the period for advance purchases of foreign exchange by importers. The Philippines removed all restrictions on the use of foreign exchange for both current and capital transactions.

Although many of these measures were encouraged by inflow surges, in many cases they represented a continuation of a liberalization process that was already under way. It is noteworthy, however, that financial reforms of a strictly domestic nature were typically not accelerated in response to inflows, and in some cases the policy response to inflows actually ran counter to previous liberalizing measures. This was true of increases in reserve requirements in many countries, for example.

Measures to Reduce Reserve Accumulation

Several countries reduced tariffs during the period of large inflows. This was the case in Korea, Malaysia, the Philippines, Thailand, Chile, Colombia, and Costa Rica, though only the Philippines, Thailand, Colombia, and Costa Rica appear to have done so specifically in response to inflows.

The experience of the Philippines presents something of an anomaly. Although trade liberalization was accelerated through reduction of quantitative restrictions and reduced tariff dispersion, a 9 percent import duty surcharge was imposed early in 1991 for fiscal reasons under an IMF-supported stabilization program.

Several countries permitted a nominal appreciation of their currencies or a slowdown in the rate of nominal depreciation. This implies reduced intervention in the foreign exchange market by the central bank, and thus less pressure on the monetary base arising from reserve accumulation. Three observations are relevant here:

- No country abandoned a predetermined peg for a freely floating regime (Costa Rica experimented with a float, but only temporarily). Official intervention continued to be practiced in all of them. On the other hand, as already mentioned, the tradeoff between holding the exchange rate steady for the purpose of stabilizing price expectations and allowing it to appreciate to absorb monetary pressures was resolved in the case of some countries by the use of exchange rate bands. Chile, Colombia, and Mexico all used bands with the intention of focusing price expectations around the predetermined central parity while allowing movements within the band to absorb some of the pressure from inflows. Colombia and Mexico introduced exchange rate bands during their surge episodes, while Chile widened its previous band.

- Nominal appreciation was more common in Latin America (Bolivia in 1991, Chile in 1990–92 and again in 1994, Colombia in 1991 and 1994, Costa Rica in 1992, and Mexico in 1991) than in East Asia (Korea in 1987–89, Malaysia in 1993, and the Philippines in 1992).[17]

- By and large, the magnitude of nominal appreciation has been small. Exceptions were revaluations of 5 and 7 percent in Colombia in 1994, and a revaluation in excess of 9 percent in Chile in 1994.

---

17. According to Calvo, Leiderman, and Reinhart (1993), nominal appreciation was also undertaken by Singapore and Taiwan.

Measures to Restrict Base Money Growth

By far the most common response to capital inflows has been sterilized intervention. This largely reflects the combination of an exchange regime characterized by predetermined official rates and concern about inflation and real exchange rate appreciation. Sterilized intervention was pursued by all of the countries examined here, with the exception of Argentina and Bolivia. Such intervention took the forms of open-market sales of government or central bank securities, central bank borrowing from commercial banks, shifts of government deposits from commercial banks to the central bank, increases in interest rates on central bank assets and liabilities, and reduced access to rediscounts. Transfers of government deposits to the central bank have been particularly common in East Asia (Indonesia, Malaysia, and Thailand). In the Philippines, the government borrowed from the private sector in order to make deposits in the central bank. A different twist was provided by Mexico, which placed its privatization proceeds in the central bank during 1991, thus sterilizing inflows by selling real assets. Reduction of access to the discount window was employed by Korea (1986–88) and Thailand (1989–90). According to Reinhart and Dunaway (1995), Chile, Colombia, Indonesia, and Malaysia were particularly aggressive initially in their pursuit of sterilization when inflows accelerated. Chile, Korea, Mexico, the Philippines, and Thailand were less aggressive, seeking only to ameliorate effects on the base.

Countries that received substantial inflows tended to use sterilized intervention soon after the inflows began to arrive, often in the first year. Indonesia, Malaysia, Thailand, Mexico, and Egypt continued the policy of sterilization longer, while Chile and Colombia eased monetary policy in the second year of inflow. Indonesia eventually eased in mid-1993 and Egypt in mid-1994. Chile had already reduced the intensity of sterilization by mid-1990, and Colombia by late 1991. Observers have attributed the change in policy to its quasi-fiscal costs, to the effects of sterilization in magnifying the size of the inflows, and to the perception that this policy deprived domestic investment of the benefits of inflows. The clear pattern in the country experience reviewed in Montiel (1995), however, is that sterilization was used in countercyclical fashion.

A notable feature of the sterilization episodes is that countries succeeded in keeping domestic interest rates high despite the capital inflows, in some cases (Colombia being a clear case) even higher than before the inflows. This suggests that, whether desirable or not, sterilization remained a realistic option for these countries, at least in the short run— i.e., international capital mobility proved less than perfect, even after substantial liberalization. There is evidence, however, that capital mobility is stronger in the long run than in the short run (Glick and Moreno 1994), so sterilization may indeed be only a temporary option in most cases.

Reduction in the Money Multiplier

Changes in reserve requirements have taken various forms, ranging from altering required reserve ratios on all domestic-currency deposits to raising marginal reserve requirements on the foreign-currency liabilities of banks. The latter are best understood as a form of capital control, since they impose a discriminatory tax on a particular class of bank liabilities that is intended not to discourage overall lending but to restrain it. Increases in general reserve requirements were implemented by Korea (1988–90), Malaysia (1989–94), the Philippines (1990), Chile (1992), Colombia (1991), and Costa Rica (1993). Beyond uniform restraints on the growth of credit, restrictions on the expansion of specific types of lending (credit controls) were used by Korea, Malaysia, and Thailand. Each of these economies has a long history of using directed credit as an instrument of monetary policy. Among countries with higher reserve requirements, broad money multipliers fell during the surge period in Korea and Malaysia, were stable in the Philippines, Colombia, and Sri Lanka, and rose only in Chile.

Restrictive Fiscal Policy

Because ongoing stabilization efforts in Latin America involved fiscal tightening, it is difficult to identify specific instances in which tight fiscal policy was adopted in response to capital inflows. Costa Rica may be such a case. Although Argentina tightened fiscal policy during the surge episodes, that country was involved in a strong stabilization program which had not yet met inflation objectives when the inflow began to materialize. By contrast, fiscal tightening was an important component of the policy response in several East Asian countries that were not struggling with inflation. Tightening occurred in Indonesia (1990–94), Malaysia (1988–92), the Philippines (1990–92), and Thailand (1988–93). Of the East Asian countries included here, only Korea did not implement additional fiscal tightening during the surge episode.

Macroeconomic Outcomes

How well did these measures succeed in preserving macroeconomic stability in the face of inflows? An overview is provided in table 2. The discussion below is based on that table as well as on the more detailed information in Montiel (1995).

Official foreign exchange reserves rose in all countries and, predictably, the increase was largest in the countries that relied most heavily on sterilized intervention. By contrast, the current account offset to capital

Table 2 Macroeconomic outcomes during inflow episodes

Country	Ratio of reserve accumulation to capital account	Base money growth	Money multiplier	Inflation	Real exchange rate	Current account deficit	Investment rate	Saving rate	Stock market boom
East Asia									
Indonesia, 1990		Restrained	Increased	Stable	Depreciated	Stable	Stable	Stable	1990–93
Korea, 1989	− 0.7 (1990–91) 0.8 (1992–93)	Restrained	Decreased	Temporary surge	Depreciated	Higher	Higher	Stable	—
Malaysia, 1988–89		Increased	Decreased	Increased	Stable	Much higher	Much higher	Stable	1988–93
Philippines, 1988	Small, 1989–90, 1993 0.6, 1991–92	Temporary surge	Stable	Temporary surge	Temporary appreciation	Higher	Higher	Stable	1993
Thailand, 1988	0.65, 1988–90 0.37, 1991–93	Stable	Higher	Low	Stable	Much higher	Much higher	Much higher	1988–1993
Latin America									
Argentina, 1991	0.3 (1992)	Lower	Higher	Much lower	Large appreciation	Higher	Higher	Lower	1991–93
Bolivia, 1990	Negative (1991–93)	Higher, 1991, 1993 Lower, 1992	Higher	Lower	Depreciated	Higher, 1992	Higher	Lower	—
Brazil, 1991	2.4 (1992)	Much higher	—	Higher	Stable	Lower	Lower	Lower	1991–93
Chile, 1990	0.57 (1989–90) Decreasing, 1991–93	Higher	Higher	Lower	Appreciation	Higher	Higher	Stable	1989–93

Colombia, 1991	—	Temporary surge	Stable	Temporary surge	Appreciation	Higher, 1992	Higher	Lower, 1992	1991–93
Costa Rica, 1991	0.6 (1991) Minimal (1992–93)	Temporary surge	Lower	Temporary surge	Depreciated	Decreased, but high	Higher	Higher	—
Mexico	0.2 (1989–93)	Temporary surge	Higher	Lower	Large appreciation	Much higher	Higher	Much lower	1989–93
Other									
Egypt, 1991	—	Higher	Higher	Lower	Appreciation	Lower	Lower	Higher	1991–93
Sri Lanka, 1990	0.3 (1991–92) 0.6 (1993)	Higher	Stable	Temporary surge	Appreciation	Stable	Higher	Higher	1991–93

inflows was largest in Argentina, Bolivia, and Costa Rica (in 1992–93), all of which sterilized either weakly or not at all.[18] However, surges in money growth do not appear to have been as universal or as persistent as elsewhere. Indonesia, Malaysia, Argentina, Bolivia, Chile, and Sri Lanka registered acceleration of base money growth on average over the surge period. Base money growth was kept in check in Thailand to a greater extent than in Malaysia and Indonesia, while broad money growth accelerated in all three countries.

As the individual country experiences described in Montiel (1995) indicate, base money growth tended to accelerate in several countries (the Philippines, Colombia, Costa Rica, and Mexico) before sterilization was undertaken in earnest. Once monetary policy adapted to the persistence of inflows, however, recipient countries were largely successful in keeping base money growth in check. As indicated above, periods of substantial acceleration in base money growth tended to respond to domestic economic conditions and thus appeared to reflect policy intentions rather than the unavoidable byproducts of surges in capital inflows. The lesson, then, is that while the threat to base money expansion from a surge in capital inflows is real, sterilized intervention was employed successfully almost everywhere to retain control over the monetary base.

The behavior of the money multiplier was quite sensitive to policies regarding reserve requirements. In seven of the fourteen countries examined, the money multiplier increased during the period, an outcome which runs counter to what would have been required to offset accelerated growth in the monetary base. However, increases in reserve requirements did not figure prominently in any of these cases (until, recently, in Malaysia). Nevertheless, sustained reductions in the money multiplier were not substantial in any of the countries examined in spite of the fact that reserve requirements were raised early in the surge episode in some of them (e.g., in both Korea and the Philippines in 1990). By and large, then, control of money supply growth has been achieved by restricting the growth of the base rather than by reducing the money multiplier.

Despite limited expansion in the monetary base, stock prices surged during the early phases of the inflow episodes in both Asia and Latin America. This suggests that controls, sterilization, and increases in reserve requirements may not have succeeded in preventing the transmission of the expansionary demand shock to the recipient economies, even if explosive monetary growth was avoided. In spite of what appears to be a widespread boom in asset markets, there were no instances in which inflation accelerated drastically during the inflow episode. This does not mean, however, that all of these countries registered a satisfactory inflation

---

18. This can be inferred from the first column of table 2. The larger the ratio of reserve accumulation to the capital account surplus, the smaller the current account offset.

performance. Several of them may have failed to reach inflation targets that could have been attainable otherwise.

Significant real exchange rate appreciation was widespread outside East Asia. In Latin America, Chile experienced a mild appreciation, but the degree of appreciation was strong in Argentina and Mexico. In Asia, all of the countries examined avoided a real appreciation, although the real exchange rate appreciated temporarily in the Philippines. By contrast, increases in current account deficits have been common during inflow episodes. Larger deficits were registered by Korea, Malaysia, the Philippines, Thailand, Argentina, Bolivia, Costa Rica, Mexico, and Egypt. In Latin America, about half of the monetary impact of the capital account surplus associated with the inflow episode was offset by an increase in the current account deficit.

Despite some increase in investment in most Latin American countries, the current wave of capital inflows does not seem to have been associated with an investment boom (private or public) in the region (see also Calvo, Leiderman, and Reinhart 1993 and 1994). Thus, the increases in current account deficits have accommodated a reduction in domestic saving. Several Latin American countries appear to have experienced consumption booms led by private sector consumption. This was true of Argentina, Brazil, Chile, Colombia, and Mexico. In contrast, saving rates increased sharply in Thailand and remained stable in the other East Asian countries. In East Asia, only the Philippines experienced a similar boom. Egypt seems to have done so as well.

Policy Lessons

What can we learn from this examination of country experience about the issues raised earlier? The broad pattern of experience in these countries suggests the following observations:

Measures to Reduce Net Capital Inflows

In the case of capital controls, potential costs consist of the microeconomic distortions introduced when such controls are neither a first- nor second-best policy response (Fernandez-Arias and Montiel 1995). Although capital controls have been implemented in several countries, no evidence has been produced to date on the magnitude of such costs for the countries involved.

More can be said, however, on the issue of effectiveness. Substantial inflows followed the removal of controls in several cases (e.g., Korea in 1992), and in other cases inflows slowed after controls were reimposed (Chile in 1991 and Malaysia in 1994). Although the evidence is by no means conclusive, it suggests that such controls can be effective, at least in some cases and at least temporarily. In both Chile and Colombia, moreover, controls have been credited by some observers with altering the composition of flows in favor of those with longer maturities.[19]

With regard to liberalization of outflows, two issues were raised previously: Does liberalization matter if previous restrictions were ineffective in constraining outflows anyway? Is liberalization effective in restraining net inflows, since it may attract more inflows at the same time that it promotes outflows? The episodic evidence suggests (weakly) that liberalization may matter but may have little effect on net capital flows.

What is clear from our study is that substantial inflows followed the removal of restrictions on outflows in many countries, an experience which has also characterized industrial countries (Bartolini and Drazen 1995). Whether the removal of restrictions on outflows diminished net inflows to any significant extent is impossible to say on the basis of present evidence, but it is clear that they did not constitute a complete solution to the inflow problem anywhere.

Measures to Restrict Reserve Accumulation

The current account deficit increased in all the Asian countries in the sample that undertook trade liberalization, as well as in two of the three Latin American countries that did so. Although this is consistent with the view that liberalization helped to reduce reserve accumulation, it is difficult to make this attribution with any degree of confidence. Too many other macroeconomic changes were occurring at the same time to make this link, especially when, even the theoretical effect of liberalization on the trade balance is ambiguous.

The strongest lesson that emerges from experience concerns trade liberalization as an endogenous, rather an exogenous, variable. Despite the theoretical ambiguities described above, it is clear that trade liberalization is often inhibited by a perceived balance of payments constraint. Thus, the surge of capital inflows presented several countries with a good opportunity to pursue trade liberalization, and at least eight of the fourteen countries examined did so (table 2). Contrary to fears expressed in the sequencing literature of the 1980s, no instances of major reversals of trade liberalization triggered by real appreciation associated with capital inflows can be documented for this group of countries.[20]

---

19. Systematic evidence to support this assertion is lacking, however, and the issue of whether this would represent an important contribution of capital controls, remains problematic.

20. Even in the case of the Philippines, where an import surcharge was imposed in the midst of the inflow episode, this happened in the context of a broad trend toward commercial liberalization.

Concerning use of the exchange rate to achieve the same result, the lessons are several:

- Apart from Mexico, the countries were not pushed to extreme exchange rate arrangements (free-floating or currency boards) by financial openness. Adjustable pegs have been widely managed successfully.

- Nonetheless, innovation in the form of exchange-rate bands has provided an option that combines the nominal anchor function of the exchange rate with a mechanism to allow nominal exchange rate movements to absorb some of the pressures exerted by capital inflows in the foreign exchange market. Among the three countries that operated bands, none experienced an acceleration of inflation as a result of the additional flexibility allowed for nominal exchange movements. One interpretation of this experience is that the additional flexibility acquired through bands was purchased at near-zero cost to the nominal anchor function of the exchange rate.

- Nominal exchange rate adjustment was essentially confined to two countries (Chile and Colombia). As a result, real exchange rate appreciation was largely effected through price-level adjustments. Nonetheless, many countries managed to avoid real appreciation over the course of the surge episode. Thus, while real appreciation may be inevitable eventually if inflows are sustained, the loss of competitiveness apparently does not have to be absorbed immediately.

- The link between real appreciation and the emergence of current account deficits is not airtight. On the one hand, avoiding real appreciation did not necessarily imply avoiding current account deficits. The ⁺ account deficits was not restricted to coun- ippreciations. Malaysia and Thailand both ts in the current account balance with stable other hand, the two countries that experi- exchange rate appreciation (Argentina and ʳ large current account deficits.

Money Growth

zed intervention are mixed:

been sterilized, the adjustment mechanism This was evident in Mexico and the Philip- their inflow episodes and was evident in episode.

This portion of the ticket should be
retained as evidence of your
journey.

NOTICE

PASSENGER COUPON

PASSENGER TICKET AND BAGGAGE CHECK

- An important lesson is that sterilization has clearly been possible despite capital account liberalization and of the large magnitude of recent inflows. Indeed, many countries registered an increase in domestic interest rates over the period of sterilization. This may reflect the operation of "pull" factors increasing the domestic demand for money (Frankel 1995). Thus, perfect capital mobility does not seem to characterize any of the countries reviewed.

- The required amount of sterilization has been massive at times, and countries have been forced to rely on a variety of instruments. This suggests that quasi-fiscal deficits generated by sterilization may have been substantial, though little information on these is available.[21]

- Changes in the intensity of sterilization responded to changes in domestic economic conditions. It is clear that for the countries in this sample, sterilization has been the most flexible and attractive countercyclical tool.

- Although sterilization may have kept the growth of the monetary base in check, its effectiveness in insulating economies from the effects of external financial shocks is open to question. Asset markets, in particular, typically recorded massive increases in value during the surge periods. This is consistent with an imperfect-substitutability story in which foreign creditors demand domestic financial assets different from those issued by the central bank in the course of its sterilization operations.

Reduction in the Money Multiplier

Significant reductions in the money multiplier have not proven easy to achieve. Nevertheless, measures to increase reserve requirements appear to have been important, since there was a close association between increases in reserve requirements and stability in the money multiplier. In the absence of measures to address reserve requirements, surges in capital inflows were associated with increases in the money multiplier.

Restrictive Fiscal Policy

This paper suggests that fiscal policy has not proven to be a very flexible instrument for responding to inflows. Few countries found it possible to engage in additional fiscal tightening in response to inflows, and where

---

21. Estimates for Chile, for example, put these in the range of 1 to 1½ percent of GDP in the early nineties.

additional fiscal tightening took place the changes in the fiscal stance were typically not large compared with previous fiscal adjustments. This may reflect a variety of factors, including "stabilization fatigue" arising from the substantial fiscal adjustment that many countries had made prior to the inflow episode and political economy considerations that make it difficult to undertake fiscal austerity when the external constraint is not binding.

Real appreciation was avoided in all of the East Asian countries that tightened fiscal policy in response to inflows. It was also avoided in Costa Rica. Nonetheless, tighter fiscal policy was not in itself sufficient to avoid real appreciation. Real appreciation accompanied fiscal tightening in Argentina and Egypt, but each of those countries was in the midst of stabilizing from high inflation, and it is likely that the behavior of the real exchange rate reflected inflation inertia. If this interpretation is correct, the implication is that real appreciation would have been more severe in those countries if fiscal policy had been looser.

The Policy Strategy

This review permits us to take stock of what we have learned from country experiences about some of the issues raised earlier. This approach, however, is less well-suited to identifying policy strategies that were a successful answer to the problems raised by capital inflows. A reasonable way to approach that subject is to look for common policy features among the countries that have adjusted successfully to the arrival of new capital inflows.

Ultimately, of course, a successful adjustment strategy is one that maximizes the discounted present value of consumption for the recipient country. Such a general criterion would not get us very far, however. An operational alternative is to define success in terms of low vulnerability to external financial crises, on the assumption that avoiding such crises is conducive to the ultimate goals of macroeconomic adjustment. Since vulnerability is only observable *ex post*, we require a standard to assess it *ex ante*. The approach adopted here will be to use the Mexican crisis of December 1994 as a benchmark, defining *ex ante* indicators of vulnerability in terms of the symptoms that were of concern to observers of the Mexican case. These consisted of a high current account deficit, a "significantly" appreciated real exchange rate, and a change in the composition of domestic absorption from investment to consumption. For the purposes of this section, I will consider the simultaneous occurrence of all three phenomena as indicative of vulnerability and thus as the characteristics typical of undesirable macroeconomic outcomes.

As table 2 indicates, high and/or increased current account deficits have been the rule among the economies reviewed. Lower deficits were recorded during the inflow episodes only in Brazil and Egypt. Omitting Brazil, the economies in the sample separate rather neatly into two groups—those which experienced *both* real exchange rate appreciation and apparent consumption "booms," and those that did not register either one.[22] Only Sri Lanka falls outside the pattern, having registered a real appreciation but no apparent increase in the share of consumption in GDP. Of the others, Bolivia, Costa Rica, Indonesia, Korea, Malaysia, and Thailand all had no real exchange rate appreciation and no sign of a consumption boom, while Argentina, Chile, Colombia, Egypt, Mexico, and the Philippines all experienced a real exchange rate appreciation and an increase in the share of consumption in GDP. The emergence of such a strong association between real appreciation and consumption booms suggests that the criteria identified on the basis of the Mexican experience are indeed meaningful.

The link between these criteria and financial vulnerability is supported by the incidence of the "Tequila effect" following the Mexican crisis. Among countries in the first group, none experienced an extended short-fall in external financing in the aftermath of the Mexican crisis, while in the second group Argentina and the Philippines were affected to a relatively much greater extent. Although Chile and Colombia weathered the crisis more successfully, they can be distinguished from other members of the second group by two features. First, their consumption booms have been nominal rather than real—that is, when measured in real terms the shift in absorption from investment to consumption is no longer apparent (Montiel 1995). Second, as indicated previously, both countries intervened directly in an attempt to influence the scale and composition of their capital inflows.

To link our criteria for defining successful macroeconomic outcomes to the policy strategies followed by the respective countries requires explaining the link between real appreciation and consumption booms in terms of the underlying policy stance. The issue is not trivial, since several alternative explanations have been offered, both in the context of the inflow episodes and previously. For present purposes, however, a suggestion is offered by policy patterns present in the data. As indicated in table 1, measures involving restrictions on capital inflows, liberalization of outflows, trade liberalization, and especially restrictive monetary policy, have been applied widely by countries in both of the groups identified above. Such policies do not help to identify differences in policy regimes. However, two important differences in policy strategy do characterize the two groups. Among countries that did not experience appreciable real appreciation and changes in the composition of absorption, nominal

---

22. Brazil is omitted because the inflow episode described in Montiel (1995) covers only a brief period in 1992.

exchange rate policy was aimed at maintaining competitiveness—that is, achieving a desired value for the real exchange rate. In addition, four of the six countries in this group tightened fiscal policy. By contrast, among the countries that registered real appreciation and consumption booms, the nominal exchange rate was managed to achieve a price-level objective (it was used as a nominal anchor), and fiscal tightening was less common during the inflow episode (only two of the six countries in the group tightened fiscal policy appreciably).[23]

How does one interpret this policy pattern? A working hypothesis is that nominal exchange rate policy has mattered during the inflow episode. Targeting the real exchange rate has been more associated with success—in the form of reduced financial vulnerability—than targeting the price level. This raises a problem, however. Targeting a real variable, such as the real exchange rate, with a nominal instrument is likely to destabilize the price level if the target real exchange rate is more depreciated than the equilibrium rate (Adams and Gros 1986). In the presence of a substantial capital inflow, the equilibrium real exchange rate is likely to appreciate, so the relative constancy of the real exchange rate among countries in the first group might be expected to be associated with increased inflation. However, such an outcome has not materialized, at least until the present time, for the countries in the first group. A possible explanation is provided by the tighter fiscal policies adopted in most of these countries. Since fiscal tightening causes the equilibrium real exchange rate to appreciate, tight fiscal policy may have contributed to the success of the strategy by avoiding (or at least ameliorating) the undervaluation of the domestic currency among the countries in the first group.

Overall, then, a policy strategy consisting of using nominal exchange rate policy to sustain competitiveness, together with tightened monetary *and* fiscal policies to achieve an inflation objective, has been associated with avoidance of the emergence of real appreciation and consumption booms among the countries examined here. The Mexican experience and its aftermath suggest that these outcomes have left these countries less vulnerable to external financial shocks. The alternative strategy of using the exchange rate as a nominal anchor while relying primarily on monetary policy to restrain domestic inflation and prevent excessive real appreciation, has more often been associated with the emergence of the macroeconomic symptoms associated with financial vulnerability.

Conclusions

The recent policy experience of the developing countries that have received substantial capital inflows in recent years has helped to shed

---

23. Of the six countries in this group, clear indications of the use of the exchange rate as a nominal anchor exist in each case but that of the Philippines.

some light on some of the issues that were raised during the early stages of the episode regarding the efficacy and/or optimality of specific policies in the menu of potential domestic responses. On many of these issues, however, experience has spoken less clearly, and strong conclusions must await both further investigation and the accumulation of additional experience.

It may be more useful to conclude by addressing an important issue that arises in connection with the lessons on general policy strategies. The message there was that a strategy of using the nominal exchange rate to promote competitiveness while targeting domestic inflation through tight fiscal and monetary policies represents a more robust policy mix—that is, one less vulnerable to financial shocks—than a strategy which uses the exchange rate as a nominal anchor and relies on tight money to prevent the real exchange rate from getting out of line, with fiscal policy unchanged. If so, why have some countries opted for the latter course rather than the former?

The short answer is that almost all of the countries that did so were engaged in inflation stabilization at the time that capital flows began to arrive.[24] Much fiscal adjustment had already been undertaken in these countries, making additional fiscal tightening more difficult, and the use of the exchange rate as a nominal anchor had proved an effective way to promote inflation stabilization. Thus, the choice of differing policy strategies can be explained at least in part on the basis of differing initial macroeconomic conditions.

Does this mean that countries that attempt to stabilize in the midst of an inflow episode are forced to adopt policy strategies that leave them financially vulnerable? The strong suggestion from the experience to date is that such countries may face a difficult policy trade-off. While using the exchange rate as a nominal anchor is an effective complement to a policy of sound fundamentals in reducing the costs of stabilizing from high inflation, adopting this strategy under circumstances of high capital mobility may indeed put the economy in a precarious position, since the perception of overvaluation may trigger a Mexican-style financial crisis. Such countries may face a choice between abandoning the use of the exchange rate as a nominal anchor earlier in the stabilization process or reconsidering whether the process of stabilizing from high inflation should be conducted in a context of financial openness. Mexico avoided this choice, while Chile and Colombia chose the second option.

However, both the effectiveness of capital controls in the Chilean and Colombian contexts, as well as their contributions to the relative success of these economies in weathering the Mexican crisis, are at present open

---

24. The Philippines is the exception. Although inflation stabilization arose there as a policy issue during the course of the inflow episode, low rates of inflation had already been achieved when capital flows surged.

questions. Whether reconsideration of financial openness is a viable option in the present international context remains problematic. This issue may determine the viability of using the exchange rate as a tool of inflation stabilization, and it should figure prominently on the future research agenda.

References

Adams, Charles, and Daniel Gros. 1986. *The Consequences of Real Exchange Rate Rules for Inflation: Some Illustrative Examples*. International Monetary Fund Staff Papers 33. Washington: International Monetary Fund.

Baldwin, Richard, and Paul R. Krugman. 1989. "Persistent Trade Effects of Large Exchange Rate Shocks." *Quarterly Journal of Economics* 104: 635–54.

Bartolini, Leonardo, and Allan Drazen. 1995. "Capital Account Liberalization as a Signal." International Monetary Fund. Photocopy (April).

Calvo, Guillermo. 1989. "Incredible Reforms." In G. Calvo et al., *Debt, Stabilization, and Development*. Cambridge, MA: Basil Blackwell.

Calvo, Guillermo, Leonardo Leiderman, and Carmen Reinhart. 1993. *Capital Inflows to Latin America: The Role of External Factors*. IMF Staff Papers 40, no. 1: 108–51. Washington: International Monetary Fund.

Calvo, Guillermo, Leonardo Leiderman, and Carmen Reinhart. 1994. "The Capital Inflows Problem: Concepts and Issues." *Contemporary Economic Policy* (July): 54–66.

Fernandez-Arias, Eduardo, and Peter J. Montiel. 1995. "The Surge in Capital Inflows to Developing Countries: An Overview." World Bank. Photocopy (March).

Frankel, Jeffrey A. 1995. "Sterilization of Money Inflows: Difficult (Calvo) or Easy (Reisen)?" University of California, Berkeley. Photocopy.

Glick, Reuven, and Ramon Moreno. 1994. *Capital Flows and Monetary Policy in East Asia*. Pacific Basin Working Paper Series No. PB94-08. San Francisco: Federal Reserve Bank.

Haque, Nadeem, and Peter J. Montiel. 1990. "How Mobile is Capital in Developing Countries?" *Economics Letters* 33: 359–62.

King, Robert G., and Ross Levine. "Finance, Entrepreneurship, and Growth: Theory and Evidence." *Journal of Monetary Economics* 32: 513–42.

Laban, Raul, and Felipe Larrain. 1993. "Can a Liberalization of Capital Outflows Increase Net Capital Inflows?" Department of Economics, Pontifica Universidad Catolica de Chile (June).

Mathieson, Donald J., and Liliana Rojas-Suárez. 1993. *Liberalization of the Capital Account: Experiences and Issues*. International Monetary Fund Occasional Paper No. 103. Washington: International Monetary Fund.

McKinnon, Ronald, I., and Donald J. Mathieson. 1981. *How to Manage a Repressed Economy*. Essays in International Finance No. 145. Princeton, NJ: Princeton University, International Finance Section, Department of Economics.

Montiel, Peter J. 1994. "Capital Mobility in Developing Countries: Some Measurement Issues and Empirical Estimates." *World Bank Economic Review* 8 (September): 311–50.

Montiel, Peter J. 1995. "The New Wave of Capital Inflows to Developing Countries: Country Policy Chronologies." World Bank. Photocopy (April).

Montiel, Peter J. 1995. "The Mexican Crisis of December 1994: An Interpretation." Oberlin College. Photocopy (September).

Ostry, Jonathan. 1991. *Trade Liberalization in Developing Countries, Initial Trade Distortions, and Imported Intermediate Inputs*. International Monetary Fund Staff Papers 38 (September): 447–80. Washington: International Monetary Fund.

Reinhart, Carmen, and Steven Dunaway. 1995. "Dealing with Capital Inflows: Are There Any Lessons?" International Monetary Fund. Photocopy.

Thomas, Vinod, John Nash, and Associates. 1991. *Best Practice in Trade Policy Reform*. London: Oxford University Press.

Comment

Johnny Åkerholm

Peter Montiel has equipped us with a clear, concise analysis of the links between capital inflows and economic policy management. The sequencing of the process forms the basis for a useful analytical framework. It also provides solid ground for analyzing experiences and for the presentation of empirical results. However, one should be careful when taking measures out of their economic context and, hence, in giving universal answers as to the usefulness of different measures. The effectiveness of these depends to a large extent on the economic circumstances under which they are being implemented. A few examples:

Capital controls. The possibilities for resorting to capital controls hinge largely on the circumstances under which capital flows have been liberalized in the first place. If they have been deregulated as part of efforts to create well-functioning financial markets and these have not yet emerged, a temporary reintroduction of capital controls might well be effective. However, if the liberalization has been undertaken because financial markets have developed and become increasingly integrated with the rest of the world, it might turn out to be a futile process to try to re-regulate markets. In that case, market participants have the technical knowledge to circumvent controls, and they typically also have access to well-developed financial instruments which are not easily regulated by the authorities. Although controls could be effective in reducing certain activities, capital inflows come through many different channels. One big hole in the regulatory framework may suffice to allow for capital flows large enough to

Johnny Åkerholm is permanent undersecretary of state for economic affairs, Ministry of Finance, Helsinki.

upset monetary balance. Controls will in these circumstances only reduce the transparency of financial markets and in the end complicate monetary management.

The exchange rate. As is documented in the paper, effects on the nominal exchange rate are typically resisted by the authorities because of the effects that a nominal appreciation has on the competitive position. This is not welcome for both short- and long-term, structural reasons. However, there are certainly circumstances where a nominal appreciation would seem to provide the right remedy. If capital inflows emanate, for example, from an increase in the terms of trade and a concomitant boom in export industries, an appreciation of the exchange rate is the right answer. This is particularly true if the increase in export prices is conceived by the authorities to be only temporary, and hence could give rise to an "overinvestment" in certain branches.

Fiscal policies. I would tend to agree with Montiel's suggestion that fiscal policy is not a flexible enough instrument to be effectively used to counter the effects of large capital inflows. This is particularly true because capital inflows will tend to support demand and growth in the short run and hence to strengthen the budget balance. Experience shows that in these circumstances it is extremely difficult to find political support for further restrictive budget measures.

But it is also highly uncertain that a tightening of fiscal policy would affect capital flows in themselves. There is a fair chance that a tightening of fiscal policy will add to the credibility of economic policy and, hence, further boost capital inflows.

It is also easy to agree with Montiel's suggestion that monetary sterilization is effective only if foreign and domestic assets are less than full substitutes. However, the emergence of a capital inflow problem is at the same time a sign of the fact that substitutability between domestic and foreign currencies is high.

The Bank of Finland sterilized in the early 1980s by intervening in the forward exchange market. This forced the banks to cover their currency positions by making deposits abroad. As a result, an increase in the reserves of the central bank and of the monetary base could be avoided. However, by the same token, the forward rates remained attractive and the forward market became a major avenue for capital inflows. The net result is difficult to assess.

Reserve requirements can certainly be used to some extent, in particular if different requirements are applied to different items on banks' balance sheets. Higher requirements can be put on items classified as narrow money because these have few, if any, substitutes. However, in order to effectively reduce monetary expansion, high requirements are necessary. These will no doubt lead to circumvention and a loss of transparency in the financial markets.

It holds also more generally that if measures like these are effective, they also tend to have some other, and usually unwanted, impact. If they do not have any side effects, they are probably not effective in inhibiting capital inflows or the effects that these give rise to.

Since capital inflows by their very nature tend to sooner or later strengthen the real exchange rate, which is also confirmed in Montiel's analysis, it would in many cases seem to be most effective to counter capital inflows by allowing the moninal exchange rate to appreciate. Whether this should take place by allowing the exchange rate to fluctuate within a fluctuation band is difficult to judge. The band has the attraction of maintaining a longer term reference for investment and pricing decisions. But in order to achieve these effects, the fixity of the band must be fully credible. This is not very often the case.

Comment

Liliana Rojas-Suárez

Over the last few years, the magnitude and volatility of capital flows have been important items on the economic agenda of policymakers in a number of developing countries. Authorities have attempted to design policies that ameliorate the impact of sudden flow reversals, such as those experienced during the most recent financial crises in Mexico and Argentina. However, even in the absence of such reversals, the sheer magnitude of capital flows can interfere with key policy objectives, such as achieving domestic price stability or improving domestic competitiveness. As policymakers in developing countries consolidate gains made in their stabilization programs and pursue further structural reforms, they face an additional challenge: how to design policies that meet domestic objectives while at the same time protecting the economy from the impact of a rapidly changing international financial marketplace.

The paper by Peter Montiel is a most comprehensive study of these issues. In a very systematic way, the paper reviews the policy alternatives for dealing with macroeconomic problems created by capital flows and the advantages and disadvantages associated with each. The paper then analyzes the experience of individual countries in order to derive lessons on the feasibility, usefulness, and limitations of each of the policies considered.

Briefly stated, the policies analyzed in the paper can be classified as: (a) those that attempt to directly control the flows of external capital, and (b) those that minimize the impact of the flows on the macroeconomic

Liliana Rojas-Suárez is principal adviser, office of the chief economist at the Inter-American Development Bank (IDB), Washington.

aggregates of the domestic economy. Capital controls and widening exchange rate bands belong to the first group of policies, while sterilized intervention, reserve requirements, and fiscal contraction belong to the second group.

The paper admirably fulfills its purpose. Indeed, the coverage and depth of the discussion has made my job a very hard one, as I found myself largely agreeing with both its analysis and its conclusions. Therefore, rather than being critical of the paper, I will attempt to complement the analysis by addressing another element of the relationship between capital flows and macroeconomic policies—the role of the domestic financial sector.

In my view, the impact of capital flows on a particular country, and the effectiveness of policies designed to deal with these flows, are largely influenced by the state of the domestic financial sector, particularly the banking system. For example, policymakers may be concerned that bank loans financed by the expansion of money are not sound enough to stand a reversal of the inflows, which would provide an additional motivation for controlling the expansion of monetary aggregates associated with capital inflows. That is, the policy issue concerns not only the quantity but also the quality of domestic credit expansion.

Because financial markets are relatively more fragile in developing countries than in industrial countries, the quality of bank credit is more important in the former. Indeed, in contrast to the experience in most industrial countries (where turbulence in foreign exchange markets has not resulted in serious banking problems),[1] recurrent evidence in the recent history of a number of developing countries, especially in the Latin American region, shows that balance of payments crises associated with a reversal of capital inflows have been followed by severe difficulties in the banking system. The recent events in Mexico and Argentina are cases in point.

The argument that I want to advance here is that the strength of the domestic banking system matters for the effectiveness and limitations of macroeconomic policies designed to control the expansion of credit. A corollary to this is that the quality of the banks also plays an important role in determining the extent of the appreciation of the real exchange rate during periods of capital inflows.

To develop this argument, I focus on the experiences of some Latin American countries with two policies commonly used to control the potential expansion of domestic monetary aggregates associated with capital inflows: sterilization and reserve requirements.

---

1. The exception is the experience of three Nordic countries (Finland, Norway, and Sweden), where severe banking crises followed the exchange rate crisis of the Exchange Rate Mechanism (ERM) in late 1992.

Sterilization

The purpose of a sterilization policy when used by countries following fixed or actively managed exchange rates is to limit the impact of capital inflows on the expansion of the monetary base. The degree to which a country sterilizes can be measured by the ratio of foreign reserves to the supply of base money. This measure captures the intent of sterilization, which is to control the growth of credit by controlling the growth of base money as foreign currency assets are purchased by the central bank.

To identify the degree to which countries have relied on sterilization, figure 1 presents the recent evolution of the ratio of foreign reserve assets to monetary base for six Latin American countries during the recent capital inflows period. Consistent with the evidence presented elsewhere, the data indicate that Chile was the most aggressive and consistent sterilizer among this group. Colombia was the second most active sterilizer throughout the period, while Brazil sterilized heavily during 1992–93. Mexico and Peru followed with somewhat lower average ratios of international reserves to monetary base. In Argentina, consistent with the establishment of the "Convertibility Law," that requires that the monetary base be fully backed by foreign exchange reserves, the ratio of these two variables has remained close to one since 1991. This implies that Argentina was the least active sterilizer among the six countries.

Although the lack of perfect capital mobility has allowed sterilization to have an impact on the monetary base, as discussed in Montiel's paper, the real question is whether this policy has been effective in controlling the expansion of broader monetary aggregates, which is, after all, the final aim of the policy. Have the most active sterilizers also been the most successful in controlling monetary expansion? Although an exhaustive treatment of this question would require extensive systematic research, a simple analysis of the evidence indicates no significant relationship between the degrees of sterilization and of monetary expansion.

Figure 2 plots the average annualized growth of a broad domestic monetary aggregate, adjusted for exchange rate changes, and the average ratio of international reserves to the monetary base for the period 1992 through mid-1994. Broad money is defined to include currency held by the public and both bank deposits and nonbank liquid assets held by the nonbank public.[2] Figure 2 indicates that Mexico experienced the slowest growth in broad money, even though it was a much less vigorous sterilizer than Chile. Brazil, an active sterilizer, experienced the highest growth in broad money. On the other hand, Argentina, an inactive sterilizer, experienced a very high growth rate in liquidity. Hence, the figure reveals

---

2. A detailed definition of broad money for each country is contained in Rojas-Suárez and Weisbrod (1996).

Figure 1 Ratio of international reserves to monetary base, 1989–93

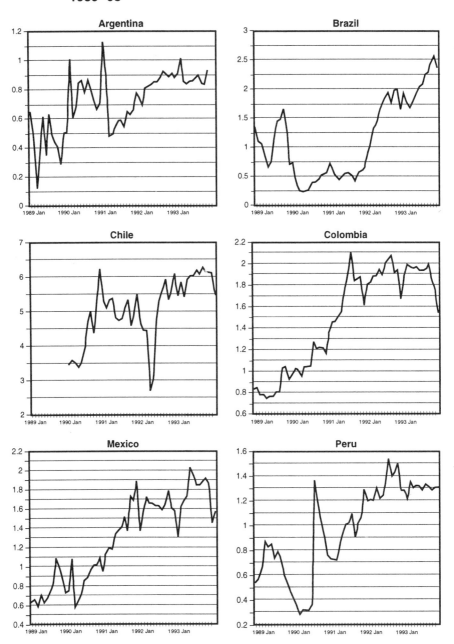

Source: IMF, *International Financial Statistics.*

Figure 2 Averaged liquidity growth and ratio of reserves to base, 1992–94

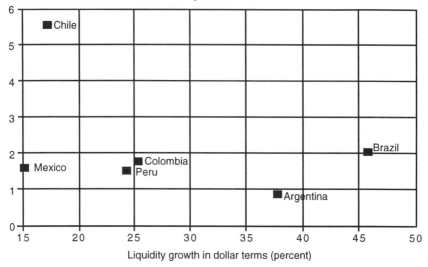

ratio of international reserves to monetary base

Liquidity growth in dollar terms (percent)

Sources: Banco Central de Chile, *Boletin Mensual;* Banco Central de Reserva del Perú, *Nota Semanal;* Banco Central do Brasil, *Boletin;* Banco Central de la Republica Argentina, *Boletin Estadistico;* Banco de la República Colombia, *Revista del Banco de la República;* Banco de Mexico, *Indicadores Económicos.*

no obvious relationship between the extent of sterilization and the growth rate of broad money.

I believe that to explain the lack of relationship between sterilization and the growth of money, it is necessary to understand the recent evolution of the process of financial intermediation in those countries. As is well known, domestic investors' view of the quality of a country's banking system is an important factor in determining the demand for liquid assets. If investors believe that banks make good credit decisions, they will also believe that banks will pay off their deposit liabilities in real terms. Hence, they will demand more bank deposits. Since bank deposits constitute the largest component of broad money in the Latin American region, one would expect that countries with a strong banking system are those where the banking system plays a major role in intermediating capital inflows. Therefore, the relative strength of the banking system needs to play a role in determining the expansion of monetary aggregates.

To characterize the banking systems of individual countries as strong or weak, I rely on a recent study by Steven Weisbrod and myself in which we attempt to classify five of the Latin American countries in the sample according to the strength of their banking systems (Rojas-Suárez and Weisbrod 1995). Brazil was not included in the analysis.

Based on a comprehensive analysis of the behavior of commercial banks and the central bank during the 1980s and early 1990s, we concluded that by 1994, Chile had the strongest banking system among the sample countries, followed by Colombia. Peru and Argentina were at the opposite end, while Mexico was in the middle. As a point of clarification, it is important to note that our definition of bank soundness was not confined only to the analysis of traditional bank ratios (which in some of the countries analyzed did not have too much meaning); we also examined the incentive structure established by policymakers to deal with possible bank difficulties. In our view, where policymakers put mechanisms in place to motivate banks to perform their role of maintaining borrower creditworthiness, bankers become well-equipped not only to evaluate properly the risks they take but also to develop workout programs with their borrowers if sudden adverse shocks lead to banking difficulties. Thus, we view a strong banking system not as one that can prevent difficulties altogether but as one where problems are faced promptly and bankers have incentives to restore defaulting borrowers to performing status.[3]

Consistent with the ordering described above, the countries classified as having the strongest banking system were those where bank intermediation, reflected in the ratio of bank deposits to GDP, was the highest. For example, Chile, classified as having the strongest banking system in the group, also had the highest ratio of deposits to GDP (figure 3). In spite of being an active sterilizer, Chile displayed a sustained increase in the ratio of deposits to GDP during most of the capital inflows period. This is also true for Colombia, where the period of more aggressive sterilization policies (1990–93) coincided with the fastest rate of growth of deposits to GDP in the last decade. In contrast, Argentina's low ratio of deposits to GDP is consistent with the large bank disintermediation that followed the hyperinflation period of the mid-1980s. Although this ratio has been increasing over the last few years, the extremely low point reached in 1991 suggests that the increase in the ratio largely reflects a partial recovery from the unprecedented disintermediation. A similar pattern of behavior is shown in Peru and Mexico, the two other countries in the sample that experienced large financial disintermediation during the 1980s. In the case of Mexico, however, the process of re-intermediation occurred earlier than in Argentina and Peru. As a result, the highest rate of growth of deposits to GDP took place during the period 1989–91. The improvement in this ratio decelerated during 1992–93.

---

3. The recent banking difficulties in Mexico and Argentina provide an excellent opportunity to fully assess the strength of these systems. Although some have argued that the shocks faced by these economies were too large to enable the banking sector to avoid problems, the way the crisis was managed and the capacity to quickly solve current problems will provide an indicator of the long-term soundness of the banking sectors in these countries.

Figure 3 Total deposits as a percentage of GDP, 1982–93

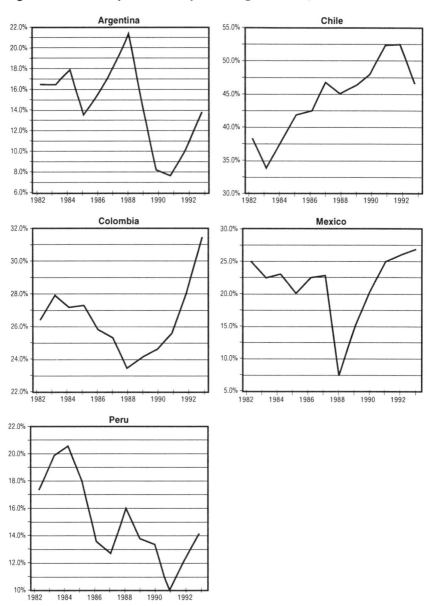

Source: IMF, *International Financial Statistics.*

These results shed added light on figure 2. Argentina shows a very high rate of expansion of liquidity, largely because of the extremely low ratio of deposits to GDP reached in 1991. Indeed, while the recent pattern of liquidity growth in Chile and Colombia is consistent with the continued expansion of financial systems that are perceived as being relatively strong, the rapid growth of liquidity evident in Peru and Argentina during 1992–94 largely reflected the success of stabilization efforts in improving public confidence. Thus, the extent of real bank activity in a particular country seems to be influenced more by the quality of the banking system than by the sterilization policy chosen by the central bank.

Capital Inflows and Reserve Requirements

The argument would not be complete without reviewing the experience with reserve requirements. Could it be that the extent of domestic monetary expansion reflects only the policy stance regarding reserve requirements? In other words, even if controlling the growth of the monetary base through sterilization is not enough to control the expansion of broad money, have the policy objectives been achieved with high reserve requirements? After all, the main argument advanced by supporters of high reserve requirements is that as an effective tool for controlling liquidity growth, high reserve requirements allow for a high ratio of international reserves to liquidity. This in turn protects the central bank in the event of an attack on the exchange rate because the demand for international reserves by investors holding domestic-currency denominated assets can be satisfied without having to resort to high interest rates to defend the parity.

Figure 4 displays the real annualized growth in a broad liquidity aggregate versus reserve requirements on demand deposits for the six countries discussed in this note. The comparison is undertaken for the most recent period of capital inflows, 1993 through mid-1994.[4] The figure shows that there is no clear relationship between these two variables. Indeed, the negative relationship expected by advocates of high reserve requirements is not in evidence. Brazil, with the highest reserve requirement, was one of the countries with the highest rate of liquidity growth. In contrast, Mexico, with a zero reserve requirement ratio, experienced a moderate rate of growth of liquidity during this period.

Concluding Remarks

The conclusion that I derive from the discussion above is that the strength of the banking system is an important determinant of the evolution of

---

4. A similar picture is obtained if reserve requirements on time deposits are used. The analysis is largely based on Rojas-Suárez and Weisbrod 1996.

Figure 4   Average liquidity growth and reserve requirements, 1993–94

reserve requirements on demand deposits (percent)

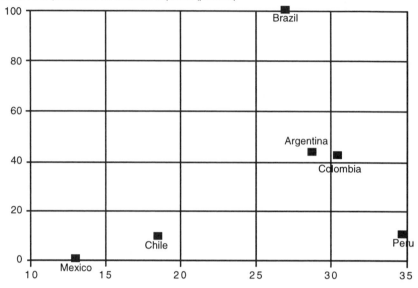

Liquidity growth in dollar terms (percent)

Sources: Banco Central de Chile, *Boletin Mensual;* Banco Central de Reserva del Perú, *Nota Semanal;* Banco Central do Brasil, *Boletin;* Banco Central de la Republica Argentina, *Boletin Estadistico;* Banco de la República Colombia, *Revista del Banco de la República;* Banco de Mexico, *Indicadores Económicos.*

domestic monetary aggregates; indeed, it may even surpass the importance of some policies used to control its expansion. In addition, there is a related question that the analysis in this note might help to answer: Can a sound banking system contribute to ameliorating the appreciation of the real exchange rate associated with capital inflows?

I believe that the answer to that question is yes. If the financial system has strong mechanisms in place to control the quality of credit, banks will have an incentive to properly evaluate the risks associated with extending loans. Sound banks will take into account the probability of a reversal of flows when extending credit to economic agents whose real net income depends largely on revenues from the nontradeable economic sector. If this risk is properly assessed, banks will need to accumulate more capital when extending loans to finance activities related to the nontradeable sector. This, in turn, will act as an incentive to limit credit to this sector and will therefore contribute to minimizing the appreciation of the real exchange rate. By focusing on the quality of credit and not only on its volume, sound banks can contribute to a stable macroeconomic environment.

References

Rojas-Suárez, Liliana, and Steven Weisbrod. 1995. *Financial Fragilities in Latin America: The 1980s and 1990s.* IMF Occasional Paper No. 132. Washington: International Monetary Fund.

Rojas-Suárez, Liliana, and Steven Weisbrod. 1996. *Achieving Stability in Latin American Financial Markets in the Presence of Volatile Capital Flows.* In Ricardo Hausmann and Liliana Rojas-Suárez, *Volatile Capital Flows: Taming Their Impact on Latin America.* Washington: Inter-American Development Bank.

7

What Role for the Official Sector?

Morris Goldstein and Guillermo A. Calvo

Like the developing-country debt crisis of the early 1980s, the global stock market crash of October 1987, and the 1992–93 crises of the Exchange Rate Mechanism (ERM), the Mexican economic crisis of 1994–95 provided a powerful impetus for reassessment and stock taking. The search is on for policy "lessons" that could help other emerging-market economies avert a repetition of Mexico's difficulties, as well as for institutional reforms that would strengthen the system's arsenal of crisis prevention and crisis management instruments.

Among the questions on the front burner are the following: How much of the vulnerability to financial crisis was unique to Mexico and how much reflects current or prospective vulnerabilities that a wider set of emerging market economies share? What policy guidelines in host countries stand the best chance of reducing future vulnerabilities while maintaining much of the benefit of international financial integration? Why didn't either private market forces or surveillance by official watchdogs identify Mexico's difficulties earlier and bring sufficient corrective pressures to bear before a crisis erupted? All things considered, was the unprecedented, large ($50 billion plus) official support package for Mexico justified, and did the difficulties associated with arranging it suggest the need either for new mechanisms for emergency financial assistance or for new formal or informal workout procedures for sovereign debt crises?

Morris Goldstein is Dennis Weatherstone Senior Fellow at the Institute for International Economics, Washington. Guillermo A. Calvo is a professor of economics at the University of Maryland.

At their economic summit in Halifax last June, the Group of Seven (G-7) countries offered their own initial recommendations on how to forestall and/or deal with future Mexicos. In brief, they proposed, inter alia:

- that the International Monetary Fund (IMF) establish benchmarks for the timely publication of economic and financial data and identify publicly the list of countries meeting these benchmarks;

- that the IMF give sharper, franker messages to countries whose policies are going off track;

- that a new "emergency finance mechanism" be established within the IMF for quick, surgical responses to crises with systemic implications and that this mechanism be subject to strong conditionality and be financed via roughly a doubling of the General Agreements to Borrow (GAB);

- that G-10 authorities review procedures that might facilitate the orderly resolution of international debt crises in a financial environment characterized by greater diversity of creditors and financial instruments;

- that countries continue to be encouraged both to remove capital market restrictions and to develop appropriate supervisory and regulatory systems.[1]

Do these G-7 recommendations go in the right direction? Are they likely to be adequate to deal with the risks at hand? What potential problems do they hide under the carpet?

In this chapter, we reflect on the role of the official sector in preventing and managing crises associated with large and volatile private capital flows to emerging markets. These reflections are organized along the following lines. We first highlight the role of financial vulnerabilities—particularly maturity and currency mismatches in public-debt management and in banking—in provoking Mexico-type crises. In addition, we draw attention to the way in which "temporary," large private capital inflows can lead to an overly optimistic reading of the adequacy of international reserves and the government's fiscal position. The following section turns to existing early warning arrangements. We identify several of the key constraints on both private market discipline and official surveillance and offer a few suggestions on how to improve early warning arrangements. We then review the rationale for multilateral official lending and consider issues (eligibility, size, speed, and moral hazard) associated with proposals to reinforce the mechanisms for providing emergency financial

---

1. See Halifax summit (1995) and US Treasury (1995) for the full communiqué, as well as for background documentation on its main features.

assistance. In that connection, we also discuss the attraction of formal and informal workout procedures for sovereign debt default, along with some of the thorny problems that plague its early implementation.

Financial Vulnerabilities in Host Countries

Economists will no doubt be debating the origins and lessons of the Mexican economic crisis for a long time. If one had to draw up a representative "top 10" list of lessons based on the studies done to date, it might look as follows:

- Even with its strong policy track record, Mexico allowed its current account deficit (at about 8 percent of GDP in 1994) to become far too large (the safe limit would be on the order of 3 or 4 percent of GDP).

- Mexico used too much of its foreign borrowing for private consumption and not enough for investment.

- Mexico subscribed too readily to the Lawson thesis that current account deficits originating in the private sector are inherently benign and self-correcting.

- In view of the significant cumulative real appreciation of the peso and the large and climbing current account deficit, Mexico permitted the nominal anchor role of the exchange rate to overstay its welcome (it should have devalued or moved to a much wider band, by the latest March or April 1994).

- Mexico let monetary and fiscal fundamentals slip somewhat in 1994 and was slow to correct these slippages even in the face of market nervousness.

- Mexico received an unusual dose of bad luck in 1994, in the form of both a turn in the international interest rate cycle and unfortunate domestic political developments.

- Mexico shows that even the best trained and mostly highly regarded technocrats are not immune to political pressures that can delay needed exchange rate and macroeconomic policy measures.

- Mexico went too fast and too far in liberalizing its capital account (it should have made greater recourse to controls and/or taxes on short-term inflows, or at least discouraged portfolio capital inflows relative to inflows of foreign direct investment).

- Mexico relied too heavily on short-term and foreign-currency indexed debt in 1994.

- Mexico suffered lapses in supplying the market with up-to-date and transparent information and hence blunted the market discipline that could in turn have prompted an earlier and less costly correction (for further discussion, see Bergsten 1995; Bergsten and Cline 1995; G. Calvo 1995a, 1995b; Cline 1995a; Dornbusch and Werner 1994; Frankel 1995; Sachs, Tornell, and Velasco 1995; Solomon 1995; Williamson 1995; see also chapter 1).

We concur with much of the underlying message in the top 10 list. That being said, it seems to us that the emerging consensus on the crisis runs the danger of giving insufficient emphasis to financial vulnerabilities, particularly mounting maturity and currency mismatches in public debt and in the banking system that together rendered the Mexican government illiquid and produced not only a currency crisis but a debt crisis as well. Concentrating on these financial vulnerabilities and elevating "stock"-type disequilibria above "flow"-type disequilibria (the current account) also make it easier to explain several key characteristics of the crisis, especially the country pattern of attacks.

Monetary Policy and Debt Management

A crucial chapter in the Mexican story occurs in early 1994 when the private capital markets become markedly more pessimistic about the economic outlook in Mexico (as indicated, inter alia, by a much higher risk premium on Mexican securities and a sharp falloff in net private capital inflows).[2] From that point on and until the outbreak of the crisis in December, the Mexican authorities made a strategic decision not only to stick with the quasi-fixed exchange rate but also to minimize the rise in domestic interest rates that would otherwise have ensued (if there was little or no sterilization of capital flows).[3] They implemented this decision in two ways. First, they allowed domestic credit to expand enough to offset declining international reserves and hence kept the monetary base on a relatively even keel (figure 1). Second, they engaged in large-scale substitution of lower-yielding, short-term, dollar-indexed government securities (the now infamous *tesobonos*) for higher-yielding, short-term, peso-denominated ones (*cetes*; see figure 2).[4]

By thwarting the classical monetary adjustment mechanism, the Mexican authorities implicitly accepted the risk that continued deteriorations

---

2. A similar story emerges if one emphasizes the negative effects of an upward turn in US interest rates combined with Mexican political developments on the demand for money in Mexico in 1994; see G. Calvo and Mendoza (1995).

3. For more extensive treatment of this strategy, see G. Calvo (1995a, 1995b), IMF (1995), Sachs, Tornell, and Velasco (1995), and chapter 1.

4. The expansion in issuance of *tesobonos* is pronounced between March and August 1994 and then again in October and November.

Figure 1   Mexico: central bank sterilized intervention

end-of-month stocks in billions of new pesos

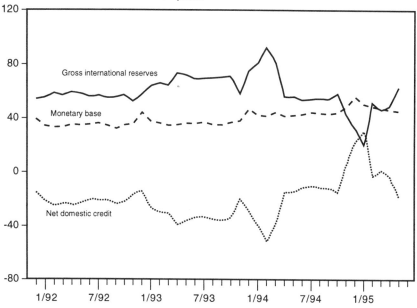

**Figure 2   Public debt held by the private sector and
commercial banks, December 1993–December 1994**

percent of total

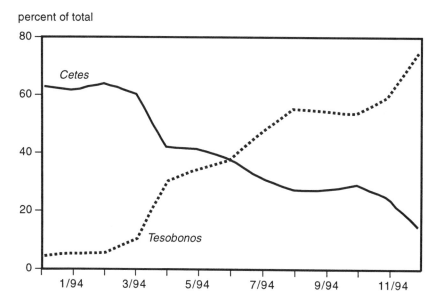

in confidence, as manifested in reduced net capital inflows, would be translated into a continuing decline in international reserves. By substituting *tesobonos* for *cetes*, they assumed the currency risk that had previously been carried by creditors.

It is not entirely clear *why* the Mexican authorities decided against accepting the interest rate consequences that would have gone along with a tighter monetary policy. Perhaps they thought the decline in net private capital flows would be only short-lived (e.g., because the election results would bolster confidence and the overvaluation was being reduced by a depreciation in the real exchange rate for the peso that amounted to about 10 percent in first three-quarters of 1994). Almost surely, they were worried about the impact of higher interest rates on the banking system (with potential spillovers to capital flight). After all, overdue loans (relative to both total loans and bank capital) were already quite high at Mexican banks in mid-1994.[5] A likely related concern was that an increase in short-term rates would raise mortgage rates, reduce economic growth, and alienate key sources of electoral support prior to the elections.

In any case, the result of this monetary and debt management tandem was to open up an increasing mismatch between the government's short-term liabilities and its liquid assets, particularly in terms of foreign exchange. After expanding by nearly tenfold between February and November 1994, the stock of *tesobonos* outstanding grew (by late summer/ early fall) to exceed the (rapidly declining) stock of international reserves. By the beginning of December, when reserves had fallen to less than $13 billion, that gap was on the order of $9 billion to 10 billion.

Unlike debt denominated in domestic currency terms, in these circumstances the government's liquidity problem cannot be eased by the central bank printing currency and supplying it to the government; if the stock of international reserves is inadequate to meet obligations coming due, foreign exchange would have to be borrowed. Also note that a devaluation will not lower the government's foreign currency–denominated obligations (by definition). True, a devaluation will help reduce the need for further borrowing and permit the debtor to earn foreign exchange in the future (by contributing to a current account surplus), but those resources may not be available soon enough to avoid a default if a large amount of foreign-currency debt is maturing in the very near term. The shorter the time horizon and the larger the existing stock disequilibrium, the less relevant will be flow remedies.

A similar picture of a liquidity mismatch in public debt and reserve management emerges if we look at private holdings of Mexican short-

---

5. IMF (1995) reports that the ratio of past due loans to total loans at Mexican banks increased steadily from about 4½ percent at end-1991 to about 8½ percent in mid-1994; during the same interval, the ratio of overdue loans to bank capital increased from 46 to 97 percent.

Figure 3　Mexico: domestic debt[a] (in dollars) and international reserves

billions of dollars

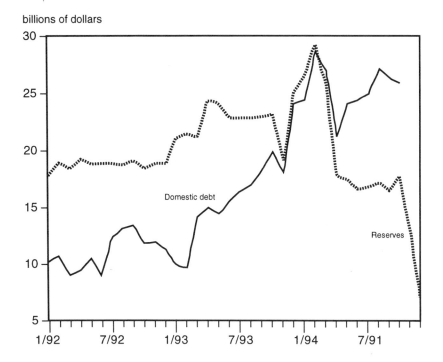

a. *Cetes* plus *tesobonos*.

term public debt (the sum of *cetes* and *tesobonos*).[6] Even though the 1994 expansion of *tesobonos* came largely at the expense of *cetes* (the stock of *cetes* fell by over 50 percent between February and November 1994), *cetes* outstanding stood at a high level (equal to roughly 100 percent of net international reserves) at end-1993. When a country has a quasi-fixed exchange rate regime, it has to stand ready to redeem liquid short-term public debt with international reserves.

Figure 3 compares outstanding short-term government debt to Mexico's gross international reserves. Note that the gap grows progressively larger from the second quarter of 1994 on, and widens appreciably in October and November.[7] To be sure, the government could try to reduce the real

6. Little would be altered if we added other peso-denominated short-term government debt (pagafes and bondes) to the sum of *cetes* and *tesobonos* (G. Calvo and Mendoza 1995).

7. Granted, there have been other periods (e.g., especially mid-1990 and, to a lesser extent, late-1993) when the mismatch between short-term public debt and international reserves in Mexico was also large and no attack occurred; however, in those earlier episodes, other factors (e.g., the share of dollar-denominated debt, the main holders of debt, the strength of net capital inflows, etc.) were more favorable.

value of its debt denominated in domestic currency by engineering a surprise increase in inflation. But that would jeopardize maintenance of the fixed exchange rate, raise serious questions with investors about its longer-term prospects, and probably yield relatively little relief on short-term debt since bond holders could soon recontract at much higher interest rates. Additional resources to meet domestic-currency obligations could be raised by tightening the government's fiscal position, but again, the reduction of flow disequilibria may not take place fast enough to avoid a default if the stock disequilibria is large enough and near-term enough.

In our view, the size and prospective trend of this short-term mismatch between government liabilities and assets helps pin down the *timing* of the Mexican crisis. Once investors became aware that Mexico's ability to meet its maturing short-term debt obligations was in doubt, rollover of that debt became problematic and a financial panic was soon in train.[8]

This vulnerability on government debt also offers insight into a wide range of questions: why the official rescue operation had to be mounted with such haste, why market pressures responded strongly to good and bad news about prospects for agreement on an official support package (both in the US Congress and the IMF), why devaluation by itself in December (in the absence of an official support package that would address the stock disequilibria) would *not* have been adequate to restore the confidence of investors, why that support had to be in the form of reserve currencies, why European countries (Sweden, Italy, the United Kingdom) that devalued or floated their currencies during the ERM crises of 1992–93 (before their reserves had gotten so low relative to their near-term debt obligations) had an easier time of it than Mexico, and why consideration of formal and informal approaches to more orderly resolution of sovereign bond defaults has become such a hot ticket.

Liquidity considerations associated with the maturity and currency composition of debt also shed light on why countries may be attacked even if broad indicators, like the ratio of total debt to GNP, suggest they are comfortably solvent.[9] For one thing, potential mismatches (at one end of the yield curve) are likely to be obscured by aggregate indicators. For another, a failure of current bond holders to roll over maturing debt may be interpreted by other investors as a signal that the country is suffering from solvency difficulties (even if the true problem is only one of illiquidity); since solvency takes time to prove, other investors may also refuse to refinance, adding to the run. In addition, solvency is not independent

---

8. About $29 billion of *tesobonos* were scheduled to mature in calendar year 1995, almost $10 billion in the first quarter alone. By end-December, Mexico's gross international reserves stood at roughly $6 billion.

9. Mexico's ratio of total gross public debt to GDP jumped from 34 percent in 1993 to 51 percent in 1994—but this latter figure was still well below the OECD average of 71 percent (Sachs, Tornell, and Velasco 1995).

**Figure 4   Scheduled public-sector debt service/exports ratio,[a]
1992–94 (foreign and domestic)**

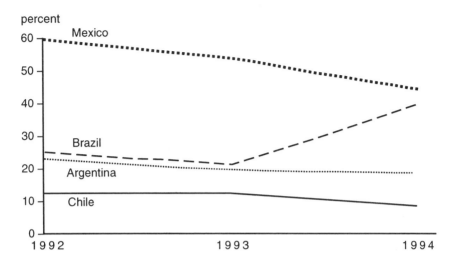

a. Excludes amortization.

of the measures taken by authorities during a liquidity crisis. For example, the country may react by imposing taxes that are easy to collect in the short run but that have a deleterious longer-term effect on output (G. Calvo 1995a).

Perhaps the greatest advantage of focusing on vulnerabilities associated with government debt positions is that it offers some clues as to why some countries were more likely targets of attack than others. It is just as important to try to understand who was *not* attacked and why as to understand why Mexico was at the top of the hit list.

Suppose we compare Mexico to other countries in the region with respect to the size of the public debt maturing in 1995. Figure 4 shows scheduled public debt service, excluding debt amortization, as a share of exports for the period 1992–94.[10] The difference between Mexico and three other large, emerging-market countries in Latin America (namely, Argentina, Brazil, and Chile) is striking. While this ratio hovers around 60 percent for Mexico over the whole period, it is much lower for Argentina and particularly low for Chile. It hits 60 percent for Brazil, but not until 1994. Argentina engaged in much less sterilization of capital inflows during the 1990–93 period than did Mexico, and this helped limit its marketable public-sector debt.

---

10. The qualitative conclusion would not be different if we replaced exports in the denominator with gross international reserves.

Figure 5 Potential public-sector debt service/exports ratio,[a] 1992–94 (foreign and domestic)

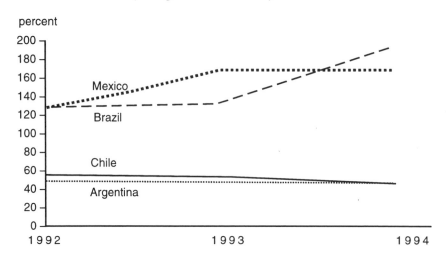

percent

a. Includes amortization.

Figure 5 introduces debt amortization into the picture by adding it to scheduled debt-service payments. Again, Mexico emerges as much more vulnerable than either Argentina or Chile, with a ratio reaching almost 180 percent in 1994. Brazil again joins Mexico at the top; indeed, Brazil's ratio even exceeds Mexico's in 1994. This reflects the fact that a large share of Brazilian public-sector *domestic* debt is of very short maturity. In contrast, the ratios for Argentina and Chile remain below 60 percent, suggesting that not much debt was scheduled to mature during those years.

But if Brazil had a debt ratio similar to Mexico's in 1994, why didn't Brazil get attacked first or at least simultaneously?[11] One conjecture is that the type of debt holder may matter. Brazilian debt (outside the central bank) was largely in the hands of Brazilian commercial banks and Brazilian firms. When debt is held by banks, the ultimate holders are depositors who typically place a high value on liquidity services. As such, they may be less yield conscious than some other types of holders. Similarly, if debt is being held by Brazilian firms, chances are that it is being utilized for repurchase agreements that enhance firms' liquidity; again, this may suggest a relatively low degree of yield sensitivity. In contrast, a significant share of Mexico's *tesobonos* was held by foreign institutional investors,

11. Cline (1995a) offers some other reasons Brazil may have been less vulnerable to attack than Mexico in 1994.

who are generally believed to be highly sensitive to changes in expected returns.

Banking Sector Difficulties

A second puzzle raised by figure 5 is why Argentina ran into serious difficulties (requiring emergency help from the Fund) whereas Chile did not—even though the two had debt-service ratios in the same ballpark. To answer that puzzle, as well as to generate a fuller account of Mexico's vulnerability, one has to bring the vulnerability of the banking sector and the behavior of monetary aggregates into the equation. In addition, financial vulnerability will be affected by the type of exchange arrangements maintained by the country.

Banks are of course in the business of maturity and liquidity transformation. Indeed, the traditional explanation for why banks are "special" is that only they issue liquid short-term liabilities *and* hold illiquid long-term assets (typically, business loans). But banks' ability to sustain such a maturity and liquidity mismatch requires that they maintain the confidence of depositors and creditors; otherwise, they are vulnerable to a run. Bank capital, deposit insurance, and the existence of a lender of last resort can each serve to boost confidence—but the cushion (capital/insurance) may not be large enough and the central bank's monetary policy stance may not be unconstrained enough to carry the day.

Note should be taken too of the advances in technology and information processing that have made it easier for residents of emerging markets (like their counterparts in industrial countries) to alter the currency composition of bank deposits when they sense that a significant change in relative yields is in the making. In this regard, the IMF (1995) reports that most of the pressure on Mexico's foreign exchange reserves in 1994, and particularly just before the devaluation, came not from foreign investors but rather from Mexican residents sending their funds abroad. This is a useful reminder that with increasingly liberalized and integrated capital markets, *domestic* investors also have the potential to initiate a crisis. Capital flight counts.

It is also important to recognize that bank liabilities can be a key component of the *government's* potential financial vulnerability. Whatever the de jure arrangements for uninsured deposits and for providing government assistance to banks, we observe very few cases (in either developing or industrial countries) where governments allow large banks to fail. For this reason, bank liabilities are often realistically regarded as a *contingent* liability of the government.

Back to the story. As noted earlier, Mexican banks already had accumulated a large burden of overdue loans by the middle of 1994. This followed a period in which the (marked-to-market) value of bank assets was undergoing increasing strain while bank liabilities were increasing rapidly. The

Figure 6   Mexico: M2 (in dollars) and international reserves, 1985–94

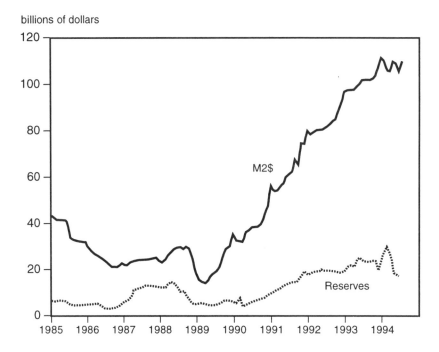

billions of dollars

growth of monetary aggregates relative to GDP had been spurred over the past four years by capital account liberalization, by banking reforms that liberalized bank interest rates and eventually eliminated reserve requirements, by disinflation, and by capital inflows themselves. On top of this, depositors had a good deal of familiarity with foreign currencies. Roughly a quarter of commercial bank liabilities in 1994 were dollar denominated; the corresponding figure for the state development banks was about two-thirds (Sachs, Tornell, and Velasco 1995).

No surprise then that with international reserves falling markedly in 1994, rising ratios of monetary aggregates to international reserves pointed to another financial mismatch. Figure 6 shows Mexican M2 deflated by the peso/dollar exchange rate (henceforth denoted M2$), along with gross international reserves (in US dollars). Beginning in 1989, the gap between M2$ and gross international reserves widens progressively. Before the 20 December devaluation, M2$ had climbed to a level almost five times higher than the maximum level of international reserves ever recorded in Mexico. You might ask why the numerator of that ratio did not fall in 1994, as the upward turn in US interest rates and the expenditure implications of a decline in net capital inflows reduced the demand for money (G. Calvo and Mendoza 1995). The answer—as suggested earlier—

**Figure 7 Argentina: monetary aggregates (M3) and
international reserves, January 1991–January 1994**

billions of dollars

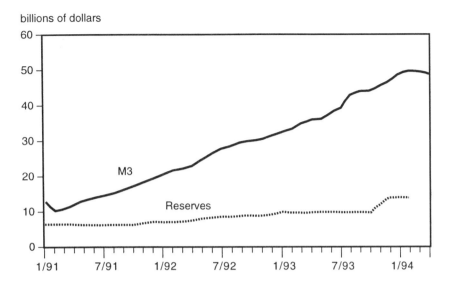

is that the Bank of Mexico followed an active policy of credit expansion
during this period to offset deposit withdrawals and to rein in an incipient
increase in domestic interest rates. This was successful in preventing a
fall in M2—but again, at the cost of creating the conditions for a run
against *tesobonos* (G. Calvo and Mendoza 1995).

Returning to cross-country variations in financial vulnerability, we note
that the 1994 ratio of M2$ to gross international reserves was around 3
in Brazil and only about 1.5 in Chile—far below Mexico's 1994 ratio of
close to 5. Here too, Mexico emerges as the most vulnerable. But why
might Argentina appear to be more vulnerable than Chile? There are two
complementary clues. First, the relevant monetary aggregate for Argentina in 1994 (M3, which includes US dollar-denominated deposits) was
very high as a ratio to gross international reserves—in fact, not much
different from that for Mexico. Second, monetary aggregates in Chile
moved almost in tandem with international reserves over the 1991–94
period, whereas the growth of monetary aggregates in Argentina exceeded
considerably the growth of international reserves over this same period
(figures 7 and 8). As it turned out, banks in Argentina did undergo a
fairly serious liquidity crisis in 1995 (right after the Mexican crisis), when
total deposit withdrawals accounted for almost 18 percent of the stock of
bank deposits. At that time, Argentinean banks were assisted by relaxing
reserve requirements within the band allowed by the Convertibility Law.

Exchange arrangements also matter. The main point is that countries
with "hard" exchange rate commitments provide very limited scope for

Figure 8   Chile: M2 (in dollars) and international reserves, January 1991–July 1993

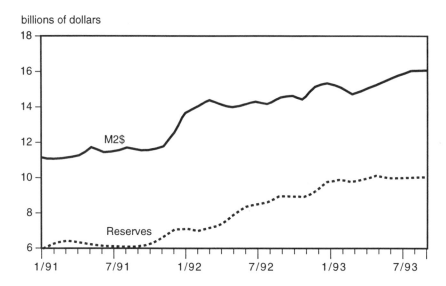

billions of dollars

the central bank to act as lender of last resort at times of weakness in the banking system. On this count, Argentina with its currency board arrangement and Mexico with its quasi-fixed exchange rate, were more vulnerable, *ceteris paribus*, to banking difficulties than were Brazil and Chile (where monetary policy was not so constrained by exchange arrangements). It's more than coincidence that both Mexico and Argentina had to arrange outside official support packages within the last year to help alleviate problems in their banking systems.

Capital Flow Volatility, External Factors, and Underlying Fiscal and International Reserve Positions

Financial mismatches are not the only source of vulnerability. The Mexican economic crisis also illustrates how easy it is for host countries to be lured into a sense of overconfidence—both about the permanence of private capital flows and about the size of the protective cushion against potential outflows.

By now, there is an impressive array of country case studies and multi-country econometric evidence to support the proposition that countries with better policy fundamentals find it easier to attract and to hold foreign and domestic saving—as well as to access that saving on better terms (spreads, maturities, offering prices, etc.)—than do countries with weaker policy fundamentals (Chuhan, Claessens, and Manning 1993; Cline 1995b; Dooley, Fernandez-Arias, and Kletzer 1994; Edwards 1991; Goldstein

1995a; and Goldstein et al. 1994). Nor is there much doubt that the $500 billion cumulative net private capital inflow into developing countries over the 1990–94 period owes a good deal to the improved macroeconomic structural and policy performance in the host countries themselves.[12]

But recent empirical research has also established firmly that these net private capital flows to emerging markets are heavily influenced by interest rates and business cycle conditions in major creditor countries.[13] Recall that during the surge of inflows in 1990–93, US short-term nominal interest rates fell from over 7½ percent to about 3 percent.[14] It was not until February 1994 that US short-term rates began to move in the other direction.

G. Calvo, Leiderman, and Reinhart (1993) demonstrated that international reserve accumulation and real exchange rate appreciation in Latin American host countries were highly correlated with various US financial variables. Later studies, using data for a wider sample of host countries on net private capital flows and secondary market prices of bank debt, found that foreign financial variables typically accounted for at least half (and sometimes as much as 85 percent) of the variation in capital flows or secondary market prices (Chuhan, Claessens, and Mamingi 1993; Dooley, Fernandez-Arias, and Kletzer 1994; Fernandez-Arias 1994).

The clear implication is that so long as we continue to have business and interest rate cycles in industrial countries, net private capital flows to emerging markets will be subject to considerable volatility (albeit perhaps around a secularly rising trend) that is partly beyond the host countries' control. In other words, some significant share of capital inflows is likely to be "temporary." And if part of the inflows is temporary, then part of the effects of these capital inflows is also temporary. Failure to take this into account can lead to false optimism in the host country in at least two important areas of policy.

One is in the size of the international reserve cushion. As is well known, the surge of capital inflows into emerging markets in 1990–93 was accom-

---

12. For a discussion of these policy changes, see Corbo and Hernandez (1993), Fernandez-Arias and Montiel (1995), Goldstein (1995a), and Schadler et al. (1993).

13. Lower interest rates in creditor countries induce greater capital flows to developing countries through two channels. First, they make investing at home less attractive at the margin than investing abroad (the asset substitution channel). Second, they improve the creditworthiness of debtor countries, either by reducing the present discounted value of their contractual debt payments or by increasing the present discounted value of the resources available for making external payments, or both (Fernandez-Arias and Montiel 1995).

14. When the industrial countries are taken as a group, the weighted short-term interest rate fell from over 9 percent in 1990 to a little over 5 percent in 1993. Long-term interest rates showed somewhat less variation but followed the same trend. Substituting real for nominal interest rates, or interest rate spreads for interest rate movements in creditor countries alone, or relative stock market performance for rate of return differentials on fixed

panied by large increases in international reserves (often accounting for 40 percent or more of the net inflow; see G. Calvo, Leiderman, and Reinhart 1993, 1995; Fernandez-Arias and Montiel 1995). This reflected the conscious policy decision in host countries not to be completely passive with respect to either an appreciation of the nominal exchange rate or a monetization of the inflow. This decision was implemented by engaging heavily in sterilized exchange market intervention; hence, the large increase in international reserves.

The rub is that when industrial-country interest rates move in the opposite direction, as they did in 1994, a symmetrical policy of intervention on the outflow side implies that reserve *de*-accumulation will also be substantial. As noted earlier in this section, Mexico followed just such a sterilization policy in the face of reduced inflows. It is instructive that what looked like a huge cushion of international reserves in February–March 1994 ($29 billion) was nearly depleted (80 percent, down to $6 billion) only nine months later.

A second area of policy affected by the temporary nature of inflows is fiscal policy. Another empirical regularity of capital inflow episodes is that the host country typically experiences an increase in aggregate demand, often marked by a consumption boom. Because fiscal revenue tends to be positively associated with aggregate demand, the fiscal balance tends to improve during episodes of capital inflow, particularly for countries that place relatively high reliance on consumption taxes. But again, part of the revenue improvement is unsustainable because part of the capital inflow is temporary. If the fiscal balance is therefore not "corrected for volatility," there is a danger that authorities may expand government expenditure unduly—a policy that may be difficult and costly to reverse when external factors switch sign and induce an outflow. In Mexico's case, the government's underlying fiscal position for 1994 was actually somewhat weaker than suggested by the observed data because aggregate demand was still reflecting the expansionary effect of earlier inflows and because the interest saving associated with the substitution of *tesobonos* for *cetes* was unsustainable (G. Calvo 1995a).

Implications for Policy and Surveillance

The first line of defense against Mexico-type financial crises should be to reduce the homegrown component of vulnerability. From the perspective of the observations outlined above, at least three lessons stand out.

First, emerging market countries ought to *be cautious in managing public debt*. Debt management strategies that produce a bunching of short maturities and relatively heavy reliance on foreign currency–denominated (or indexed) liabilities carry a shadow price (to the borrower) significantly

---

income assets, doesn't alter the qualitative nature of the conclusion; (G. Calvo, Leiderman, and Reinhart 1993).

above current borrowing costs.[15] As argued by Dooley (1995), in a world in which rollover and currency risk can be influenced strongly by events beyond the borrower's control (such as changes in international interest rates), asset markets are subject to multiple equilibria, emerging market borrowers (as a group) have a spottier track record on default than do industrial countries, and constraints elsewhere in the financial system limit the scope for aggressive defensive action on interest rates, borrowers have to worry about the *variance* of borrowing costs—not just about average cost. It's quite possible to drown in a lake that has an average depth of three feet. To be sure, sticking more closely to longer term, nominal, domestic-currency debt will be expensive—but probably less expensive than the costs over the longer-term of having an imprudent debt management policy facilitate a financial crisis.

Lesson number two is to *beware of the weakness in the domestic banking system*, which can be a serious handicap to avoiding a crisis in an environment of liberalized capital markets and of sharp changes in risk/return outlook for traded assets.[16] If the Mexican banking system had been in better shape in early 1994, it is quite possible that monetary authorities would have felt more comfortable about allowing reduced capital inflows to pass through unimpeded into higher interest rates, which itself would have moderated the decline in reserves. But when the banking system is already laboring under a high burden of overdue loans, there will be concern that large increases in interest rates, via their contractionary effect on economic activity and on property and equity prices (which serve as the collateral for loans), will exacerbate those weaknesses—to say nothing of the political fallout. With open capital markets and low transactions costs of switching the currency composition of deposits, questions about the government's ability to meet both short-term government debt obligations and potential recapitalization costs in the banking system can easily generate a run. If fixed exchange rate commitments severely constrain the central bank's ability to act as lender of last resort and if the deposit insurance fund is small relative to the amount of bad loans, the situation is more fragile still.

The best solution, of course, is not to allow the banking system to get into serious trouble to begin with. This means, inter alia, requiring banks to hold adequate risk-weighted capital; limiting the concentration of loans

---

15. A distinction needs to be drawn here between established and new borrowers. When countries first get access to the capital markets, they may have little choice but to borrow short term; this is their toe in the water. But after they have been active participants in the market for some time and have established some reputation, they have a wider maturity menu at hand. Mexico clearly was in this latter category.

16. Banking system weaknesses also acted as a binding constraint on the defense of fixed exchange rates for some ERM countries during the crises of 1992–93; (Goldstein et al. 1993).

to highly interest-rate-sensitive sectors; maintaining good accounting standards; and ensuring that banking supervisors have the information and authority they need to monitor risk, to issue cease and desist orders, and, if necessary, to close troubled banks before they become insolvent. If serious banking difficulties are already at hand, a second-best approach is to tighten oversight and prudential regulations so that banks don't engage in double-or-nothing risk taking behavior. Such regulations might include higher reserve requirements (especially on short-maturity deposits), temporary restrictions on foreign currency–denominated borrowing by banks, and tighter limits on open foreign exchange positions.[17] Arranging outside financial assistance to help recapitalize weak banks may also help calm nervous depositors—especially where the exchange rate regime limits the central bank's room for maneuver.

The third lesson is that surveillance exercises need to *pay more attention to indicators of financial vulnerability*. For starters, the concept of adequate international reserves needs to be revised to take greater account of capital flows, financial stocks, and explicit and contingent government liabilities. For countries that are increasingly involved with private capital markets, assessing reserve adequacy with respect to imports alone makes less and less sense. If figuring "net" international reserves is intended to capture proximity to a balance of payments crisis, then *all* short-term public obligations should be considered as candidates for subtraction from gross reserves. Some obligations should presumably carry lower weights than others, depending on country-specific institutional characteristics. For example, domestic currency–denominated obligations of the government should carry less weight than foreign currency–denominated ones, since the government can reduce the value of the former by devaluation. However, if exchange rate stability is highly prized, then the devaluation option would be very costly, making the two types of debt close substitutes on that count. This is clearly the case in Argentina, where by law, the peso bears a 1-to-1 exchange rate against the US dollar.

In the case of an exchange rate band, perhaps the best way to proceed would be to use the upper limit of the band to value short-term domestic-currency obligations of the government in terms of foreign exchange. If government debt is held primarily by economic agents who value highly its liquidity services, then it should carry a lower weight (as a liability) than if the holders are more sensitive to changes in expected yields. If some public assistance to the banking system (beyond what is available from deposit insurance and outside official creditors) is likely to be extended over the short term, that too might be subtracted. In a similar vein (but more qualitatively), judgments about the adequacy of reserves should be conditioned by assessments of the government's room for

---

17. Mexico did impose restrictions on banks' foreign liabilities (see Buira, chapter 11).

maneuver to increase domestic interest rates during an attack. Low growth, high unemployment, a high share of nonperforming loans in the banking system, and a large public-sector deficit imply that reserves will, *ceteris paribus*, be under greater strain during an attack than if those conditions were not prevailing.

The Early Warning System

In a sense, every financial crisis can be regarded as a failure of the early warning system.[18] By the early warning system, we mean the set of signals and pressures on participants in financial markets to modify excessive borrowing or lending and/or to alter misaligned exchange rates *before* a crisis occurs.

For our purposes, it is convenient to think of the early warning system as having two components: private market discipline and surveillance by the official sector. In the former case, it is private creditors who are exerting pressure on borrowers, whereas in the latter case, it is official creditors (major creditor governments plus the IMF, the World Bank, the Organization for Economic Cooperation and Development [OECD], the Bank for International Settlements [BIS], etc.) who are exerting peer pressure, sometimes supplemented with conditional access to official lending.

In this section, we first review the conditions affecting market discipline and then discuss their relevance in the Mexican context. This is followed by some remarks on surveillance by the IMF, again drawing on the perspective of Mexico. Finally, we offer some suggestions on how the working of the early warning system could be improved.

Market Discipline

Market discipline means that financial markets provide signals and incentives for borrowers to behave in a manner consistent with their solvency (Lane 1993). Specifically, the underlying notion (as applied to the fiscal behavior of sovereign borrowers) is that as borrowing proceeds progressively beyond prudent limits, the market initially insists on an increasing interest rate spread and eventually excludes the borrower from additional credit altogether. The increase in the cost of borrowing, along with the threat of being rationed out of the market, then provides the incentive for the borrower to correct imprudent behavior.

---

18. A financial crisis itself can of course enforce greater discipline on economic policy; indeed, sometimes a crisis is the only way to obtain that discipline. But generally, the idea is to take corrective actions *before* they are imposed by a crisis in a more disorderly and costly way.

Market discipline will tend to more effective, *ceteris paribus*, when six conditions are satisfied. First, financial markets should be free and open so that interest rates can respond to the level and kind of borrowing. Capital controls or restrictions on competition that allow governments to create a captive market for their debt and weaken discipline.

Second, market participants should be aware of the full magnitude of the debtor's obligations (so that they can accurately assess debt-servicing obligations relative to capacity); for governments, it is useful if such information includes off-balance-sheet liabilities. The poorer the quality of information, the harder it is for creditors to accurately price risk, the easier it is for rumors to incite runs, and the greater the scope for the borrower to engage in manipulation.

Third, market participants should *not* expect the authorities to intervene routinely and to guarantee the survival of insolvent firms (institutions, countries) in the case of actual or impending default; otherwise, creditors will have little incentive to monitor the health of the borrower, borrowers themselves will have less incentive to maintain solvency, and interest rates will reflect the creditworthiness of the guarantor—not that of the borrower. It has been argued, for example, that the main reason for relatively narrow spreads on commercial bank loans to developing countries in the 1970s was the expectation that large commercial banks would be "bailed out" by creditor governments in case of difficulties (Folkerts-Landau 1985).

Fourth, the financial system has to be strong enough to withstand a default by the borrower. If the borrower is "too large to fail," then authorities will be driven to provide assistance to the borrower to prevent any systemic repercussions of a default. Also, if failure by the borrower would adversely affect a line of business, then individual firms who count heavily on that line may face a conflict of interest in blowing the whistle on the borrower's difficulties.

Fifth, the borrower's debt should not be *monetized* via central bank purchases; otherwise, inflation and depreciation will erode the real value of the debt. For sovereign borrowing, this condition is particularly relevant in cases in which debts are denominated in the borrower's own currency. Sixth and finally, higher interest rate spreads and/or lower availability of credit should induce the borrower to adopt more prudent behavior. Higher interest rate spreads alone, for example, may not restrain insolvent borrowers who never intend to repay or governments who have very short time horizons (Lane 1993).

In the Mexican case, interest rate spreads did widen appreciably between the first and second quarters of 1994. Specifically, the spread on *cetes* relative to three month US Treasury bills increased from about $5\frac{1}{4}$ percent in the first quarter to over 9 percent in the period from April–July 1994. But then the spread receded back to the 7 percent ballpark and stayed there almost up to the outbreak of the crisis.[19] What could have prevented market discipline from carrying the day?

One contributing factor may well have been inadequate information. Data on Mexico's international reserves (in 1994) were apparently released to the market late—sometimes as much as six months late.[20] This delay by itself probably should have been regarded as a signal, but apparently it wasn't taken seriously. Presumably, earlier release of those data could have induced an earlier and more gradual increase in interest rate spreads and/or earlier pressure on the exchange rate. Interestingly enough, as the crisis unfolded, the Mexican authorities decided to increase public disclosure about key economic developments: as of mid-April 1995, the Bank of Mexico began publishing daily data on money supply, intervention in foreign exchange markets, and current account developments.[21]

Incentive compatibility problems associated with blowing the whistle on Mexico's problems and overestimation of the effects of economic policy reform in emerging markets may also have played a part in market failure. Kaufman (1995, 3) offers the following perspective on the former point:

> Every firm wants to do deals in emerging markets when margins are high. Analysts become part of the deal-making and are reluctant to speak up about problems that might derail a deal. They are also under pressure from sales and corporate finance executives to come up with ideas that might lead to a sale, not ideas that might stop one. The research function is not in the upper echelons of the firm. Getting the message of impending trouble to top management requires getting it past more senior executives who are responsible for dealing, trading, and other functions. It is tough to move bad news up the chain of command.

On the latter point, Krugman (1995) argues that the mutually reinforcing interaction between huge private capital inflows and policy reform in emerging markets is best characterized as a "bubble" that was bound to be pricked once too high expectations about the effects of policy reforms met reality.[22] Both investors and reformers were overoptimistic in predicting how fast hard currency policies could bring down inflation, as well

---

19. Looking at the interest rate spread between one-year *cetes* and one-year *tesobonos* over the period July 1993 to December 1994, Obstfeld and Rogoff (1995) show that this indicator of expected peso depreciation usually exceeded the government's promised maximum depreciation under its announced crawling peg. Nevertheless, this indicator suggests that the credibility of the exchange rate target was at its weakest in April and in the May–August period—not just before the crisis in the late fall-early winter.

20. According to the Group of Thirty (1995), market participants also pointed to data on Mexico's *tesobonos* borrowing as being subject to significant publication delays—but subsequent investigation suggests that these data were available from financial news services (e.g., Bloomberg).

21. The Bank of Mexico now also releases many economic and financial data series on the Internet.

22. Gilibert and Steinherr (chapter 4) come to the same conclusion.

as how quickly growth and income distribution would respond to large capital inflows and trade policy reform. Mexico provided the "reality check" that burst the bubble when it refused to accept either currency devaluation or slower growth.

Note that under both these explanations of market failure, the key problem is not inadequate information. In Krugman's story, investors misinterpret the fundamentals; that is, they behave like chartists. In Kaufman's story, (some) market analysts recognize that fundamentals in the borrowing country have deteriorated but are discouraged from sharing that view with other market participants; hence, the bubble continues until a crisis occurs.

Yet a third possible source of market failure is expected official financial assistance. Market participants may have reasoned through much of 1994 that Mexico was too large—or at least, too important to the United States—to be allowed to default on its bonds. This could explain why the measured default premium on *tesobonos*, defined as the difference between the *tesobono* interest rate and the rate on comparable maturity US Treasuries never rose above 3 percent (between April and December 1994) until the week of the crisis.[23] In the end, of course, the $50 billion official support package did allow *tesobono* holders to get out whole.

A fourth possibility worth mentioning is garden-variety politics. As noted earlier, the market discipline hypothesis assumes a rational borrower whose fiscal policy decisions are sensitive to variations in cost and/or availability. Indeed, as Lane (1993) pointed out, if the rational borrower had the same information as lenders, he would not even wait for the market signal: he would know that higher borrowing would produce a higher interest rate spread and that unappetizing prospect would induce him to refrain from excessive borrowing in the first place. But when the borrower is a government, optimal behavior is harder to define. In the Mexican case, the coming election in August 1994 presumably reduced the response to what market signals were there.

Going beyond the Mexican case, the empirical evidence on the market discipline hypothesis (for sovereign borrowers) is mixed. There is fairly strong support from studies on US states, Canadian provinces, and countries (both industrial and developed) that less-disciplined fiscal policies (as proxied by higher debt ratios and larger fiscal deficits) do lead to higher borrowing costs (Bayoumi, Goldstein, and Woglam 1995; Edwards 1986; Goldstein and Woglam 1992; Lane 1993). Where the empirical evidence can speak with much less authority is on the slope of the interest rate/government borrowing curve: that is, do spreads respond in a gradual, continuous way or alternately, is the response best characterized as

---

23. An alternative explanation is that market participants simply never considered seriously the risk of default until very late in the day.

abrupt and highly nonlinear? It is even less clear regarding the response of governments to these changing market signals.

Official Surveillance

All emerging-market countries have their economic policies reviewed and evaluated at least once a year by the international financial institutions (IFIs). As a rough approximation, the IMF concentrates on macroeconomic and exchange rate policies and the World Bank on structural policies.[24] If a country's policies are heading seriously off track, such official surveillance is supposed to identify the nature and extent of the problem, point out the risks (for both the home country and its trading partners) of a continued deterioration, and make specific recommendations for policy changes that will help correct current and prospective shortcomings.

Via what channels would such surveillance be expected to have an effect—particularly in countries that are at the time *not* operating under policy-based lending programs with the IFIs? Persuasion and peer pressure might work. Persuasion might be enhanced by the professional and objective nature of the analysis, and by the staff's ongoing relationship with member countries. Peer pressure relies on the propositions that misguided and unsustainable policies ultimately generate negative spillovers for other countries and that countries generally value good relations with their neighbors. Another potential channel of influence is publication of information. The data and analysis of economic developments published by the IFIs can influence the private market's evaluation of the creditworthiness of individual countries. Since net private capital flows now account for the dominant share of total capital flows to developing countries (roughly three-quarters in 1993), he who influences private flows could in principle have a large effect on policies even if his own lending were small.

But why should the IFIs have a comparative advantage in monitoring and evaluating such policies and sharing that evaluation with others? Rodrik (1995) provides three answers. One is that information about the quality of government policies is a public good: such information benefits all potential investors, regardless of their specific projects. Given the public nature of the benefit, individual investors have inadequate incentives to devote resources to information gathering of this kind and little incentive to share it with others. In contrast, the IFIs can internalize these externalities. A second answer is that the IFIs have good access to government data and analytical talent of the right kind. Third, unlike credit-rating agencies, the IFIs frequently have financial transactions with their

---

24. The OECD also conducts economic surveillance (over macroeconomic and structural policies) for its member countries. Mexico became a member of the OECD in April 1994.

developing-country member countries. Because they are frequently "putting their money where their mouth is," they have an incentive to promote truthful reporting.

Now, to consider the negative side of the ledger, what factors operate to reduce the effectiveness of official surveillance? In the case of the Fund, at least five come to mind.

First, countries may not only withhold or delay reporting unfavorable economic and financial data to the market, they may withhold it from the Fund too—notwithstanding their obligations under the Fund's Articles of Agreement (Article VIII, section 5). After all, the Fund is obligated to take into account the varying ability of members to furnish the data requested, the Articles do not mention a specific time frame for reporting, and the process of censuring members who are not living up to the letter or spirit of the law has probably been too uncertain and too time-consuming to act as much of a deterrent.

Second, neither the frequency, focus, nor allocation of resources in Fund surveillance may be up to the task at hand. Developing countries that are operating under Fund-supported adjustment programs are subject to near-continuous monitoring, evaluation, and performance criteria. Not so with emerging-market countries that do not have programs and thus may only be subject to a comprehensive review at the annual Article IV consultation. Similarly, while the Fund sends a capital markets mission to major financial centers in order to discuss capital market issues with a range of private financial institutions and official regulatory bodies, that mission too is an annual one. Given how quickly key economic developments can change, the existing frequency of surveillance may be inadequate. Furthermore, as the arguments in the previous section made clear, surveillance may not be focused enough on financial vulnerabilities and banking problems. And surveillance resources may be spread too thin across nearly 180 member countries to give systemic threats in the larger emerging-market economies the attention they merit.

Third, as with private markets, incentive incompatibility problems may constrain timely whistle-blowing. The subjects of surveillance are also the shareholders of the IFIs. Most countries are firm supporters of strict surveillance—until it is aimed in their own direction. The IFIs count on major shareholder support for funding and other initiatives. All of this may create a bias toward "pulling punches" and "clientitis" when it comes to delivering a frank and transparent surveillance message to large shareholders—even if the message is delivered in secret.

Fourth, the ability of Fund surveillance to affect the behavior of private lenders is sharply constrained by the fact that at present most of the surveillance message (at least for emerging-market countries) is delivered confidentially. No doubt, this reflects concerns that going public with an adverse appraisal would both lay the Fund open to the charge that it precipitated a crisis and make member countries more reluctant to provide information on brewing or existing economic problems to the Fund in the future.

The Fund's *International Financial Statistics* appears monthly but contains only data. The biannual *World Economic Outlook* offers Fund assessment of macroeconomic and structural policies in a global perspective, but the discussion there, when it gets down to the level of individual countries (as opposed to country groups), focuses more on major industrial countries than on emerging markets. The Fund's annual *International Capital Markets Report* discusses systemic issues in international finance but again rarely goes into problems at the individual-country level except for major industrial countries. Since November 1994 the Fund has been making publicly available that part of every Article IV country report that describes recent economic developments, conditional upon the country giving its consent to publication.[25] But *not* now published are the Fund's Article IV staff appraisals, which provide a comprehensive assessment of the country's economic policies and prospects.

Fifth and finally, the same political considerations that can blunt the response of governments to variations in the cost and/or availability of market borrowing could also be expected to blunt the effectiveness of official surveillance. Without the requisite political will to change policies, nothing will happen.

Unfortunately, the effects of Fund surveillance are not easily amenable to empirical testing, because much of the "treatment"—either embedded in confidential documents or transmitted orally through confidential channels—is unobservable to outsiders. That same problem limits what can be said (at least by us) on how and where official surveillance may have faltered in the Mexican crisis. Maybe data supplied to the Fund were less timely and less transparent than they should have been. Maybe the error was methodological, in the sense that not enough attention was given to analyses of debt management vulnerabilities, banking problems becoming worse, and exchange rate misalignment.[26] Maybe the message of increasing risks wasn't conveyed forcefully enough—or maybe it was transmitted repeatedly but was not taken seriously on the receiving end. Maybe a combination of these factors was at work. The set of recommendations offered by the G-7 in Halifax is suggestive of that conclusion. The postmortem offered by one insider—Karin Lissakers, the US executive director at the IMF—goes in the same direction: "The whole surveillance process [in Mexico] did not work the way it should have. . . . We were too tolerant"

---

25. As of July 1996, reports for over 154 countries have been released.

26. After all, there were a few private-sector analysts who (on the basis of existing data) emphasized the risk of a Mexican currency/financial crisis before the fact; see, for example, Williamson (1993), Dornbusch and Werner (1994), and G. Calvo (1994).

(*New York Times*, 19 March 1995, E3). And Michel Camdessus (1995), the Fund's managing director, has conceded that the Mexican crisis revealed a problem with the "culture" of the Fund. Specifically, prior to Mexico, the Fund didn't give enough emphasis to the capital account in the balance of payments, and at times it gave too much of the benefit of doubt to member countries.

Strengthening the Early Warning System

The Mexican crisis provides strong support for the view that efforts to improve the early warning system should carry a higher priority than heretofore. Once the early warning system fails, the remaining courses of action—for example, requiring the borrowing country to undergo a very deep recession to generate a current account surplus; permitting a potentially chaotic, unilateral, involuntary rescheduling; attempting to orchestrate a "workout" without the benefit of an internationally agreed code or informal understanding; mounting a large, official support package)—are far from appealing.[27]

The behavior of the early warning system in the run-up to the Mexican crisis also shows why efforts to improve it should proceed along two fronts. As argued earlier, both private market discipline and official surveillance are prone to weaknesses that can reduce their effectiveness; therefore, relying exclusively on one or the other would be ill-advised. But what specific measures would be helpful in improving both market discipline and official surveillance? In our view, three steps stand out.

First, incentives should be increased for supplying the markets with economic and financial data in a more timely, transparent, and comprehensive way. Admittedly, better information is no panacea for avoiding financial crisis: in some cases (e.g., the ERM crises of 1992–93 and the bond market turbulence of early 1994), faulty economic analysis and/or unexpected developments—not imperfect information—was the driving force. Even with better information, private credit markets will still sometimes be subject to (misguided) self-fulfilling prophecies. Nevertheless, the G-7 members in Halifax were on the right track; they just didn't go far enough.

They were on the right track because providing the markets with better information may well help moderate abrupt changes in market sentiment that often accompany delayed release of adverse country data. The point is to get changes in the cost/availability of credit to shock the borrower into corrective action—not to electrocute the borrower with a massive crisis. More timely provision of economic and financial data to the market should also make it less seductive to pump up monetary and fiscal policy

---

27. As Goldstein (1995b, 40) has put it, "Once the milk is on the floor for a large market borrower, it is now a much messier and more costly operation for the official sector to mop it up."

before elections, since such excesses would then become a matter of public knowledge more quickly.

Getting the IMF to establish benchmarks for timely publication of a uniform set of economic and financial data, including more demanding standards for countries heavily involved with international capital markets as well as having the Fund identify publicly the countries that meet the more demanding standard (as agreed in October 1995 by the IMF's Interim Committee), should up the ante for good disclosure. It remains to be seen, however, how long it will take countries to qualify for a gold star. The outcome is not assured, because while the obligation of countries to supply data to the Fund is laid out clearly in the Articles of Agreement, it is our understanding that requirements to *publish* data are not set forth in black and white. But even if signing on to the publication standard is only voluntary, market pressures should operate to encourage compliance: once a few large borrowers comply, others may well face pressure to join the club—much in the same way that the market came to regard conforming to the Basel capital adequacy standards (for internationally active commercial banks) as the norm. As a fallback measure, some market incentive could be obtained by supplying a notation—"dd," for "data delayed"—in *International Financial Statistics* when an entry to a key series was missing without an adequate explanation; after Mexico, the market might well read this as a signal.

The G-7 Halifax proposal on information does not go far enough. As argued in several recent studies (Goldstein 1995b; Group of Thirty 1995; Minton-Beddoes 1995; Rodrik 1995), the Fund should be authorized to begin timely publication of its staff appraisals for individual countries. This would help market participants get a better picture of current economic fundamentals, potential vulnerabilities, and medium-term prospects in individual countries. As demonstrated in the previous section, the *interpretation* of economic and financial data can be as crucial to detecting vulnerability to a crisis as the data themselves. Granted, the market is already full of forecasts and policy analyses. But if, as is generally assumed, the IMF has a particular expertise in the analysis of policy fundamentals, then that analysis ought to be shared with the private markets. Also, as noted earlier, the Fund's financial transactions with countries may give it a credibility advantage over credit-rating agencies.

The chief objection to releasing these reports is that it will lay the Fund open to charges of precipitating a crisis. While this is a legitimate concern, we do not see it as decisive.[28] For one thing, there is the counterfactual to consider. Once country policies get sufficiently off track, some market correction is almost inevitable. Is it not better to catch a problem at an

---

28. See Goldstein (1995b) for a fuller discussion of the case for sharing IMF views with the private markets.

early stage, when the correction is relatively small, than to have the market at a later stage force a less orderly and more costly adjustment? For another, it is not necessary in these reports for the Fund to flash in neon lights the message, "Country A has overborrowed and is in danger next year of not being able to service its maturing public debt," or "Currency X is vastly overvalued." As in reports issued by other official agencies (e.g, the Federal Reserve on monetary policy), the drafting can be done in a way that permits market participants to read between the lines. Recall too that Fund (staff) appraisal of economic policies for individual G-7 countries already appears in the *World Economic Outlook*; wider publication of staff appraisals would provide more in-depth analysis for all countries, thus supplying markets with increased information on those emerging-market economies whose interaction with private capital markets has potentially significant spillover effects.

The influence over economic policies that IFIs obtain from their own lending activities is likely to shrink in the future as private capital flows continue to expand relative to multilateral lending. Thus, the potentially most promising channel for increasing the effectiveness of official surveillance is to influence the private market's assessment of country economic policies. But to do that, the IFIs will have to be less reluctant to communicate their views. In the end, we agree with Rodrik (1995, 11–12) that the best policy for the IFIs is "to play it straight with market participants."

In a second constructive step, the IMF should modify its internal operating procedures so as to deepen its contacts with private capital markets; intensify its surveillance over debt management, banking, and financial-sector developments; and increase the frankness of its advice, especially when it comes to exchange rate policy.

At present, an annual Fund capital-markets mission visits major financial centers in North America, Europe, and Asia to discuss potential sources of systemic risk with both private market participants and regulatory officials. Given the rapidity with which assessments of country situations can change, however, it probably makes sense for there to be a brief interim capital market visit to keep closer tabs on areas of increasing market concern. We have already indicated why we think the Fund should speak more to private capital markets; the other side of that coin is for it to *listen* more to private capital markets as well.

A frank Fund view on exchange rate policy is especially desirable because this is an area in which delays in adjustment, at least in fixed and quasi-fixed exchange regimes, occur all too commonly. The 1990s track record includes not only the Mexican case but earlier delayed adjustments in the ERM crises of 1992–93 and in the CFA franc zone. In most cases, delays are linked to the perceived political costs of devaluing. Since the Fund has more political independence than do governments, it needs to be a clear voice for timely adjustment—before misalignments become so large as to threaten a crisis. Major shareholders of the Fund should encourage the Fund to speak more frankly on these matters by holding it more accountable for identifying large misalignments. In this connection, the G-7's call in Halifax—that "wherever feasible, the Fund should be more open and transparent in its assessments and policy advice"—is right on the money.

Third, a way needs to be found to limit the frequency and scope of emergency financial assistance to cases where there is a genuine market failure, where the official lender faces a relatively low risk of being repaid, where such assistance is being provided at market or penalty rates inclusive of conditionality, and where failure to provide such assistance has expected costs for the system in excess of the benefits.[29] Otherwise, market discipline will not be a very effective component of the early warning system. Since all this is tied closely (for sovereign borrowers) to arrangements for an international lender of last resort, we take it up in the next section.

Emergency Financial Assistance, the International Lender of Last Resort, and Workouts for Sovereign Bond Defaults

It would be too optimistic, some might say naive, to assume that even an improved early warning system would be able to prevent all crises linked to large-scale shifts in private capital flows. For this reason, the instruments of crisis management also warrant examination, particularly in light of the experience of the Mexican crisis. In this section, we first review the rationale for using multilateral conditional lending to relieve balance-of-payments crises. We then discuss the issues raised by large and volatile private capital flows for the design of mechanisms for emergency financial assistance and for so-called international bankruptcy or workout procedures.

The Rationale for Multilateral Lending

When the IMF was established 50 years ago, the expectation was that private international capital flows would be quite limited. Thus the rationale for Fund lending was straightforward: by providing official financing, it would permit countries to adjust to balance of payments pressures in ways that helped preserve national and international prosperity—that is,

---

29. Most of this parallels Bagehot's advice to lend freely to an illiquid borrower upon good collateral and at penalty rates—amended to account for policy conditionality and for the difficulties in attaching collateral for sovereign governments.

with less deflation of output and employment (at home and abroad) and with less use of trade restrictions.

Some developing countries still do not have much recourse to private capital flows. But for those that do—which are the main subjects of this paper—what rationale for multilateral lending remains? In particular, why can't private capital flows, with or without bilateral official flows, do the job? The answer that has emerged from the literature is linked to public goods, market imperfections, conditionality, and political acceptability.

In the previous section, we characterized information on the quality of government programs as a public good (which would be undersupplied by private markets). An analogous claim can be made for openness to trade and capital flows (Masson and Mussa 1995). Because gains from trade accrue to all parties, private lenders cannot fully appropriate the benefits; hence, they will supply too little insurance (in the form of financing) against adverse shocks to prompt a sufficiently outward-looking policy orientation. In contrast, the Fund (or other official lenders) can internalize these externalities. In addition, it can use coinsurance and conditionality to limit excessive risk taking associated with the provision of such insurance.

When we turn our attention to market imperfections, we find credit rationing due to imperfect information about borrowers, absence of an international bankruptcy code for enforcing sovereign loan and debt contracts, multiple (good and bad) equilibria in asset prices, herd behavior on the part of lenders, and distortions due to the availability of (domestic) too-big-to-fail bailouts for banks together with weak banking supervision (Frankel 1995; Masson and Mussa 1995; Sachs 1995). Those who focus on these issues often draw attention to such factors as the large (excessive) swings in sovereign lending over the past 100 years (Eichengreen 1991), the protracted nature of negotiations over rescheduling and forgiveness of bank debt after the 1982 debt crisis, and contagion of equity price movements among emerging markets during periods of market turbulence (including directly after the December 1994 outbreak of the Mexican crisis).

The argument is that official lending can help compensate for such private market imperfections. In addition, multilateral official lenders are said to possess a comparative advantage over both private lenders and bilateral official lenders in one important area, namely, the exercise of *policy conditionality* over sovereign borrowers; such conditionality is important, in turn, for overcoming time-inconsistency problems that arise between lenders and borrowers. As Rodrik (1995) emphasizes, in an era when national sovereignty is highly prized and zealously guarded, multilateral conditionality is more politically acceptable (in part because developing countries are shareholders of the IFIs) than either bilateral conditionality or private-sector conditionality.[30] As illustrated by the Mexican case, multilateral lending may also offer burden-sharing advantages for official lenders if the amounts involved become very large.

Issues in Crisis Management Lending

So much for justifying the continued existence of an international lender of last resort. The key question then becomes: Does the Mexican crisis point to the need for both larger financial resources and greater speed in the institutional arrangements for crisis-management lending? If so, what characteristics should such arrangements possess?

It is not hard to understand why Mexico would have brought these issues to the fore. In the end, the official sector was able to mobilize a $50 billion support package. But consider the two main components of that package.

The largest piece of the pie ($20 billion) represented a conditional, collateralized loan, funded from the US Treasury's Exchange Stabilization Fund (ESF). Recall that the Clinton administration was driven to this mode of financing only after it proved impossible to garner sufficient congressional support to obtain approval for an earlier $40 billion loan guarantee proposal—impossible despite the special stakes involved for the United States. Moreover, in the aftermath of the US loan, several bills have recently been introduced in the Congress to sharply constrain future use of the ESF for Mexico-type rescues.

The second-largest slice was a $17 billion standby loan from the IMF. Mexico's quota in the Fund is SDR1.75 billion (roughly $2.5 billion). Under current Fund access policy, maximum cumulative access is 300 percent of quota. Mexico not only received that maximum, which is itself unusual, but also received an additional $10 billion under the "exceptional circumstances" provision. In addition, the funds were front-loaded more than in the normal case. This loan for 700 percent of quota was the largest standby in Fund history. It was also widely reported in the press that several European executive directors of the Fund abstained in the voting for the Mexico loan.

No doubt this background weighed on the minds of G-7 leaders in Halifax last July when they proposed establishment within the Fund of a new standing procedure, the Emergency Financing Mechanism. This procedure would involve a fund arrangement with strong conditionality, high upfront access, and faster access—all for crisis situations under the "exceptional circumstances" clause. To help finance this means of dealing

---

30. We speak here of *direct* private-sector conditionality, as illustrated, say, by negotiations between bondholders' councils or commercial banks and sovereign debtors. Indirect private-sector conditionality, as reflected in changes in the cost and/or availability of credit, is much less politically sensitive.

with financial emergencies, which would be now beyond the Fund, the G-7 proposed doubling the resources currently available under the GAB ($27 billion).

The issues that come up in designing official financing for crisis management can be conveniently addressed under the following headings: eligibility, size, speed, and moral hazard.

Eligibility

Beyond the general notion that volatile private capital markets can create various types of balance-of-payments pressures, at least three different eligibility concepts have been put forward as a rationale for new or additional forms of official assistance. One model is the short-term financing facility proposed on several occasions by the managing director of the Fund (Camdessus 1994a, 1994b). Its main purpose would be to help member countries cope better (including avoiding resort to exchange restrictions) with very short-term balance of payments or exchange market pressures. To be eligible, a country would have to have been pursuing satisfactory policies and be facing a viable external payments situation. In other words, it would be a facility to counter short-term speculative attacks *un*justified by economic fundamentals. Qualifying countries would be able to obtain financing much more quickly and perhaps in larger amounts than under existing Fund facilities and practices.

In a sense, this facility is reminiscent of the Fund's old Compensatory Financing Facility (which provided compensation for temporary shortfalls in export receipts)—amended to include "exogenous" private capital flows. Note that if such capital flows were being driven by temporary factors beyond the member's control, then balance-of-payments pressures should be essentially self-correcting.[31] Similarly, if the country has satisfactory prospects, there is little worry about the Fund getting its money back.

On the positive side, as noted earlier, there is strong empirical evidence that private capital flows to emerging markets are heavily influenced by external factors (especially interest rates and business cycle conditions in major creditor countries). Likewise, the Mexican crisis illustrates that some "contagion" of capital market pressures can occur in the short-term—even affecting countries with sound policies (IMF 1995). Those suffering from such contagion would therefore be good candidates for such a facility.

On the negative side, a number of considerations could materially reduce or complicate the facility's usefulness. For one thing, when pres-

---

31. This also implies that no conditionality would be necessary. In practice, however, the "temporariness" of capital market pressures may be hard to ascertain *ex ante* and the borrower could create new problems by following inappropriate policies after receiving assistance; for these reasons, some review of the borrower's policies would probably be a feature of such a facility.

sures are short-term and policies are sound, it will be easier to provide financing via other existing assistance channels (including central bank swap lines). For another, some external factors driving capital flows will be medium- to long-term and thus will require adjustment (even if they are beyond the borrowing country's control); financing could unduly delay adjustment of such pressures. Much more often than not, speculative attacks will reflect, at least in part, *un*sound policies in the borrowing country. And if economic conditions and policies are changing rapidly, it will be difficult to precertify a country for eligibility based on a review of policies at a previous Article IV consultation; this in turn is likely to reduce the facility's speed advantage relative to existing procedures.

Had it been in existence in 1994, Mexico presumably would *not* have been eligible to draw from such a short-term facility (Williamson 1995): as already demonstrated, capital and exchange market pressures reflected in part unsatisfactory domestic (monetary, exchange rate, and debt management) policies, and its large, current account deficit and banking-sector difficulties clouded the medium-term horizon.[32] Also, Mexico needed medium-term assistance to transform its short-term government debt obligations into longer maturity ones. Had access to such a short-term facility been available in early 1994, it might have delayed Mexican adjustment further, increasing the size of the disequilibrium.

A second approach is a facility tailored to a particular kind of market failure associated with private capital flows. For example, if the lack of an international bankruptcy code for sovereign debt is the main problem, then eligibility for the facility should be restricted to "emergent borrowers" (Frankel 1995). Those emerging-market countries who had not reached a threshold amount of sovereign borrowing would not be eligible; nor would emerging markets suffering from, say, speculative attacks on fixed exchange rate regimes (even if those attacks could not be justified by weak fundamentals). The advantage of such an approach is that it overlaps the least with existing arrangements because it is targeted at a specific deficiency in the official safety net. The disadvantage is that it excludes from eligibility countries suffering from other kinds of capital flow vulnerabilities, even if those vulnerabilities are larger now than when existing arrangements were put in place. Mexico would have been a potential user of such an emergent borrower facility because of its problems in meeting maturing *tesobonos* obligations (for more on formal and informal workout procedures, see below).

Finally, a third approach—and the one that has so far garnered most attention—is to define eligibility in terms of the systemic consequences of not intervening. This is the GAB model. The basic rationale is to limit

---

32. Williamson (1995) has argued that a country should not be eligible to use such a short-term facility if its current account deficit (relative to GDP) is excessive.

adverse *spillover* effects from the troubled borrower to others so as to reduce the likelihood of either a wider disruption in the global financial system or a deterioration in macroeconomic performance of the regional or global economy. The closest analogy is emergency lending by central banks (in a domestic context) to limit systemic risk. The tacit assumption is that balance-of-payments pressures in nonsystemic borrowing countries can be handled adequately via existing arrangements.

An advantage of the systemic approach is that it limits activation of the implicit and explicit official safety net to serious spillover threats, thereby producing the least adverse effects on private market discipline. In this regard, it should be noted that the GAB has not been activated since the late 1970s. The disadvantage (relative to an approach that targets assistance to the nature of the market failure) is its bias in favor of sovereign borrowers who are "too large to fail" (for whatever reason) and against smaller sovereign borrowers.

An interesting question in this context is whether, with the benefit of hindsight, Mexico's difficulties should have been regarded as "systemic." Anyone trying to answer that question immediately encounters two difficulties. One is that the counterfactually,—that is, what would have happened in the *absence* of the $50 billion official support package—is unobservable; thus the endeavor is something of a conjectural exercise. The other difficulty is that very different definitions of "systemic risk" currently coexist in the literature.[33] While practically all of them capture the notion of shocks in one part of the financial system spreading and causing difficulties elsewhere, they imply quite different behavior for the lender of last resort. For example, Schwartz (1994) sees systemic risk as arising only via contractions in the money supply (e.g., flights to currency or fears that liquidity will be unavailable at any price during a stock market crash); she therefore would sharply limit the activity of the lender of last resort to preventing such contractions from taking place. In contrast, some others (e.g., Kindleberger 1978) see a much wider variety of circumstances adversely affecting the national or global economy and consequently envision a more active role for the lender of last resort. Notwithstanding these difficulties, it is useful to consider the various kinds of potential spillovers from Mexico's currency and debt problems.

In our view, Mexico was *not* systemic with respect to endangering banking and payments systems in the major industrial countries. Unlike the 1982 debt crisis, this time the creditor claims and institutions most affected were not commercial bank loans and money center banks but rather securitized instruments (bonds and portfolio equity) held mainly

---

33. See Bartholomew and Whalen (1994), Bordo, Mizrach, and Schwartz (1995), Eichengreen and Portes (1987), Goldstein (1995c), and Mishkin (1994) for a review of alternative conceptions of systemic risk and/or of a financial crisis.

by institutional investors.[34] Thus, losses were much more distant from the banking and payments system than in 1982.[35] Also, the weight of emerging markets in these diversified institutional portfolios is still rather small (on the order of 1 to 2 percent; see Goldstein and Mussa 1994; IMF 1995); falling asset values should therefore have translated into only small declines in wealth. One thus would have expected relatively small effects on consumption and the real economy (because the United States has large trade links with Mexico relative to other G-7 countries, it faced spillovers to the real economy via US exports and the value of the dollar that did not apply to others). Nor do we think that there was a serious danger at the time that losses on Mexican or emerging-market securities as a whole would ignite a large-scale sell-off of mutual fund shares more generally. The limited scale of redemptions during the height of the crisis suggests that most final holders of US mutual funds seem to regard their claims as longer-term investments. Capital account and asset price spillovers are much larger from industrial countries to emerging markets than those going in the opposite direction.

Both actual and potential spillovers of the Mexican crisis were more significant with respect to other emerging markets, the so-called tequila effect. Yields on internationally traded equity and bonds tend to show higher correlations during periods of market turbulence than during normal periods (Goldstein and Mussa 1994), and the Mexican crisis followed that same pattern. IMF (1995) and Masson and Mussa (1995) show, for example, that returns on Brady bonds were much more highly correlated between Mexico and three other large emerging markets in Latin America (Argentina, Brazil, and Venezuela) during the crisis period (mid-December 1994 to March 1995) than during either 1993 or 1994. Across emerging markets, so Calvo and Reinhart (chapter 5) find evidence that the spillover or contagion effect on capital flows is significant from larger countries to smaller ones (but not in the other direction), and especially so from Mexico to others. The latter finding may reflect Mexico's importance as a destination for private flows over the 1990–94 period and its de facto role as a "benchmark" for pricing emerging-market securities (Goldstein et al. 1994).

As it turned out, Latin American emerging markets were subject to earlier and larger spillover effects from Mexico than Asian ones. Within

---

34. This changing composition of private capital flows extends more generally to host developing countries as a group. During the run-up to the debt crisis (1978–81), commercial bank loans accounted for more than three-quarters of net private capital flows to developing countries. In contrast, during the 1990–93 period, the corresponding figure was 17 percent. The remaining shares are accounted for by foreign direct investment (51 percent), portfolio equity flows (16 percent), and bonds (15 percent); see Goldstein (1995a).

35. Eichengreen and Portes (1987), in discussing the financial crisis of the 1930s, highlight the linkages running from debt defaults and exchange market disturbances to the instability of banking systems.

Latin America, the rebalancing of institutional portfolios seemed to fall hardest on Argentina (where stock and bond prices fell on the order of 50 percent in the first trimester following Mexico), and next hardest on Brazil. In Asia, Thailand, the Philippines, Indonesia, and Hong Kong took relatively brief but nontrivial hits. A recent IMF report (1995) shows that after the initial reaction, those emerging markets with weaker fundamentals (low saving rates, large current account deficits, significant volumes of short-term debt, and weak banking systems) were subject to greater pressure than those with stronger fundamentals. By May–June of 1995, equity markets and international reserves in most of the affected countries were back to, or higher than, the precrisis level. Mishkin (1994) has suggested that perhaps the best signal of a true financial crisis is an increased interest rate spread between low and high quality bonds; on that score, the immediate aftermath of the Mexican crisis would seem to have qualified.[36]

If the official support package had not been mobilized and Mexico had turned to a unilateral default on *tesobonos*, spillover effects to other emerging markets probably would have been more severe than those actually observed (at least over the first year or so after the crisis). This would have required stronger adjustment measures in the affected countries, and trade and growth in the affected regions would likely have been weaker.[37]

Yet another spillover channel is the policy demonstration effect. This has both a short-term and longer-term aspect. As noted by Cline (1995a), the specter of a Mexican outcome strengthened the hand of policy authorities in the near term for obtaining fiscal adjustment in Argentina and Brazil—and probably in Hungary as well. What will be the longer-term demonstration effect of the Mexican crisis on the "Washington policy consensus" is harder to figure. Some might see the official rescue as an indication that those who make a serious, long-term effort at reform will get strong backing from the international community if they temporarily "fall off the wagon;" others may see it as adding strong banking supervision and prudent debt management to the consensus. And still others will regard it either as reducing the hype about the medium-term payoffs to the consensus (Krugman 1995) or as giving a new legitimacy to controls or taxes on short-term capital inflows (Cline 1995a). The notion that a default or difficult rescheduling by Mexico would have returned much of the developing world to the statist, inward-looking policies of an earlier era strikes us as highly implausible.

In the end, the potential spillover effects from Mexico's impending default in December 1994 were significant enough—and the prospects of official lenders being repaid good enough—to justify the official rescue

---

36. See IMF (1995) for an analysis of interest rate spreads during the crisis.

37. The most severe deflationary effects would of course have taken place in Mexico itself.

package, if only, as Chairman Alan Greenspan then characterized it, as the "least worst" of the available options.

Size

A question closely related to who should get emergency financial assistance under what circumstances is how much assistance is needed to do the job. For now, we are content to identify some of the key factors that would need to be taken into account in addressing the problem.

One factor is the increased integration and agility of international capital markets. While the increased openness and liberalization of capital markets offers significant benefits to liberalizing countries and their trading partners, it also exposes countries to vulnerabilities associated with large and sudden changes in risk/return outlook for internationally traded assets. Moreover, a number of studies have shown that the scale of private capital flows has grown faster than either the stock of international reserves or wider measures of international liquidity (Group of Ten Deputies 1993; Masson and Mussa 1995). As but one indicator of potential vulnerability, Masson and Mussa (1995) show that roughly a third of 49 industrial and middle-income developing countries suffered a maximum, *monthly* reserves loss equal to 100 percent or more of their Fund quotas during the 1985–93 period. The implication is that resources needed for emergency financial assistance are apt to be larger today than, say, a decade or two ago when capital flows were smaller and capital markets less integrated.

A second factor that should be taken into account is the likely covariance of requests for assistance. *Ceteris paribus*, the more coincident are individual country crises, the greater the strain on official resources. For example, if difficulties of major market borrowers were regularly associated with contagion to other (smaller) emerging markets, we would need a larger emergency kitty than otherwise. Mishkin (1994) shows that the incidence of financial crises has historically been much higher during periods of increasing interest rates, stock market declines, increases in uncertainty, bank panics, and unanticipated decline in inflation—but more empirical work is needed to determine how these factors have operated in the case of emerging markets.

The exchange rate regime is a third factor. As the ERM crises of 1992–93 amply demonstrated, attempts to defend a fixed exchange rate against a concerted assault by private capital markets can be an extremely costly (and largely fruitless) operation. This suggests that if emergency assistance is to be used in part to defend against (allegedly unjustified) speculative attacks on fixed exchange rates, the facility will need to be *extremely* careful that the rates being defended are equilibrium ones; otherwise, the resources would simply be used to delay adjustment and no feasible facility or line of credit would be big enough to do the job.

A fourth factor is the availability of coinsurance and of official and private lenders of earlier resort. Unless one is very confident that the shock is purely temporary, it should be accompanied by adjustment—not just financing. The fact that this adjustment imposes some costs on the borrower also serves to restrain excessive risk taking in the future. Likewise, if other insurance mechanisms (e.g., deposit insurance, reserve requirements) and/or other official lenders (national central banks) take up more of the risk, the line of credit needed for the international lender of last resort can be smaller.

A quick approach to the size issue is to ask oneself whether the vulnerabilities that led to Mexico's $50 billion support package are likely to be "unique." Cline (1995a), for one, answers that question in the affirmative. He argues that no country other than Mexico managed to convince foreigners to hold large short-term government debt denominated in domestic currency (albeit indexed to the dollar), and that the systemic risk associated with the "first major shock" to the capital market of the early 1990s cannot by definition, be repeated. The market has now been chastened. As argued earlier, we agree with Cline (1995a) that Mexico's public-debt vulnerabilities helped to put it at the top of the hit list. It may also be the case that Mexico turns out to be unique in the sense that no other emerging-market country can generate the political support in major creditor countries needed to support very large (say, $25 billion plus) emergency financial assistance. But we are not as sanguine as Cline that Mexico is unique as regards the scale of future financial vulnerabilities. Specifically, weaknesses (actual and latent) in banking sectors are anything but an isolated event in emerging-market countries (Folkerts-Landau et al. 1995; Rojas-Suárez and Weisbrod 1994). When you combine those banking weaknesses with a liberalized capital market, increasingly savvy depositors, little or no deposit insurance, a memory of earlier stabilization failures, and international reserves much smaller than bank liabilities, you cannot rule out large-scale future demands on an emergency facility or line of credit. Whether you would want to accommodate those demands is another story.

Speed

As much as anything else, the Mexican crisis put the spotlight on the speed of access to emergency financial assistance. Here too, consideration of a few key questions is sufficient to convey the options.

The natural place to start is to ask under what circumstances speed of access to emergence assistance is so crucial as to make recourse to existing Fund facilities problematic. Williamson (1995) identifies two cases: when a country is trying to defend an exchange rate peg, and when a country is so illiquid that without international help it will have little alternative but to default. We agree but would add a third case: when a country's large banks are undergoing a run and without international help will have little alternative but to suspend payment. In these three cases, an all-or-nothing decision is required. If the emergency assistance arrives even a little late, it may not be possible to affect the desired results. In all other cases, the consequences of delayed access to emergency assistance are better regarded as lying on a continuum, where later assistance implies a greater need for adjustment prior to its arrival. To illustrate the point, if Mexico had in late 1994 not faced a short-term *tesobono* funding crisis and had not been operating under a quasi-fixed exchange rate, there would presumably have been more breathing room either to negotiate an official support package or to try to arrange a workout between creditors and the borrower.

But what constrains existing Fund procedures from responding more quickly to demands for such assistance? One key constraint is the need to review the borrowing member's economic situation and to negotiate the policy conditionality for such assistance. That conditionality serves both as "commitment technology" to overcome potential time-inconsistency problems and as a means of generating the foreign exchange that will allow the Fund to be repaid on time. Even in crises, such a review with negotiation of conditionality would be expected to take a few weeks.

One possible way around this time problem would be to preapprove the borrower for the loan, perhaps at the time of the most recent Fund Article IV consultation—akin to the preapproved line of credit that individuals and firms routinely have available from their banks. It is sometimes argued that public knowledge of the availability of such emergency financing assistance might also help deter speculative attacks not based on fundamentals.

The rub is that preapproval also carries certain risks that on-the-spot decision making does not. An obvious one is that economic conditions may change markedly for the worse between the time that the line was preapproved and the time the borrower wishes to draw on it. For example, the risk of lending to Mexico *before* the turn in US interest rates and before the large-scale substitution of *tesobonos* for *cetes* was different than that after those events. Changes in risk over time also complicate the publication of a list of eligible borrowers. If a country's creditworthiness changes over time, will the facility be prepared to accept the market reaction associated with downgrading a country (that is, removing it from the list)? A second disadvantage of preapproval is the moral hazard on the borrower's side; that is, the borrower will have an incentive to take more risks because insurance is preapproved. In contrast, if the decision is made on the spot, these potential moral hazard problems are reduced.

Once policy authorities in the borrowing country and the IMF staff and management have agreed on conditionality, a second potential source of delay emerges. Other countries, especially creditor countries, need to approve the loan and its conditions. Activation of the GAB, for example, requires approval by a (weighted) majority of GAB participants, followed by approval from the IMF's Executive Board. While there is no reason in principle why agreement could not be reached very rapidly, in practice there can be disagreements among creditors. For burden-sharing reasons, there are advantages in having a large creditor group. But the larger the group, the more diluted becomes the control of any subgroup of creditors and the less likely it becomes to reach agreement quickly. Some creditors, for example, may see the debtor's problems as more "regional" or "bilateral" than "systemic" and may therefore propose that it be either financing via other channels or handling by stronger adjustment measures. Some may feel more strongly than others about the adverse moral hazard effects of extending assistance. And some others may be willing to extend assistance only for very short maturities.

But if such disagreements among creditors cannot be resolved quickly, then the character of the emergency financing as a rapid response mechanism will be compromised. In those circumstances, an increase in the facility's financial resources could also present a misleading impression of its likely effectiveness, since one couldn't be confident that those resources could actually be mobilized during the relevant time frame of the crisis.[38] In this regard, it is an open question whether in Mexico's case it would have been possible to secure agreement to activate the GAB.

Some of these trade-offs have come to the fore in the proposed expansion of the GAB. Expanding membership to include a group of developing countries with ample reserves would permit a doubling of GAB resources without having to place heavy additional assessments on existing members (the G-10 countries plus Saudi Arabia). But enlarging the creditor base would dilute the say of existing members about who should get emergency assistance and under what conditions; indeed, if the G-10 weren't so concerned about maintaining such control, they would presumably opt for an increase in Fund quotas as a way to fund any needed increase in emergency financial assistance. In any case, enlarging the creditor base could also decrease the probability of reaching a quick consensus in real time. For their part, new creditors are likely to be reluctant to pledge their money if they are denied a fair share in the vote on how that money is going to be used.

In cases in which these types of delays conflict with a country's urgent liquidity needs, G-10 countries have sometimes found it necessary either to arrange short-term bridge loans via the BIS or to extend short-term loans directly on a bilateral basis.

---

38. If market participants expect the emergency financing mechanism to be activated but agreement cannot be reached among creditors, news about this lack of expected external support could actually exacerbate the crisis (at least in the short term).

Moral Hazard

As emphasized during our earlier discussion of market discipline, a potentially adverse by-product of efforts to increase the official sector's capacity to contain financial crises is that they may encourage just the kind of excessive risk taking that contributes to such crises in the first place.

In principle, the moral hazard problem can be handled by insisting that those receiving insurance or assistance bear costs that tend to offset their incentive to take on more risks. But many of the mechanisms that operate to impose such costs in a domestic financial context (e.g., higher capital requirements, risk-weighted capital requirements, risk-weighted deposit insurance, restrictions on financial firms' assets and activities, and structured early intervention and resolution for banks) are not directly transferable to sovereign borrowers in an international context.[39] For example, countries cannot be closed down, nor can outside bodies legally restrict their assets and activities (at least prior to requests for financial assistance). Nevertheless, following Masson and Mussa (1995), one can regard strong policy conditionality as a form of "coinsurance" designed to make the borrower assume a fair share of the costs of excessive risk taking. These costs include not only the short- to medium-term output and employment costs that typically accompany a tightening of monetary and fiscal policies but also the reduction in policy independence that is necessary to convince official creditors that they will be repaid on time. In Mexico's case, for example, recent figures suggest that real GDP in the third quarter of 1995 had declined by approximately 8 percent from the level of a year earlier, and surveillance of the economy by both official and private creditors has no doubt increased by an order of magnitude.

Still, creditors will consider the probability and size of emergency financial assistance as elements in their risk/return calculations. Even though coinsurance by the borrower should limit excessive risk taking, investors may reckon that some borrowers will be unresponsive to such prospective costs during certain periods (say, right before an election). Creditors will be less careful in monitoring those borrowers who are the most likely recipients of such assistance. For example, if systemic borrowers are more likely to be bailed out than smaller ones, the former will be able to attract more private capital and at lower cost, *ceteris paribus*, than if emergency financial assistance were not linked to perceived systemic risk.

In the end, the only way to remedy such lax monitoring of risk by creditors is for experience to teach that expectations of official emergency assistance will frequently turn out to be incorrect, with significant adverse consequences for the investor. Toward this end, we agree with Masson

---

39. See Benston (1993) for a discussion of these measures as protection against moral hazard in banking.

and Mussa (1995) that governments should try to maintain the principle that the risks associated with private investments in private-sector assets are not the responsibility of governments. Since private-to-private capital flow transactions account for roughly 70 percent of all net long-term private capital flows to developing countries, this by itself would go a long way. When emergency financial assistance is extended, the authorities can try to convince market participants that this action is no guide for intervention in future crisis situations.

Market expectations of bailouts are also not independent of what alternative courses of action are available to authorities during the crisis. For example, if investors believe that the *only* alternatives to emergency financial assistance are severe economic contraction in the borrowing country and chaotic and costly default, then it will be difficult to convince them that emergency assistance is not in the cards. Here, formal or informal workout (or bankruptcy) procedures for sovereign debt could make an important difference by giving authorities another option. We turn to such procedures next.

Formal and Informal Workout (or Bankruptcy) Procedures

Just as the Mexican crisis induced the official sector to consider whether existing arrangements for emergency financial assistance needed to be overhauled, it also focused attention on a hole in the existing framework for rescheduling debt at times of financial distress. On a national level, the procedures to be followed are laid out in bankruptcy law. For example, chapter 11 of the US Bankruptcy Code specifies what is to be done for corporate bankruptcies and chapter 9 extends those principles and procedures to municipal governments (but not to states or the federal government). On the international level, there is no formal law or code for state insolvency; nevertheless, an informal institutional framework has emerged to handle certain types of rescheduling and restructuring. Specifically, the Paris Club deals with government-to-government debt and the London Club addresses commercial bank debt.

But there is no organized framework to deal with rescheduling of sovereign bonds and/or to conduct an ongoing dialogue between sovereign debtors and nonbank international investors (namely, mutual funds, pension funds, hedge funds, insurance companies, and security houses). Yet the (gross) funds raised through bond issues by developing countries in international capital markets have increased from about $3.5 billion in 1989 to over $50 billion annually in both 1993 and 1994, and institutional investors have simultaneously emerged as the new muscle in global capital markets (Goldstein et al. 1993; Group of Ten Deputies 1993).

Equally to the point, Sachs (1995) has argued that the problems and pressures faced by sovereign borrowers at times of distress are very similar to those faced by corporations and municipalities in a domestic context—and that the principles and mechanisms that have evolved to guide reorganization in domestic bankruptcy law are just what the doctor ordered for dealing with sovereign default at the international level. The three crucial principles are that (1) the chaotic creditor race to grab assets has to be prevented by an "automatic stay," (2) provision of working capital to the restructuring country (so called debtor-in-possession financing) has to be facilitated by granting repayment seniority to new loans over old (prebankruptcy) ones, and (3) holdout and free riding by creditors have to be precluded by making acceptance of the restructuring plan by all creditors subject either to majority vote or to "cramdown" by the bankruptcy court or agent.

If these principles were adopted at the international level and if the IMF acted more like a bankruptcy judge than an international lender of last resort, then—so the argument goes—all parties could avoid protracted, costly, and inefficient debt renegotiations (like those that characterized the aftermath of the 1982 debt crisis); debtors would be able to maintain essential state services (with dividends for political and economic stability); and less taxpayer money would be put at risk by large, emergency official support packages.

Suffice it to say that not everyone is convinced. There are two objections. The main one is that implementation of either a formal bankruptcy code or an informal workout procedure for sovereign debt is fraught with serious difficulties for the foreseeable future. Among the difficulties often mentioned as bedeviling best efforts are the following: (1) great diversity in the new (nonbank) creditor base, particularly as regards attitudes toward risk and legal requirements for rescheduling; (2) the absence of a powerful single regulator for these diverse creditor groups at the national level that could encourage them to "play ball;" (3) the potential for rogue creditors to torpedo any informal approach by challenging its legality in court; (4) the dim prospects for separating external from domestic debt in any rescheduling (given the nontrivial holdings of "external" and foreign currency–denominated debt by domestic residents and the scope for using domestic proxies to escape rescheduling of external debt); (5) the reduced restraining effect of the "sharing clause" (common in sovereign bank loan agreements) on litigation, now that bank loans account for a smaller share of sovereign debt; (6) the time-consuming and uncertain prospect of trying to override national bankruptcy laws (recall how long it took to get legal certainty in major creditor countries for a master agreement on "netting" in derivative contracts); (7) problems of defining insolvency and of distinguishing "can't pay" from "won't pay" when dealing with sovereigns who can raise taxes (for the latter, see Orange County); (8) the questionable acceptability of using Article VIII, Section 2B, of the Fund's Articles of Agreement to sanction an "automatic stay" and the time delay associated with amending the Articles to remove that legal uncertainty; and (9) the absence of a natural candidate to serve as the bankruptcy court (only the IMF and World Bank have the universality of membership that would be required, but their own claims on debtor countries and their susceptibility to political pressure from major shareholders could preclude them from being perceived as impartial).

Hurlock (1995) has argued that one may be able to retain the essential part of international bankruptcy reform, while vaulting over many of the hurdles, by amending sovereign immunity laws. Under such an amendment, either a foreign state would be immune from suit or its property immune from attachment if, in the context of a sovereign debt workout, the litigating creditor was attempting to overturn a restructuring plan supported by a majority of creditors. Another idea for a clean rescheduling mechanism is that of Cline (1995a). He proposes that major creditor countries require that any bonds issued on their markets by sovereign states incorporate a clause providing for majority bondholder approval of rescheduling without recourse to default claims by dissenting minority bondholders.[40] Since existing bonds do not carry such a clause, Cline's proposal would not help with the existing stock of sovereign debt—but it would make rescheduling easier for future debt.

Even if international bankruptcy reform had smooth sailing ahead, there is a second objection. An important question that would still need answering is what would such reform imply for the interest rate spreads paid by sovereign debtors. On the one hand, the reduction in uncertainty associated with bankruptcy reform should work against higher spreads. On the other, such reform might be seen by debtors as reducing the penalties (relative to the status quo) associated with recontracting; and if (bond) creditors were to see such reform as reducing their expected return, they would presumably seek compensation by charging higher spreads. Which of these two opposing forces would dominate the behavior of spreads strikes us as largely an empirical question. It would be a useful line of inquiry for future research to examine both earlier bankruptcy reform at the national level and the (much earlier) historical experience with bondholders' councils.

Evaluation

In view of the increasing openness and integration of international capital markets, we think it makes sense to give the international lender of last resort an updated capability to respond forcefully and quickly to potential financial crises.

---

40. Cline (1995a) notes that since *tesobonos* were not issued in foreign markets, such a clause would not have been relevant for the Mexican case.

The G-7's proposal at Halifax to double the size of the GAB is a useful one—not least because by requiring strong conditionality for borrowers, by rejecting prequalification and evaluating each threat on a case-by-case basis, and by insisting that intervention be tied to significant spillover effects it avoids some of the worst culprits for exacerbating moral hazard. An open question is whether this (perhaps increasingly) diverse group of creditors will really be able to agree in real time on which situations deserve such emergency financial support.

Despite the formidable obstacles involved, we also believe it would be well worth the effort to see what can be done to bring some more order and organization to the process of sovereign debt rescheduling. Existing arrangements not only are costly to debtors but they also make it more likely that mechanisms of emergency financial assistance will be employed too often (because the alternative prospect of unilateral default and deep recession in the borrowing country is so grim). If investors knew that losses associated with "writing down" official-sector assets at times of distress were an element of risk associated with investing in emerging markets, maybe the swings in those flows would be less pronounced.

We would go farther. Looking down the road, we see two ways in which mechanisms of emergency financial assistance can be strengthened.

One is to tighten the preconditions for their use so that likely draws on these resources will be smaller and so that riskier borrowers face larger coinsurance payments and closer official monitoring than less risky ones. In exchange for greater access when they need it, perhaps participants can be persuaded to agree to undertake stronger preventive measures. These might include tougher than average data disclosure standards for economic and financial data, closer IMF monitoring of exchange rate and debt management policies (particularly when the country chooses to maintain a fixed exchange rate regime), intensified efforts to improve banking supervision, and maintenance of deposit insurance and adequate reserve requirements. Moreover, when *ex ante* risk increases (e.g., international reserve levels fall below a prespecified minimum), closer IMF surveillance could be automatically triggered. The idea would be to put in an international context some of the same structured intervention procedures that now apply to financial firms in a domestic context (Benston 1993).

A second improvement (albeit probably one way down the road) would be to get better coordination between emergency financing and debt write-down mechanisms, perhaps even combining them within the same facility. To facilitate that, an initial step would be to follow Cline's (1995a) suggestion and have major creditor countries agree that all sovereign bonds issued (by developing countries) in their markets include provisions for majority bondholder approval of rescheduling. If an emerging-market economy then found itself in financial distress, it could apply to the emergency financial mechanism for assistance. Upon application, the administrator of the facility or credit line (say, the IMF) could then decide on a case-by-case basis whether the situation was one of illiquidity or insolvency, and whether it manifested systemic risk. Depending on the nature of the problem, the administrator could recommend a mix of adjustment, financing, and writing down of official debt. The mix would differ from country to country. Since investors would not know in advance what the final combination would be, they would be less quick to presume that a bailout was the likely course of action. At the same time, the possibility of temporary emergency financing should counter any tendency for the cost of external finance to rise when more liberal workout procedures were introduced. The fact that the administrator was frequently putting its own money where its mouth was would add to its credibility in monitoring the borrower's compliance with the policy conditionality accompanying any temporary financing. Again, there are parallels here with the resolution of banking problems in a domestic context (Kaufman 1994).

Concluding Remarks

A strong underlying theme of this paper is that if real progress is to be made in preventing and managing financial crises linked to volatility in private capital markets, improvements will be needed across several fronts. There is no silver bullet that can do the job by itself.

On the host-country side, greater preventive measures are needed to avoid the increase in banking problems and other sources of financial vulnerability. Once the banking system becomes fragile, the host country will be handicapped in using the interest rate as an equilibrating mechanism to deal with shifts in market sentiment. In addition, the perception of mounting banking problems in a liberalized capital market adds to the likelihood of runs by domestic investors, and the resolution of banking problems presents governments with the prospect of a large public-sector liability. In a similar vein, host countries should avoid being penny wise and pound foolish in their debt management practices. Too much reliance on short-term debt and too liberal a recourse to foreign currency–denominated debt can leave the borrowing country hostage both to a sudden deterioration in the external factors driving private capital flows and to short-term domestic setbacks. What once seemed like a more than comfortable cushion of international reserves can dissipate quickly, making a rollover of maturing debt problematic and adding to pressures on the domestic currency. More conservative debt management will cost more in the short term but will provide the breathing room necessary to deal with unforeseen developments. Gauging the equilibrium exchange rate can be difficult for a country undergoing large structural changes that affect the profitability of investment. Still, when the exchange rate looks to be significantly out of line and needs to be adjusted to protect competitiveness, it is better to do it before international reserves have dropped so far that the authorities are facing both a currency crisis and a debt crisis.

The stakes involved in improving the functioning of the early warning system have become higher. Improvements should be sought both for private market discipline and for multilateral surveillance. Faulty economic analysis and self-fulfilling prophecies can initiate financial crises even with good information. Nevertheless, setting more rigorous standards for the publication of economic and financial data and making public the list of countries who meet these standards should increase incentives for disclosure and help markets in pricing risk better. Timely and regular publication of data should reduce the chances of abrupt shifts in private capital flows resulting from the overdue receipt of accumulated bad news. Market discipline would similarly be enhanced by a better picture of the fundamentals driving capital flows and prices of internationally traded assets. Toward that end, the IMF should begin sharing its evaluation of country policies and prospects with the private markets. Multilateral surveillance could come closer to living up to its potential if the IFIs—and particularly the IMF—deepened and increased the frequency of their contacts with private capital markets, intensified surveillance over financial-sector developments and debt management policy, and increased the frankness of their advice to their member countries, particularly on exchange rate policy (where political factors have too often in the past unduly delayed adjustment).

Experience suggests that there will be cases when neither host countries nor the early warning system will act early enough or strongly enough to avert a financial crisis. In some of those cases, bilateral official efforts at crisis management will not be sufficient to handle the task themselves. In such circumstances, it is highly desirable that the international lender of last resort have the capability to intervene quickly and forcefully so that the crisis does not deepen and/or spread far beyond its initial locus. In that connection, the proposed doubling of the GAB—with its accompanying emphasis on strong conditionality and activation only in cases of systemic risk—strikes us as well suited to the task at hand. The toughest nut to crack is how to prevent such emergency financial assistance from exacerbating moral hazard. It is partly for this reason that we favor efforts to bring more order and organization to the workout of sovereign debt defaults—notwithstanding the hurdles involved. This would add another option to the current menu of official responses and bring the resolution of financial difficulties on the international level more closely in line with domestic practice.

References

Bartholomew, Phillip, and Gary Whalen. 1994. "Fundamentals of Systemic Risk." Paper presented at conference on Banking, Financial Markets, and Systemic Risk, sponsored by US Office of the Comptroller of the Currency, 2 December, Washington.

Bayoumi, Tamim, Morris Goldstein, and Geoffrey Woglom. 1995. "Do Credit Markets Discipline Sovereign Borrowers? Evidence from US States." *Journal of Money, Credit, and Banking* 27, no. 4 (November): 1046–59.

Benston, George. 1993. "Safety Nets and Moral Hazard in Banking." Paper prepared for conference on Financial Stability in a Changing Environment, sponsored by the Bank of Japan, 28–29 October, Tokyo.

Bergsten, C. Fred. 1995. "Lessons of the Peso Crisis." Statement before the Committee on Banking and Financial Services, US House of Representatives, 10 February.

Bergsten, C., and William Cline. 1995. "The Peso Crisis and Financial Support for Mexico." Statement before the Committee on International Relations, US House of Representatives, 1 February.

Bordo, Michael, Bruce Mizrach, and Anna Schwartz. 1995. "Real Versus Pseudo International Systemic Risk: Some Lessons from History." Paper prepared for Third Conference on Pacific Basin Business, August, Taipei, Taiwan.

Calvo, Guillermo. 1994. "Comment." In Dornbusch and Warner, *Brookings Papers on Economic Activity* 1: 298–303.

Calvo, Guillermo. 1995a. "Managing Economic Reform Under Capital Flow Volatility: Main Issues." Paper presented at World Bank conference on Managing Economic Reform under Capital Flow Volatility, sponsored by the World Bank, 30 May–2 June, Washington.

Calvo, Guillermo. 1995b. "Varieties of Capital Market Crises." University of Maryland. Photocopy (April).

Calvo, Guillermo, Leonardo Leiderman, and Carmen Reinhart. 1993. "Capital Inflows and Real Exchange Rate Appreciation in Latin America: The Role of External Factors." *IMF Staff Papers* 40, no. 1 (March) 108–50.

Calvo, Guillermo, Leonardo Leiderman, and Carmen Reinhart. 1996. "Inflows of Capital to Developing Countries in the 1990s." *Journal of Economic Perspectives* 10: 123–40.

Calvo, Guillermo, and Enrique Mendoza. 1995. "Reflections on Mexico's Balance-of-Payments Crisis: A Chronicle of Death Foretold." University of Maryland. Photocopy (August).

Camdessus, Michel. 1994a. "The Future of the IMF." In Bretton Woods Commission, *Bretton Woods: Looking to the Future*. Washington: Bretton Woods Commission.

Camdessus, Michel. 1994b. "The IMF at Fifty—An Evolving Role But Constant Mission." Speech at the Institute for International Economics, June, Washington.

Camdessus, Michel. 1995. Remarks at 24 April press conference, Institute for International Economics, Washington.

Chuhan, Punam, Stijn Claessens, and Niandu Mamingi. 1993. *Equity and Bond Flows to Asia and Latin America: The Role of Global and Country Factors*. World Bank Policy Research Paper 1160. Washington: World Bank.

Cline, William. 1995a. "Capital Markets after the Peso Crisis." Paper presented for the Annual World Bank Conference on Development in Latin America and the Caribbean, 12–13 June, Rio de Janeiro.

Cline, William. 1995b. *International Debt Reexamined*. Washington: Institute for International Economics.

Corbo, Vittorio, and Leonardo Hernandez. 1993. "Macroeconomic Adjustment to Portfolio Capital Inflows: Rationale and Some Recent Experiences." In Stijn Clessens and Sudarshan Gooptu, *Portfolio Investment in Developing Countries*. Washington: World Bank.

Dooley, Michael. 1995. "Managing the Public Debt." Paper presented at conference on Managing Economic Reform under Capital Flow Volatility sponsored by the World Bank, 30 May–2 June, Washington.

Dooley, Michael, Eduardo Fernandez-Arias, and Kenneth Kletzer. 1994. *Recent Private Capital Inflows to Developing Countries: Is the Debt Crisis History?* NBER Working Paper 4792. Cambridge, MA: National Bureau of Economic Research.

Dornbusch, Rudiger, and Alejandro Werner. 1994. "Mexico: Stabilization, Reform, and No Growth." *Brookings Papers on Economic Activity* 1: 253–97.

Edwards, Sebastian. 1986. "The Pricing of Bonds and Bank Loans in International Markets." *European Economic Review* 30 (June): 565–89.

Edwards, Sebastian. 1991. "Capital Flows, Foreign Direct Investment, and Debt-Equity Swaps in Developing Countries." In Horst Siebert, *Capital Flows in the World Economy*. Tubingen, the Netherlands: J. C. B. Mohr.

Eichengreen, Barry. 1991. "Trends and Cycles in Foreign Lending." In Horst Siebert, *Capital Flows in the World Economy*. Tubingen, the Netherlands: J. C. B. Mohr.

Eichengreen, Barry, and Richard Portes. 1987. "The Anatomy of Financial Crises." In Richard Portes and Alexander Swoboda, *Threats to International Financial Stability*. Cambridge, UK: Centre for Economic Policy Research.

Fernandez-Arias, Eduardo. 1994. *The New Wave of Private Capital Inflows: Push or Pull?* World Bank Policy Research Paper 1312. Washington: World Bank.

Fernandez-Arias, Eduardo, and Peter Montiel. 1996. "The Surge in Capital Inflows to Developing Countries." *World Bank Economic Review* 10, no. 1 (January): 51–77.

Folkerts-Landau, David. 1985. "The Changing Role of International Bank Lending in Development Finance." *IMF Staff Papers* 32, no. 2 (June): 317–63.

Folkerts-Landau, David, Gary J. Schinasi, Marcel Cassard, Victor K. Ng, Carmen M. Reinhart, and Michael G. Spenser. 1995. "Effect of Capital Flows on the Domestic Financial Sectors in APEC Developing Countries." In Mohsin Khan and Carmen Reinhart, *Capital Flows in the APEC Region*. IMF Occasional Paper 122. Washington: International Monetary Fund.

Frankel, Jeffrey. 1995. "Lessons from the Mexican Crisis," Paper presented at meeting of Council on Foreign Relations, 10 April, New York.

Goldstein, Morris. 1995a. *Coping with Too Much of a Good Thing: Policy Responses for Large Capital Inflows to Developing Countries*. World Bank Policy Research Working Paper 1507. Washington: World Bank (September).

Goldstein, Morris. 1995b. *The Exchange Rate System and the IMF: A Modest Agenda.* POLICY ANALYSES IN INTERNATIONAL ECONOMICS 39. Washington: Institute for International Economics.

Goldstein, Morris. 1995c. "International Financial Markets and Systemic Risk." Washington: Institute for International Economics. Unpublished, December.

Goldstein, Morris, and Michael Mussa. 1994. "The Integration of World Capital Markets." In Federal Reserve Bank of Kansas City, *Changing Capital Markets: Implications for Monetary Policy*. Kansas City: Federal Reserve Bank of Kansas City.

Goldstein, Morris, David Folkerts-Landau, et al. 1993. *Exchange Rate Management and International Capital Flows*. IMF World Economic and Financial Surveys. Washington: International Monetary Fund.

Goldstein, Morris, David Folkerts-Landau, et al. 1994. *International Capital Markets: Developments, Prospects, and Policy Issues*. IMF World Economic and Financial Surveys Washington: International Monetary Fund.

Goldstein, Morris, and Geoffrey Woglom. 1992. "Market-Based Fiscal Discipline in Monetary Unions: Evidence from the US Municipal Bond Market." In Matthew B. Canzoner, Vittorio Grilli,, and Paul Masson, *Establishing a Central Bank: Issues in Europe and Lessons for the United States*. Cambridge, UK: Cambridge University Press.

Group of Ten Deputies. 1993. *International Capital Movements and Foreign Exchange Markets*. Rome: Bank of Italy.

Group of Thirty. 1995. *Mexico: Why Didn't Wall Street Sound the Alarm?* Washington: Group of Thirty.

Halifax Summit. 1995. "Review of International Financial Institutions: Background Document." 15–17 June.

Hurlock, James. 1995. "A Chapter 9 Process for the Global Financial System?" New York: White and Case. Manuscript.

International Monetary Fund (IMF). 1995. *International Capital Markets: Developments, Prospects,and Policy Issues*. IMF World Economic and Financial Surveys. Washington: International Monetary Fund.

Kaufman, George. 1994. "FDICIA: The Ongoing Evidence." *Challenge Magazine*, July/August: 53–57.

Kaufman, Henry. 1995. "Opening Remarks." In Group of Thirty, *Mexico: Why Didn't Wall Street Sound the Alarm?* Washington: Group of Thirty.

Kindleberger, Charles. 1978. *Manias, Panics, and Crashes: A History of Financial Crises*. New York: Basic Books.

Krugman, Paul. 1995. "Dutch Tulips and Emerging Markets." *Foreign Affairs* 74, no. 4 (July/August): 28–44.

Lane, Timothy. 1993. "Market Discipline." *IMF Staff Papers* 40, no. 1 (March) 53–88.

Masson, Paul, and Michael Mussa. 1995. "The Role of the Fund: Financing and Its Interactions with Adjustment and Surveillance." Washington: International Monetary Fund. Photocopy.

Minton-Beddoes, Zanny. 1995. "Why the IMF Needs Reform." *Foreign Affairs* 74, no. 3 (May/June): 123–33.

Mishkin, Frederic. 1994. *Preventing Financial Crises: An International Perspective*. NBER Working Paper 4636. Cambridge, MA: National Bureau of Economic Research.

Obstfeld, Maura, and Kenneth Rogoff. 1995. "The Mirage of Fixed Exchange Rates." *Journal of Economic Perspectives* 9, no. 4: 73–96.

Rodrik, Dani. 1995. *Why Is There Multilateral Lending?* CEPR Discussion Paper 1207. London: Centre for Economic Policy Research.

Rojas-Suárez, Liliana, and Steven Weisbrod. 1994. *Financial Market Fragilities in Latin America: From Banking Crisis Resolution to Current Policy Challenges*. IMF Working Paper 94/117. Washington: International Monetary Fund.

Sachs, Jeffrey. 1995. "Do We Need an International Lender of Last Resort?" Frank D. Graham Lecture, 20 April, Princeton University.

Sachs, Jeffrey, Aaron Tornell, and Andres Velasco. 1995. "The Collapse of the Mexican Peso: What Have We Learned?" Harvard University. Photocopy (May).

Schadler, Susan, Maria Carkovic, Adam Bennett, and Robert Kahn. 1993. *Recent Experiences with Surges in Capital Inflows*, IMF Occasional Paper 108. Washington: International Monetary Fund.

Schwartz, Anna. 1994. "Systemic Risk and the Macroeconomy." Paper presented at conference on Banking, Financial Markets, and Systemic Risk sponsored by US Office of the Comptroller of the Currency, 2 December, Washington.

Solomon, Robert. 1995. "The Mexican Financial Crisis." *International Economic Letter* 15, no. 1 (15 January).

US Treasury. 1995. "Halifax G-7 Economic Summit." Fact Sheet RR-379. Washington: Office of Public Affairs (June).

Williamson, John. 1993. Statement on Exchange Rate Policy in Mexico before the Committee on Small Business, US House of Representatives, 20 May.

Williamson, John. 1995. "A New Facility for the IMF?" Paper prepared for the Group of Twenty Four. Washington: Institute for International Economics (June).

Comment

Richard Portes

The main argument in the paper for the official rescue package is contagion. I find that argument unconvincing.

I do agree with the authors that in the framework that Barry Eichengreen and I developed several years ago for analyzing international financial crises, it is clear that Mexico posed no systemic risk.

They accept the IMF conclusion that the main spillover effect was on countries with weaker fundamentals. They then say it would have been worse, at least initially, had there been default—stronger adjustment would have been needed. But perhaps stronger adjustment *is* needed in those countries with weaker fundamentals, regardless, and perhaps that is being delayed by easy access to short-term capital that *ought* to be scared away.

Looking forward, suppose it were possible to have an "endorsed" debt-service standstill. That is, a country in financial distress could ask an independent body—the Fund or another agency advised by the Fund but acting independently—to endorse a payment stay for a limited period, during which it would negotiate a debt workout. If that agency could certify that there were particular circumstances *not* common to other debtor countries, this could help to limit contagion. Moreover, if in addition there were known orderly workout procedures to follow, they too would reassure the markets that chaos was not around the corner.

It is sometimes argued that the contagion problem is much worse now—that the increase in size and speed of reaction of international capital

Richard Portes is director at the Centre for Economic Policy Research, London.

markets and the overall globalization of finance have created a qualitatively different environment. But looking back as far as the interwar period, we see that the markets reacted quickly then too and forced the hand of governments. There was evident contagion in the wave of defaults that swept through Latin America in 1931 and Europe in 1932 (Eichengreen and Portes 1987). And in that earlier period, many countries did not have central banks that could act effectively as lenders of last resort to limit the domestic effects of capital market shocks.

The paper points out conflicts in the roles of the IMF, in particular the problem that the subjects of surveillance are IMF shareholders. I think the problem is somewhat worse than they suggest, especially when we turn to considering the Fund's role in proposed innovations such as procedures for an "endorsed" payments standstill, mediation and conciliation among the debtor and various classes of creditors, and of course the extreme case of the Fund acting as an international bankruptcy court.

It seems evident that there might be significant incentive incompatibilities among some subset of the Fund's activities, if they were to include all of the following: (1) monitoring and surveillance, (2) acting as *ex ante* policy adviser to a debtor whose policies may subsequently be judged to have "failed" (might the IMF have some responsibility?), (3) being a priority creditor, (4) being the major source of information to other lenders, (5) acting as negotiator and/or arbiter of a debt restructuring that might impose write-downs on dissident creditors, (6) acting as the authority imposing conditionality on the debtor, and (7) serving as the source of new lending. "Policeman, judge, jury and executioner—or dispenser of pardons."

My third and final remark is about the international bankruptcy court. I agree with our authors, up to a point. But not entirely.

They are right to say that there are two ways of convincing agents that there will not be a bailout. One is to establish case law—to demonstrate with several examples that the authorities are willing to see a debtor default and to let investors take the hit. Some of us think this should have happened even in the 1980s—that is, that the first five years of the "debt strategy" were overly influenced by concerns about systemic risk (or indeed by less objective arguments).

The development of emerging markets and the securitization of debt bring both advantages and disadvantages. Since debt is now widely held by mutual funds, pension funds, and individuals, losses can be absorbed and unserviceable debts can be and are written down without jeopardizing the stability of creditor-country financial institutions. Moreover, good news can have powerful effects: new investors in search of yield may be prepared to jump quickly into emerging markets when credible policy reforms are put in place, notwithstanding a history of debt-servicing difficulties.

At the same time, the speed with which markets move and the large number of investors mean that bad news, or even the possibility of bad news, creates problems of collective action even more serious than those of the 1980s. Bad news can provoke a powerful rush for the exits, with devastating effects on the debtor in the short run. As the authors suggest, we must offer an alternative to *dis*orderly workouts, if only so investors will not believe in the implicit guarantee.

They are right to rule out an international bankruptcy court or any other mechanical analogy with chapter 11. I accept their first set of reasons, that implementation would be very difficult—I would indeed say impossible in the foreseeable future, because to override national commercial law and extend sovereign immunity in the necessary way would require a most unlikely international treaty. And that is in part because chapter 11 is not such a great idea. Even in the United States, it has come under increasing criticism in recent years—large firms that go into chapter 11 stay there for three years, on average; the debtor is in an exceptionally favorable position; and so on. And other countries have bankruptcy codes so different from the American code as to suggest that agreement at the international level is out of the question.

But their second reason is misconceived. They suggest that any such reform would increase the cost of borrowing: "If (bond) creditors were to see such reform [officially recognized workout procedures] as reducing their expected return, they would presumably seek compensation by charging higher spreads." It can be argued, however, that debt contracts do not really make sense when they fail to mention the word "default" and to specify an insolvency process—as is typical of sovereign debt. Think of a corporate debt contract that did not specify what happened in the event of default: it is hard to imagine that the interest rate would be lower as a result of this uncertainty. In practice, corporate debt contracts do normally include provisions for dealing with default, in consonance with the relevant national bankruptcy code. Private debt contracts are signed in the knowledge that defaults will be adjudicated by specific courts. Far from deterring lenders, this reassures them.

The magnitude of spreads on bank loans to sovereign borrowers and on the bond issues of governments and quasi-public enterprises clearly indicates the existence of a significant perceived probability of capital loss due to default. And yet there exist no recognized procedures for dealing with that contingency when it arises, as it inevitably does (for otherwise the lending would be risk free, at the risk-free rate). Procedures that reduce *ex ante* the uncertainty of how default will be resolved, providing orderly as opposed to disorderly workouts, will improve the *ex ante* position of lenders and therefore the market terms. Debt contracts without such provisions are exceptional. With the increasing globalization of markets, it is more important now than before that sovereign debt contracts should no longer be exceptional in this regard.

The reduction of the risk premium that results from making provision for orderly workouts and minimizing uncertainty will dominate any increase in the risk premium due to any perceived weakening of the *ex ante* bonding role of debt. And it would be possible to supplement orderly workouts with other measures that would strengthen the incentive to adhere to the *ex ante* terms of loan contracts.

So I believe that orderly workout procedures could be good for both debtors and creditors. But the authors' suggestion of combining emergency financing and write-down mechanisms in the same facility (administered, for example, by the IMF) is dangerous and probably not feasible. It would create incentive incompatibilities (or conflicts of interest), as suggested above. It would override the Paris Club, and not only the French would object. Moreover, it ignores what might be the most important single feature of a bankruptcy-like procedure in the sovereign context: the payments standstill or "automatic stay." As the authors suggest, however, there are various ways forward, and I believe it is important to follow as many of them as possible (Eichengreen and Portes 1995).

References

Eichengreen, Barry, and Richard Portes. 1987. "The Anatomy of Financial Crises." In Richard Portes and Alexander Swoboda, *Threats to International Financial Stability.* Cambridge, UK: Cambridge University Press.

Eichengreen, Barry, and Richard Portes. 1995. *Crisis? What Crisis? Orderly Workout Procedures for Sovereign Debtors.* London: Centre for Economic Policy Research.

Comment

Edwin M. Truman

This is an excellent paper—thorough, insightful, and provocative. I will concentrate my comments on my points of disagreement, but I would not want that concentration to be interpreted as reflecting on the paper's overall high quality.

The appropriate threshold question that the authors ask is what was unique about Mexico—or, more precisely, what was not unique about Mexico. Calvo and Goldstein take the view that this is a contest between the "fundamental model," which would imply the response to the crisis should have been left to the market, and their own "financial fragility model," which more clearly justifies extraordinary international intervention. It is difficult to disentangle these two views, for the financial fragility of the Mexican economy in the end was a reflection of a weakness in economic fundamentals: an exchange rate anchor that was held too long, a banking system that was in bad shape, a domestic debt management strategy that was misguided in terms of its excessive reliance on short-term debt in which foreigners invested heavily (*cetes* in 1993 and *tesobonos* in 1994), a fiscal policy and a monetary policy that ultimately were incompatible with the maintenance of the peso's peg with the dollar.

My view about what was not unique about Mexico starts from the proposition that policymakers are human and will make mistakes despite their best efforts and the well-intentioned advice of the international

---

Edwin M. Truman is staff director, Division of International Finance, Board of Governors of the Federal Reserve System. These comments represent the view of the author and should not be interpreted as reflecting the views of the Board of Governors of the Federal Reserve System or other members of its staff.

financial community, including the International Monetary Fund (IMF). Ariel Buira (chapter 11) amply illustrated this thesis. Mexican policymakers thought they were taking the right steps, given that they were living in an uncertain economic and political world in 1994.

Furthermore, today's financial markets will make mistakes as well. The lack of the prompt availability of comprehensive information about the Mexican financial situation contributed on the margin to the crisis by limiting the force and scope of market discipline. However, Calvo and Goldstein greatly exaggerate this feature. For example, information on the outstanding stock of *tesobonos* was readily available on the financial news services (Reuters and Bloomberg), and analysts could easily calculate by the end of July 1994 that *tesobonos* in the hands of the public exceeded the previously announced level of Mexican foreign exchange reserves. From this perspective, and the perspective of the speculative attack literature, the puzzle is that it took almost five months before the crisis broke.

The Mexican crisis had a great deal in common with the behavior of financial markets during the crisis of the Exchange Rate Mechanism (ERM) of the European Monetary System (EMS) in 1992. In that sense, Mexico definitely was not unique, and Calvo and Goldstein underemphasize this important point about today's financial markets. In both cases, investors operated on the basis of largely false premises about the viability of an exchange rate regime and their collective ability to get out of their investments at the last moment. Investors were influenced by a common view about regimes involving rigid exchange rates and their durability that was rooted in Europe and was spread by the IMF management and staff to Latin America (a point to which I return below). Moreover in the ERM crisis, as well, there were important elements involving the weakness of the financial system (in the United Kingdom and Sweden), and there were important elements involving weakness in debt management policies (in Italy and Sweden).

Therefore, the Mexican peso crisis was not a unique event in financial market terms, and although Calvo and Goldstein are right to stress Mexico's financial vulnerabilities in terms of its financial system and debt management policy, Mexico was hardly unique in that respect either. In addition, it is not clear from their paper what the mechanism is that connects financial vulnerabilities to the outbreak of the Mexican crisis. In the conventional view, the connection is simple: the weak financial system served as one of the important constraints on Mexican monetary policy.

Having established what was not unique about the Mexican peso crisis, I turn to the issue of how such a crisis might be prevented in the future, or more precisely how the probability of its occurring might be reduced. Calvo and Goldstein are right to stress the role to be played by better information—a theme of the Halifax economic summit of 1995. Better data are unlikely to affect adversely the functioning of markets. There is also a role for the IMF in this process. Where I part company with Calvo and Goldstein is in the emphasis they place on that role. It would be impossible for the IMF to specify all the relevant data series that should be available *ex ante* to reveal problems well before they are obvious, because *ex post* this number is likely to be very large. This does not mean that the IMF should not try to establish standards for their members for the release of data. However, the IMF should audit the results only by working with member countries on their statistical systems; it should not place itself in a position of certifying the data or certifying that a particular set of data are all that are relevant to judging any country's financial situation. I would suggest that the issue of certifying the accuracy of the data is much more serious than simply certifying that countries are releasing the data according to IMF-established standards. The second issue is contentious, but it is a red herring because the markets can police this level of compliance.

A more controversial question concerns what the IMF should be saying in public about a country's policies. The issue here is not whether the so-called recent economic developments documents prepared by the IMF staff should be released; more than 80 countries have already agreed to their release, and these analyses can be used by the market to help inform its judgments. The issue is whether the associated policy appraisal documents prepared by the IMF staff should be released. I strongly disagree with Calvo and Goldstein on this point.

I am not principally concerned about diluting the influence of the IMF over members' policies but rather about the IMF's credibility: whether its word can be believed on those occasions—for example, during international financial crises—when it can and should speak out. I am unconvinced by Calvo and Goldstein's arguments that the IMF has a comparative advantage in the area of policy analysis. First, even if one accepts the argument that analyses of economic and financial policies are an undersupplied public good, this has nothing to do with theory of comparative advantage per se. Second, while the IMF might now have access to better data, the thrust of the prevention argument is that those data should be provided by countries directly to the market. Third, while the IMF has good analysts (many of whom did their postgraduate training at the Federal Reserve), that institution does not have and should not be perceived as having a monopoly on generally sound analysis in a world where there is considerable economic and financial uncertainty and to err is human.[1] Finally, the IMF's record in the 1980s in separating its

---

1. With humility I would argue as well that Calvo and Goldstein's analogy with the Federal Reserve's success in presenting its analyses is misplaced. The focus of Federal Reserve official publications is on accountability for past actions and clarity about current actions, not on presenting documents that allow market analysts, and particularly not that special class of readers, to "read between the lines."

analysis from considerations of its financial stake was poor; the IMF shifted to a policy of lending into the arrears of countries with commercial banks and to a policy favoring debt reduction by the commercial banks, not because of the quality of its staff analysis but because it was concerned that it would be left holding the financial bag as commercial banks exited.

The IMF has a "culture problem" and always will have one; like other large groupings, including groupings of economists, it will be swept with fads, like the late 1980s' enthusiasm for exchange rate anchors. These people are human and potentially flawed in their judgments, especially their collective, institutional judgments. The fundamental issue in Mexico was the sustainability of the exchange rate regime given Mexico's economic and political situation and its other policies: the Mexican crisis was, after all, a Mexican *peso* crisis. This point is downplayed too much by Calvo and Goldstein. Moreover, and importantly for my argument, the IMF was not in agreement about the Mexican exchange rate regime; its staff, its management, and its Executive Board were divided. As a consequence, the IMF was not in a position to give clear advice to Mexico, in public or in private, about the risks associated with its exchange rate regime; by early 1993, when such advice might have been given, any message from the IMF would have been blunted because the institution as a whole had not yet fully absorbed the lessons of the ERM crisis.[2] In this sense, one can argue that the Mexican peso crisis was made in Europe!

Aside from its policy blinders, the IMF in Mexico was also dealing in a world of uncertainties and probabilities. Should it have said in public during 1994 that there was a 20 percent probability that Mexico would need to devalue the peso by 10 percent? That was what the market "expected." If it had done so, it might have precipitated an adjustment or a crisis earlier, but as was well demonstrated in Ariel Buira's remarks at this conference (see chapter 11), the IMF might have been wrong. Where would that have left the IMF's credibility?

Consider the recent example of public IMF advice to the G-3 countries (Germany, Japan, and the United States)—and I am not here taking issue with the advice, only its public delivery. In April 1995, the IMF management advised Japan and Germany to lower interest rates and the United States to raise interest rates. From the vantage point of September 1995, it appears that the IMF was right about Japan, wrong about the United States, and the jury is still out about Germany. The IMF's advice was essentially rejected at the time, and for better or worse the public nature of the advice on the margin inhibited action. Although the advice was couched in terms of the domestic needs of the countries in question, the recipients of the advice knew full well that it was motivated almost

---

2. More fundamentally, the major shareholders in the IMF remain divided on the issue of fixed versus flexible exchange rates and the global exchange rate regime.

exclusively by exchange rate concerns. The authorities of the G-3 countries have not embraced the notion that monetary policy should be guided primarily by exchange rate considerations, as opposed to taking into account the effects on domestic economies of actual and prospective movements in exchange rates. Moreover, the G-3 authorities suspected that if they acted on the advice of the IMF management their actions would come back to haunt them, because the author of the advice would cite this example as a case in which external-rate considerations were and should have been dominant. Thus, in the G-3 case the IMF damaged its credibility with its public, and it does not have excess credibility to lose.

The answer to this problem of public policy advice is not to think in terms of the creation of a single, monolithic early warning system directed by the IMF. The answer lies in the establishment of three robust early warning systems. One would be by and for the country itself, focusing on its financial vulnerabilities and the influence of external stocks. The second would be by and for participants in the private markets, incorporating views as diverse as Rudi Dornbusch's and Moody's. The third would be by and for the official sector and should involve the IMF, other international organizations, and governments, with the information kept to themselves, at least on an *ex ante* basis. While these early warning systems should exploit the same database (this is where the public good aspect is relevant), their analyses should be separate because their perspectives and interests frequently differ in terms of their time horizons and their loss functions.

Calvo and Goldstein correctly emphasize that something more is needed from the official sector, beyond incentives and mechanisms, to improve the chances of preventing crises of the Mexican type. They also make the case very clearly why something is needed in addition to or instead of large-scale external financing packages, which in the future are likely to prove neither feasible nor desirable. There will not be enough funding in official hands to repeat the Mexican experience, and the authorities, including those outside of the country in question, will also not want to live with the risk of systemic fallout.

Thus, there is a need for another option, for considering improved workout arrangements that emphasize order not disorder, that emphasize a range of potential arrangements not a particular imposed solution. As Calvo and Goldstein note, the principal objection to this approach is that it would be complex. However, that does not mean that it would not be a good idea to explore some of the more structured alternatives. A second objection that Calvo and Goldstein cite, but do not endorse, is that the existence of such as-yet-undefined arrangements would raise the cost of borrowing for developing countries. This is not a very convincing argument: full-blown bankruptcy arrangements exist for corporate borrowers in our countries, and it is difficult to believe that the cost of borrowing would be lower without them; reduced uncertainty does not increase costs.

What is insufficiently recognized in the Mexican case is that two types of moral hazard were involved. First, there was the hazard for Mexico, and countries like it in the future, thinking that the international financing cavalry would come to their rescue. Given all that the Mexican economy has gone through and is likely to go through, it is difficult to argue convincingly that Mexico was the principal beneficiary of the IMF-US package.[3] The principal beneficiaries were the holders of a certain class of Mexican securities (*tesobonos*) and external claims on Mexican banks. It would appear that the institutions involved and their lawyers would like to perpetuate the fiction that investors can get out or will be "bailed out" of such investments. Sooner or later they will be wrong. If a better "middle way" to handle these situations has not been found by that time, they will be clamoring for one!

---

3. It was not even Mexico that benefited most in macroeconomic terms, in the sense of the ratio of economic output lost to what would have been lost in the absence of the package, but the other emerging-market countries for whom the spillover effects were minimized.

8

Managing Capital Flows in the Czech Republic

Josef Tošovský

The Czech Republic's episode of capital inflows started in the second half of 1993, continued throughout 1994, and culminated in 1995 when the capital inflow-to-GDP ratio in net terms exceeded 18 percent. During this period, official external reserves witnessed an unprecedented increase, from almost zero after the breakup of Czechoslovakia in 1993 to $14 billion by the end of 1995.

From a real-economy standpoint, the massive capital inflow unequivocally speeded economic recovery by closing the gap between the insufficient level of domestic capital and domestic savings on the one hand and the restructuring needs of the business sector on the other hand. One might further claim that the extent of incoming capital was insufficient in the face of the vast investment requirements to replace obsolete technology or to upgrade underdeveloped infrastructure.

However, "standard" monetary side effects soon dominated the policy debate. Among the most important issues facing the Czech monetary authorities were the following:

- the impact of capital inflows on the money supply, associated with weakening of monetary control and resulting inflationary pressures;

- a widening current account deficit, as a result of higher domestic absorption financed by capital inflows;

Ing. Josef Tošovský is governor of the Czech National Bank, Praha.

- a strong real appreciation of the domestic currency, caused both by inflation differentials and the excess supply of convertible currencies with negative impact on the country's competitiveness;

- the increased risk of a reversal of capital flows, due to abrupt shifts in expectations with the threat of higher exchange rate instability;

- the need to avert reckless credit extension by the banking sector, given the greater liquidity accompanying higher capital inflows.

Systemic and institutional discontinuities and changes, all taking place within a relatively short time span, added uncertainty to the evaluation of how these side effects would affect current and future economic development. To some extent, these unusual conditions and rigidities helped shield the economy from fundamental mismatches with major trade partners—reconciling, for example, the fixed exchange rate regime with a relatively wide interest-rate differential or pursuing monetary targeting more or less independently of interest rate or exchange rate policies.

It should be noted, however, that Czech policymaking had been firmly on the liberalization and deregulation track since the beginning of the transition. Within a short period, the legal framework for liberalization of the external sector gradually changed from a policy of internal convertibility to one of assuming obligations, as required by IMF's Article VIII on convertibility. Many capital controls, both on the inflow and outflow side, were further relaxed so that only a handful of "last resort" regulations remained (e.g., credits extended by residents to nonresidents, accounts of Czech entities held in a foreign bank, access of foreign securities to the domestic primary and secondary financial markets, and purchases of domestic real estate by nonresidents).

The liberalized environment provided a foundation for coping with the challenges of excess capital inflows. A wide range of policy responses was considered and applied. The Czech National Bank resorted to sterilized intervention as its first line of defense, at a high cost to both the central bank and the commercial banking sector. The means for monetary tightening were expanded gradually, embracing buying up foreign currencies and selling central bank bills on a certain proportion of acquired reserves, increasing reserve requirements as applied to bank deposits, switching government-owned deposits to the central bank, and curbing central bank refinancing facilities.

Initially, considerable support came from tight fiscal policies; eventually fiscal policy was eased, mainly in response to the logic of the political cycle. Consequently, the Czech National Bank felt it necessary, together with some frowning, to signal some tightening in its stance because rigidities and bottlenecks remained in the supply-side response to demand incentives.

As part of the policy package, the bank also experimented with measures for "throwing the sand in the wheels" in the form of controls on the nonresident, short-term open position of commercial banks. We understand that such controls tend to be ineffective in the longer run, but they seem to work, at least to some extent, in the short run.

Although authorities meant chiefly to deal with the temporary effects of capital controls, a breakthrough in exchange rate policy was accomplished in February 1996 when the 5-year-old regime of fixed exchange rates was modified by adopting a wider band (plus or minus 7.5 percent of the central parity) for permissible exchange rate fluctuations. The immediate impact was an outflow of hot money in the amount of $0.6 billion. Since then, the exchange rate pressures seemed to have subsided. In any case, the Czech monetary authorities entered a new era of exchange rate management as well as an era of more pronounced linkages between monetary, exchange rate, and interest rate policies.

9

Lessons from the Mexican Crisis

Andrew Crockett

The Mexican crisis and its aftermath provide a number of lessons, both for the authorities of emerging-market countries and for the international community at large.

For those in emerging-market countries, the key question is how to obtain the benefits of integration in global capital markets while minimizing vulnerability to a disruptive reversal of capital flows, such as that suffered by Mexico. It would certainly be a mistake, in my view, to conclude that the costs of liberalization outweighed the benefits and to therefore retreat into renewed controls.

Integration in world capital markets has brought, and is bringing, substantial advantages. First, it allows countries making major structural reforms to tap into additional sources of savings to finance growth-enhancing investment. Second, it facilitates capital flows that promote the transfer of managerial and technological know-how. Third, it fosters the development of domestic financial institutions and markets that contribute to domestic savings mobilization. And fourth, it helps discipline macroeconomic policies. By increasing the rewards for good policies and the penalties for bad policies, it can help limit the risks of policy slippages.

By the same token, of course, integration into world capital markets raises the stakes when policy failures occur or when a country is hit by external shocks. As the Mexican episode demonstrates, confidence can be fickle. If it erodes, selling pressure can quickly become intense, forcing a disruptive process of adjustment. Policymakers need to ask themselves

Andrew Crockett is general manager at Bank for International Settlements (BIS), Basel.

what aspects of economic performance might make them vulnerable and how their resilience to shocks can be increased.

There is, of course, no infallible recipe for how to avoid financial crises. Nevertheless, certain rules of thumb can be discerned from the Mexican experience as well as this book. None of them is very novel, but that does not make them less important.

A general requirement is to pursue credible and sustainable macroeconomic policies oriented toward medium-term stability. If markets believe that the fiscal position will be kept under firm control and monetary policy is committed to price stability, it is harder for external shocks to spark a self-fulfilling loss of confidence.

There are, however, more specific lessons that can be drawn from recent experience. First, governments should be very wary of issuing short-term foreign currency debt (whether to finance a deficit or by conversion of existing obligations). The *tesobono* experience in Mexico shows clearly that circumstances can arise in which such debt is virtually impossible to roll over. When that happens, it is hard to avoid the choice between moratorium and bailout.

Second, it is desirable to build up a safety margin of foreign reserves that is related, not just to the traditional yardstick of so many months' import cover, but also to the scope for adverse capital movements. Governments are sometimes unwilling to incur the quasi-fiscal cost of reserve accumulation. What recent experience has shown is that the consequences when markets perceive reserves are inadequate can be even more costly.

A third lesson is the need to pay attention to current account position. For a while at the end of the 1980s, it was fashionable to say that the current account was unimportant, provided the budget was in balance. This was because a current account deficit would then be the counterpart of private capital inflows, which could presumably be serviced out of the income from the investment they financed. While there is something to this view, it should not be pushed too far. When a deficit reaches as much as 8 percent of GDP, as in the case of Mexico before the crisis, a country becomes uncomfortably dependent on the continuation of favorable conditions.

It is one thing to say that a current account deficit is dangerously high and another to do something about it. A fourth lesson is therefore the need to take opportunities for avoiding excessive appreciation of the real exchange rate. This involves actions to strengthen domestic saving relative to investment. Fiscal action is part of this process and may indeed involve running a fiscal surplus for a while.

A fifth lesson is the importance of structural changes that promote private saving. The relatively low level of private saving in Mexico may be contrasted with the much higher levels in most East Asian countries and in Chile. This contrast may have something to do with the differential success with which different countries weathered the disturbances that followed the initial Mexican crisis.

Sixth, consideration needs to be given to the speed and sequencing of the removal of capital restrictions. Liberalization of the capital account remains an important medium-term goal and a fundamental support to reform. Nevertheless, some countries have found it useful to control the pace at which controls over capital inflows are removed. In some cases, this can help avoid excessive overvaluation of the currency in circumstances in which foreign investors respond to the reform process by trying to invest more money than a country can easily absorb.

A seventh and final point concerns the resilience of the domestic financial system. Participation in global capital markets means being willing to respond to unanticipated events by adjusting interest rates to maintain confidence in the domestic currency. Such adjustments are more difficult when domestic financial institutions and structures are weak or underdeveloped. So it is crucial for appropriate supervisory mechanisms to be developed and for financial institutions (especially banks) to have a strong, resilient capital base.

Let me conclude with some reflections on lessons for the international community. Confronted with an actual or potential financial crisis, there are two opposing dangers. One is a situation in which there is a genuine risk of systemic disruption and the authorities fail to respond in a timely or adequate way. The other is a situation in which a disruption would be contained, if left to market forces, but the authorities intervene to prevent the market from working. Mistakes of the first kind, if they were made, would be immediately damaging and highly visible. Mistakes of the second kind are unknowable (it is never possible to assert categorically that a systemic crisis would have developed in the absence of preventive action). Nevertheless, they have well-known moral-hazard costs.

Given international financial authorities' risk aversion, there is likely to be a bias in favor of preventive action when the costs of a crisis are large, even though the probability of its materializing is small.

To state the problem does not do much to resolve it. Clearly the authorities of the leading countries need to have procedural mechanisms in place that enable them to respond rapidly when a crisis seems to be developing. Moreover, these mechanisms should be developed at a global level and not left dependent on regional political considerations. Yet there is danger in working out too precisely in advance how to deal with a particular development. Too much precision risks increasing moral hazard. To quote a phrase Jerry Corrigan has made familiar in a domestic context, there is a virtue in the authorities' maintaining a stance of "constructive ambiguity" about their willingness to provide last-resort finance.

10

Explaining the Crisis and Preventing Future Crises

Sushil Wadhwani

My remarks address the following questions: Is the crisis really over? What should one do to prevent a future crisis? In particular, what role is there for better information? Why did the market get Mexico wrong? Are capital controls and other related measures to restrict the power of markets a good idea?

Is the Crisis Really Over?

Some conference participants argued that the recovery in Latin American equity markets is proof that the crisis is over. However, while share prices have bounced from their oversold levels, one should not interpret that as signifying that the Latin American region will have ready access to foreign inflows.

Much of the price recovery is a technical bounce, and at least some of the buying is therefore unlikely to have been carried out by long-term holders. Further, existing holders of Latin American securities include those the crisis caught wrong-footed who now desperately want to believe that everything is fine again—that is, there is a type of cognitive dissonance at work here.

At current levels, Latin American equities appear unattractive relative to East Asian equities. A commonly used rule of thumb to value equities

---

Sushil Wadhwani is director of research, Tudor Proprietary Trading, London.

Table 1   East Asia and Latin America: price-earnings ratio versus GDP growth

Country	P/E[a] ratio	Long-term[b] growth rate	P/E to growth rate
East Asian markets			
Hong Kong	10.9	5.3	2.1
Indonesia	13.2	6.2	2.1
Korea	16.1	9.0	1.8
Malaysia	17.9	6.8	2.6
Philippines	17.8	4.5	4.0
Singapore	15.5	6.2	2.5
Thailand	15.8	9.0	1.8
Latin American markets			
Mexico	13.7	2.0	6.9
Argentina	11.0	3.0	3.7
Brazil	9.7	3.5	2.8

a. 12-month forward P/E ratio (16 October 1995), based on SBC Warburg estimates.
b. Goldman Sachs forecasts.

Source: The Tudor Group.

is to compare the price-earnings ratio of a country's market to its underlying long-term GDP growth rate.

Table 1 suggests that, in general, one pays rather less for each unit of growth in East Asia than in Latin America (with the exception of the Philippines). Similar results can be obtained for alternative valuation measures. Conceptually, an economist would prefer a measure of total return based on adding the dividend yield to long-term growth forecasts. Such a computation would yield similar results. Attempts to adjust the price-earnings ratios for industrial-mix differences across countries also does not change the fact that the East Asian equity markets appear much more attractive than the Latin American markets. Note that the Latin American markets appear overvalued, even though we have used assumptions about long-term GDP growth that assume an economic recovery. Hence, there is no room in these valuations for banking sector problems that might hold back GDP growth or for speculative attacks on countries that imply that interest rates stay too high to permit much GDP growth.

To summarize, a backdrop of poor valuation, political instability, and potentially serious banking sector problems does not fill me with confidence that the crisis is really over.

Whether Latin America sees a resumption of durable, sustained foreign inflows over the next few years must remain an open question.

What Should Be Done to Prevent a Future Crisis?

It has been suggested that the provision of better information may prevent the recurrence of such crises. There is little doubt that better and more timely information about Mexico would to some extent have affected Wall Street's perception of that economy. Guillermo Calvo and Morris Goldstein are also surely right in pointing out that research provided by the modern-day integrated investment bank is sometimes compromised by the need to facilitate a deal. Fund managers have some recognition of this problem, and that is why many already receive research from more-independent consultants.

The Calvo-Goldstein proposal that the International Monetary Fund's country assessments be published should be welcomed; high-quality economic research can promote better decision making. However, there are some obvious limitations on what might be learned from these assessments. Stanley Fischer has already reminded us that some countries believe that publication of these assessments would inhibit frank discussions with the Fund. Moreover, although I am a great fan of the IMF's *World Economic Outlook* (WEO hereafter), I look to it for the many economic insights it contains and not for its forecasts. One often cannot help thinking that the numerical forecasts are not entirely driven by economic considerations. A prominent recent example of this was when the IMF suggested a surprisingly optimistic outlook for the Japanese economy in the May 1995 issue of *WEO*. They suggested GDP growth of 1.8 percent in 1995 followed by 3.5 percent in 1996. This was at a time when the markets had already been looking for much lower growth. Unsurprisingly, the next issue of *WEO* (October 1995) revised these projections down to 0.5 percent for 1995 and 2.2 percent in 1996.

Hence, while more information from the IMF will be extremely useful, the limitations associated with it suggest that one should not exaggerate the expected benefits.

Why Did the Market Get It Wrong?

An understanding of why the market got it wrong is surely necessary to any attempt to prevent other crises. Undoubtedly, misperceptions played some role. I know several investors who thought that the North American Free Trade Agreement (NAFTA) implied a de facto monetary union and that therefore the peso would never be devalued. Hence various danger signals about the Mexican economy were ignored. Undoubtedly there were also many investors who were relatively new to the Mexican market and had only invested there as part of the emerging-markets fad. These are the real-world analogs of the "noise traders" in our theoretical models of financial markets. They can and do help drive market prices away from "fair value." Although policymakers can endeavor to ensure that the market is in general better-informed, one cannot legislate these noise traders away. Further, it would be wholly misleading to characterize the

Mexican crisis as wholly resulting from a lack of information and/or generalized ignorance.

Several market participants were aware that the peso was overvalued. The financial markets read the Brookings Institution's *Papers on Economic Activity* too and had duly noted the argument, advanced by Rudiger Dornbusch and Alejandro Werner in April 1994, that the real exchange rate was too high. However, most market participants lack confidence in purchasing power parity calculations of equilibrium exchange rates as a predictor of short-term exchange rate changes. Obviously, it is often rational for an individual to buy an overvalued currency if he expects it to become even more overvalued.

This is why markets sometimes appear to react too slowly to emerging imbalances but can eventually move excessively in the direction of the underlying economic fundamentals. Often, an overvaluation can persist until a catalytic event boosts participants' confidence that there is a good chance that the overvaluation might be corrected. Hence, while there was widespread recognition that both sterling and the Italian lira were overvalued in 1992, it took a no vote in the Danish referendum before market participants were emboldened to bet against these currencies.

It seems to me almost inevitable that market prices will not always be closely aligned to market fundamentals, and the availability of more accurate economic information will not change that. Instead, a world in which the economic fundamentals have sometimes been a poor guide to future price moves is also a world in which smart investors will continue to rely on technical indicators as a guide to future price moves.

Should the Power of Markets Be Restricted?

For me, a striking feature of the conference was the frequency with which support was expressed for measures that restrict the power of markets (e.g., capital controls to deter foreign inflows). This is a huge change from the days when the IMF was in the vanguard of the movement to get countries to liberalize and deregulate.

We have already noted that financial markets are sometimes mistaken and/or they can and sometimes do set prices far from any reasonable notion of underlying fundamental value. However, the growing power of financial markets has not all been bad. Surely, by raising the penalties associated with poor government policies, the markets now play an even more important role in keeping governments on the straight and narrow.

In my experience, multinational corporations that are considering direct investment often pay attention to whether a country has liberalized portfolio investment. The reason for this is that foreign portfolio investors can make it much more costly to reverse economic reforms.

Conclusions

To summarize, let me simply answer the questions with which I began. Is the crisis really over? Probably not. Is there a role for better information in preventing future crises? Better information would be extremely valuable, but don't expect it to prevent crises. Why did the market get Mexico wrong? A variety of reasons explain it, including misperceptions and the fact that the market routinely can and does ignore economic fundamentals for long periods. But are capital controls a good idea? Probably not.

11

Reflections on the Mexican Crisis of 1994

Ariel Buira

The recent Mexican experience and its aftermath have prompted a proliferation of explanations about its origins. This conference is a good example of the interest that the Mexican devaluation crisis has generated among policymakers, academics, and financial analysts. Understanding this crisis is important, among other things, because of the implications it might have on the prospects for emerging economies. This requires a careful analysis that avoids oversimplifications and does not leave out any relevant aspect.

The paper by Leonardo Leiderman and Alfredo Thorne, followed by the very interesting comments by Bill Cline and Rogelio Ramirez de la O, was good. As you might expect, I do not share their views on certain points. In what follows, I will present an assessment of the origins of the crisis in which both coincidences and differences will become apparent.

I believe, as they do, that it is difficult to rationalize this currency crisis and its causes within the traditional models. One cannot treat this crisis merely as one more example of lax monetary and fiscal policies leading to an overvalued currency, or of an overvalued currency leading to a growing current account deficit and finally to a payments crisis.

Beginning in the mid-1980s, Mexico undertook a far-reaching process of macroeconomic stabilization and structural economic reform. The intent

Ariel Buira is deputy governor of the Bank of Mexico. This is the text of his address to the conference on 7 September 1995.

was to improve Mexico's prospects by increasingly allowing market forces to determine economic activity. This process included the strengthening of public finances, deregulation of economic activity, privatization, financial reform, the restructuring of external debt, trade liberalization, and the signing of the North American Free Trade Agreement (NAFTA). After almost a decade of low growth and high inflation, these policies allowed economic activity to recover (averaging 3.1 percent between 1989 and 1994) and in 1993 brought inflation down to single-digit levels for the first time in more than 20 years. This performance, which earned the country international recognition, suggested that Mexico was ready to enjoy the fruits of economic growth with stability. Economic reforms had increased the country's attractiveness to investors and attracted unprecedented net private capital inflows, which between 1990 and 1994 reached $104 billion.

Hence, it came as a shock—not only to Mexicans but also to most observers worldwide—that this model economy could fall into a crisis of the depth and magnitude of that which emerged in December 1994.

Peso Appreciation and the Current Account Deficit

It has become a stylized fact that the currency tends to appreciate in exchange rate-based stabilization programs, and Mexico's currency was no exception. Some observers have argued that the real appreciation of the peso led the Mexican currency to become overvalued. In their view, this overvaluation of the peso, by hurting the competitiveness of Mexican exports and encouraging imports, gave rise to expanding current account deficits. As the degree of overvaluation increased, the external imbalance grew larger and became more difficult to finance. Eventually, the situation became unsustainable, and the exchange rate regime finally collapsed. Proponents of this thesis point to the following to support their view:

- the substantial real appreciation of the peso that followed the launching of the stabilization program, known as the Pacto, in December 1987 (figure 1);

- Mexico's increasing current account deficit, which averaged 6.7 percent as a proportion of GDP between 1991–94 and reached 7.8 percent in 1994 (figure 2).

While the logic of the above argument is indisputable and overvaluation in fact often arises when authorities follow expansionary monetary and fiscal policies, a current account deficit need not reflect an overvalued currency. Indeed, there is ample evidence, most recently in Southeast

Figure 1 Mexico: real exchange rate, 1981–95

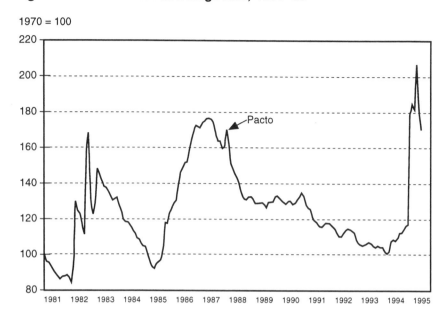

1970 = 100

Figure 2 Mexico: current account balance, 1985–94

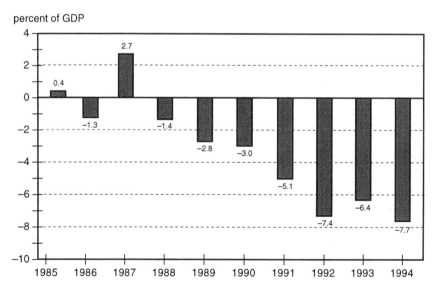

percent of GDP

Asia, that a country can run large current deficits for prolonged periods without major strains on its foreign exchange markets or concerns about its currency being overvalued.[1]

A careful analysis of the data demonstrates that the direction of causality in the Mexican case goes from the massive foreign capital inflows since 1990 to the expansion of the current account deficit, a large accumulation of international reserves, and the appreciation of the currency.

Regardless of the level of the exchange rate, a current account deficit will appear whenever domestic saving falls short of investment. Obviously, this gap may emerge as a result of increased investment opportunities or from a decline in the saving rate. In Mexico's case, both factors played a role. Structural reform not only improved the efficiency of the economy, it also created profitable openings for investment—well in excess of what could be financed by domestic sources. The response of international markets to these increased investment opportunities, along with other factors, such as the reduction in US interest rates, unleashed an unprecedented flow of foreign capital into the country.

The increased availability of external funds fueled aggregate expenditure—both investment and consumption—and contributed to a reduction in national saving, thus widening the external disequilibrium. In fact, the inflow of foreign capital had but two possible uses: an increase in imports or an accumulation of international reserves. Logic dictated resorting to both. Had the choice been to sterilize inflows fully and to accumulate international reserves, an opportunity to expand domestic productive capacity would have been lost. Furthermore, large-scale sterilization would have entailed enormous costs. On the other hand, not to sterilize would have meant added pressure on the price level and an even larger current account deficit.

In addition to capital inflows, Mexico's financial markets experienced an abundance of loanable funds due to the strengthening in public finances, the rise in confidence following the restructuring of the external debt in 1990, financial deepening following the liberalization of interest rates and the elimination of reserve requirements on banks' peso liabilities, and the use of privatization revenues to retire public debt (to the tune of $23.6 billion between 1989 and 1993).

The increased supply of funds eased the budget constraints of individuals and of firms and created an incentive for commercial banks to expand credit. Banks had no trouble in finding demand for these resources, for several reasons: economic reforms had created abundant investment opportunities, there was pent-up demand for plant and equipment following a decade of low investment, improved expectations caused an upward

---

1. For instance, Singapore ran current account deficits averaging more than 10 percent of GDP between 1970 and 1982, while its currency appreciated 46 percent in nominal terms vis-à-vis the US dollar.

revision of perceived permanent incomes that led to an increase in consumption, there was a wealth effect associated with higher values of both the stock market and real estate, and, after a decade of low growth, there was pent-up demand for durable goods and housing. As a result, investment recovered, and the growth of consumption was reflected in lower private-sector saving. Note, however, that positive growth rates of private saving have been observed since 1993.

The huge injection of resources Mexico received between 1990 and 1994 turned Mexico from a net exporter into a net importer of capital and created strong upward pressures on the peso. The same outcome would have obtained regardless of the prevailing exchange rate regime. The fact that Mexico was using a preannounced exchange rate band as part of its strategy to reduce inflation is irrelevant since, even under a regime of clean floating, large capital inflows would have strengthened the currency. Whether through nominal appreciation or via domestic inflation exceeding the rise of external prices, a real appreciation of the currency is the inevitable result of sizable capital inflows. Moreover, recall that by the end of 1987—at the starting point of its appreciation—the peso was grossly undervalued and Mexico was running a current account surplus. Appreciation was inevitable as the real exchange rate moved to equilibrium.

Currency appreciation, unless compensated by substantial improvements in total factor productivity, will reduce competitiveness, hurt export performance, and stimulate imports. In Mexico, as a result of structural reform and trade liberalization, labor productivity in manufacturing increased by 6.7 percent a year over 1991–94. The latest IMF consultation report shows that despite the stronger peso, Mexico's unit labor costs (in dollar terms) were on average 2.2 percent lower in 1994 than in 1992. Mexican competitiveness was thus not eroded by the peso's appreciation.

Over 1992–94, manufacturing exports increased on average, by 17 percent per year, and their share in total exports climbed from 37.6 percent in 1985 to 83 percent in 1994.[2] Moreover, exports of manufactures to the United States were 21 percent higher in 1994 than in the previous year (figures 3 and 4). This strong export performance provides another clear indication of competitiveness. Note that even before NAFTA became effective, rates of growth of Mexican exports greatly exceeded those of world trade (6.9 percent per year between 1989 and 1993) as well as the expansion of major Mexican markets (i.e., US imports increased on average 5.7 percent per year).

Turning to the exchange rate anchor, recall that in 1991 the speed at which the band was widened increased. Also, the inner intervention band was abandoned toward the end of 1993.

Finally, the overvaluation argument appears even weaker if one considers that in 1994 the real exchange rate depreciated by 14 percent in real

---

2. This led total exports to increase 12.6 percent per year, despite the stagnation of oil exports.

Figure 3   Mexico: merchandise exports, rates of growth and share of manufacturing, 1985–94

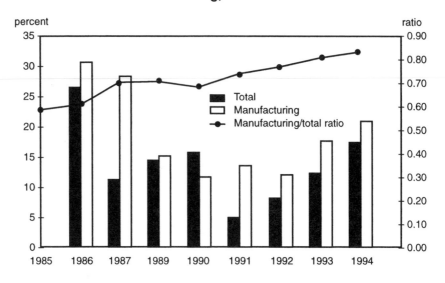

Figure 4   Export volume: Mexico versus other countries, 1985–1995

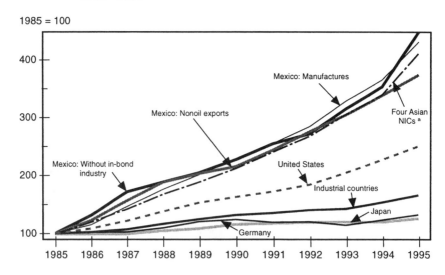

a. Hong Kong, Korea, Singapore, and Taiwan.

Sources: Banco de Mexico; IMF, *World Economic Outlook.*

Figure 5 Mexico: annual growth rates of monetary aggregates, 1993–94

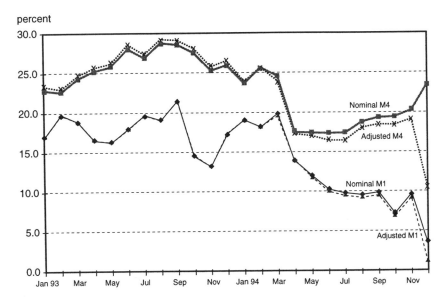

percent

terms prior to the crisis.[3] If the peso was not overvalued in 1992, the central bank's accumulation of reserves throughout 1993 and up to February 1994 and the peso's depreciation in 1994 made this argument even less persuasive on the eve of the crisis.

Appropriateness of Fiscal and Monetary Policies

Turning to macroeconomic management, there is no evidence of a fundamental deterioration in Mexico's monetary and fiscal policies. Rates of growth of monetary aggregates in 1994 were significantly lower than in the previous year (figure 5). Since the aggregates include items denominated in foreign currencies, appropriate measurement of their growth requires that the effect of the peso depreciation on the value of the stock of domestic currency be eliminated. When this is done, not only is the alleged acceleration nowhere to be seen, but in fact credit expansion is seen to decline further in relation to 1993. Indeed, the fact that interest rates were rising along with the quantity of money in 1994 rather than falling suggests that currency growth responded to demand shocks. This

---

3. Based on consumer prices from 133 countries, using GDP weights.

Figure 6 Mexico: nominal annual growth rates in domestic financing,[a] December 1992–December 1994

percent (adjusted to eliminate the effect of exchange rate variations)

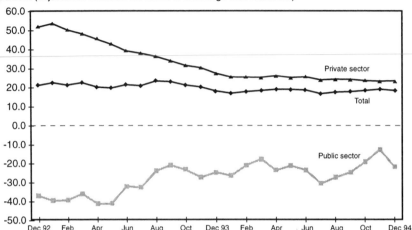

a. Includes total credit from the banking system, government securities, commercial paper, and other private-sector paper.

is borne out by econometric estimates, which have found little evidence of a relaxation of monetary policy in 1994 (see, e.g., Rogers 1995).

Nominal and real interest rates remained high during 1994. For instance, the interest rate on 28-day *cetes*—the money market's leading rate—doubled from 9 to 18 percent in the aftermath of Luis Donaldo Colosio's assassination, with other interest rates rising accordingly. Even after they later declined as calm returned to markets and inflation fell, there were repeated private-sector complaints about the high level of real interest rates.

Furthermore, beginning in the second half of 1993, commercial banks adopted a more prudent policy regarding credits to firms and individuals. This prudence continued in 1994. This slower pace of credit expansion to the private sector probably reflected the rise in past-due loans. Moreover, the credit figures include refinancing of interest obligations (due to the high level of interest rates charged on loans; see figure 6).

The available data also show that fiscal policy in 1994 continued to be fundamentally sound. Although the nonfinancial public sector showed a cash deficit of 0.3 percent of GDP (compared with a surplus, equivalent to 0.7 percent of GDP in 1993), inclusion of nonrecurrent revenues from privatization in the fiscal accounts turns that deficit into a small cash surplus equal to 0.1 percent of GDP. On the basis of these figures, fiscal policy, though somewhat less restrictive than in 1993, can hardly be considered "loose."

Leiderman and Thorne attribute the Mexican crisis to inadequate policy responses to shocks. In hindsight, they may be right. However, policies should be judged in the light of the information available at the time they were adopted.

When this perspective is adopted, it is clear that the crisis was fundamentally the outcome of a series of unpredictable political and criminal events. Of these, it was the Chiapas uprising that finally undermined the confidence of domestic and foreign investors—leading to a lower availability of foreign capital and eventually to a reversal of capital flows in an economy that was heavily dependent on them.

Note that up to 22 March—that is, the day before the assassination of the ruling party's presidential candidate—a totally different set of issues was in the minds of investors and authorities. Given the large inflows of capital recorded after the US Congress's approval of NAFTA, there were strong market pressures for a revaluation of the nominal exchange rate and for a reduction in interest rates. Inflation was declining, and there were signs that a recovery of economic activity was in the making. At the time, the central bank had to sterilize large inflows of capital since the potential expansion of the monetary base would have occurred when seasonal money demand was at its weakest.

The political events of 1994, the likes of which Mexico had not experienced for two generations, dramatically altered prospects. These events increased uncertainty and resulted in the loss of a sizable fraction of the country's international reserves. Uncertainty produced this loss, not expansionary policies. The uncertainty preceded the Bank of Mexico's sterilization measures, which it undertook to compensate for the large contractionary effects that international reserve losses otherwise would have imposed on the Mexican economy. The Bank of Mexico's increases in net domestic credit during 1994 reflected the need to satisfy the larger demand for the monetary base and to offset the loss of international reserves.

In the aftermath of Colosio's death, an 8 percent nominal depreciation of the exchange rate within the band was allowed, interest rates increased sharply, and *tesobonos* were issued. Even though the change in the composition of short-term public debt helped maintain stability in financial markets, this admittedly was a strategy that involved a degree of risk—particularly as short-term, dollar-denominated debt approached the level of international reserves. This debt management strategy has been severely criticized. However, a fair assessment should take into account the fact that two-thirds of bank deposits were very short-term and that, in any case, there is no interest rate high enough to compensate investors for the increased perceived risk of a devaluation. Recall that authorities had successfully resorted to the substitution of *tesobonos* for *cetes* just before the NAFTA vote in the US Congress in November 1993. Once the

Figure 7   Mexico: stock of net international reserves, 1994

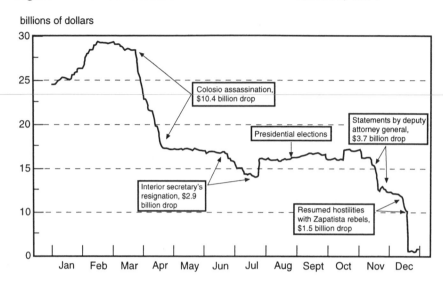

billions of dollars

uncertainty about the outcome of the vote was removed, *tesobonos* were converted back into *cetes* and the exchange rate and interest rates swiftly returned to their previous trend values.

From the end of April to mid-November 1994, the policies that were pursued prevented further reserve losses (figure 7). Capital inflows throughout this period were large enough to finance the current account deficit. For more than seven months, with no new political shocks or crimes, there was no capital outflow, international reserves remained stable, and the central bank's domestic credit did not expand. It was only when new shocks hit that reserves were lost and the Bank of Mexico allowed net domestic credit to expand in order to satisfy the demand for base money by replacing the resulting lost liquidity.

Faced with what then appeared to be transitory shocks, the authorities decided to draw on the stock of international reserves rather than to adjust policies significantly. Initially, it was believed that political uncertainties would be largely resolved by a clean electoral process. After elections, which had been both credible and had produced clear-cut results, the expectation was that economic policies would continue along the same broad lines. Thus, confidence was expected to be fully restored. Following major structural reform and with NAFTA's coming into effect, medium-term prospects for the Mexican economy continued to look very bright. Using a fraction of the central bank's international reserves to smooth out the effects of the transitory shocks seemed an appropriate policy response. After all, this is the purpose of holding reserves.

In hindsight, as Leiderman and Thorne point out, the policy combination turned out to be inadequate. Yet at the time, further political turmoil was not expected. Had the authorities known that the turbulence would continue, they would in all probability have acted to avoid the sharp adjustment that followed. Unfortunately, perfect foresight is not possible. At the time, tough choices had to be made, and erring on either side could be costly. Higher interest rates would impede the recovery of activity and add to the difficulties of the financial system, while greater exchange rate flexibility would add to inflationary expectations and thereby sacrifice the hard-won progress made toward stabilization. If shocks turned out to be nonrecurrent, as suggested by historical experience, stronger policy actions would not have been warranted. In the light of available information, the authorities made what then seemed to be a reasonable bet.

Breaking Investors' Faith

The process of structural change that culminated both in the passage of NAFTA and Mexico's admission to the Organization for Economic Development and Cooperation (OECD) held for many a symbolism that went beyond its immediate economic significance: Mexico, with what some foreign observers regarded as the "best economic management in the world," was leaving underdevelopment behind and entering the First World. A new economic power had appeared on the world scene. Expectations of sustained economic progress and prosperity rose rapidly—not only in Mexico but also abroad.

An excessive surge in optimism and overblown expectations, which official statements did not discourage, were to contribute in no small measure to the depth of the crisis that followed devaluation, as both domestic opinion and foreign investors felt not simply disappointed but also deceived.

The Chiapas uprising underscored that developing-world poverty still prevailed in some regions of the country. Chiapas, together with the political assassinations, gave rise to questions about the stability of the political system. The devaluation was seen by many as a breach of faith. The ensuing disappointment may explain why exchange rate adjustment, rather than restoring confidence in the country's ability to correct the external imbalance, gave rise to or exacerbated a confidence crisis of major proportions. The virulence of the reaction to the devaluation by both domestic investors and international investment managers has to be given considerable weight if the depth of the crisis is to be understood.

The Mexican crisis is a reminder that while large current account deficits can be financed for prolonged periods when they result from a country doing things "the right way," these deficits significantly increase the economy's vulnerability to variations in international capital flows.

Indeed, when an important fraction of the funds used to finance the deficit is short-term and volatile, the vulnerability is even greater. Although determining the sustainable level of the current account deficit is by no means an easy task, awareness of this vulnerability can lead authorities to limit the deficit.

A country that becomes very attractive to foreign investors confronts a paradoxical situation. As capital inflows eventually translate into a growing current account deficit, the very same investors who were so eager to bring in their capital may look at the size of the deficit and become nervous. Investors may overreact to any unfavorable development by withdrawing their funds. In this way, they can contribute to the emergence of a payments crisis. Thus, as capital inflows—a symbol of success—give rise to a current account deficit they ironically become the country's weakness. Reducing the exposure of the country to the volatility of external capital, while sustaining a healthy level of investment, requires increased national saving. One way to accomplish this, which has proved effective in countries such as Chile, is through the development of pension programs.

The liberalization of cross-border flows has led to the internationalization of investment by institutional funds. This has generated a large supply of funds that tend to be yield-sensitive and that respond swiftly to changes in sentiment about the recipient economies. Abrupt, massive changes in capital flows leave policymakers and private agents little time to adjust. The December devaluation of the peso triggered a run on the country; both foreign mutual funds and domestic investors were involved. The result was a liquidity crisis of huge proportions, as capital flows were not only interrupted but reversed. The depth of the crisis would call for massive external support and extreme economic measures.

Such a reversal in capital flows may call for measures to discourage the entrance of so-called hot money. For prudential reasons, the Bank of Mexico had in fact imposed a limit on the foreign currency-denominated liabilities that commercial banks could take on. By narrowing this avenue for foreign capital to enter the country, the regulation may have contained somewhat the increase in the current account deficit. In hindsight, additional restrictions might have discouraged short-term foreign capital inflows—for instance, limits on the acquisition of debt instruments by nonresidents. In fact, such a restriction had applied to foreign purchases of government paper from December 1980 to December 1990, but it eliminated in the tide of the liberalization then sweeping the country. Recall that Mexico further liberalized its capital account in 1993 because the OECD Codes of Liberalization require the full elimination of all restrictions on capital movements.

Measures to discourage short-term capital inflows, including the adoption of a floating exchange rate, might be viewed as a means of reducing the risks of a large current account deficit and of neutralizing the effects of market imperfections. Indeed, in the event of a capital withdrawal, a difference may arise between individual and social costs. While an investor bears a market-imposed reduction in the value of his investment in an emerging market—a reduction that often covers only a small proportion of his portfolio—a massive capital outflow may cause the financial collapse of an entire economy. Moreover, during the run, investors who get out first increase the cost of getting out for others who react less quickly. This in turn places a premium on volatility, an undesirable result for all.

The Mexican crisis raises several issues for emerging countries that have undertaken internal reforms and external opening. Can a danger level for the current account deficit be determined? What are the appropriate policies to cope with short-term capital movements and sudden changes in market sentiment? How is one to distinguish between temporary and permanent shocks? Is the blanket removal of restrictions on capital inflows always the good thing that it is often presumed to be? Is it possible to sterilize massive capital inflows? Finally, can a country be expected to offset capital inflows by running large fiscal surpluses?

Conclusion

Mexico suffered a series of far-reaching political shocks sufficient to jar the system, displace expectations, and alter the economic outlook. The ensuing sudden halt in foreign lending and the reversal of capital flows were bound to generate a financial crisis.

When a change in expectations arises from events as disparate as political assassinations and interest rate movements abroad and where there is no systematic, underlying monetary weakness, there is some basis for suggesting it is largely accidental. This abrupt change in expectations, which in the context of NAFTA had perhaps reached unrealistically optimistic levels, may be seen as the cause of the crisis. Alfred Marshall's comment on bank failures may apply equally well to investment fund managers: "Their trust had been ignorant, their distrust was ignorant and fierce. Such a rush often caused a bank to fail which might have paid them gradually."

References

Banco de Mexico. 1995a. *Informe Anual 1994.* Mexico City.

Banco de Mexico. 1995b. *The Mexican Economy 1995.* Mexico City.

Banco de Mexico. 1995c. *Report on Monetary Policy, 1 April 1994–31 December 1994.* Mexico City.

Banco de Mexico. 1996. *Report on Monetary Policy. 1 January 1995–31 December 1995.*

Buira, Ariel. 1994. "The Main Determinants of Savings in Mexico." Paper prepared for conference on the Role of Savings in Economic Growth, Federal Reserve Bank of Dallas, 18–19 March, Houston, Texas.

Calvo, Guillermo A., Leonardo Leiderman, and Carmen Reinhart. 1993. "Capital Inflows and Real Exchange Rate Appreciation in Latin America." IMF Staff Papers (June). Washington.

Dornbusch, Rudiger, and Alejandro Werner. 1994. "Mexico: Stabilization, Reform, and No Growth." *Brookings Papers on Economic Activity*: 1.

Gil-Díaz, Francisco. 1995. "A Comparison of Economic Crisis: Chile in 1982, Mexico in 1995." Paper presented at Forum 95 of the Managed Futures Association, Chicago, July. Mexico City: Banco de Mexico.

International Monetary Fund (IMF). 1995. *International Capital Markets: Developments, Prospects and Policy Issues*. Washington.

Krugman, Paul. 1995. "Dutch Tulips and Emerging Markets." *Foreign Affairs* 74, no. 4 (July/August): 28–44.

Leiderman, Leonardo, and Alfredo Thorne. 1995. "Mexico's 1994 Crisis and Its Aftermath: Is the Worst Over?" Paper prepared for the Conference on Private Capital Flows to Emerging Markets After the Mexican Crisis, jointly sponsored by the Institute for International Economics and the Oesterreichische Nationalbank, Vienna, 7–9 September.

Mancera A., Miguel. 1995a. "Ajustes de Politicas Frente a Turbulencias Financieras [Policy Adjustments in the Face of Financial Turmoil]." Remarks at the seminar, 70 anos del Banco Central de Chile, Santiago.

Mancera A., Miguel. 1995b. "Desafios de la Banca Central Hacia el Ano 2000." Roundtable remarks at the seminar, 70 anos del Banco Central de Chile, Santiago.

Reisen, H. 1995. "Managing Temporary Capital Inflows: Lessons from Asia and Latin America." Working Paper. Paris: OECD Development Centre, March.

Rogers, John H. 1995. "Mexican Money Demand." Presentation to the Board of Governors of the Federal Reserve System, June.

Turner, Philip. 1995. *Capital Flows in Latin America: A New Phase*. BIS Economic Papers No. 44. Basel: Bank for International Settlements.

12

Summing Up

Stanley Fischer

The discussion in this conference has been dominated, appropriately so, by the aftermath of the Mexican crisis. I will take up seven questions, the first of which is whether what hit Mexico was simply bad luck. Specifically, if it had not been for political events—beginning with the assassination of presidential candidate Luis Donaldo Colosio and extending until the day before the devaluation, with the renewal of troubles in Chiapas, would Mexico have come through 1994 unscathed? Of course, we will never know, but it is certain that if Mexico had not had to devalue, it would have been easy to write a story that explained its success—a story that would have heavily stressed the radical reforms that had taken place in the Salinas administration, the credibility of the authorities with foreign investors, the sound fiscal situation, and the success in reducing inflation to the single-digit range.

Nor is it so obvious what should have been done differently and when. I believe that the massive current account deficit means there should have been more devaluation in 1993. But it has to be admitted that Mexico was at that time receiving net capital inflows and market pressures were for appreciation, not depreciation. Nor did Mexico have many policy tools that could have produced a devaluation. The budget was balanced, and running large surpluses is politically difficult, especially given the pressing social needs in Mexico. Comprehensive capital controls were probably

Stanley Fischer is first deputy managing director at the International Monetary Fund (IMF), Washington.

not feasible, though perhaps tax measures could have been used to reduce the rate of inflow. While the macroeconomic situation in 1993 would have made devaluation difficult, that was not the case after the spring of 1994—then it was the political situation that made devaluation difficult, but the economics would have supported it.

The second question I will discuss was raised by Val Koromzay: was the exchange rate regime the source of evil in this case? It is true that a crisis on this scale would not have occurred with a truly floating rate. Although big shocks that impose enormous costs on the system can occur in a floating rate system, the sort of crisis that makes it obvious the country has to go to the International Monetary Fund (IMF), and that leads to midnight phone calls, tends to be associated with fixed exchange rates.

That does not lead me to the conclusion that a country should never have a fixed rate. Argentina would not have achieved what it has in terms of adjustment, growth, and stability if it had not been for the convertibility plan. The Czech Central Bank governor, Josef Tošovský, believes—and I share that belief—that the fixed exchange rate played an important role in the success of the Czech stabilization. There are countless other examples of countries that benefited from fixing the exchange rate.

The difficult question is how and when to shift away from the fixed rate—that is, the exit strategy. Some say that Mexico proves Russia should not fix the exchange rate: what it actually proves is that Russia should not try to fix the exchange rate forever. And it is possible to exit successfully without a crisis, as several countries have done, Israel and Poland among them.

A third question about Mexico is, what exacerbated the crisis? Were the investors rational, or was there a herd instinct at work? The investors cannot have been rational both before and after the devaluation. The stories that Sushil Wadhwani told in this conference could be multiplied with regard to investors in Mexico. In this case, the capital markets obeyed my first law of institutions, which is that every institution (except, of course, the IMF) looks better from a distance.

Another factor that exacerbated the situation was the weakness of the banking system—and that point has been heavily and rightly emphasized in this conference. Of course, there is also the other side of the coin: that the crisis exacerbated the condition of the banking system, so that banking problems that could probably have been dealt with in normal times made a difficult situation far worse.

A fourth question is, were there contagion effects? Yes. Were they appropriate? To some extent, yes: there was information during the Mexican crisis that related to what could happen in other countries. But I doubt that the conclusions the markets drew were all the right ones. For instance, I could not understand why Brazil came under repeated attack in a situation that looked very different from Mexico's. Some aspects of the capital-market reaction—for instance, that Chile and Colombia were relatively less affected—seemed about right. But remember as we applaud this wisdom of the capital markets that much of this wisdom was shown after the Mexican situation stabilized. The IMF's *Capital Markets Report*, which was widely misreported, pointedly said that the capital markets did a pretty good job of discriminating *after the crisis was stabilized*. But before that, there were clear elements of panic, including the temporary spread of difficulties to some countries in Asia.

The fifth question: was official action justified? The consensus of the authors is the correct one: yes. It has been a very grudging yes, but with all the grumbling, that is everyone's conclusion.

Why was official action appropriate? It is important to emphasize that official action would have been appropriate even if there had not been contagion effects. Mexico is suffering from a massive recession. Without official intervention, the recession could have lasted four or five years. With official intervention, the recession is likely to be over within 18 months. International intervention would have been amply justified even if the effects had been confined to shortening the inevitable Mexican recession.

It is common to say that this was a costly bailout. It is not so clear what the direct costs to the international community are. These loans will be repaid. The international community makes these loans available through the IMF at times when the private markets will not lend—for whatever reason. But they are loans, not grants. The obligation of the international community to act in this way is enshrined in the IMF's Articles of Agreement.

I must confess that as I listened earlier to some of the discussion about how salutary it would have been not to have helped, and even taking into account the importance of moral hazard, that some people sounded like World War I generals who were sacrificing not only their own troops but also other country's troops. It would no doubt have been salutary for the Mexican policymakers and for the investors to pay the right price for their sins. But the problem is that ordinary Mexicans would have borne much larger costs. That's justification enough for the international action.

Of course, there was another justification: contagion effects. They were there, and they were substantial. You could see that by tracking the correlations of interest rates and stock prices across markets. The contagion effects imply that official intervention was justified not only to help Mexico but also to minimize the recession that did or could have affected other countries.

Some have argued that the Mexican intervention may have worsened the contagion because it was clear that an operation on that scale could not be mounted for any other country. That argument misses on two scores. In the first place, if the international community was not willing to help Mexico, who would it have been willing to help? Further, I have no doubt that without official assistance, the crisis would have been much worse and much wider. And second, although the United States was doubtless not willing to intervene again, the IMF was and it did, as was demonstrated in Argentina in April 1995.

While the discussion in this volume about systemic risk has been very interesting, it also has been potentially extremely dangerous. The authors seem to accept the premise that official lending should take place only if there is a risk to the system. That is wrong and is certainly counter to the spirit and the Articles of Agreement on which the IMF is founded. That view is unfortunate and inappropriate, for there is good reason for *conditional* international lending to countries in trouble that cannot access the capital markets. The implicit equation—"there was no systemic risk, therefore the loans were unjustified"—is fallacious and dangerous.

Question six: are we living in a brave new globalized world for capital markets? Even adjusting for the normal hype, the answer is yes. What is new is the size and speed of private capital flows, the new types of investors, the new instruments, and the innovations that are certain to come in this area. But there is also an element of hype, because all of the problems we are now dealing with—overborrowing and contagion—have been around a long time.

The critical difference is that for the first time in 70 years, private capital flows are playing the dominant role in financing developing countries. In the long run, there will be globalized capital markets, dominated by private capital, and countries will have to adapt their policies to that fact.

Question seven: how should we adapt? We all have to behave better. That means, first, that countries have to behave well. The idea this book presents of what is needed should make the IMF very happy: macroeconomic stability is critical, and that is shorthand for policies the Fund has pushed for years. The authors recognize that the banking sector is far more important than was once thought. They struggled with the difficult question of how large a sustainable current account is. The discussion is analytically straightforward in a world of certainty but less so when potential shocks—to interest rates, terms of trade, or export demand—have to be taken into account. Further, the answer will differ among countries, depending on the growth rate, the responsiveness of exports and imports to the exchange rate, and the nature of the capital inflows.

The authors also emphasize microeconomic reforms to increase domestic saving, on which, unfortunately, little of substance is presented beyond pointing to the Chilean pension scheme. There was some approval of controls on capital flows. The authors and participants at the conference had surprisingly little to say on what recipient countries ought to be doing to make it better and easier for investors to invest in them. They said, "Provide information." Upgrading of accounting rules, of transparency in the equity markets, and in private as well as official business also ought to be emphasized.

They did not address whether industrialized countries should regulate mutual fund investments in emerging markets. I have a very uneasy feeling that the regulators assume that the information mutual funds obtain from and about foreign companies is as good as what they get in their home markets.

But not even all the information in the world can guarantee efficient markets. My MIT colleague Bob Solow tells the story of a lieutenant in the army who seemed a reasonable enough fellow to him, who knew a lot, but whom the men hated. When Bob asked one of the soldiers what was wrong with the lieutenant, the answer was, "This is a guy who knows everything and realizes nothing." Even where the information is provided, realizing or seeing what is happening is always difficult.

We need to do better on crisis prevention and also on crisis response. Better, more timely, data are needed for crisis prevention, and IMF surveillance is being improved. But still there will be crises, and there is a need to ensure that the IMF has the necessary resources for emergencies. The expansion of the General Arrangements to Borrow (GAB) is the short-run answer to the question, how do you get through the next year or two? But the GAB is a complicated piece of machinery, and it may be unwieldy in an emergency. That is one of the many reasons that IMF quotas need to be increased.

Finally, there is the interesting and very complicated idea of improving workout procedures. There are some ideas that are so simple that they can be applied as soon as the light goes on in someone's head, and they can make a real difference immediately. There are other ideas that are very complicated to work out and that may eventually make a difference. The workout idea falls into the second category. We will see elements of the workout proposal being discussed and something useful emerging, but not next year—perhaps over five or ten years.

Other Publications from the
Institute for International Economics

BOOKS

IMF Conditionality
John Williamson, editor/*1983*   ISBN cloth 0-88132-006-4   695 pp.

Trade Policy in the 1980s
William R. Cline, editor/*1983*
(out of print)   ISBN paper 0-88132-031-5   810 pp.

Subsidies in International Trade
Gary Clyde Hufbauer and Joanna Shelton Erb/*1984*
      ISBN cloth 0-88132-004-8   299 pp.

International Debt: Systemic Risk and Policy Response
William R. Cline/*1984*   ISBN cloth 0-88132-015-3   336 pp.

Trade Protection in the United States: 31 Case Studies
Gary Clyde Hufbauer, Diane E. Berliner, and Kimberly Ann Elliott/*1986*
(out of print)   ISBN paper 0-88132-040-4   371 pp.

Toward Renewed Economic Growth in Latin America
Bela Balassa, Gerardo M. Bueno, Pedro-Pablo Kuczynski,
and Mario Henrique Simonsen/*1986*
(out of stock)   ISBN paper 0-88132-045-5   205 pp.

Capital Flight and Third World Debt
Donald R. Lessard and John Williamson, editors/*1987*
(out of print)   ISBN paper 0-88132-053-6   270 pp.

The Canada-United States Free Trade Agreement:
The Global Impact
Jeffrey J. Schott and Murray G. Smith, editors/*1988*
      ISBN paper 0-88132-073-0   211 pp.

World Agricultural Trade: Building a Consensus
William M. Miner and Dale E. Hathaway, editors/*1988*
      ISBN paper 0-88132-071-3   226 pp.

Japan in the World Economy
Bela Balassa and Marcus Noland/*1988*
      ISBN paper 0-88132-041-2   306 pp.

America in the World Economy: A Strategy for the 1990s
C. Fred Bergsten/*1988*   ISBN cloth 0-88132-089-7   235 pp.
      ISBN paper 0-88132-082-X   235 pp.

Managing the Dollar: From the Plaza to the Louvre
Yoichi Funabashi/*1988, 2d ed. 1989*
      ISBN paper 0-88132-097-8   307 pp.

United States External Adjustment and the World Economy
William R. Cline/*May 1989* ISBN paper 0-88132-048-X   392 pp.

Free Trade Areas and U.S. Trade Policy
Jeffrey J. Schott, editor/*May 1989*   ISBN paper 0-88132-094-3   400 pp.

Dollar Politics: Exchange Rate Policymaking in the United States
I. M. Destler and C. Randall Henning/*September 1989*
(out of print)   ISBN paper 0-88132-079-X   192 pp.

Latin American Adjustment: How Much Has Happened?
John Williamson, editor/*April 1990*
      ISBN paper 0-88132-125-7   480 pp.

Measuring the Costs of Protection in Japan
Yoko Sazanami, Shujiro Urata, and Hiroki Kawai/*January 1995*
ISBN paper 0-88132-211-3   96 pp.

Foreign Direct Investment in the United States, Third Edition
Edward M. Graham and Paul R. Krugman/*January 1995*
ISBN paper 0-88132-204-0   232 pp.

The Political Economy of Korea-United States Cooperation
C. Fred Bergsten and Il SaKong, editors/*February 1995*
ISBN paper 0-88132-213-X   128 pp.

International Debt Reexamined
William R. Cline/*February 1995*
ISBN paper 0-88132-083-8   560 pp.

American Trade Politics, Third Edition
I. M. Destler/*April 1995*   ISBN paper 0-88132-215-6   360 pp.

Managing Official Export Credits: The Quest for a Global Regime
John E. Ray/*July 1995*   ISBN paper 0-88132-207-5   344 pp.

Asia Pacific Fusion: Japan's Role in APEC
Yoichi Funabashi/*October 1995*
ISBN paper 0-88132-224-5   312 pp.

Korea-United States Cooperation in the New World Order
C. Fred Bergsten and Il SaKong, editors/*February 1996*
ISBN paper 0-88132-226-1   144 pp.

Why Exports Really Matter!   ISBN paper 0-88132-221-0   34 pp.
Why Exports Matter More!   ISBN paper 0-88132-229-6   36 pp.
J. David Richardson and Karin Rindal/*July 1995; February 1996*

Global Corporations and National Governments
Edward M. Graham/*May 1996*   ISBN paper 0-88132-111-7   168 pp.

Global Economic Leadership and the Group of Seven
C. Fred Bergsten and C. Randall Henning/*May 1996*
ISBN paper 0-88132-218-0   192 pp.

The Trading System After the Uruguay Round
John Whalley and Colleen Hamilton/*July 1996*
ISBN paper 0-88132-131-1   224 pp.

**Private Capital Flows to Emerging Markets
After the Mexican Crisis**
Guillermo A. Calvo, Morris Goldstein, and Eduard Hochreiter/*September 1996*
ISBN paper 0-88132-232-6   352 pp.

WORKS IN PROGRESS

Liberalizing Financial Services
Michael Aho and Pierre Jacquet

Trade, Jobs, and Income Distribution
William R. Cline

China's Entry to the World Economy
Richard N. Cooper

Assessing the National Economic Council
I.M. Destler

Canadian customers can order from the Institute or from either:

RENOUF BOOKSTORE	LA LIBERTÉ
1294 Algoma Road	3020 chemin Sainte-Foy
Ottawa, Ontario K1B 3W8	Quebec G1X 3V6
Telephone: 613 741-4333	Telephone: 418 658-3763
Fax: 613 741-5439	Fax: 800 567-5449

Visit our website at: http:/ / www.iie.com   E-mail address: orders@iie.com